LIBRARY OF HEBREW BIBLE/
OLD TESTAMENT STUDIES

705

Formerly Journal for the Study of the Old Testament Supplement Series

THEODICY AND HOPE IN THE BOOK OF THE TWELVE

Edited by

**George Athas, Beth M. Stovell,
Daniel C. Timmer and Colin M. Toffelmire**

t&tclark

LONDON · NEW YORK · OXFORD · NEW DELHI · SYDNEY

T&T CLARK
Bloomsbury Publishing Plc
50 Bedford Square, London, WC1B 3DP, UK
1385 Broadway, New York, NY 10018, USA
29 Earlsfort Terrace, Dublin 2, Ireland

BLOOMSBURY, T&T CLARK and the T&T Clark logo
are trademarks of Bloomsbury Publishing Plc

First published in Great Britain 2021
This paperback edition published in 2023

A catalogue record for this book is available from the British Library.
Library of Congress Control Number: 2021932641.

ISBN: HB: 978-0-5676-9535-2
         PB: 978-0-5677-0171-8
         ePDF: 978-0-5676-9536-9

Series: Library of Hebrew Bible/Old Testament Studies, volume 705
ISSN 2513-8758

Typeset by: Trans.form.ed SAS

To find out more about our authors and books visit www.bloomsbury.com
and sign up for our newsletters.

CONTENTS

LIST OF CONTRIBUTORS

George Athas is Director of Research, Lecturer in Old Testament and Hebrew at Moore College, New South Wales, Australia.

Mark J. Boda is Professor of Old Testament at McMaster Divinity College, Hamilton, Ontario, Canada.

Michael H. Floyd is retired and was formerly a Professor of Old Testament at Centro de Estudios Theológicos in Santo Domingo, Dominican Republic.

David J. Fuller is the Managing Editor of McMaster Divinity College Press, Hamilton, Ontario, Canada and is currently an adjunct faculty member at Thorneloe University at Laurentian, Horizon College and Seminary, and Ambrose University.

Rainer Kessler is Emeritus Professor of Old Testament at Marburg University, Marburg, Germany.

Brittany Kim is an adjunct professor of Old Testament and spiritual director-in-training based in Chicago, Illinois, United States. She has taught at Roberts Wesleyan College, Northeastern Seminary, Bethel Seminary, and North Park Theological Seminary.

Grace Ko is an adjunct professor of Biblical Studies for the Canadian Chinese School of Theology at Tyndale University, Toronto, Ontario, Canada.

Chelsea D. Mak is a PhD student in Graduate Division of Religion at Emory University, Atlanta, Georgia, United States.

Anthony R. Petterson is a Lecturer in Old Testament and Hebrew at Morling College (Australian College of Theology) in Macquarie Park, New South Wales, Australia.

Beth M. Stovell is Associate Professor of Old Testament and Chair of General Theological Studies at Ambrose Seminary of Ambrose University, Calgary, Alberta, Canada.

Heath A. Thomas is President and Professor of Old Testament at Oklahoma Baptist University, Shawnee, Oklahoma, United States.

Daniel C. Timmer is Professor of Biblical Studies for the PhD program at Puritan Reformed Theological Seminary in Grand Rapids, Michigan, United States and serves at the Faculté de théologie évangélique in Montreal, Quebec, Canada.

Colin Toffelmire is Associate Professor of Old Testament and Chair of Ministry at Ambrose University, Calgary, Alberta, Canada.

ABBREVIATIONS

AB	Anchor Bible
ABR	*Australian Biblical Review*
ABRL	Anchor Bible Reference Library
ANEM	Ancient Near East Monographs
AOTC	Abingdon Old Testament Commentaries
AYB	Anchor Yale Bible
BA	*Biblical Archaeologist*
BAR	Biblical Archaeology Review
BBR	*Bulletin for Biblical Research*
BBR Sup	Bulletin for Biblical Research Supplements
BDB	Brown, Francis, S. R. Driver, and Charles A. Briggs. *A Hebrew and English Lexicon of the Old Testament*. Oxford: Clarendon, 1907
BETL	Bibliotheca Ephemeridum Theologicarum Lovaniensium
Bib	*Biblica*
BibInt	Biblical Interpretation Series
BibRes	*Biblical Research*
BT	*Bible Today*
BthSt	Biblisch-Theologische Studien
BZAW	Beihefte zur Zeitschrift für die alttestamentliche Wissenschaft
CBET	Contributions to Biblical Exegesis & Theology
CBQ	*Catholic Biblical Quarterly*
CBR	*Currents in Biblical Research*
ConBOT	Coniectanea Biblica Old Testament Series
COS	*The Context of Scripture*. Edited by William W. Hallo. 3 vols. Leiden: Brill, 1997–2002
CTR	*Criswell Theological Review*
CurTM	*Currents in Theology and Mission*
FAT	Forschungen zum Alten Testament
FCB	Feminist Companion to the Bible
FOTL	Forms of the Old Testament Literature
FRLANT	Forschungen zur Religion und Literatur des Alten und Neuen Testaments
HALOT	Koehler, Ludwig, Walter Baumgartner, and M. E. J. Richardson (eds). *The Hebrew and Aramaic Lexicon of the Old Testament*. 5 vols. Leiden: Brill, 1994–2000
HAR	*Hebrew Annual Review*

HBM	Hebrew Bible Monographs
HBT	*Horizons in Biblical Theology*
HCOT	Historical Commentary on the Old Testament
HebAI	*Hebrew Bible and Ancient Israel*
HSM	Harvard Semitic Monographs
HThKAT	Herders Theologischer Kommentar zum Alten Testament
HTS	Harvard Theological Studies
ICC	International Critical Commentary
IECOT	International Exegetical Commentary on the Old Testament
IEJ	*Israel Exploration Journal*
INJ	*Israel Numismatic Journal*
Int	*Interpretation*
IRT	Issues in Religion and Theology
ITC	International Theological Commentary
JANER	*Journal of Ancient Near Eastern Religions*
JAOS	*Journal of the American Oriental Society*
JBL	*Journal of Biblical Literature*
JBQ	*Jewish Bible Quarterly*
JETS	*Journal of the Evangelical Theological Society*
JHS	*Journal of Hebrew Scriptures*
JNES	*Journal of Near Eastern Studies*
JNSL	*Journal of Northwest Semitic Languages*
JQR	*Jewish Quarterly Review*
JSOT	*Journal for the Study of the Old Testament*
JSOTSup	Journal for the Study of Old Testament: Supplement Series
JSS	*Journal of Semitic Studies*
JSSR	*Journal for the Scientific Study of Religion*
KTU	*KTU: The Cuneiform Alphabetic Texts from Ugarit, Ras Ibn Hani, and Other Places.* Edited by Manfried Dietrich, Oswald Loretz, and Joaquin Sanmartín. Münster: Ugarit-Verlag, 1995
LHBOTS	Library of Hebrew Bible/Old Testament Studies
LSTS	Library of Second Temple Studies
NAC	New American Commentary
NIBC	New International Bible Commentary
NICOT	New International Commentary on the Old Testament
NIDOTTE	VanGemeren, Willem A., ed. *New International Dictionary of Old Testament Theology and Exegesis.* 5 vols. Grand Rapids: Zondervan, 1997
NIVAC	NIV Application Commentary
NSBT	New Studies in Biblical Theology
NTT	New Testament Tools
OBO	Orbis Biblicus et Orientalis
OBT	Overtures to Biblical Theology
ORA	Orientalische Religionen in der Antike
OTL	Old Testament Library
OtSt	*Oudtestamentische Studiën*
PRSt	*Perspectives in Religious Studies*

RelS	*Religious Studies*
RelSoc	*Religion and Society*
ResQ	*Restoration Quarterly*
SBL	Society of Biblical Literature
SBLAB	Society of Biblical Literature Academia Biblica
SBLAIL	Society of Biblical Literature Ancient Israel and Its Literature
SBLDS	Society of Biblical Literature Dissertation Series
SBLMS	Society of Biblical Literature Monograph Series
SBLRBS	Society of Biblical Literature Resources for Biblical Study
SBLSPS	Society of Biblical Literature Seminar Papers
SBLSymS	Society of Biblical Literature Symposium Series
SBLWAW	Society of Biblical Literature Writings from the Ancient World
SBT	Studies in Biblical Theology
SemeiaSt	Semeia Studies
SHBC	Smyth & Helwys Bible Commentary
SJOT	*Scandinavian Journal of the Old Testament*
SSN	Studia Semitica Neerlandica
StBibLit	Studies in Biblical Literature
STI	Studies in Theological Interpretation
SVT	Studia in Veteris Testamenti
THOTC	Two Horizons Old Testament commentary
TLOT	*Theological Lexicon of the Old Testament.* Edited by Ernst Jenni, with assistance from Claus Westermann. Translated by Mark E. Biddle. 3 vols. Peabody, MA: Hendrickson, 1997
VT	*Vetus Testamentum*
VTSup	Supplements to Vetus Testamentum
WBC	Word Biblical Commentary
WMANT	Wissenschaftliche Monographien zum Alten und Neuen Testament
ZAW	*Zeitschrift für die alttestamentliche Wissenschaft*
ZTK	*Zeitschrift für Theologie und Kirche*

Introduction

Beth M. Stovell and Daniel C. Timmer

Countless realities in the world around us prove daily that evil is all too present, and that measures taken to counter or undo it are often insufficient or ineffective. This has been especially true at the time of this book's writing in 2020 as the coronavirus (COVID-19) pandemic rages around the world. The questions why good things happen to bad people and why bad things happen to good people, while simplistic, are hardly trite or irrelevant. At present, on almost every continent dictators and political strongmen build and retain their grasp on power by oppressing or even pursuing the extermination of people under their control. At the same time, the novel coronavirus brings sickness and death indiscriminately on a scale comparable to other scourges like cancer, famine, and interpersonal violence—all of which continue to bring chaos, grief, and death. All of these evils afflict individuals, groups, and societies regardless of moral, ethnic, or other criteria, and inevitably give rise to questions concerning justice, both human and divine.

As the long history of questions dealing with divine justice and human suffering show, these concerns are not unique to our contemporary setting.[1] Although it is almost a reflex to turn to the wisdom and exilic literature for material in the Hebrew Bible/Old Testament that bears on theodicy (especially Job and Lamentations), the prophetic literature is also concerned to understand God's actions in a world where evil often seems to have the upper hand and even judgment of it involves (at least) immediate causes that are almost inevitably compromised and corrupted by sin. Despite their cultural, epistemological, and historical distance from the present-day reader, the writings that make up the Book of the

---

1. See, e.g., Michael W. Hickson, "A Brief History of Theodicy," in *The Blackwell Companion to the Problem of Evil*, ed. J. P. McBrayer and D. Howard-Snyder (Chichester: John Wiley & Sons, 2013), 1–18.

Twelve propose a variety of challenging yet compelling responses to the problem of evil and YHWH's actions with respect to it.

The essays in this volume explore the interrelated themes of theodicy and hope in individual writings of the Twelve and across the Book of the Twelve as a whole. As explained below, the authors have adopted a generally heuristic, inductive approach, especially by adopting somewhat different definitions of theodicy and by pursuing a delicate balance between the diversity and unity of the texts studied. In doing so, attention is given to literary analysis of the extant texts in dialogue with synchronic and diachronic perspectives, to the historical settings connected to the text's production and referents, and to the different ways that the authors and redactors of these books have formulated their respective theodicies and (in most cases) hope-filled responses to them. Given the relative dearth of literature dealing with these twin themes in the Twelve, the contributors hope that these essays will promote continued reflection on evil's presence, persistence, and limits while fostering realistic, holistic responses to it.[2]

This introduction briefly surveys a number of issues that situate the volume, both methodologically and conceptually, in several contemporary discourses. In the domain of method, we discuss the positioning of the following essays with respect to the synchronic–diachronic spectrum. We then explore how a thematic approach allows a focus on the topics of theodicy and hope while doing justice to the different ways that these issues are treated in the biblical texts under investigation. Next, we sketch how the volume uses theodicy in particular as a heuristic lens through which to see how the texts studied raise and answer questions related to

---

2. Theodicy is not directly addressed in Lena-Sofia Tiemeyer and Jakob Wöhrle (eds), *The Book of the Twelve: Composition, Reception, and Interpretation*, VTSup 184 (Leiden: Brill, 2020); it is intersected by articles on justice and violence in Julia M. O'Brien (ed.), *The Oxford Handbook of the Minor Prophets* (Oxford: Oxford University Press, 2021). It is dealt with directly by James L. Crenshaw, "Theodicy in the Book of the Twelve," in *Thematic Threads in the Book of the Twelve*, ed. Paul L. Redditt and Aaron Schart, BZAW 325 (Berlin: de Gruyter, 2003), 175–91. Individual books within the Twelve are more frequently studied with attention to theodicy; for example, Ruth Scoralick, *Gottes Güte und Gottes Zorn: Die Gottesprädikationen in Exodus 34,6 F und ihre intertextuellen Beziehungen zum Zwölfprophetenbuch*, HBS 33 (Freiburg: Herder, 2002), and Catherine L. Muldoon, *In Defense of Divine Justice: An Intertextual Approach to the Book of Jonah*, CBQMS (Washington, D.C.: Catholic Biblical Association of America, 2010). Studies of the closely related theme of utopia are also relevant, including Ehud Ben Zvi (ed.), *Utopia and Dystopia in Prophetic Literature*, Publications of the Finnish Exegetical Society 92 (Göttingen: Vandenhoeck & Ruprecht, 2006).

the existence of evil and the respective roles of YHWH and humanity in relation to it and to one another. Finally, we consider several contested and challenging issues that intersect theodicy broadly considered, especially anthropodicy, violence, gender, and xenophobia. We then reflect briefly on the utility of retaining theodicy and hope as mutually clarifying lenses through which to view these and the other issues the volume raises. Concise overviews of each chapter complete the introduction.

1. *Methodology*

a. *The Synchronic/Diachronic Spectrum*

In order to locate this volume's contribution to the domain of Biblical Studies, some attention to questions of method is necessary. One of the dominant methodological landscapes in Hebrew Bible/Old Testament studies is that bounded by the synchronic and diachronic horizons. As commonly used within Biblical Studies, this pair circumscribes crucially important features of the biblical texts themselves and of readers' methodological commitments, particularly with respect to the kinds of diversity these texts exhibit. The synchronic–diachronic pair itself derives from the linguistic theory of Ferdinand de Saussure, which notably did not present them as mutually exclusive or incompatible.[3] Both perspectives are historical in nature, and are required if one is to grasp both difference over time (cf. diachronic) and similarity within a single temporal cross-section or period (cf. synchronic) in a language. When employed within the field of Biblical Studies, these two perspectives typically focus attention on the nature of textual formation (holistic or compositional) and the resultant level of overall unity that the text exhibits. This is determined, in turn, by the presence or absence of surface-level cohesion (grammar, syntax, etc.) and semantic-level coherence (theme, theology, etc.) that a text exhibits, and leads to determinations of the historical circumstances in which and processes by which these texts were produced.[4]

---

3. See K. P. Hong, "Synchrony and Diachrony in Contemporary Biblical Interpretation," *CBQ* 75 (2013): 521–39.

4. Jacob Hoftijzer, "Holistic or Compositional Approach? Linguistic Remarks to the Problem," in *Synchronic or Diachronic? A Debate on Method in Old Testament Exegesis*, ed. J. C. de Moor, OtSt 34 (Leiden: Brill, 1995), 98–114; Elizabeth Robar, "Cohesion and Coherence," in *Encyclopedia of Hebrew Language and Linguistics*, ed. Geoffrey Khan, 4 vols. (Leiden: Brill, 2013), 1:471–3; Ted Sanders and Henk W. L. Pander Maat, "Cohesion and Coherence: Linguistic Approaches," in *Encyclopedia of Language and Linguistics*, ed. Keith Brown, 2nd ed. (London: Elsevier, 2006), 591–95.

Regardless of the terms in which the synchronic–diachronic spectrum
is presented, it is crucially important to recognize that it is a continuum.[5]
Its theoretical foundations prevent the interpreter from focusing on one
perspective to the exclusion of the other. Even when that fundamental
point is granted, there remains widespread disagreement as to the criteria
used to identify diachronic processes by which literary texts pass through
phases of growth, and thus of the historical circumstances in which this
took place.[6] As a result, current study of the Book of the Twelve reflects
a wide variety of opinion as to whether individual books and their
constituent parts are better viewed holistically or compositionally and as
to the nature of the collection itself.[7] Recognizing these complexities, the
essays in this volume engage these issues inductively, giving attention
to diversity of kinds (literary formation, theology, etc.) and integrating it
in their treatments of the themes of theodicy and hope. The potential for
coherence or holism is inevitably the point of departure for any critical
reading, but simultaneously makes possible the recognition of difference
or incoherence.[8] This means that while many of the essays are more
synchronic (holistic) than diachronic (compositional) in orientation, the
various kinds of diversity on which diachronic approaches characteristically focus is not neglected. The interplay of unity and diversity that
appears throughout the volume is a reflection of the diverse nature of the
texts themselves, and each essay attempts to capture both facets of the
text(s) in question as well as their relative priority.

5. See the essays in J. C. de Moor (ed.), *Synchronic or Diachronic? A Debate
on Method in Old Testament Exegesis*, OtSt 34 (Leiden: Brill, 1995), and Hong,
"Synchrony."

6. See most recently Raymond F. Person and Robert Rezetko (eds), *Empirical
Models Challenging Biblical Criticism*, SBLAIL (Atlanta: SBL, 2016), and Benjamin
Ziemer, *Kritik der Wachstumsmodells: Die Grenzen alttestamentlicher Redaktions-
geschichte im Lichte empirischer Evidenz*, VTSup 182 (Leiden: Brill, 2019).

7. See the illuminating methodologically focused exchange of Ehud Ben Zvi
and James Nogalski, *Two Sides of a Coin: Juxtaposing Views on Interpreting the
Book of the Twelve / Twelve Prophetic Books*, ed. T. Römer, Analecta Gorgiana 201
(Piscataway: Gorgias, 2009). Martin Beck proposes a tertium quid of sorts in "Das
Dodekapropheton als Anthologie," *ZAW* 118 (2006): 558–83.

8. See Northrop Frye, *Words with Power* (Toronto: University of Toronto Press,
2008), 98, who argues that "holism is the practical working assumption that every
act of criticism must begin with." Francis Landy, "Three Sides of a Coin," *JHS* 10
(2010), article 11, esp. 16–17, reaches a similar conclusion by arguing along generally
linguistic lines.

Despite the general preference of the following essays for unifying rather than separating the various parts of the texts they treat, their findings will still be valuable for scholars who favor a diachronic (or any other) approach, not least because their respective differences will foster discussion of points of agreement and disagreement.[9] Indeed, such varied reception seems inevitable given the methodological diversity of Hebrew Bible/Old Testament interpretation at present. In the context of the Book of the Twelve and with respect to the synchronic–diachronic spectrum in particular, different readers will surely propose different histories of formation for the collection and for the individual books.[10] For the same reason, different readers will find coherence, tension, or outright incompatibility at different points and for different reasons. The authors recognize this reality, and the conclusions reached in each essay are amenable to adjustment, reconfiguration, or even radical change in accord with the reader's engagement with the biblical text. At the same time, the essays focus on the text's linguistically expressed, historically situated meaning and so preserve the foundational commitments of the historical-critical tradition while guarding against the imposition of extraneous meanings upon the text.[11]

b. *Themes and Theology*

(1) *Theme and Themes*

The present volume's thematic focus contributes to what has become a sizable body of literature in the last few decades dealing with themes that

9. This dialogical approach to difference is advanced by Rolf Rendtorff, "The Book of Isaiah: A Complex Unity: Synchronic and Diachronic Reading," in *New Visions of Isaiah*, ed. R. F. Melugin and M. A. Sweeney, JSOTSup 214 (Sheffield: Sheffield Academic, 1996), 32–49.

10. For a spectrum of views on the Twelve's formation, compare Rainer Albertz, James Nogalski, and Jakob Wöhrle (eds), *Perspectives on the Formation of the Book of the Twelve: Methodological Foundations—Redactional Processes—Historical Insights*, BZAW 433 (Berlin: de Gruyter, 2012); Elena Di Pede and Donatella Scaiola (eds), *The Book of the Twelve—One Book or Many?*, FAT 2/91 (Tübingen: Mohr Siebeck, 2016); Heiko Wenzel (ed.), *The Book of the Twelve—An Anthology of Prophetic Books or The Result of Complex Redactional Processes* (Göttingen: Vandenhoeck & Ruprecht, 2017); and Tiemeyer and Wöhrle (eds), *The Book of the Twelve*. Surveys of theories for the formation of individual books can be found in the relevant chapters of Tiemeyer and Wöhrle (eds), *The Book of the Twelve*.

11. John Barton, *The Nature of Biblical Criticism* (Louisville: Westminster John Knox, 2007).

run through some or all of the Twelve.[12] "Theme" in this context derives its definition from literary studies rather than from discourse analysis, and simply refers to what a text says about its subject matter, or to a developed treatment of one of the text's subjects (since there may be more than one theme).[13] With respect to the interpretation of the literature of the Hebrew Bible/Old Testament, it is significant that literary themes are generally implicit.[14] Particularly because the concept of theodicy was developed in the modern era but is used herein as an heuristic interpretative optic, this volume's thematic orientation encourages the use of theme as an optic to perceive where and how the text's semantics and pragmatics resemble those of the theme while guarding against the imposition of an artificial hermeneutical grid.[15] A thematic approach to the Twelve is also well-suited to the highly diverse nature of the books or writings that constitute the collection. Because a theme is able to capture both continuity (one theme) and discontinuity (development of that theme over time and/or different texts), the essays can grapple with linguistic, conceptual, developmental, and theological diversity.[16] The inherently complex yet inclusive potential

---

12. In chronological order, note Terence Collins, *The Mantle of Elijah: The Redaction Criticism of the Prophetic Books*, The Biblical Seminar 20 (Sheffield: JSOT, 1993); James D. Nogalski and Marvin A. Sweeney (eds), *Reading and Hearing the Book of the Twelve*, SBLSymS 15 (Atlanta: Scholars Press, 2000); Paul L. Redditt and Aaron Schart (eds), *Thematic Threads in the Book of the Twelve*, BZAW 325 (Berlin: de Gruyter, 2003); Jason T. LeCureux, *The Thematic Unity of the Book of the Twelve*, HBM 41 (Sheffield: Sheffield Phoenix, 2012); Aaron Schart and Jutta Krispenz (eds), *Die Stadt im Zwolfprophetenbuch*, BZAW 428 (Berlin: de Gruyter, 2012); Daniel C. Timmer, *The Non-Israelite Nations in the Book of the Twelve: Thematic Coherence and the Diachronic–Synchronic Relationship in the Minor Prophets*, BINS 135 (Leiden: Brill, 2015); Lena-Sofia Tiemeyer (ed.), *Priests and Cult in the Book of the Twelve*, ANEM 14 (Atlanta: SBL, 2016).

13. This use is advocated by see LeCureux, *Thematic Unity*, 27; for its relation to other uses of the term, see Jan van Kuppevelt, "Topic and Comment," in *Concise Encyclopedia of Philosophy of Language*, ed. P. V. Lamarque (Oxford: Elsevier Science, 1997), 191–8.

14. D. J. A. Clines, *The Theme of the Pentateuch*, 2nd ed., JSOTSup 10 (Sheffield: Sheffield Academic, 1997), 19–22.

15. See, on the complicated but unavoidable relationship between semantics and pragmatics, Emma Borg, "Semantics without Pragmatics?" in *The Cambridge Handbook of Pragmatics*, ed. K. Allen and K. M. Jaszczolt (Cambridge: Cambridge University Press, 2012), 513–28.

16. Note the thematic nature of the redactional levels proposed by Jakob Wöhrle, which he argues are highly diverse with respect to chronology and theology in particular. Among others, *Fremdvölker I* announces judgment for non-Israelites as a

of a theme yields interpretations that invite the reader to look along the author's interpretative trajectory and to bring it into fruitful contact with other perspectives. It is hoped that this will enrich the texture and complexity of the themes explored while promoting productive, mutually correcting and illuminating interaction between different interpretative perspectives.

(2) *Theology*

As the plurals in the title of a recent collection of essays on the Twelve implies (*The Books of the Twelve Prophets: Minor Prophets, Major Theologies*[17]), there is no shortage of theological reflection on this corpus, nor can its theologies be easily summarized, harmonized, or tamed. This volume seeks to contribute to this growing engagement with the theologies that are present in the Book of the Twelve.[18] This task involves reckoning with these theologies within the same optic of unity and diversity introduced earlier. The integrative methodological direction of this volume allows it to draw various themes into conversation with the bifocal optic of theodicy and hope, much like Rolf Rendtorff did with the theme of the Day of YHWH in a landmark essay two decades ago.[19] Methodological grounding for this undertaking can be found, among other places, in the recent re-articulation of form criticism with its commitment to understand prophetic books as complex compositions that

whole, *Fremdvölker II* foresees the judgment of particular nations, and the *Hiel-für-die-Völker* redaction promises deliverance for at least some non-Israelites. See his *Die frühen Sammlungen des Zwölfprophetenbuches: Entstehung und Komposition*, BZAW 360 (Berlin: de Gruyter, 2006), and *Der Abschluss des Zwölfprophetenbuches: Buchübergreifende Redaktionsprozesse in den späten Sammlungen*, BZAW 389 (Berlin: de Gruyter, 2008).

17. Heinz-Josef Fabry (ed.), *The Books of the Twelve Prophets: Minor Prophets, Major Theologies*, BETL 295 (Leuven: Leuven University Press, 2018).

18. Note James D. Nogalski, "God in the Book of the Twelve," in *The Oxford Handbook of the Minor Prophets*, ed. Julia M. O'Brien (Oxford: Oxford University Press, 2021), 103–16; Heinz-Josef Fabry, "'Gewalt über Gewalt': Die dunklen Seiten Gottes im Zwölfprophetenbuch," in Fabry (ed.), *The Books of the Twelve Prophets*, 3–32; Jerry Hwang, "'My name will be great among the nations': The *Missio Dei* in the Book of the Twelve," *TynBul* 65, no. 2 (2014): 161–80; Paul House, "Endings as New Beginnings: Returning to the Lord, the Day of the Lord, and Renewal in the Book of the Twelve," in Redditt and Schart (eds), *Thematic Threads in the Book of the Twelve*, 313–38.

19. Rendtorff, "How to Read the Book of the Twelve as a Theological Unity," in Nogalski and Sweeney (eds), *Reading and Hearing the Book of the Twelve*, 75–87.

"communicate a particular, comprehensible message."[20] This theological orientation is foundational, in turn, for the exploration of theodicy and hope in the Book of Twelve.[21]

2. *Theodicy and Hope*

Unlike hope, the term theodicy has a relatively short but complex history. In their robust treatment of the topic, Laato and de Moor propose six "typologies" of theodicy: retributive, educative, eschatological, mysterious, communion (human–divine), and deterministic.[22] Together with the fact that the term itself is of recent coinage, the challenges of complexity and potential anachronism require a brief explanation of how the concept of theodicy is used in this volume.

The term "theodicy" appeared for the first time in the title of G. W. Leibniz's *Essais de Théodicée: Sur la Bonté de Dieu la Liberté de l'Homme et l'Origine du Mal* (1710). Despite the important differences that came to characterize many treatments of theodicy in the modern era, there is a significant continuity between these approaches and biblical ones.[23] Consider, as an example of the former, the "fundamental premises" of Leibniz's theodicy as identified by Laato and de Moor: one God, who "represents goodness and justice," who "has power in this world" in which "suffering and evil are a reality."[24] As an example of the latter, the worldview assumed by the prophetic books of the Hebrew Bible/ Old Testament is firmly rooted in monotheism and (with minor and rare qualifications) the assumption that YHWH is the ultimate source and standard of justice. The prophetic books are equally committed to the belief that YHWH can and does act unhindered in this world, and they repeatedly affirm the moral imperfection of human beings with a robust array of vocabulary and metaphors.

20. Michael H. Floyd, "Introduction," in *The New Form Criticism and the Book of the Twelve*, ed. M. Boda, M. Floyd, and C. Toffelmire, ANEM 10 (Atlanta: SBL, 2015), 1–15 (9). Many of the essays in that volume offer theological reflection that is interwoven with historical, literary, and other components.

21. Note the arguments for the inseparability of theodicy and theology in Daniel Castelo, *Theological Theodicy*, Cascade Companions (Eugene, OR: Cascade, 2012).

22. Antti Laato and Johannes C. de Moor, "Introduction," in *Theodicy in the World of the Bible*, ed. A. Laato and J. C. de Moor (Leiden: Brill, 2003), vii–liv (xxx).

23. Some emphases of modern treatments of theodicy are noted by Marcel Sarot, "Theodicy and Modernity: An Inquiry into the Historicity of Theodicy," in Laato and de Moor, *Theodicy in the World of the Bible*, 1–26.

24. Laato and de Moor, "Introduction," xx.

However, important differences exist between ancient Israelite and generically modern approaches to theodicy. For example, Sabot argues that in pre-modern thought, "fathoming the problem of evil led man *to doubt himself*," whereas modern treatments of theodicy tend "*to doubt God* and God's justice instead."[25] This fundamental shift, nowhere more evident than in philosophy, has significant effects on interpreters who find themselves in, and to varying degrees in accord with, whatever aspects of their context and outlook are modern.[26] The same is true for postmodern approaches to theodicy, which are arguably more varied than the modern discussion surveyed by Laato and de Moor. In addition to drawing into question overarching attempts to account for evil and human suffering, postmodern approaches emphasize the "interaction between God and created reality in which the divine is affected by the created" and occasionally concede that God is simply unknowable, making theodicy a moot issue.[27] In light of these realities, the authors of this volume have striven to appropriately define theodicy in light of the texts they study while forming their conclusions in the context of their own epistemological commitments. If these provisos are kept in mind, there is no reason to deny to theodicy, appropriately defined, its role as an interpretative optic for biblical and other ancient literature.

The essays in this volume generally incorporate the "fundamental premises" of theodicy noted above, although, like the biblical authors, the authors of these essays give more prominence to some elements than to others and occasionally question or propose refinements or limits to a particular premise. There is widespread recognition that the biblical authors believed that YHWH possesses unique deity and unlimited power over all that exists. There are occasional doubts that YHWH is perfectly and constantly good. This perspective is advanced unashamedly in Habakkuk 1, and made even more forcefully by the prophet Jonah (as found in the essays of Floyd, Fuller, Ko). The latter voice, however, seems to be countered not only by YHWH's response to Jonah, but by the overall argument of the Twelve. The Twelve repeatedly claims that the problem of theodicy cannot be resolved apart from the related question of anthropodicy, specifically as it bears on human benevolence (or lack

---

25. Sabot, "Theodicy and Modernity," 6 (emphasis original).

26. Paul S. Fiddes, "Suffering in Theology and Modern European Thought," in *The Oxford Handbook of Theology & Modern European Thought*, ed. N. Adams, G. Pattison, and G. Ward (Oxford: Oxford University Press, 2013), 169–91.

27. John Culp, "Overcoming the Limits of Theodicy: An Interactive Reciprocal Response to Evil," *International Journal for Philosophy of Religion*, 263–76 (272, 273).

thereof).[28] In the Twelve, human wrongdoing, whether against YHWH, other human beings, or the earth, is the reason that YHWH, the ultimate source of justice, cannot remain unconcerned or inactive. Yet divine patience is present and crucially important even in the many warnings of the prophets, and renders possible the delay between an offense and its punishment (as shown in the essays of Boda, Kessler, and others). This is true of the non-Israelite nations but especially of Israel and Judah, which enjoyed a special relationship with YHWH as his chosen people and covenant partner. YHWH also uses, or creates, benevolent human behavior as part of the divine response to evil (explored by Kessler, among others). This captures an interesting difference between anthropodicy, which is typically dependent on human goodness, and the prophetic books explored here, which see both good and evil in human behavior in concert with an overarching divine plan and will.[29] As noted below, however, the authors of the Twelve arrange these pieces in various ways as they construct their often hopeful responses to evil and suffering.

The reliability of YHWH's promises to deliver those who trust in him, even if they are negatively affected by the punishments inflicted upon fellow Israelites who refuse to follow YHWH, is the ground of the hope that frequently blossoms in the apparently unpromising soil of divine judgment. For the authors of the Twelve, these promises, whether to the patriarchs, the nation (Timmer and others), or David (Athas), ensure that judgment is not YHWH's last word. Rather, judgment itself is a necessary but penultimate point on a trajectory that culminates in permanent, superlative well-being for those who maintain trust in YHWH's promises and remain faithful to him.

This brings into view one of the central elements in the Twelve's treatments of theodicy: the goodness and constancy of the divine character. Constancy involves YHWH's absolute reliability, and his unchanging goodness sustains the faith of his people. In the face of human evil, his compassion and grace repeatedly offer forgiveness to the guilty if they recognize the self-destructive nature of their current direction and turn toward YHWH. In the Twelve, citations, allusions, and echoes of Exod. 34:6-7 contribute prominently to this theme, and by their very presence reinforce its theological importance. The essays in this volume

---

28. See Ionut Untea, "Anthropodicy and the Fate of Humanity in the Anthropocene: From the Disenchantment of Evil to the Re-enchantment of Suffering," *Journal of Agricultural and Environmental Ethics* 32 (2019): 873–89.

29. Frederick Sontag, "Anthropodicy or Theodicy? A Discussion with Becker's *The Structure of Evil*," *JAAR* 49 (1981): 267–74.

find different theological explanations for the predominance of mercy, including but not limited to the following: divine mercy invariably triumphs over divine justice (in Kessler, Ko); grace is a divine choice (in Boda, Floyd, Fuller, Petterson); and judgment serves the larger purpose of restoration (in Kim, Petterson).

3. *Theodicy and Anthropodicy*

As noted, theodicy and anthropodicy function in relationship with one another in the Twelve. Several chapters in this volume point to this relationship specifically. In her chapter "The Lawlessness of the Lion-God: Theodicy in the Book of Amos," Mak argues that rather than seeing Amos as theodicy, it is more correct to see it as anthropodicy. On this point Mak follows James Crenshaw. Mak explains Crenshaw's point as follows: "Crenshaw argues that such challenges [of evil, suffering, and death] to the religion's coherence occasionally led to questions about God's character (theodicy), but more often produced answers located also on the character of human beings (anthropodicy)."[30]

Questioning the character of human beings is a foundational counterpoint throughout this volume even when scholars do not name it as "anthropodicy" per se. In his chapter on "The Hope of Habakkuk in the Anthropocene Age," Floyd focuses not only on the character of God, but the character of human beings as he explores themes of theodicy and hope. Exploring the implications of human greed and destructive human interactions with their environment allows Floyd to point to God's responses to these problems of human character in Habakkuk.

Such an exploration of anthropodicy argues that, in the Twelve, understanding the character of God and the nature of his actions is not completely separate from the exploration of the character of human beings and their actions in relation to God. In fact, due to the covenantal relationship between God and the Israelite people, anthropodicy can sometimes form the justifications stated in theodicy. For example, God's responses of violence against the land can be seen as clearing the way for the land's renewal and as being a direct response to the violence and neglect that the humans with whom God is interacting have shown to the land. Other scholars have pointed to this exploration of anthropodicy

---

30. James L. Crenshaw, "Introduction: The Shift from Theodicy to Anthropodicy," in *Theodicy in the Old Testament*, ed. James L. Crenshaw, IRT 4 (Philadelphia: Fortress; London: SPCK, 1983), 5.

within Job and other forms of wisdom literature that show a theme of critique of human character and a justification for human character.[31]

As Balentine explains the concept of anthropodicy in relation to theodicy, he states, "theodicies in the Hebrew Bible clearly embrace the notion of human sinfulness as explanation of and legitimation for pain and suffering. It is the controlling idea, for example, in the Deuteronomistic tradition... Yet this view, though prominent in the Hebrew Bible, does not meet with uniform acceptance, as the prayers presented here make clear."[32] Balentine points to prayers that "raise questions that challenge the traditional view—and even change it."[33] While Balentine cites the example of Abraham speaking of Sodom and raising questions that aim to turn God's attention from the wicked to the righteous, the voice of challenge and questioning is also present in the Book of the Twelve as Amos and Habakkuk alike respond to God's judgments with debates on their harshness. In this volume, Ko points to these debates with God in the Twelve in her chapter "Theodicy and Hope in the Twelve." As Balentine explains, "It is just here, in people having their say before God, that these prayers for divine justice contribute to a dissenting voice to orthodox dogma concerning the acceptable boundaries of divine–human engagement."[34] In a similar vein, this volume at times poses the question whether, in the Twelve, the biblical texts should affirm that God's judgments are fair and right due to the actions of human sinfulness or if the biblical authors are right to question God's divine justice when they find God's judgments to be too harsh.

A focus on theodicy also has epistemological implications for the Twelve. As already noted, the prophetic voices that make up the Book of the Twelve generally assume without hesitation that YHWH is just, and the few exceptions eventually reach the same conclusion after treating protests like Habakkuk's. This is epistemologically significant in itself, and several essays press the limitations of human understanding of self, God, and the world further to prioritize anthropodicy over theodicy in this corpus. Indeed, the very category of deity suggests inherent limits in humanity, and the prophets' insistence on human moral imperfection and self-absorption imply that these limits are neither harmless nor inconsequential for an accurate understanding of evil in the world. From

31. For more on Job as anthropodicy, see Mayer I. Gruber, "The Book of Job as Anthropodicy," *BN* 136 (2008): 59–71.

32. Samuel Eugene Balentine, *Prayer in the Hebrew Bible: The Drama of Divine–Human Dialogue* (Philadelphia: Fortress, 1993), 141.

33. Ibid.

34. Ibid., 142.

another perspective, this is simply to recognize, as postmodernism has for different reasons, that modern attempts to ground certainty in the self, sense perception, history, or other imminent foundations come with their own limits.[35]

The question of the relationship between theodicy and anthropodicy is not resolved within the Twelve, nor do the authors of our volume fully agree on their position in relation to these questions. Instead, this movement back and forth between theodicy and anthropodicy plays a key role in the wrestling with simplistic theodic responses or calls for hope in the Twelve and in this volume.

4. *Key Recurring Questions*

Related to the intertwined questions of theodicy and anthropodicy are the recurring questions that explorations of theodicy and hope in the Twelve raise. One such question is whether the biblical authors are right in their various justifications of God throughout the Twelve. These recurring questions arise in several hermeneutical responses to the Twelve, including feminist and environmental responses. Unlike prophetic books like Isaiah, Jeremiah, and Ezekiel, which depict both the blessings and the judgments from God, parts of the Twelve are nearly bereft of blessing and focus entirely on the judgments of God. Nahum and Obadiah fit in this category and Amos is very similar. These thorough and consistent depictions of violence raise important ethical questions. The pervasive nature of this violence in the Twelve is central to the specific questions of violence against women and violence against "the nations," but other forms of violence also flow through the Twelve. Some scholars would go as far as to argue that it is violence itself in the Twelve that raises questions about the book's continuing value for today.

a. *Treatment of Women, Theodicy, and the Twelve*

Feminist responses to the Twelve frequently raise questions about the specific imagery used to judge Israel and its implicit and explicit depictions of violence against women.[36] Both metaphorical and literal depictions of

---

35. These shifts are explored in Leo G. Perdue, *The Collapse of History: Reconstructing Old Testament Theology* (Minneapolis: Fortress, 1994), and idem, *Reconstructing Old Testament Theology: After the Collapse of History*, OBT (Minneapolis: Fortress, 2006).

36. Examples include Gerline Baumann, *Love and Violence: Marriage as Metaphor for the Relationship between Yhwh and Israel in the Prophetic Books* (Collegeville: Liturgical, 2003); Julia M. O'Brien and Chris Franke, *The Aesthetics*

violence against women run throughout the Twelve. Some have suggested that Hosea's depiction of God as the aggrieved husband and Israel as the unfaithful wife is the foundation for depictions of Israel as unfaithful wife in Jeremiah and Ezekiel. There is debate by many about whether metaphorical depictions of women should be read in the same way as the literal violence depicted in the ripping open of pregnant women's bodies in passages such as Hos. 13:16 and Amos 1:13. As scholars like Cogan have suggested, depictions of violence against pregnant women likely serve the purpose of depicting the violence of war and the cruelest punishments inflicted by the Assyrians.[37]

Yet pointing to the violence of war does not fully answer the questions associated with the judgment that falls on Hosea's unfaithful wife, who is tied metaphorically to Israel. While such violence exists in the Twelve specifically, it is part of the larger structures of violence against women found throughout the Hebrew Bible. One way of tackling this issue is to compare ancient Near Eastern practices of marriage to the depictions in Hosea and elsewhere.[38] While this provides helpful historical context for the situation in Hosea, it does not answer whether such imagery is justifiable, especially when God is the one inflicting these punishments against a metaphorical bride.

Questions of this sort are highlighted in some of the chapters in this volume. For example, Mak's approach to theodicy in Amos points to the question of God's lawlessness and its justification within Amos. Ko's chapter also points to the voice of the people (*vox populi*) that responds to God's harsh judgments. While not directly feminist readings, these essays raise an awareness of key questions that feminist hermeneutics also ask.

In line with Third Wave and later approaches to feminism comes another avenue for feminist responses to the Twelve: highlighting the

---

of Violence in the Prophets, LHBOTS 517 (New York: T&T Clark, 2010); Julia M. O'Brien, *Challenging Prophetic Metaphor: Theology and Ideology in the Prophets* (Knoxville: Westminster John Knox, 2008); Julia M. O'Brien, *Nahum*, 2nd ed., Readings (Sheffield: Sheffield Academic, 2009); L. Juliana M. Claassens, *Mourner, Mother, Midwife: Reimagining God's Delivering Presence in the Old Testament.* (Louisville: Westminster John Knox, 2012).

37. Mordechai Cogan, "'Ripping Open Pregnant Women' in Light of an Assyrian Analogue," *JAOS* 103 (1983): 755–7. For more recent discussion of this topic see Cynthia Chapman's chapter "Daughter Zion: The Gendered Presentation of the Assyrian Crisis in First Isaiah, Zephaniah, and Nahum," in her *The Gendered Language of Warfare in the Israelite–Assyrian Encounter*, HSM 62 (Leiden: Brill 2004), 60–111.

38. See, e.g., Baumann, *Love and Violence.*

under-represented scholarship of female imagery within the Twelve. For example, scholars such as Claudia Bergmann, L. Juliana Claassens, and Christl Maier explore the maternal imagery in the Twelve in relation to this imagery in other parts of the Hebrew Bible.[39] Within this volume, scholars like Anthony Petterson take these readings seriously and incorporate their insights into their work.

b. *Xenophobia, Theodicy, and the Twelve*

Xenophobia is another relevant concern with respect to the portrayal of theodicy in the Book of the Twelve. Books like Nahum and Obadiah are explicitly and almost entirely devoted to calling for divine violence against the neighboring nations or regions of Nineveh and Edom. Meanwhile books like Amos echo with oracles against the nations like those found in Isaiah and Ezekiel. Such calls for violence against the nations prompt careful reflection and difficult questions among scholars about the ethics of divine violence and retribution. Are the people justified in their condemnation of neighboring nations? Is God justified in his promises of the nations' destruction (or at least the text's depiction of God's promises)? Are such attitudes against the nations undergirded by a general xenophobia, or, worse, does the Hebrew Bible in books like the Twelve perpetuate genocidal tendencies? In light of the topic of this volume, one could further ask if the notion of hope is possible when such calls for violence are present.

Responses to these questions are varied, but this volume seeks to engage the question of xenophobia in the Twelve responsibly in at least two ways. First, these books are a call for justice in situations of injustice with authors and communities who are victims of trauma.[40] Second,

---

39. Claudia D. Bergmann, *Childbirth as a Metaphor for Crisis: Evidence from the Ancient near East, the Hebrew Bible, and 1QH XI, 1–18*, BZAW 382 (Berlin: de Gruyter, 2008); L. Juliana M. Claassens, "From Traumatic to Narrative Memories: The Rhetorical Function of Birth Metaphors in Micah 4–5," *Acta Theologica Supplementum* 26 (2018): 221–36; Claassens, *Mourner, Mother, Midwife*; L. Juliana M. Claassens, "The Rhetorical Function of the Woman in Labor Metaphor in Jeremiah 30–31: Trauma, Gender, and Postcolonial Studies," *Journal of Theology for Southern Africa* 150 (November 2014): 67–84; Christl Maier, *Daughter Zion, Mother Zion: Gender, Space, and the Sacred in Ancient Israel* (Minneapolis: Fortress, 2008).

40. Among scholars who explore the impact of trauma in books within the Twelve, see Claassens, "From Traumatic to Narrative Memories"; L. Juliana M. Claassens, "Rethinking Humour in the Book of Jonah: Tragic Laughter as Resistance in the Context of Trauma," *OTE* 28 (2015): 655–73; Alphonso Groenewald, "'Trauma Is

these books do not only call for justice against the injustices done by the nations, but also call for justice against the injustices done by the nations of Israel and Judah themselves.

The first of these responses points out that the power dynamics between Israel and the "nations" are frequently unequal. Israel is the smaller nation who has frequently been the victim of violence by the larger surrounding empires of Assyria, Babylon, and Persia. When anger is directed at these nations, it is a response to how power has been misused and abused against the weaker and smaller nation of Israel. This is not by itself a reflection of xenophobia, but rather an expressed desire for God to protect the smaller and weaker nations against the nations who oppressed them who were stronger, more prosperous, and larger than Israel/Judah. In the cases where Israel is not the weaker in terms of power dynamics such as Obadiah's call for judgment against Edom, the reasons for this judgment have to do not with race or ethnicity, but rather with Edom's choice to provide a pathway for the stronger powerful nation of Assyria to attack the nation of Israel.

The second of these responses (and the more common in this volume) is to point to the judgments that are placed on the nation of Israel alongside their neighboring nations. If the judgment in the Twelve were only outward facing, one could point to the clear injustice and the us versus them dynamic. But the Twelve consistently points to the unjust and oppressive actions of the nations of Israel and Judah who also deserve God's judgment alongside the descriptions of their neighbors. This approach argues that ethnicity is not the key question: injustice is. Wherever injustice is found—whether outside of Israel or within it—the prophets condemn it and ask for it to be eradicated. This is consistent with the broader tension within prophetic literature which calls for judgment against the nations and against Israel.[41]

Suffering that Remains': The Contributions of Trauma Studies to Prophetic Studies," *Acta Theologica Supplementum* 26 (2018): 88–102; Alphonso Groenewald, "'For Her Wound Is Incurable: It Has Come to Judah' (Micah 1,9): Reflections on *Trauma* in Micah 4,1-5," in Fabry (ed.) *The Book of the Twelve Prophets*, 26, 353–64.

41. For discussions on the nations in prophetic literature and the tensions therein, see Matthew Lynch, "Zion's Warrior and the Nations: Isaiah 59:15b–63:6 in Isaiah's Zion Traditions," *CBQ* 70 (2008): 244–63; Paul Nadim Tarazi, "Israel and the Nations (According to Zechariah 14)," *SVTQuarterly* 38 (1994): 181–92; Rikki E. Watts, "Echoes from the Past: Israel's Ancient Traditions and the Destiny of the Nations in Isaiah 40–55," *JSOT* 28 (2004): 481–508; John Barton, *Amos's Oracles against the Nations*, SOTSMS 6 (Cambridge: Cambridge University Press, 1980);

There is still the remaining question whether violence is the appropriate response to such injustice. Does eradication of injustice justify God's violent actions in the Twelve? This question remains an open question, one that scholars would answer in different ways depending on their own disposition towards the moral status/authority of the Hebrew Bible/Old Testament and their beliefs about its representation of God.

5. *The Interrelationship of Theodicy and Hope*

Such lingering questions could cause scholars to question whether it is reasonable to speak of theodicy and hope in the same breath. One might argue that these concepts are at the heart of tensions within the Twelve and function as concepts at war with one another. Yet in his work, *Suffering and Hope: The Biblical Vision and the Human Predicament*, J. Christiaan Beker argues for a way of reading the biblical story that does not see suffering and hope as opposing forces, but instead sees them as intimately and irrevocably linked to one another.[42] According to Beker, the biblical story points to hope within suffering and even to "redemptive suffering." Behind this book lay Beker's own experiences of suffering from the time when he was imprisoned and forced to be a slave laborer during the Nazi occupation of the Netherlands. Based on his reading of the biblical texts, Beker turns from a philosophically driven version of theodicy that focuses on justification of God's ways and instead encourages his reader to embrace a biblical picture of the complexity of suffering, its causes, its results, and its uses by God.

While Beker does not address the Twelve specifically in his analysis, his exploration of suffering and hope in the Hebrew Bible provides a bridge for approaching these issues in the Book of the Twelve. Throughout this volume, scholars demonstrate how theodicy and hope function as partners rather than as opposing factions. Grace Ko and Anthony Petterson argue in their chapters examining the Twelve as a corpus for the interweaving of theodicy and hope as a whole and how hope arises in the midst of the dark places of suffering.

Richard L. Schultz, "Nationalism and Universalism in Isaiah," in *Interpreting Isaiah: Issues and Approaches*, ed. David G. Firth and H. G. M. Williamson (Downers Grove: IVP Academic, 2009), 122–44.

42. Johan Christiaan Beker, *Suffering and Hope: The Biblical Vision and the Human Predicament* (Grand Rapids: Eerdmans, 1994).

6. *Chapter by Chapter*

This volume begins with chapters that focus on the overarching themes of theodicy and hope in the Twelve as a whole and then shifts to chapters focusing on these themes in specific books within the Twelve following the order of the Jewish canon. While all of the books within the Book of the Twelve are covered in some way, Hosea, Joel, Amos, Micah, Nahum, Habakkuk, Zephaniah, Zechariah, and Malachi have a sizable portion of the entirety of a chapter dedicated to their study.

In Chapter 2, Ko provides the first of the chapters that explore the Twelve as a whole. Ko explores these concepts of theodicy and hope by examining the voice of the people (*vox populi*) which questions God's justice. She then highlights the responses of the prophets in situations of foreign invasion, the loss of national security, and environmental catastrophe. In the second half of her chapter, Ko points to the "salvation sayings that raise hope amidst atrocity in the Book of the Twelve." Her chapter argues for the underlying use of Exod. 34:6-7 throughout the Twelve that contributes to the picture of divine mercy and compassion providing hope in the Twelve.

Like Ko, in Chapter 3 Petterson also examines the Twelve as a corpus with the themes of theodicy and hope in mind. Petterson's specific focus for this chapter is exile and re-exile in the Book of the Twelve. His chapter explores the theodicy raised in the Twelve in response not only to the geographical dislocation and the loss, pain, and suffering associated with the exile, but also the continuing experiences of exilic effects in the "postexilic" period as the Israelites do not see the full restoration they had hoped for, which Petterson terms "re-exile." Alongside these themes, Petterson points to the emerging themes of salvation and blessing on the other side of that experience in the future hope of covenant renewal and restoration.

The focus shifts from all of the Twelve to Hosea in Chapter 4 with Kim's examination of the contributions from Hosea to theodicy in the Twelve. Kim argues that Hosea provides three key contributions to theodicy: (1) the vindication of God's character, emphasizing the just punishment of Israel in right measure to their sin; (2) Hosea's use of metaphorical depictions of Israel's judgment with God as aggrieved husband and rejected parent in order to generate sympathy; and (3) Hosea's depiction of God's ultimate aims in God's judgment for the purpose of repentance of the people and restoration to flourishing life.

In Chapter 5, Thomas also confronts complex imagery in the Twelve and questions of just punishment and theodicy as he examines the depictions of human trafficking in Joel 4:4-8. Thomas's approach reads discussion of human trafficking in Joel 4:4, 6, and 8 in relation to the surrounding descriptions of divine questions, human crimes, and divine verdict that characterize the literary structure of the section. Thomas points out that Joel 4:5 disrupts the literary flow and purely retributive model of theodicy otherwise present in Joel 4. Instead, Joel 4:5 only finds its fulfillment when read in light of Haggai 2. This connection between Haggai 2 and Joel 4 allows the reader to see how God "turns the violation back upon the violators" of those who performed human trafficking. Because of this, Thomas argues that Joel, read in light of Haggai, provides a theodicy that moves beyond a retributive approach towards a hope deferred. In this way, Thomas shows the interweaving of theodicy and hope created by reading the Twelve as a book.

As with Thomas and Kim, in Chapter 6, Mak focuses on the implications for theodicy through the imagery within a specific book within the Twelve. Her chapter's focus is on the lion imagery and its impact on theodicy in Amos. Mak uses Jacques Derrida and his work in *The Beast and the Sovereign* as a dialogue partner for her study. This allows Mak to ask questions about the beastly nature of God's depiction in Amos and the ability of this leonine metaphor to conceptualize God as "being-outside-the-law." Mak notes that Amos's rhetoric does not question this notion of God's lawlessness or his justice, but instead affirms that such Otherness of God needs no justification. Thus, for Mak, Amos is not actually a book that is concerned with theodicy. As she states, "If there is a theodicy here, it is the dismantling of theodicy altogether." However, Mak notes that this does not remove the reader's responsibility of questioning and even deconstructing this divine imagery and its complex implications within systems of power and violence.

Kessler's contribution, in Chapter 7, explores theodicy in Micah. He begins by dating a penultimate form of Micah 1–3 to the Assyrian attack on Jerusalem in 701, and against that background explores how that unit justifies the prophet as well as God. He then explores the ethical difficulty of divine punishment falling on a group when only some of those who constitute it are guilty, and proposes a solution based on the phrase "because of you" in Mic. 3:12. The rest of the essay explores two further responses to the destruction of Jerusalem, one based in the oracles of salvation that appear at several points in the book and the other on the importance of human repentance alongside divine purification.

Timmer focuses, in Chapter 8, on the variety of theodicies in the book of Nahum. The first involves Judah, whose past punishment and restoration are both asserted with no explicit explanation. YHWH's punishment of Assyria, by contrast, is justified by a number of accusations and condemnations. Timmer identifies several varieties of retribution in the divine punishment of Assyria, and then critically examines the moral propriety of punishing violence with more violence in light of multiple causation (divine and Medo-Babylonian). He then explores the different types of punishments that fall on the guilty and on those in the group of which they are part, and closes by highlighting the importance of divine mercy amid the violence Nahum describes.

In Chapter 9 Fuller offers a close linguistic analysis of two passages in Habakkuk that express hope (2:1; 3:18). He begins by exploring ch. 3, and especially 3:17, as the context for the following affirmation of hope. Comparing 3:17 with other descriptions of infertility in the Twelve, he notes the relative absence of divine accusation and calls for repentance in Habakkuk. Similarly, the expression of hope in 3:18 is set before agricultural infertility has been remedied, and is presented as the prophet's direct speech. Fuller concludes by arguing that the expectant attitude described in 2:1 is likewise hopeful, and serves as a pivot between the first and second sections of the book.

The interweaving of divine and human causes of evil and responses to it is at the heart of Floyd's discussion of Habakkuk 3 (Chapter 10). He begins by observing that our responses to the environmental, socio-economic, and moral problems that attend the Anthropocene age in which we live depend on "our vision of the natural world and our place in it." Against this background, he interprets Habakkuk's retelling of the combat myth and its seismic and environmental features in Chapter 3 as symbolizing Babylon's inevitable collapse. From Habakkuk 3 as a whole, he concludes that the prophet claims that YHWH will act against evil on a cosmic scale, but that those actions themselves create further chaos and so do not fully resolve the issue of theodicy. Nonetheless, Floyd concludes that YHWH's personal involvement with and actions in the world, and our own response to current problems, have the potential to usher in a new epoch that affirms life and promotes harmony after the destruction and disorder of the Anthropocene epoch.

Boda's essay, in Chapter 11, explores the theme of theodicy in connection with the empires that brought weal or woe upon Israel/Judah. After surveying several proposals for the diachronic formation of parts of the Twelve collection, he first observes that Babylon appears only twice in Hosea–Zephaniah while references to Assyria are far more frequent. This changes in the post-exilic presentation of Haggai and Zechariah 1–8, where Babylon comes to prominence, but in Zechariah 9–14 and Malachi both Assyria and Babylon are nearly absent. Boda goes on to explore the "jump" from Assyria (over Babylon) to Persia in light of the calls to silence (rather than protest over destruction) and the calls to joy that connect Habakkuk–Zephaniah with Zechariah, and finds in this dynamic a response to questions of theodicy.

In the final chapter, Athas examines the intriguing role of Zerubbabel in connection with the apparent failure of the divine promise to David and his descendants. Against the chaotic political background of Cambyses's death in 522 BCE, and in light of the king–temple link in Israel/Judah and elsewhere, Athas argues that Zerubbabel's rebuilding of the temple constituted a step toward the restoration of a Davidic kingdom in Yehud, and proposes that Zerubbabel's removal was a response to his eventual declaration of independence. These events, and the placement of Joshua the High Priest in a royal role, are reflected in passages like Zech. 9:9-12, but that optimism waned as both Davidides and priests failed to realize Judah's restoration. Athas closes by showing how Hosea, Joel, and Malachi contribute to a trajectory in the Twelve that moves toward a divine purification of the priesthood, and how Amos and especially Malachi point beyond Zechariah's disappointment with the Davidic hope. In both cases, the Twelve as a whole shows that YHWH keeps his promises to priests and king alike, despite the delays and detours in their fulfillment.

Chapter 1

Theodicy and Hope in the Book of the Twelve

Grace Ko

Introduction

Searching for meaning in the face of anomalies, especially during calamity and when good deeds are not rewarded and bad deeds are not punished, inevitably gives rise to the question of theodicy.[1] James L. Crenshaw suggests that there are three answers given to the apparent injustice of God in the ancient Near East: (1) human beings are innately evil, therefore they deserve what they get; (2) the gods are unjust, by allowing the innocent to suffer, they are not upholding justice; and (3) human knowledge is limited, since the gods are hidden.[2] All these responses may be found in some forms in Israelite attempts to grapple with the problem of theodicy.

In the first part of this chapter, I will examine the prophetic struggle to deal with the issue of theodicy in the Book of the Twelve. In order to

---

1. Theodicy is a term first coined by Gottfried von Leibniz (1646–1716). The word "theodicy" is derived from two Greek words meaning "God's righteousness." For a definition of theodicy, see R. L. Sturch, "Theodicy," in *New Dictionary of Christian Ethics and Pastoral Theology*, ed. D. J. Atkinson, D. F. Field, A. Holmes, and O. O'Donovan (Downers Grove: InterVarsity, 1995), 954–5. For a discussion of God's justice, see J. L. Crenshaw, "Popular Questioning of the Justice of God in Ancient Israel," *ZAW* 82 (1970): 380–95 (380–2).

2. J. L. Crenshaw, *Prophetic Conflict: Its Effect upon Israelite Religion*, BZAW 124 (New York: de Gruyter, 1971), 38. See also S. E. Balentine's helpful summary of perspectives on theodicy in the Hebrew Bible in *Prayer in the Hebrew Bible: The Drama of Divine–Human Dialogue*, OBT (Minneapolis: Fortress, 1993), 190.

do that, I will investigate the prophetic disputation with the *vox populi*[3] as expressed in most of the prophetic sayings in the Twelve, and the prophetic attempts to justify divine judgment. I will also discuss the relationship between prophecy and covenant to understand why the prophets' view is so fundamentally different from the view of the people. Then I will look into some of the prophetic complaints to see if any of the prophets share the same sentiment and inquisitive spirit as the populace. Since divine judgment is never the last word in the prophetic literature, the second part of this essay will focus on the salvation sayings that raise hope amidst atrocity in the Book of the Twelve, especially during the time when the national security is threatened and catastrophe brought on by the foreign invasion is at hand. I will pay special attention to the attributes of divine mercy and compassion (stated in Exod. 34:6-7) as hope for Israel.

Prophetic Disputation with Vox Populi in the Twelve

When facing calamity, the most popular sentiment displayed by the people is to blame God and to accuse him of injustice. Most of the classical prophets engage in justifying God by disputing with the *vox populi* which questions God's justice.[4] In the Book of the Twelve, Hosea accuses the Israelites of harassing the prophets, God's spokespersons, and treating them like fools and madmen (Hos. 9:7).[5] He uses his own personal experience as a betrayed husband by his adulterous wife, Gomer, to indict Israel of harlotry by forsaking God and attributing God's gifts to her lovers, the idols (1:5-13).[6] Israel's idolatry (13:2, 4) breaks the first three commandments of the Decalogue (Exod. 20:2-5a), which then leads to many social and political crimes among them. False swearing, lying, murder, stealing, adultery, bloodshed and violence break out in the society (Hos. 4:2),[7] which are direct transgressions of divine covenant and

---

3. For a detailed discussion on *vox populi*, see Crenshaw, *Prophetic Conflict*, 21–36.

4. Ibid., 30–1.

5. All Scripture quotations, unless otherwise stated, are taken from The Holy Bible, *New Revised Standard Version* (1989).

6. Hans Walter Wolff explains that the simile of Yahweh as husband is, first, "to clarify the indictment against Israel" and, secondly, "to elucidate the fact that Yahweh is the exclusive bestower of all gifts." See "Guilt and Salvation: A Study of the Prophecy of Hosea," trans. Lloyd Gaston, *Int* 15 (1961): 274–85 (278).

7. In this verse alone, Israel has broken five of the Ten Commandments, which are: nos. 3, 9, 6, 8, and 7 (Exod. 20:1-17; Deut. 5:1-21). M. Daniel Carroll R. mentions that if the verb פרץ, "break out," is counted as another violation, then the

law (8:1). On the political front, the people prefer to make alliance with foreign powers than turn to the Lord (5:13; 7:8-11; 8:9). Domestically, they change kings and dynasties through deception and violence, but never bother to seek God's counsel (7:3-7; 8:4a). Hence, according to Hosea, it is Israel's pervasive sins that cause God to terminate his covenant with them. This termination of covenant is symbolized by the naming of two of Hosea's children Lo-Ruhamah (לא רחמה), which means "not-pitied" (1:6), and Lo-Ammi (לא עמי), meaning "not my people" (1:9). Both names indicate God's relationship with Israel. The former one focuses on God's attribute as merciful, illustrating a broken relationship between God and Israel, and that God will no longer have mercy on his people.[8] As a consequence, the latter name is a reversal of Exod. 6:7: "I will take you as my people, and I will be your God."[9]

Amos also indicts Israel of her religious and social sins. Sins include oppression of the righteous and the poor, profaning the Lord's name by sexual impurity, taking garments and keeping them as pledge from the poor and drinking wine beside the altar, making the Nazirites drink wine and commanding the prophets not to prophesy (Amos 2:6-12). He declares that in spite of many catastrophes, such as famine, drought, flooding, disease, locust, plague, war, fire, which he attributes to Yahweh, Israel still refuses to turn back to God: "Yet you did not return to me" (Amos 4:6, 8, 9, 10, 11). This blatant disregard of divine warnings, which Crenshaw calls "wasted opportunity," then leads to the "doxologies of judgment" in Amos 4:13; 5:8-9; 9:5-6.[10] These doxologies, which explicitly mention Yahweh's name, function as judgments in order to exonerate God's punishment on Israel as just and righteous;[11] and to give a universal aspect

---

number of sins adds up to seven, i.e., Israel commits "perfect sin." See his "Hosea," in *The Expositor's Bible Commentary 8: Daniel–Malachi*, ed. T. Longman III and D. Garland, rev. ed. (Grand Rapids: Zondervan, 2008), 244.

8. The word "compassionate" (רחמה) may allude to Exod. 34:6.

9. John T. Willis, "'I am your God' and 'You are my People' in Hosea and Jeremiah," *ResQ* 36 (1994): 292–8, gives five metaphorical backgrounds for these terms: (1) Israel borrowed them from other ancient Near Eastern nations describing their relationship with their gods; (2) covenantal terms based on Hittite suzerainty treaties; (3) the shepherd–sheep relationship; (4) the father–child relationship; and (5) the husband–wife relationship.

10. J. L. Crenshaw, "Theodicy in the Book of the Twelve," in *Thematic Threads in the Book of the Twelve*, ed. Paul L. Redditt and Aaron Schart, BZAW 325 (New York: de Gruyter, 2003), 175–91 (190).

11. Amos also debunks Israel's spurious belief that Yahweh would deliver them because of their covenant with him, by telling them that God would punish them precisely because of their privileged position of being God's people (Amos 3:2).

to his justice.[12] Moreover, the rejection of Amos by Amaziah seals the fate of the Northern Kingdom of Israel (Amos 7:10-17).[13]

Micah accuses the people of stopping the prophets from preaching so as to avoid bringing disgrace upon the people (Mic. 2:6). He then engages in arguing with them, "Should it be said, O house of Jacob: 'Is the spirit of the Lord impatient? Are these his doings?' Do not my words do good to one who walks uprightly?" (Mic. 2:7). This shows that the people are so callous that they simply do not want to hear the prophetic message. Later Micah, representing Yahweh, launches a "covenant lawsuit" (ריב) against the people (6:1-16).[14] The structure of the lawsuit has five constituent parts:[15] (1) an introduction describing the scene of judgment, which usually involves summoning the heaven and earth, and other natural elements such as hills and mountains, as witnesses to hear Yahweh's accusation against Israel for breaking his covenant (Mic. 6:1-2); (2) an accusation by the plaintiff stating Yahweh's case against his people (Mic. 6:3, 10-12); (3) a refutation of the defendant's possible arguments (Mic. 6:6-8); (4) a pronouncement of guilt (Mic. 6:16a); and (5) a sentence or warning (Mic. 6:13-15, 16b). Micah disputes their claim that Yahweh is interested in many sacrifices, even human sacrifice (Mic 6:6-7), but rather what God required of them is simply "to do justice, to love kindness, and to walk humbly with your God" (Mic. 6:8).

The dispute over God's justice continues even in the post-exilic period when Malachi argues with the people: "You have wearied the Lord with your words. Yet you say, 'How have we wearied him?' By saying, 'All who do evil are good in the sight of the Lord, and he delights in them,' or by

12. J. L. Crenshaw, "Theodicy and Prophetic Literature," in *Theodicy in the World of the Bible*, ed. A. Raato and J. C. de Moor (Leiden: Brill, 2003), 236–55 (252–3).

13. Hetty Lalleman-de Winkel, *Jeremiah in Prophetic Tradition: An Examination of the Book of Jeremiah in the Light of Israel's Prophetic Traditions*, CBET 26 (Leuven: Peeters, 2000), 237–8, explains that the rejections of the prophetic words by the kings in both Amos' and Jeremiah's days render the prophetic intercessions ineffective and the divine judgment irreversible.

14. For a detailed discussion on the use and the meaning of the word ריב in the Old Testament, see J. Limburg, "The Root ריב and the Prophetic Lawsuit Speeches," *JBL* 88 (1969): 291–304.

15. For a detailed discussion on the form of the prophetic covenant lawsuits and their possible origins, see H. B. Huffmon, "The Covenant Lawsuit in the Prophets," *JBL* 78 (1959): 285–95. See also L. C. Allen's discussion on Mic. 6:1-8 as a covenant lawsuit in his commentary, *The Books of Joel, Obadiah, Jonah, and Micah*, NICOT (Grand Rapids: Eerdmans, 1976), 363–4; and M. O'Rourke Boyle's discussion on Amos 3:1–4:13 in "The Covenant Lawsuit of the Prophet Amos: III 1–IV 13," *VT* 21 (1971): 338–62.

asking, 'Where is the God of justice?'" (Mal. 2:17). The prophet's quotations of the people's complaints not only show that the people doubt divine justice because of the prosperity of the wicked, they also use them as an excuse to deal treacherously with each other.[16] Malachi responds to the people's charge of divine injustice by announcing that the Lord is sending his messenger to prepare his way and that he will come suddenly to purify his temple by refining the Levites and judging the evildoers, namely, the sorcerers, adulterers, perjurers, and those who defraud the laborers as well as the oppressors of the weak (3:1-5). The disputation intensifies as the prophet accuses the people of robbing God by withholding tithes and offerings. The people justify their rejection to serve the Lord by saying: "It is vain to serve God. What do we profit by keeping his command or by going about as mourners before the Lord of Hosts? Now we count the arrogant happy; evildoers not only prosper, but when they put God to the test they escape" (Mal. 3:14-15). The people's complaint reveals an underlying problem: their disappointment over the unfulfilled promises when the expected prosperity of the restored Jerusalem never materialized. It also shows that they view religious piety as a means to obtain material blessings from the Lord. But when the expected blessings do not materialize, they refuse to serve the Lord. Also, they implicitly accuse God of not carrying out justice and letting the evildoers get away with murder, as it were. Recognizing that there may be some honest doubters among the people and that the prosperity of the wicked may be too damaging to their continued trust in the Lord, Malachi reminds them that the Lord is the ultimate Judge who knows the conduct of all people. He encourages them to remain loyal to the Lord regardless of the situation, for their righteous deeds will not be in vain, because a "scroll of remembrance" is written before the Lord and that the righteous and the wicked will have two very different destinies in the Day of Judgment (3:16-21 [3:16–4:3 Eng.]).[17]

16. E. Ray Clendenen divides the book of Malachi into three main sections corresponding to the three main themes of the book: 1:2–2:9; 2:10–3:6; and 3:7–4:6. Such division links the people's complaint about divine justice to their unfaithful acts in 2:10–16, and their question on theodicy can be taken to mean that they are justifying their own treacherous acts, since God either delights in the evildoers or he does not care to mete out justice. See his essay, "C. J. H. Wright's 'Ethical Triangle' and the Threefold Structure of Malachi," in *Annual Meeting of the Evangelical Theological Society 2003* (Nashville: Broadman & Holman, 2003), 10.

17. Some scholars view this as an attempt to avoid the question of failed prophecy by mentioning such a scroll so as to push the matter to a future eschaton whereby divine justice will finally take place. See the discussion in Crenshaw, "Theodicy in the Book of the Twelve," 185–6. Nogalski, however, argues that the "book of remembrance" is not the same as the "book of life," which records the name of the righteous

Prophecy and Covenant

The people's rejection of the prophetic messages is due to their delusion that their covenant with Yahweh would guarantee them Yahweh's protection regardless of their morality. They consider the prophetic warnings as the prophets' way of trying to impose unnecessary laws on them.[18] However, Clements mentions that from the earliest stage, Israel's covenant with Yahweh has consisted of a foundation of law expressed in decalogic form to establish a standard of conduct among the people.[19] Thus the prophets are not the inventors of the law, but rather they aim to remind Israel of her covenantal obligation as a people of Yahweh. Clements also comments that the prophets are not teachers of a new doctrine of God or of a new morality. Rather they are God's messengers reminding the people of their covenantal tradition which is not "devoid of theological insights and moral value."[20]

Crenshaw opines that the prophetic emphasis on a covenantal and "holy war" tradition, together with the ancient Near Eastern worldview of a moral world governed by the retribution principle, may have given rise to the question of theodicy; and that the principle of grace fits poorly into such a worldview.[21] However, the covenant between Yahweh and Israel entails reciprocal responsibilities between both parties.[22] Yahweh elects Israel to be his people by delivering them from servitude and by granting them his covenant. Israel, as people of Yahweh, must live out the ethical demands imposed on them as expressed in the covenant law. The purpose of the law is to ensure the continuance of the covenantal relationship between Yahweh and his people. Thus the law is a gift of grace for it gives

whom the Lord will remember in the judgment day. It is, rather, a book which reminds the God fearers of God's grace, patience, and justice so that they will be able to distinguish between the righteous and the wicked, and to live accordingly. See J. D. Nogalski, "Recurring Themes in the Book of the Twelve: Creating Points of Contact for a Theological Reading," *Int* 61 (2007): 134–45.

18. A modern example is the dismissal of human deeds affecting global warming by some, thinking that it is fabricated by scientists to promote the conservation agenda.

19. R. E. Clements, *Prophecy and Covenant*, SBT 43 (London: SCM, 1965), 23. In "Ancient Oriental and Biblical Law," *BA* 17 (May 1954): 26–46 (28), G. E. Mendenhall stated the belief that the Decalogue was the foundation of the Sinai covenant, from which laws and stipulations were derived.

20. See Clements, *Prophecy and Covenant*, 16.

21. Crenshaw, *Prophetic Conflict*, 36.

22. Clements (*Prophecy and Covenant*, 69) comments that "the existence of a covenant implied of necessity the existence of a series of obligations into which the covenant members were contracted."

Israel a moral and ethical standard to regulate her life as the people of Yahweh, and to protect the covenant from annulment.[23] Israel's obedience to the law is not a precondition of the covenant, but is an expression of her loyalty to Yahweh.[24] Israel has no right to accuse Yahweh of injustice when she is the one who breaks the covenant and, as a result, experiences the covenantal curses.[25]

Prophetic Complaint against Yahweh

The populace's complaint about God's justice is usually dismissed as due to their lack of the knowledge of the Lord or due to their rebellious nature. However, when the protest comes from God's own called ones—the prophets—then the issue of theodicy becomes too acrid to ignore. When we examine the prophetic complaints against Yahweh, we will find that they share the inquisitive sentiment of the populace and raise the same questions concerning God's justice. In the Book of the Twelve, two prophets, Jonah and Habakkuk, stand out to challenge God's actions and raise the theodic cry[26] against Yahweh.[27]

Jonah challenges divine compassion toward the Assyrians, the notorious enemy of Israel, who commit atrocities against other ancient Near Eastern countries and inflict great pain on Israel.[28] Jonah does not question

---

23. Ibid., 77.

24. Ibid., 74.

25. Clements states that it was not Yahweh, but Israel, who broke the covenant by disobeying the law, and that this caused Yahweh to terminate the covenant. See his discussion in ibid., 76.

26. "Theodic crisis" is a term coined by Brueggemann, by which he means that there is a theodic settlement within a community, which teaches that moral behavior is rewarded and evil behavior is punished. But when the lived reality does not accord well with this settlement, then a theodic cry arises to challenge it. See W. Brueggemann, "Some Aspects of Theodicy in Old Testament Faith," *PRSt* 26 (Fall 1999): 253–68 (257).

27. E. Ray Clendenen opines that, according to 2 Kgs 17:13, all prophetic writings have a hortatory function "to 'warn Israel and Judah' to 'turn from [their] evil ways and keep [Yahweh's] commandments and statutes.'" In Jonah and Habakkuk, they serve their hortatory function "by inviting the ideal reader to assume the identity of the prophet himself." See the discussion in his article, "Textlinguistics and Prophecy in the Book of the Twelve," *JETS* 46 (2003): 385–99 (398).

28. Assyrians are well known for their cruelty towards their enemies. For a concise summary of ancient documents and pictorial depictions of their brutality, see Erika Bleibtreu, "Grisly Assyrian Record of Torture and Death," *BAR* 17, no. 1 (1991): 52–61.

God's compassion *per se*, for he knows full well God's compassionate nature. This is reflected in his prayer to God, "O Lord, is not this what I said while I was still in my own country? That is why I fled to Tarshish at the beginning, for I knew that you are a gracious God and merciful, slow to anger and abounding in steadfast love, and ready to relent from punishing" (Jon. 4:2). Jonah knows from Israel's experience that God is willing to pardon people and relent from sending judgment when they repent from their sins.[29] That is why he runs away to Tarshish in an attempt to flee from the Lord, so as to avoid his mission to Nineveh (1:1-3). Jonah's action shows that he does not want Nineveh to repent, for he questions the justness of proffering divine mercy to such an evil nation as Assyria,[30] under whose hand Israel has suffered tremendous loss.[31] To Jonah, God's compassion toward Assyria, a nation whose wickedness has come to God's attention (1:2), indicates divine caprice and injustice.[32] Thus, theodicy is a central issue in Jonah.[33]

In response to Jonah's resentment, God twice questions Jonah's right to be angry: "Is it right for you to be angry?" (4:4, 9).[34] He uses the growing up and withering of a vine as an object lesson to teach Jonah that he has no right to question God's justice and sovereignty; "You are concerned about the bush, for which you did not labor and which you did not grow; it came into being in a night and perished in a night. And should I not be concerned about Nineveh, that great city, in which there are more than a hundred and twenty thousand persons who do not know their right hand from their left, and also many animals?" (4:10-11). God's argument is twofold.[35] First, since the vine does not belong to Jonah, its growth is

---

29. Fretheim explains that Israel's very life depends on God's repentance of sending calamity, so it is not the changeableness of God that bothers Jonah. See Terrence E. Fretheim, "Jonah and Theodicy," *ZAW* 90 (1978): 227–37 (228).

30. Ibid., 227.

31. During the reign of Jeroboam II (793–753 BCE), Assyrian's power was declining under the reigns of several weak kings and Israel was able to enjoy a period of peace and prosperity. But historically Assyrian aggression had caused great grievances to Israel and other ancient Near Eastern nations. So Jonah's hostility towards Assyria is understandable. Eventually in 722 BCE, Assyria conquered and ended the Northern Kingdom of Israel.

32. Fretheim, "Jonah and Theodicy," 234.

33. Ibid., 229.

34. Fretheim insightfully mentions that while the divine questions in Jon. 4:4 and 4:9 are set in parallel, their content is quite different: 4:4 concerns God's deliverance of Nineveh, and 4:9 concerns divine destruction of the vine. See ibid., 233.

35. For a detailed discussion, see ibid., 234–5.

purely a gift from God. Therefore, Jonah has no right to be angry when it is taken away by God. Secondly, the plant is only short-lived and insignificant ("came into being in a night and perished in a night"), yet Jonah is concerned about its existence; how, then, can he blame God for being concerned about the well-being of the city of Nineveh when so many lives are at stake? Moreover, Jonah's story also reveals that Yahweh, as a universal sovereign, cares for the other nations just as much as he cares for Israel. Since Israel has experienced divine saving acts despite their continuous rebellious acts, they do not have the right to raise questions of divine justice with regard to Nineveh.[36]

Habakkuk is unique among the Twelve in his message. While most of the other prophets engage in warning Israelites against breaking the covenant with Yahweh, and prophesying foreign invasion as the just divine judgment, Habakkuk accuses God of his aloofness and even obliviousness to rampant wickedness (Hab. 1:1-4). When God reveals that he is using the Babylonians as his tool of judgment (Hab. 1:5-11), Habakkuk further challenges God's justice for his appointment of brutal Babylon as a judgment on Judah (Hab. 1:12-17). According to Habakkuk, this is incongruous with Yahweh's nature, and a gross miscarriage of divine justice, since Judah is a more righteous nation than Babylon (Hab. 1:13). To him, God, as a righteous judge, is supposed to calculate degrees of righteousness and favor the less unrighteous. But, in reality, this is not the case; hence he challenges theodicy on behalf of the people by complaining against God. The questions raised by Habakkuk indeed give voice to the honest doubters who earnestly seek to reconcile the hard reality of life with belief in a benevolent God. This open challenge against divine justice reflects the popular sentiment and would certainly attract attention and gain approval from his audience. It is this bold challenge against God, on behalf of the people, that makes Habakkuk unique among his peers. I will address his resolution on the issue of theodicy in the second half of this study.

Hope in the Book of the Twelve

Although the classical prophets usually warn the Israelites of the certainty of divine judgment, the message of doom will never be their last word.[37] In the midst of doom and destruction, the prophets always look beyond the

36. Ibid., 230.

37. Clendenen ("Textlinguistics and Prophecy," 388) sees the judgment oracles as one of the elements of the prophetic hortatory discourse, which serves to deter Israel and Judah from disobeying Yahweh and to motivate their repentance.

judgment and pronounce a future salvation plan for Israel.[38] This message of hope in the Book of the Twelve is not missed in Jewish interpretation of the prophetic message, but is affirmed in Sir. 49:10: "May the bones of the twelve prophets revive from where they lie, for they comforted the people of Jacob and delivered them with confident hope."[39]

This "confident hope," which concerns Israel's salvation, is made possible by the divine attributes as proclaimed in Exod. 34:6-7:

> The Lord, the Lord, a God compassionate (רחום) and gracious (חנון), slow to anger, and abounding in steadfast love (חסד) and faithfulness (אמת). Keeping steadfast love for thousands, forgiving iniquity and transgression and sin. Yet he by no means clearing the guilty, but visiting iniquity of the fathers on the children, and on the children's children to the third and fourth generations.[40]

Raymond C. Van Leeuwen argues convincingly that the final redactor of Hosea–Micah uses this passage "as a base text in developing an overarching theodicy vis-à-vis the incidents of 722 and 586 B.C."[41] In addition to that purpose, I suggest that this passage, which describes divine attributes, is also the basis of Israel's hope. We shall now examine how this passage helps to arouse hope in the Book of the Twelve.

Hosea

While in Hosea there is no direct reference to Exod. 34:6-7, the hope of salvation is seen in the re-naming of Hosea's children in Hos. 2:1-3 [1:10–2:1 Eng.] and 2:24-25 [22-23 Eng.], where Lo-Ammi (לא עמי), "not my people," is changed to Ammi (עמי), "my people," and Lo-Ruhamah (לא רחמה), "not-pitied," is renamed Ruhamah (רחמה), "pitied." And the indictment and judgment of Israel in Jezreel (1:4-5) will become a day when

---

38. Most of the prophetic books end with a positive hope for the future of Israel as a whole. In most cases these words of hope likely come from the prophets themselves, but it is possible that these could be from later editors as well.

39. R. E. Clements, "Patterns in the Prophetic Canon," in *Canon and Authority: Essays in the Old Testament Religion and Theology*, ed. G. W. Coats and B. O. Long (Philadelphia: Fortress, 1977), 42–55 (44). He explains that it is the "canonical form of prophecy that brings together the various sayings and messages of individual prophets and coordinates them into a unified 'message.' Likewise, it is this canonical form and structure which make prophecy as a whole a message of coming salvation."

40. Translation here is mine.

41. Raymond C. Van Leeuwen, "Scribal Wisdom and Theodicy in the Book of the Twelve," in *In Search of Wisdom: Essays in Memory of John G. Gammie*, ed. Leo G Perdue et al. (Louisville: Westminster John Knox, 1993), 31–49.

God will answer and sow (יזרעאל)[42] the land by bringing back the people and granting them bountiful agricultural products (2:22-23). The reason for this reversal is due to divine compassion for Israel, which accords well with Yahweh's compassionate attribute as described in Exod. 34:6-7a.

God's love and compassion for Israel come through most vividly in Hos. 11:1-11.[43] Here Yahweh is portrayed as a pained father dealing with his rebellious son, Israel, who goes on his wayward way by committing idolatry, despite divine loving care and guidance. Israel's apostasy leads to judgment. Yet this hurts Yahweh so much to see Israel in distress that he cries out, "How can I give you up, Ephraim? How can I hand you over, Israel? How can I make you like Admah? How can I treat you like Zeboiim? My heart is turned over within me, my compassions are kindled" (v. 8).[44] The divine pathos is shown in this soliloquy as he deliberates over what to do. Then he resolves to withdraw his wrath (v. 9), which may allude to Yahweh's slowness of anger in Exod. 34:6. Indeed, divine mercy always prevails over his justice when there is a tension between them.[45]

Joel

After a severe locust plague that ruins all the crops in Judah, Joel tells the people that the plague is a divine warning of an upcoming devastating judgment and urges the Judeans to repent and return to God.[46] Joel's

42. A play on Jezreel's name, which mean "God sows."
43. I see a chiasmus in this passage as follows:
   A. God calls and delivers Israel out of Egypt (v. 1)
     B. Israel refuses to follow Yahweh and her apostasy (v. 2)
       C. God's loving care for Israel but Israel does not know (v. 3)
         D. God's merciful guidance and providence for Israel (v. 4)
           E. Israel's refusal to return to Yahweh leads to exile to Assyria (v. 5)
             F. The consequence of rebellion (v. 6)
           E' Israel's forsaking God leads to heavy burden (v. 7)
         D' Divine deliberation and compassion for Israel (v. 8)
       C' God's resolution to recede his anger against Israel (v. 9)
     B' God roars and Israel follows (v. 10)
   A' God lets Israel return and settles them in their homes (v. 11)
44. J. Gerald Janzen quotes Mays in calling this form of questioning an "intense impassioned self-questioning by Yahweh," which is in full view. See Janzen, "Metaphor and Reality in Hosea 11," *Semeia* 24 (1982): 7–44 (10).
45. So, Crenshaw when he says, "the belief in justice stands in tension with mercy, and when the two come into conflict mercy will prevail" ("Theodicy in the Book of the Twelve," 189).
46. Richard D. Patterson, "Joel," in Longman and Garland (eds), *The Expositor's Bible Commentary*, 8:307–46 (313).

advice is based on Yahweh's attributes and he quotes Exod. 34:6: "Rend your hearts and not your garments, and return to the Lord your God, for he is gracious and merciful, slow to anger, and abounding in steadfast love and relents from [sending] calamity" (Joel 2:13). Although he does not take God's mercy for granted,[47] his firm belief in God's attributes leads him to trust that repentance is the only way to move God to have compassion (חוס) on his people (2:14, 17).[48] Joel's ministry seems to be successful and he ends the book with a glorious hope of Zion becoming the permanent residence of Yahweh (4:17, 21 [3:17, 21 Eng.]).[49]

Amos

Amos is usually regarded as a "preacher of judgment and doom,"[50] since his messages are mostly on divine judgment of human sins, particularly the sins of Israel. These judgments are Yahweh's warnings to stimulate Israel's repentance to return to him.[51] Amidst all the doom sayings, there are at least two incidents whereby Amos pleads to Yahweh, appealing to his compassionate nature and his love for Israel: "O Lord God, please forgive/stop! How can Jacob stand? For he is so small!" (Amos 7:2, 5). Amos' success in changing Yahweh's heart in these two instances shows that Yahweh is open to the prophetic intercession for the salvation of Israel. Although Amos' message is mainly "doom and gloom," the book ends with the hope of Israel's future restoration (Amos 9:11-15).[52] This restoration is made possible due to divine compassion for Israel and his faithfulness to his covenant.

Obadiah

Obadiah accuses Edom of collaborating with the Chaldeans during the Babylonian invasion of Jerusalem in 586 BCE. Edom's lack of familial

47. This is confirmed by Joel's use of "who knows?" in 2:14, which allows divine sovereignty to take place (cf. Jon. 3:9)

48. Patterson, "Joel," 330.

49. Nogalski, "Recurring Themes in the Book of the Twelve," 132, comments that by changing the recipient of divine wrath to the nations in Joel 4:21 (3:21 Eng.), both Joel 2:13 and 4:21 (3:21 Eng.) then complete the hope and judgment parts of Exod 34:6–7. Moreover, judgment on Israel's enemies signifies hope and salvation for Israel.

50. Walter Brueggemann, "Amos' Intercessory Formula," *VT* 19 (1969): 385–99 (385).

51. Crenshaw, "Theodicy in the Book of the Twelve," 190.

52. The descriptions in Amos 9:11—the fallen booth of David, breached wall and ruins—presuppose a time after the fall of Judah in 586 BCE.

loyalty and treachery against Judah are the main reasons for divine punishment (vv. 10-16).[53] While Edom will face destruction, Israel as a whole on the other hand, will be restored (vv. 17-21).[54] Their distinct destiny is due to divine attributes. God shows his justice by meting out judgment when Edom fails to carry out the familial loyalty (חסד) and faithfulness (אמת);[55] and he demonstrates divine compassion (רחום) on Israel because of his covenant with them.

Jonah

God's sovereignty and his compassion on all nations are demonstrated most clearly in Jon. 4:10-11. Jonah obviously understands God's nature, for he quotes Exod. 34:6 in his complaint against God (4:2). What bothers him is the issue of theodicy that God would extend forgiveness to such a brutal nation as Assyria.[56] However, what he fails to see is that God's provisional pardon on Assyria is also an implicit call for Israel's repentance. If God would pardon even a brutal nation like Assyria, how much more would he do for Israel if she would only return to him?

Micah

Hope in Micah can be seen from its repetitive pattern of alternating arrangement of judgment and salvation. I follow Leslie C. Allen and see an intentional chiastic structure in the whole book by repeating the catchwords.[57]

---

53. In this section Judah is called "your brother Jacob" (יעקב אחיך), emphasizing their ancestral familial relationship, for Esau and Jacob are twin brothers.

54. The mention of "Mount Zion" in v. 17 and "house of Joseph" in v. 18 indicate that the whole Israel is in view.

55. Historically Edom was hostile to Israel since the days when Israel first came out of Egypt. They refused to let Israel pass through their territory (Num. 20:14-21; cf. Deut. 2:4-8; Judg. 11:17-18). Edom was among Israel's enemies to plunder and oppress them (1 Sam. 14:47). The subjugation of Edom by David in 2 Sam. 8:13-14 is seen as part of the fulfillment of the Lord's promise to grant Israel peace and security (2 Sam. 7:10). In prophetic literature, Edom is singled out to represent those who oppose God's people, due to its relationship with Israel.

56. Stephen Derek Cook, in his unpublished dissertation "'Who Knows?' Reading the Book of Jonah as a Satirical Challenge to Theodicy of the Exile" (PhD diss., University of Sydney, 2019), 315, argues that the main concern of Jonah's story is not about theodicy, but that God's mercy is unpredictable and unknowable. But his argument contradicts Jonah's complaint in 4:2, for he knows full well of God's mercy and his proclivity to forgive when people repent.

57. Leslie C. Allen, *The Books of Joel, Obadiah, and Micah*, NICOT (Grand Rapids: Eerdmans, 1976), 260.

I. Judgment against Samaria and Jerusalem, 1:2–2:11 (שמעו)
   Promise of deliverance, 2:12-13
II. A. Judgment against Israel's leader, 3:1-12 (שמעו)
   Hope for Zion's future, 4:1-5 (והיה)
      B. Remnant's hope: restoration of ruler, 4:6-8 (שארית, אתה)
         C. Present dire situation in Zion with hope of deliverance,
         4:9-10 (עתה)
         Present siege by nations but eventual victory, 4:11-13 (עתה)
         Present helpless judges and the future ideal king, 4:14–5:5
         (5:1-6 Eng.) (עתה)
      B'. The future role of Israel's remnants, 5:6-8 (5:7-9 Eng.) (שארית)
   A'. God's future purge, 5:9-13 (10-14 Eng.) (והיה)
   Hope of deliverance in the future, 5:14 (5:15 Eng.)
III. God's indictment against Israel, 6:1–7:6 (שמעו)
   A prophetic liturgy: hopes and prayers, 7:7-20

The structure of the book and the presence of catchwords give enough evidence that the book does contain an internal coherence.[58] It is my opinion that the intentional arrangement of a woe–weal pattern in the book is to demonstrate that human sins can never thwart the divine sovereign plan. This theme is further supported by specific mention of those who "plan" (חשב) iniquity and God's "planning" (חשב) of disaster in 2:1, 3. Moreover, God also recalls how he thwarted the "plot" (יעץ) of Balak against Israel in 6:5. This certainty and permanence of God's sovereign plan, which always involves the redemption of the remnants, becomes the source of hope and comfort for God's people throughout history. Furthermore, Micah's paraphrasing of Exod. 15:11 and Exod. 34:6-7 in 7:18-19 celebrates God's faithfulness (אמת) to Jacob and his steadfast love (חסד) to Abraham and his descendants (7:20). Hence Israel's future depends on divine attributes as well as his plan.

Nahum

While both Jonah and Micah emphasize Yahweh's compassion (רחם) and maintain that divine mercy is the basis for Nineveh's provisional deliverance and Israel's hope for future restoration, Nah. 1:2-3 paraphrases Exod. 34:6-7 to accentuate divine justice by prophesying Yahweh's punishment on Nineveh, who destroys Israel. Not only does Nahum mention hope for Judah in Nah. 1:12-15 and Israel in 2:2, the prophetic pronouncement of the destruction of Assyria in the book, particularly the

58. Willis, "Structure of Micah," 193, affirms that the structure of Micah can be demonstrated to be coherent. Although some scholars doubt the authenticity of some parts of the book, the chiastic structure is likely from the hand of the prophet.

dirge for the Assyrian king in 3:18-19 also avenges the Northern Kingdom
of Israel's suffering and also serves as an answer to the theodicy question
raised by Jonah.[59] Moreover, most would agree that oracles against the
nations, who are the enemies of Israel, are meant to be oracles of salvation
for Israel as a whole.

Habakkuk

Habakkuk speaks of the inevitability of the Babylonian invasion but at
the same time assures the people of Yahweh's justice and the eventual
destruction of Babylon. To Habakkuk, the divine revelation in Hab. 2:4b
that "the righteous by his faithfulness will live" (וצדיק באמונתו יחיה) is a
real comfort and inspiration.[60] After God's revelation, he then understands
that Yahweh's justice will prevail and that the righteous should persevere
through extremely distressing situation. The prophetic pronouncement of
the five woe oracles against the Babylonians (2:6-19), together with the
theophanic hymn celebrating Yahweh's power over his enemy (3:3-15),
give him strength to endure the imminent atrocity. Between the woe
oracles and the theophany, we hear the prophet pleading to God, "O
Lord, I have heard of your report...In the midst of years revive it, in the
midst of years make it known. In turmoil, remember compassion (רחם)"
(3:2).[61] Thus, it is Yahweh's compassion that he appeals to and it is
God's "remembering" and presence that give him hope. Then Habakkuk
professes his resolution to trust and rejoice in the Lord even when he is
deprived of all of life's necessities (3:16-19).

Zephaniah

Zephaniah explains that the universal disregard for Yahweh and his law
leads to the coming of the "Day of the Lord" (יום יהוה). According to
Zephaniah, in this awesome day, God will bring universal judgment

59. Paul L. Redditt, "The Production and Reading of the Book of the Twelve," in
Nogalski and Sweeney (eds), *Reading and Hearing the Book of the Twelve*, 15, makes
a citation error of Mic. 7:18-19 instead of Nah. 3:18-19.

60. There is an ambiguity as to whose faithfulness the writer has in mind in the
divine response, "But the righteous (וצדיק) in his faithfulness (באמונתו) shall live"
(2:4b). There have been three proposals: (1) God's faithfulness, which is supported by
LXX; (2) the trustworthiness of the vision—see J. Gerald Janzen, "Habakkuk 2:2-4
in the Light of Recent Philological Advances," *HTR* 73 (1980): 59–62; and (3) the
faithfulness of the righteous person since he is the closest antecedent. I opt for the
third meaning for this addresses Habakkuk's existential concern for the survival of
the righteous during adversity.

61. Translation here is mine.

not just on humanity but on all earth's creatures also—all animals, birds, and fish (1:2-3). This will be a reversal of the creation account in Gen. 1:20-27.[62] Despite all these dreadful pronouncements, Zephaniah also offers safety and shelter to those righteous ones who humbly seek Yahweh (2:3).[63] The book ends with the message of a future restoration of Jerusalem with the coming of worshippers from all nations and the return of God's people (3:9-20). Israel's hope for restoration is based on God's deep love (אהבה) for them (3:17).[64]

Haggai

Haggai seeks to rally the postexilic community to complete the building of the Second Temple, which they have started since their return from Babylon some sixteen years ago.[65] He points out that their abandonment of the temple building project is the reason for their meager agricultural harvest and economic failure. He admonishes them to set their priorities straight and work on building God's temple first. Haggai further encourages them by God's promise of his presence and his blessing, as

62. The order of living things listed here is in reverse order of the creation account in Gen. 1. For a detailed discussion on the relationship between Zeph. 1:2-3 and the creation account in Gen. 1–2, see Michael De Roche, "Zephaniah 1:2-3: The 'Sweeping' of Creation," *VT* 30 (1980): 104–9.

63. So, Larry L. Walker, "Zephaniah," in Longman and Garland (eds), *The Expositor's Bible Commentary*, 8:655.

64. Here the mention of Zion and Israel together in 3:14 indicates that the restoration is for Israel as a whole.

65. Some scholars opine that the Jews did not return right after Cyrus' decree in 538 BCE, but sometime during the later days of Cambyses' reign (530–522 BCE). If that was the case, then the Jews had only returned three to five years beforehand. This view is proposed by Mark Leuchter and George Athas in an unpublished conference paper, "Is Cambyses Among the Persians?" However, most scholars take Ezra 1; 5:13-16 as describing a situation in the early period of Cyrus' reign and conclude that the returnees started to build the Temple foundation right way but abandoned it later due to the hostility from the neighboring people. See Robert B. Chisholm Jr., *Interpreting the Minor Prophets* (Grand Rapids: Zondervan, 1990), 221. John Bright stated that "eighteen years after the work on the Temple had begun, it had not progressed beyond the foundation…"; see *A History of Israel*, 4th ed. (Louisville: Westminster John Knox, 2000), 367. Pieter A. Verhoef, *The Books of Haggai and Malachi*, NICOT (Grand Rapids: Eerdmans, 1987), 31, opines that Zerubbabel led the return to Jerusalem in 537 BCE. Although we cannot be sure of Zerubbabel's return date, there is a consensus that the first return under Sheshbazzar occurred shortly after Cyrus' decree in 538 BCE, and that they started building the Temple foundation right away but left unfinished.

well as giving them hope for a glorious future (2:5-9). Haggai's message is well received by the people, and that brings out God's promise of restoration and blessing (2:19b-23).

Zechariah

Zechariah is called "the prophet of hope and encouragement in troublous time."[66] The reason is that Zechariah prophesies the bright future that awaits Jerusalem. All this is made possible because Yahweh is "jealous for Zion with great jealousy (קנאה)" and "jealous for her with great wrath" (8:2). Here the word jealous is the same word that the Lord used to describe himself as "a jealous God" (אל קנא) in Exod. 20:5; 34:14. The reason for God's jealousy is because of his love for Israel, a love that demands exclusive loyalty.[67] It is precisely because of this love that Yahweh determines to return and make Jerusalem his permanent resident and calls it a "City of Truth" (עיר־אמת) (8:3).[68] He also promises the coming of a righteous and peaceful Messiah (9:9-10), and at the end, Yahweh himself is going to be king over the whole earth (14:9), and Jerusalem will be the center for all nations to come and worship God (14:20-21).

Malachi

Malachi tries to combat the disenchantment of the postexilic community. Their disappointment comes from the difficult life in Palestine: scanty harvests (cf. Hag. 1:6, 10), a failed economy, hostile neighbors (cf. Neh. 4:1-3, 7-8), and internal division between the poor and the rich (cf. Neh. 5:1-5). The reality facing the postexilic community is not even remotely close to the rosy and glorious future prophesized by the previous prophets. This leads to a general spiritual malaise in the society, which is revealed by the six disputations between Malachi and the populace (Mal. 1:2-5; 1:6–2:9; 2:10-16; 2:17–3:5; 3:6-12; 3:13-21 [4:3 Eng.]). Despite this gloomy portrayal of the postexilic community, Malachi still gives them hope by focusing on the certainty of the coming of the Messiah, who will punish the wicked and have compassion (חמל) on those who serve the Lord (3:17-18). Thus, God's justice and compassion give the disillusioned people hope to carry on.

---

66. Kenneth L. Barker quotes Theodore Laetsch in his commentary, "Zechariah," in Longman and Garland (eds), *The Expositor's Bible Commentary*, 8:730.

67. This love is similar to the love between husband and wife, which demands exclusivity.

68. This name recalls Isaiah's words that the Lord is going to restore Jerusalem so that it will be called "the city of righteousness, the faithful city (קריה נאמנה)" (Isa. 1:26).

Conclusion

Israel's covenant with Yahweh entails reciprocal responsibilities between both parties. On the one hand, Yahweh as the suzerain sovereign promises to protect Israel and to ensure the well-being of his people. On the other hand, Israel, as God's people, should observe and keep God's covenantal law that is imposed on them. Israel violates the covenantal law by committing idolatry, social, political, and cultic crimes. Thus, they incur the covenantal curses as stated in Deut. 28:15-68. The adversity that befalls them leads the people to question God's justice. The prophets as God's spokesmen justify divine action by accusing the Israelites of breaking the covenantal law. Two prophets among the Twelve, Jonah and Habakkuk, stand on the side of the people and raise the issue of theodicy on behalf of them. Their encounters and discussions with Yahweh provide us with a better understanding of divine attributes and will.

Even though God metes out his judgment against the Israelites and gives them over to their enemies, Yahweh's compassion and mercy still remain with them. The intense self-questioning in Hos. 11:8 shows divine pathos most vividly. It is the divine attributes of compassion (רחום), steadfast love (חסד), faithfulness (אמת), and indeed his justice and righteousness as expressed in Exod. 34:6-7, that drive him to offer the Israelites future hope of salvation and restoration. And it is this confident hope that empowers and enables God's suffering righteous ones in all generations to sing the song of victory with Habakkuk:

> Though the fig tree does not blossom
> And no fruit is on the vines,
> [Though] the produce of the olive fails
> And the fields yields no food,
> Though the flock is cut off from the fold
> And there is no herd in the stalls,
> Yet I will rejoice in the Lord,
> I will exult in the God of my salvation.
> God, the Lord is my strength,
> He makes my feet like the feet of a deer,
> And makes me tread upon my heights. (Hab. 3:17-19)

Chapter 2

EXILE AND RE-EXILE IN THE BOOK OF THE TWELVE

Anthony R. Petterson

The study of exile in the Bible has become popular in recent decades, exhibited in a variety of approaches and concerns. These include historical studies that seek to uncover the nature and extent of Israel's experience of exile, sociological studies that map types of forced migration to assess things like how exile shapes a group's identity, and literary and theological studies that trace the theme of exile across the biblical material.[1] I adopt the last of these approaches in this study to trace the theme of exile across the Book of the Twelve, exploring its use and associations.

In her literary study, Martien Halvorson-Taylor argues that "exile" is much more than a state of geographical displacement and that in

---

1. This variety of approaches is reflected in the following volumes: Gary N. Knoppers, Lester L. Grabbe, and Deirdre N. Fulton (eds), *Exile and Restoration Revisited: Essays on the Babylonian and Persian Periods in Memory of Peter R. Ackroyd*, LSTS 73 (London: T&T Clark, 2009); Lester L. Grabbe (ed.), *Leading Captivity Captive: "The Exile" as History and Ideology*, JSOTSup 278 (Sheffield: Sheffield Academic, 1998); John J. Ahn and Jill Middlemas (eds), *By the Irrigation Canals of Babylon: Approaches to the Study of the Exile*, LHBOTS 526 (London: T&T Clark, 2012); Mark J. Boda et al. (eds), *The Prophets Speak on Forced Migration* (Atlanta: SBL, 2015); Brad E. Kelle et al. (eds), *Interpreting Exile: Displacement and Deportation in Biblical and Modern Contexts* (Atlanta: SBL, 2011). N. T. Wright's thesis of an ongoing exile in Second Temple Judaism as crucial background for the New Testament has sparked lively debate. See James M. Scott (ed.), *Exile: A Conversation with N. T. Wright* (Downers Grove: IVP Academic, 2017).

biblical usage it becomes a metaphor which is "the hub of a system of associations."[2] The associations she identifies are death, sterility, hunger, disease, and futility, which result from "divine wrath and a separation from the deity."[3] While exile is not a metaphor in the curses of Leviticus 26 and Deuteronomy 28, but refers to the actual deportation of captive peoples, its connection in that context with the wrath of God means that exile comes to represent a form of death even before the Babylonian exile takes place.[4] Halvorson-Taylor also observes a number of passages that limit exile to a set period (e.g., Jer. 25:11-12; 29:10; Ezek. 4:5-6; Ezra 1:1-3a; 2 Chron. 36:22-23), yet she contends that associations connected with exile (such as political disenfranchisement, social inequality, and alienation from God) continue to exist even after the people have returned from exile and so there is a sense that Israel is still in exile even though the people have returned to the land, especially since they are still slaves to foreign powers (e.g., Dan. 9:25; Ezra 9:8-9; cf. 2 Chron. 36:20).[5] The focus of Halvorson-Taylor's study is "the early, formative period in which the Babylonian exile was transformed from a historical experience into a multivalent symbol of physical, mental, and spiritual distress."[6] She examines in detail Jeremiah 30–31, Isaiah 40–55, and Zechariah 1–8.

This characterization of exile is fruitful, yet for the purposes of her study Halvorson-Taylor only looks at Zechariah 1–8 in the Book of the Twelve. In Zechariah 9–14 the theme of exile undergoes a significant development where the prophet envisages another attack on Jerusalem by the nations. The motif of exile is deployed explicitly in Zech. 13:8-9 and 14:2 to speak of the refinement and purification of God's people who are restored to the covenant blessings. Therefore, not only is there evidence

---

2. Martien A. Halvorson-Taylor, *Enduring Exile: The Metaphorization of Exile in the Hebrew Bible* (Leiden: Brill, 2011), 21.

3. Ibid., 37–8. She argues that since exile as a curse is extensively found across literature of the ancient Near East, that references to exile in biblical texts need not postdate the Babylonian exile (31).

4. Ibid., 16: "a comparison of the biblical curses with ancient Near Eastern treaties dating from the ninth to seventh centuries BCE will demonstrate that the canonical form of the biblical curses is a reliable witness to pre-exilic patterns of thinking about exile. The context of exile in the treaty curses suggests that even before the development of the 'enduring exile' motif proper, exile was never simply conceived of as geographical displacement. It was already fraught with associations and connotations, to the point where exile could function as a synecdoche for the roster of divine punishments enumerated in the treaties."

5. Ibid., 7–8.

6. Ibid., 41.

that exile endures in the so-called postexilic period (as Halvorson-Taylor demonstrates), but Zechariah 9–14 foresees another exile to come. I have termed this a "re-exile" not only to indicate that it is an exile beyond exile, but that the Babylonian exile did not bring about the restoration that the earlier prophets had spoken of and there is a sense in which it needed to be repeated.

This study seeks to set this later development in context by tracing the theme of exile across the Twelve in its Masoretic order.[7] In so doing, the implications of the theme of exile for theodicy and hope will be explored. From Hosea onwards, exile stands as an image of national punishment for sin (for Israel and the nations) and has associations of disaster and death as an outworking of the wrath of God. The hope for salvation lies on the other side of punishment when Yahweh will forgive his people. With the book of Amos, exile does not lose these associations, but also is closely associated with the idea that through exile a remnant will be refined. It is this remnant that will be restored to the land to inherit the hoped-for blessings of Yahweh. Yet after the national experience of exile and return to the land, the books of Haggai and Zechariah indicate that aspects of exile continue—certainly the full extent of the prophetic expectations for restoration after exile have not materialized. The prospect for salvation and blessing is only on the other side of another experience of exile, which will refine a remnant who experience the blessings of covenant renewal. In this way, exile is closely aligned with hope for a new salvific work of Yahweh.

Relevant passages for this study were identified by a close reading of the Twelve and a vocabulary search, beginning with the vocabulary of exile identified in Deuteronomy by Kenneth Turner.[8] He identifies two primary roots, גלה ("go into exile") and שבה ("take captive"). In addition, he identifies eleven secondary terms which employ war and agricultural imagery as metaphors for exile.[9] Since they function metaphorically, these terms do not always denote exile in the Twelve. In addition to the

---

7. This is not to disparage the order in the Greek tradition but acknowledges that it was the Hebrew tradition that was ultimately followed in the ordering of the books of the Twelve in the Christian Old Testament. See further Mark J. Boda, *A Severe Mercy: Sin and Its Remedy in the Old Testament* (Winona Lake: Eisenbrauns, 2009), 7–8.

8. Kenneth J. Turner, *The Death of Deaths in the Death of Israel: Deuteronomy's Theology of Exile* (Eugene: Wipf & Stock, 2011), 34.

9. These are: ברח, "go through, flee"; דבר, "turn, drive away; subjugate"; זרה, "scatter, fan, winnow"; טול, "hurl, cast"; נדד, "retreat, flee, depart, wander"; נדח, "impel, thrust, banish"; נהג, "drive"; נתץ, "pull down, break down"; פוץ, "be dispersed, scattered"; רדף, "pursue, chase, persecute"; רחק, "be far." See the table and explanation in Turner, *Death*, 38–46.

terms that Turner identifies, there are seven other terms in the Twelve that denote exile.[10] Elements of hope are identified from the contexts of these passages, with a particular focus on שוב as restoration and the remnant motif.[11]

Hosea

Hosea announces the punishment of Israel for their rebellion against Yahweh and their unfaithfulness to the national covenant. This punishment includes military defeat and exile.[12] The first probable reference to exile is in Hos. 5:14, which contains a metaphor of a lion carrying off its victim—"I will tear and I will go, I will carry [them off], and there is no deliverer" (cf. 11:10; 13:7-8).[13] The image portrays God "as a predator, menacing the flock he once was shepherding" (cf. 4:16).[14] It connotes fear, unstoppable power, savagery, and death.[15] It is spoken against Ephraim and Judah, where Ephraim is condemned for idolatry (5:11) and political alliances (5:13), and Judah for injustice (5:10). Exile is a consequence of God's wrath (5:10) where the people will bear the guilt of their sin (5:5, 15).[16] However, even though punishment might seem fatal, this is not the

---

10. These are: גרש, "cast out" (Hos. 9:15; Jon. 2:5; Mic. 2:9; Zeph. 2:4); הלא, "remove far away" (Mic. 4:7); זרע, "sow" (Zech. 10:9); סגר, "deliver up" (Amos 1:6, 9; 6:8; Obad. 14); סער, "blow away" (Hos. 13:3; Hab. 3:14; Zech. 7:14); פזר, "scatter" (Joel 4:2 [3:2 Eng.]); פרש, "cast" (Zech. 2:10 [2:6 Eng.]); שוב, "return" (Hos. 8:13; 9:3; 11:5).

11. Lexemes denoting the remnant in the Twelve are יתר, "to remain"; שאר, "remainder"; שארית, "remnant."

12. A sketch of the theme of exile in Hosea is provided by David L. Petersen, "Prophetic Rhetoric and Exile," in Boda et al. (eds), *The Prophets Speak on Forced Migration*, 9–18 (14–15). He identifies three primary modes of exile: forced migration/deportation (e.g., Jer. 52:28-30), voluntary migration (e.g., Jer. 42), and incarceration (e.g., Jer. 48:46).

13. Boda, *A Severe Mercy*, 299, understands the image as "an allusion to the discipline of destruction and exile."

14. Pierre Van Hecke, "'For I Will Be Like a Lion to Ephraim': Leonine Metaphors in the Twelve Prophets," in *The Books of the Twelve Prophets: Minor Prophets—Major Theologies*, ed. Heinz-Josef Fabry, BETL 295 (Leuven: Peeters, 2018), 387–402 (391).

15. Joshua N. Moon, *Hosea*, AOTC 21 (London: Apollos, 2018), 112.

16. Exile as bearing guilt is consistent with Ezek. 4:4-8. Alternatively, Marvin A. Sweeney, *The Twelve Prophets, Volume 1: Hosea, Jeol, Amos, Obadiah, Jonah*, Berit Olam: Studies in Hebrew Narrative & Poetry (Collegeville: Liturgical, 2000), 68, argues it refers to a time when the people "acknowledge their guilt."

case.[17] After the people have borne their guilt, they will seek the face of Yahweh (5:15).

Scholars debate whether Hos. 6:11 uses the word for "return" (שוב) or "captivity" (שבה) in the second word of the phrase בשובי שבות, reflected in the translations "Whenever I would restore the fortunes (שוב)" (NIV) or "When I would turn the captivity (שבה)" (JPS).[18] Variations of this phrase occur 27 times in the Hebrew Bible and five times through the Twelve (also Joel 3:1 [Eng. 4:1]; Amos 9:14; Zeph. 2:7; 3:20). A key instance is Deut. 30:3, where it refers to God gathering his people from the nations where they were scattered (30:4-5; cf. 28:64). Many scholars reject the translation "captivity" (from שבה), yet a cognate construction of שוב meaning "restore the fortunes" seems forced, especially when exile is in view in most contexts.[19] In the end, since exile can function as a metaphor for states associated with separation from God, as Halvorson-Taylor demonstrates, then the phrase "turn the captivity" may metaphorically mean "restore the fortunes."[20] A related issue in Hos. 6:11 is whether it refers to what God has done in the past ("Whenever I would restore the fortunes of my people"; NIV),[21] or what he will do ("When I restore the

17. "I will tear" in 5:14 can also be translated "I will devour."

18. John M. Bracke, "šûb šebût: A Reappraisal," *ZAW* 97 (1985): 233–44 (233), argues that it means "God's reversal of his judgment." See the discussion in Jason T. LeCureux, *The Thematic Unity of the Book of the Twelve*, HBM 41 (Sheffield: Sheffield Phoenix, 2012), 80–1.

19. LXX translates Hos. 6:11 as "when I return the captivity" (ὅταν ἐπιστρέψω τὴν αἰχμαλωσίαν), and similarly in each other instance in the Twelve. The Targums also translate this phrase in each instance in the Twelve along the lines of "bring back the exiles."

20. Interestingly, Halvorson-Taylor, *Enduring Exile*, 92, does not argue for the metaphorical sense of exile in this phrase, and proposes rather that it "is an operation distinct from the return of captives." She argues this from usage of the phrase elsewhere, particularly that it "is established by its context in Job 42:10, where no captives are in evidence." However, Gerald H. Wilson, *Job*, NIBC (Peabody: Hendrickson, 2007), 2–3, argues that the themes of Job, such as enduring faithfully in the face of extreme loss and suffering, would resonate with the situation of the Diaspora community. Hence translating Job 42:10 as "turn the captivity" is a fitting way to speak of the reversal of Job's suffering. Countering the objection that the exile does not parallel Job's situation since Job is not suffering for his sin, Wilson notes psalms that indicate some in the community saw themselves as not sharing in the wider sins that led to exile. Even if Wilson's proposal is not found convincing, many of Job's possessions are exiled in the opening chapter (Job 1:15, 17), and returning these possessions that had been taken captive may also explain the phrase "turn the captivity."

21. This can also be interpreted as expressing God's intent: "Whenever I would (intend to) restore the fortunes of my people…"

fortunes of my people"; ESV). In either case, exile is punishment for breaking the covenant. At the same time the phrase "shows how eager Yhwh is to turn towards his people."[22]

In Hosea 8, Israel is condemned for breaking the covenant and rebelling against God's torah (8:1). They have "rejected the good" with the consequence is that "an enemy will pursue him" (8:3). The language here (רדף) echoes Deut. 30:7.[23] Since Israel has failed to trust Yahweh and entered into relationship with Egypt and Assyria, they will "return" (שוב) to the lands of Egypt and Assyria (Hos. 8:13; 9:3; 11:5).[24] Behind this lies the covenant curse of Deut. 28:68, where the "return" to Egypt is a reversal of the exodus salvation and a form of punishment.[25]

Hosea 9 indicates exile is Yahweh's punishment on account of Israel's idolatry: "Because of their sinful deeds, I will drive them from my house" (Hos. 9:15). Elsewhere, the same vocabulary (גרש) describes the expulsion of Adam and Eve from the Garden of Eden (Gen. 3:24), Cain from the presence of Yahweh (Gen. 4:14), and the Canaanites from the Promised Land (cf. Deut. 33:27).[26] These associations are strengthened by Cynthia Edenburg's observation that expulsion from the land in Genesis 3–4 is a prototype for the relationship between Yahweh and Israel showing that "exile and alienation from YHWH is the inevitable consequence of violating YHWH's commandments."[27] The statement that the people of Ephraim "will be wanderers among the nations" (Hos 9:17) also mirrors Cain's fate (Gen. 4:12, 14).[28] Intertwined with these prophecies of exile are haunting threats of the death of infants and the miscarriage of babies, which starkly contribute notions of crisis and death that are associated

---

22. LeCureux, *Thematic*, 81.

23. In Deut. 30:7 it refers to a reversal of the covenant curses—after Yahweh saves his people the curses will fall on the nations who "pursued" Israel.

24. See Gert Kwakkel, "Exile in Hosea 9:3-6: Where and for What Purpose?" in *Exile and Suffering: A Selection of Papers Read at the 50th Anniversary Meeting of the Old Testament Society of South Africa OTWSA/OTSSA Pretoria August 2007*, ed. Bob Becking and Dirk Human, OtSt 50 (Leiden: Brill, 2009), 123–45.

25. See LeCureux, *Thematic*, 71–6.

26. While גרש does not always denote punishment for sin, it does in each of these contexts.

27. Cynthia Edenburg, "From Eden to Babylon: Reading Genesis 2–4 as a Paradigmatic Narrative," in *Pentateuch, Hexateuch, or Enneateuch? Identifying Literary Works in Genesis through Kings*, ed. Thomas B. Dozeman, Konrad Schmid, and Thomas Römer, SBLAIL 8 (Atlanta: SBL, 2011), 155–67 (162)

28. J. Andrew Dearman, *The Book of Hosea*, NICOT (Grand Rapids: Eerdmans, 2010), 258: "Although he [Hosea] does not use the term 'go into exile'…this is what is meant."

with warfare and exile (Hos. 9:12-14, 16).[29] They too echo the covenant curses (Deut. 28:18, 32, 41).

Hosea 13:3 gives four examples of substances that quickly dissipate (mist, dew, chaff, and smoke) to speak of Ephraim's fate on account of their sin, particularly their idolatry (13:2). The image of chaff being "blown away" (סער) from the threshing floor is one used elsewhere in the Twelve of exile (Hab. 3:14; Zech. 7:14) and may draw in this association here as well.

The only use of the verb גלה in Hosea is not in relation to people, but to the calf-idols of the people of Samaria, which will be "exiled" to Assyria (Hos. 10:5). The subsequent picture of the king of Samaria being destroyed, "swept away like a twig on the surface of the waters" (10:7), may depict him being carried into exile, or the image may be more general in portraying the demise of kingship in Israel (cf. 10:15).

In summary, exile in Hosea is associated with the punishment of God for disobedience. This is consistent with the presentation of the covenant curses in Deuteronomy which culminate in exile. These curses are the punishment God designed to bring about repentance.[30] For early readers of the book of Hosea in the Book of the Twelve, for whom the catastrophe of exile had fallen on both the northern and southern kingdoms of Israel for their failure to return to the Lord, it is clear that the warnings were not heeded and God's punishment came to pass. At the same time, the book of Hosea, like Deuteronomy, holds out the hope of restoration and new life for those who return to the Lord.[31] For instance, in Hosea 2, after Israel has borne the Lord's punishment, God promises to "allure her," to "speak to her heart" (Hos. 2:16 [2:14 Eng.]), and to "betroth you to

---

29. While not referring directly to this passage, Claudia D. Bergmann, *Childbirth as a Metaphor for Crisis: Evidence from the Ancient Near East, the Hebrew Bible, and 1QH XI, 1–18*, BZAW 382 (Berlin: de Gruyter, 2008), 100, explains how childbirth often functions in the Hebrew Bible as a metaphor for crisis: "In texts describing divine punishment, the crisis brought on by the wrath of God is seen as terrible, painful, unavoidable, and potentially lethal."

30. J. Gordon McConville, *Deuteronomy*, AOTC, 5 (Leicester: Apollos, 2002), 410: "Curses operate, therefore, rather like prophetic oracles of judgment, which intend, not to declare judgment inevitable and fixed, but to turn people from their sins."

31. The influence of Deut. 30 on Hos. 14 is noted by Douglas K. Stuart, *Hosea–Jonah*, WBC 31 (Waco: Word, 1987), 214–15; J. Gordon McConville, *Grace in the End: A Study in Deuteronomic Theology* (Grand Rapids: Zondervan, 1993), 137; Eduardo F. Eli, "The Presence of the Covenant Motif in Hosea: An Intertextual Approach for the Last Oracle in the Book," *JBQ* 45 (2017): 34–42.

me forever," with the people restored to the land and given agricultural abundance (Hos. 2:21-25 [2:19-23 Eng.]).[32] Again, after experiencing God's judgment, in Hos. 3:5 the people will return (שוב) and seek the Lord and David their king. In Hosea 14, God calls on the people to return to him (14:2 [14:1 Eng.]) and promises that he will "heal them from their turning and love them freely" (Hos. 14:5 [14:4 Eng.]).[33] A restored relationship with God will also result in the restoration of his many blessings (14:6-9 [5-8 Eng.]). Hence, while Hosea envisages exile as devastating, it is not God's final word. There is hope for restoration on the other side of exile for those who return to the Lord and seek him (cf. 5:15–6:2).

Joel

In Joel 4:2-3 [3:2-3 Eng.] the language of exile is used to describe nations that amongst other things "scattered" (פזר) Israel. They will be put on trial. The Phoenician cities of Tyre and Sidon along with the regions of Philistia are specifically identified for retribution on account of what they did in selling the people of Judah and Jerusalem to the Greeks "in order to send them (רחק) far from their border" in 4:4-6 (3:4-6 Eng.).[34] The immediate context of these references focuses on God's punishment of the nations who treated Judah and Jerusalem (and hence Yahweh) in this way (cf. Amos 1–2). The reason the inhabitants of Judah and Jerusalem were exiled is not stated, but since locusts are also a covenant curse (Deut. 28:38), this suggests covenant violations.[35] The call to return/repent in view of the coming day of Yahweh (Joel 2:12-14) certainly implies exile is the punishment of God, especially since the same call to repent marks the ending of Hosea where the sins of the northern kingdom are explicit (Hos. 14:2-5 [14:1-4 Eng.]).

32. Many see new covenant concepts here. For instance, Walter Brueggemann, *Tradition in Crisis: A Study in Hosea* (Richmond: John Knox, 1968), 116–17; Hans W. Wolff, *Hosea* (Augsburg: Fortress, 1974), 55; Moon, *Hosea*, 67.

33. McConville, *Grace*, 137, argues that this reflects the new covenant theology of Jer. 31:33, where God "will somehow enable his people ultimately to do what they cannot do in their strength, namely, to obey him out of the conviction and devotion of their own hearts."

34. In Amos 1:6-9, Gaza (Philistia) and Tyre (Phoenicia) are condemned for taking captives (presumably from Israel) and selling them to Edom in the eighth century.

35. See the discussion in Jason T. LeCureux, "Joel, the Cult, and the Book of the Twelve," in *Priests & Cults in the Book of the Twelve*, ed. Lena-Sofia Tiemeyer (Atlanta: SBL, 2016), 65–79 (69–71).

As part of a promise of salvation, in Joel 4:1 (3:1 Eng.) God promises to either "turn the captivity" (JPS) or "restore the fortunes" (NIV) of Judah and Jerusalem (cf. Hos. 6:11).[36] Since exile appears in the immediate context (Joel 4:2-3 [3:2-3 Eng.]), it seems appropriate to translate it as "turn the captivity" here. This restoration is described in marvellous terms in 3:1-5; 4:17-21 (2:28-32; 3:17-21 Eng.).

Amos

The book of Amos begins where Joel ends, with God roaring from Zion and from Jerusalem against foreign nations for their "sins" (compare Joel 4:16 [3:16 Eng.] with Amos 1:2).[37] In the opening oracles of Amos, the forced deportation of peoples is identified as both a crime and a punishment—people will reap what they sow. Gaza and Tyre (Philistine and Phoenician cities respectively; cf. Joel 4:2 [3:2 Eng.]) are condemned for exiling whole communities (גלה) and delivering them up (סגר) to Edom (Amos 1:6, 9). Edom's sin includes pursuing (רדף) his brother with a sword, and he will also suffer the punishment of Yahweh (1:11-12). In terms of punishment, because of the sins of Damascus, the people of Aram will be exiled (גלה) to Kir (1:5), and the sins of Ammon will result in her king and his officials going into exile (גולה) (1:15). These initial references to exile in Amos refer to punishment of non-Israelite nations.

The translation issues surrounding the removal of Samaria's unjust women "with hooks" in Amos 4:2-3 are complex. The image could refer to actual hooks used to forcibly take away captives,[38] or be a gruesome metaphor that likens the removal of dead bodies to captured fish.[39] In either case, the punishment is a consequence of the sin—violating the requirements of the national covenant to care for the poor and needy (4:1).

After the ironic call to "Go to Bethel and sin; multiply sin at Bethel" (4:4), the judgment is later announced that Gilgal will surely go into exile (גלה), and Bethel will become nothing (5:5). This is the first use of גלה in the Twelve to refer to a punishment on Israel, even if it is only one city. Yet by the end of Amos 5, the punishment of exile (גלה) is extended

---

36. The *ketib* is אשוב את־שבות. The *qere* is אשיב את־שבות. See my earlier discussion of this phrase in relation to Hos. 6:11.

37. A sketch of the theme of exile in Amos is provided by Petersen, "Prophetic Rhetoric," 14.

38. E.g., Terence E. Fretheim, *Reading Hosea–Micah: A Literary and Theological Commentary* (Macon: Smyth & Helwys, 2013), 132.

39. E.g., John H. Hayes, *Amos, the Eighth-Century Prophet: His Times and his Preaching* (Nashville: Abingdon, 1988), 140–1.

to Israel for its idolatry and injustice (5:27), and then in Amos 6, to the leadership in Zion and Samaria for their luxurious self-indulgence. Since they put themselves first, they will be the first to go into exile (גלה) (6:7). Yahweh will certainly deliver them up (סגר) (6:8).

In Amos 7, the priest Amaziah reports Amos as announcing the military defeat of King Jeroboam and the exile (גלה) of Israel (7:11). Amaziah makes no mention of Amos decrying Israel's sin—he simply restates the punishment Amos had announced in terms that sound treasonable. Amaziah tries to silence Amos (7:12-13) but finds himself and his family sentenced to punishment in which the prophecy of the exile (גלה) of Israel is repeated (7:17).

Amos 9:4 refers to exile or "captivity" (שבי) as part of Yahweh's punishment of Israel for acting no differently to the nations (9:7). While exile at first seems to bring complete destruction of the nation, the second half of the chapter reveals that Yahweh will not utterly destroy the house of Jacob (9:8).

Amos 9:9 marks the first time in the Twelve where exile is associated explicitly with the idea of refining and purifying the nation. It does this by employing the metaphor of a sieve. Mark Boda comments that it "reveals that ultimately it will take a total destruction and exile to purge sinners from among the people."[40] While the term "remnant" is not used here (cf. Amos 5:14-15), the concept is present.[41] While sinners will die when the people are shaken among all the nations (9:10), the implication is that it is the righteous who will be preserved. In this way the motif of a remnant seeks to resolve the tension between God's just punishment of sin and his gracious commitment to his covenant people. The remnant forms "the nucleus of the new people of God."[42]

In Amos 9:14, the phrase found in Hos. 6:11 and Joel 4:1 [Eng. 3:1] occurs again (ושבתי את־שבות עמי ישראל), which is translated either as "I will bring my people Israel back from exile" (NIV), or "I will restore the

---

40. Boda, *A Severe Mercy*, 314. Rainer Albertz, "Exile as Purification. Reconstructing the 'Book of the Four'," in *Thematic Threads in the Book of the Twelve*, ed. Paul L. Redditt and Aaron Schart (Berlin: de Gruyter, 2003), 232–51 (240), argues that exile as purification is seen in Hos. 3:1-5; 14:2-4; Amos 9:7-9; Mic. 5:9-13; Zeph. 1:4-6; 3:11-13. Yet, I am not convinced it is as clear in Hosea and Mic. 5.

41. Gerhard F. Hasel, "The Alleged 'No' of Amos and Amos' Eschatology," *Andrews University Seminary Studies* 29 (1991): 3–18 (8–12).

42. Hasel, "Amos' Eschatology," 11. See also Alison Lo, "Remnant Motif in Amos, Micah and Zephaniah," in *A God of Faithfulness: Essays in Honour of J. Gordon McConville on His 60th Birthday*, ed. Jamie A. Grant, Alison Lo, and Gordon J. Wenham (New York: T&T Clark, 2011), 130–48.

fortunes of my people Israel" (ESV). Here return from "exile" suits the context well and is elaborated upon in Amos 9:11-15, which describes the bounty of the land in that day and the restoration of David's falling shelter; most likely a reference to the Judean monarchy centred in Jerusalem (cf. Hos. 3:5).[43]

In summary, exile has negative connotations from the beginning of Amos, when non-Israelite nations stand condemned for doing this to others. Israel will suffer exile from the land as punishment for violating the terms of the national covenant, particularly for false worship, idolatry, and injustice. In effect, Israel will not be saved from judgment, but *through* judgment. Significantly, Amos introduces the idea that exile will refine the nation so that a purified remnant will emerge to inherit the blessings of a renewed world.

Obadiah

The book of Obadiah concerns Edom after Jerusalem has been destroyed and its wealth and its citizens carried off in exile (Obad. 11, 14). Edom acted violently against his brother Jacob when they were attacked by strangers—he stood aloof, gloated, rejoiced, mocked, took Jacob's possessions, cut off their fugitives, and handed over their survivors (10–14). Obadiah announces that the tables will be turned: "Just as you did, it will be done to you" (15).

Obadiah does not explain the exiling of Israel and Jerusalem as punishment for sin, nor does the book describe the process as a refining of the nation (though Zion is made holy in Obad. 17). This does not contradict the idea that God was using the nations as instruments of his punishment (e.g., Habakkuk). What Obadiah shows is that, while God used nations like Edom, this does not exonerate them from receiving punishment for their own violence (cf. Habakkuk; Zech. 1:15).

Obadiah finishes on a note of hope: Mount Zion will be delivered and made holy (17), and Edom will be destroyed with no one surviving (18). The Israelite "exiles" (גלות) and the "exiles" (גלות) from Jerusalem will repossess the land (19–20). This suggests a reunion of the nation. Anticipating themes developed more fully in Haggai, Zechariah, and Malachi, Obadiah foresees military leaders ("judges") ascending Mount Zion to rule over Edom (21). Like the preceding books of the Twelve, Obadiah indicates that exile is not the last word for God's people—God's kingdom will be restored.

43. See further Anthony R. Petterson, "The Shape of the Davidic Hope Across the Book of the Twelve," *JSOT* 35 (2010): 225–46.

Jonah

There is no explicit mention of exile in Jonah. Yet the language used elsewhere of exile is heavily associated with Jonah as he "flees" (ברח) from the Lord in disobedience (Jonah 1:10) and when he is "hurled" (טול) out of the boat by the sailors (1:15). The "storm" (סער) is also language used elsewhere to depict exile (1:4, 11, 12, 13; cf. Zech. 7:14). In his prayer Jonah says he has been "driven" (גרש) from before Yahweh's eyes, but expresses hope that he will again look towards Yahweh's holy temple (Jon. 2:5 [2:4 Eng.] cf. Hos. 9:15). It is possible that the use of this vocabulary is co-incidental, yet the echoes of exile evoked by this language likely brought to mind Israel's and Judah's experiences of exile for readers of Jonah in the Book of the Twelve.[44] Jonah's metaphorical time in Sheol (Jon. 2:3 [2:2 Eng.]) may also bring exile to mind, especially with exile's associations with death. Furthermore, Bergmann notes how Jonah's personal crisis in Jonah 2 shares several terms and ideas associated with childbirth, such as distress and feeling entrapped like a foetus in the womb.[45] This anticipates Micah where childbirth is a metaphor for exile. All these connotations of exile are even more likely to be the case if Jonah is understood as a representative of unrepentant Israel.[46] In this way Jonah underlines again that exile is a consequence of disobeying Yahweh.[47]

Micah

Micah 1 condemns Israel and Judah for idolatry (Mic. 1:5-7). This "plague" of Samaria has spread to Judah and has reached Jerusalem itself (1:9). Because of this, disaster has come from the Lord to the gate of Jerusalem (1:12), possibly reflecting the campaign of Sennacherib in 701 BCE.[48] It seems that the towns listed in Mic. 1:10-15 are Judean towns which had already been caught up in an Assyrian campaign that resulted in "exile" (גלה) for some (1:16). Yet further military action is foreseen: "I will bring the possessor against you" (1:15). The glory of Israel will

44. Kevin J. Youngblood, *Jonah: God's Scandalous Mercy* (Grand Rapids: Zondervan, 2013), 81.

45. Bergmann, *Childbirth*, 127–31, 49–52.

46. For Jonah's representative role, see Daniel C. Timmer, *A Gracious and Compassionate God: Mission, Salvation and Spirituality in the Book of Jonah*, NSBT 26 (Downers Grove: InterVarsity, 2011), 62.

47. Recently, Marian Kelsey, "The Book of Jonah and the Theme of Exile," *JSOT* 45 (2020): 128–40, traces the inner-biblical allusions in Jonah to Gen. 1–4, which underscores the connection between disobedience and exile.

48. So, Delbert R. Hillers, *Micah*, Hermeneia (Philadelphia: Fortress, 1984), 30.

"go" (בוא) to Adullam—a location to which David had fled in his exile from Jerusalem (see 1 Sam. 22:1-2; 2 Sam. 23:13). Throughout Micah 1, Yahweh is portrayed as the direct agent of coming destruction, yet it is also depicted as a military campaign, the endpoint of which is exile. A direct connection is established between idolatry (in Israel and Judah) and Yahweh's punishment (1:5, 7, 9, 12).

In Micah 4, Yahweh promises to assemble those who had been "driven away" (נדח) (4:6). The parallel phrase "those whom I have afflicted" shows again that exile was the punishment of God.[49] Like Amos, Yahweh promises salvation on the other side of judgment by making a "remnant" (שארית) of the lame (injured survivors of the judgment). In a parallel phrase, those "removed far away" (הלא) will be made a strong nation (4:7). Like Amos, Micah not only promises the restoration of a remnant from exile to Jerusalem, but also the re-establishment of kingship for Daughter Jerusalem (4:8). Reference to the "former dominion" is probably to the house of David (cf. Mic. 5:2-5).[50]

A little later in the same chapter, Micah prophesies that the people of Zion will "go" (בוא) into Babylon (4:9-10). First, the loss of their king is likened to the pain of a woman in labour (4:9)—a terrible crisis where there is "a mixture of pain and fear causing wave-like trembling in the person affected."[51] Then the crisis of the forced deportation of the inhabitants of Zion is also likened to childbirth, since it elicits writhing and trembling (4:10).[52] While childbirth, like exile, could potentially end in death (as was common in the ancient Near East), in this case God's punishment does not end in death, but rescue. In Mic. 5:2 (5:3 Eng.) "childbirth is applied as a sign that pain and suffering can lead to new life."[53] Exile is abandonment by Yahweh, until a son is born and the "remnant" (יתר) of his brothers return—the nation is reunited. The son is the future ideal Davidic king.[54]

Like other prophets, Micah ends with hope for God's restoration and return (שוב) to his people (7:19).[55] The basis for this hope is God's

---

49. James D. Nogalski, *The Book of the Twelve: Micah–Malachi*, SHBC (Georgia: Smyth & Helwys, 2011), 558, argues the period of devastation and exile "looks well past the eighth century."

50. Fretheim, *Reading Hosea–Micah*, 209.

51. Bergmann, *Childbirth*, 110.

52. Ibid., 110–11.

53. Ibid., 111.

54. See Gregory Goswell, "Davidic Rule in the Prophecy of Micah," *JSOT* 44 (2019): 153–65.

55. LeCureux, *Thematic*, 156.

character, which includes his mercy and compassion in forgiving sins, his love, and his faithfulness to his promises to the ancestors (7:18-20; cf. Hos. 2:21-22 [2:19-20 Eng.]).

Nahum

Nahum also indicates that exile is the punishment of Yahweh on the guilty, but like the opening of Amos, exile is punishment visited on non-Israelite nations. God will "pursue" (רדף) the Ninevites into darkness (Nah. 1:8). While 2:8 (2:7 Eng.) is difficult to translate, it is possibly a further reference to the "exile" (גלה) of the city. The reason for this military conquest is because the Lord of hosts is against the city on account of its violence (2:13–3:5). Nineveh is no better than Thebes (3:10), who also became an "exile" (גולה) and went into "captivity" (שבי). Nahum announces a similar fate for Assyria as punishment for their "endless cruelty" (3:19). As well as punishing Nineveh for its sin, Nahum shows that Yahweh will punish Nineveh for the sake of the northern kingdom (who destroyed by the Assyrians in 722 BCE)—God will return (שוב) the splendour of Jacob, who has been laid waste (Nah. 2:3 [2:2 Eng.]).

Habakkuk

The book of Habakkuk begins with the prophet calling on Yahweh to explain why he has not saved him from the violence and injustice of the wicked (Hab. 1:1-4). God's response is that he is raising up the Babylonians to execute his punishment, much to the prophet's dismay (Hab. 1:6, 12). This punishment contains two descriptions of exile. Habakkuk 1:9 says the Babylonians "gather captives (שבי) like sand," indicating the captives are innumerable. Habakkuk 2:5 says that Babylon "takes to himself all the nations and gathers to himself all the peoples," showing the vast extent of Babylon's conquest. Both of these references show exile is the practice of a violent and greedy nation intent on empire expansion, but at the same time God uses agents like Babylon to punish his own people for covenant violations.

While not using the term "remnant," the remnant motif is portrayed in Hab. 2:4 where through the ordeal "the righteous will live by his faith-fulness." Habakkuk 3 also exemplifies this faithfulness of the righteous as the prophet gives voice to his trust, patience, and joy in the Lord.[56] Here the prophet prays for God's wrath to come and destroy his enemies.

---

56. Boda, *A Severe Mercy*, 327.

The prayer draws on many instances in Israel's history when God acted as a mighty warrior (including creation, the flood, and the crossing of the Red Sea and the Jordan) and asks God to act in these ways again to defeat Babylon (3:2, 16). Habakkuk 3:13-14 seems to look back to the time of Moses ("your anointed one") when God crushed Pharaoh ("the leader of the land of wickedness").[57] Here the parallel between the Egyptians and the Babylonians is drawn by use of the language of exile: "when his warriors stormed (סער) out to scatter us (פוץ)." Habakkuk looks back to the exodus as a pattern to be repeated in the future when the day of calamity falls on of the king of Babylon and his armies and beyond this to the ultimate conquest of evil. It provides hope for life beyond the punishment of exile.

Zephaniah

Zephaniah begins by picturing the great day of the Lord in which all humanity will be destroyed from the face of the earth (Zeph. 1:3, 18). Within this picture there is a focus on idolaters in Judah and Jerusalem (1:4). The day is one of punishment and wrath for the sin of the people (1:12, 15, 18). Jerusalem is called to repentance (2:1-3) and foreign nations are sentenced to destruction (2:4-15). However, Jerusalem fails to heed the call to repent (3:7) and so Zephaniah declares that all the world will be consumed by the fire of Yahweh's jealous anger (3:8).

The language of exile describes those who had been "scattered" (פוץ) by God's wrath beyond the rivers of Cush (3:10), again associating exile with punishment for sin, but also "shame" (בוש) (3:11). Those who emerge from the day of wrath will have purified lips that call on the name of Yahweh. They will serve him shoulder to shoulder and bring him offerings (3:9-10). These "peoples" include non-Israelite nations.[58] Those who survive in Jerusalem are called the "remnant" (שאר) (3:12) who are purged of sin (3:13) and whose punishment has been removed (3:15).

---

57. The phrase "anointed one" seems anachronistic. So, Francis I. Andersen, *Habakkuk*, AB 24E (Garden City: Doubleday, 2001), 335. In the rhetoric of Habakkuk, it points forward to a future anointed one. See Anthony R. Petterson, "The Messiah in the Book of the Twelve: Glory Through Suffering," in *The Seed of Promise: The Sufferings and Glory of the Messiah: Essays in Honor of T. Desmond Alexander*, ed. Paul R. Williamson and Rita F. Cefalu (Wilmore: GlossaHouse, 2020), 219–41 (230–1).

58. See Daniel C. Timmer, *The Non-Israelite Nations in the Book of the Twelve: Thematic Coherence and the Diachronic–Synchronic Relationship in the Minor Prophets*, BibInt 135 (Leiden: Brill, 2015), 160–4.

Zephaniah finishes with the hopeful promise that Yahweh will assemble those who had been "driven away" (נדח) (Zeph. 3:19; cf. Mic. 4:6) and bring them home (Zeph. 3:20). He will "turn your captivity" (JPS) or "restore your fortunes" (NIV), the phrase discussed earlier (cf. Hos. 6:11; Joel 4:1 [3:1 Eng.], Amos 9:14). The phrase also occurs in Zeph. 2:7 where after the Lord has destroyed the Philistines, the remnant of Judah will possess their land and pasture their flocks there.

In summary, Zephaniah again associates exile with punishment and Yahweh's anger, but also the refining of a remnant who will inherit God's promised blessing in Jerusalem so that they are honoured and praised among all the peoples of the earth. The Book of the Twelve to this point present hope for a glorious restoration beyond exile. Yet this would have raised big questions for readers who had returned to Jerusalem after the exile for whom this was not their experience.

Haggai

Haggai does not refer to exile, yet it presupposes that the nation has been through it and the "remnant" (שארית) are the survivors who now dwell in the land (Hag. 1:12, 14). Given the expectation raised earlier in the Twelve that exile will sift and refine God's people, it is reasonable to expect that the remnant will exhibit obedience to the Lord. Indeed, the people are reported as obeying the message of Haggai as Yahweh stirs up their spirit (1:12-14).

However, much of the book exhibits evidence that the experience of exile has not changed the hearts of the people. Their failure to prioritize the building of the temple is a cause of displeasure to the Lord and they have suffered drought and adversity as a consequence (1:6, 9-11). Their deeds and their offerings are defiled (2:14). They suffer covenant curses as a warning to repent (2:17). Hence there is some ambiguity in Haggai about the heart of the people and whether exile has truly refined a righteous remnant. Yet the book holds out hope that since the foundation of the temple has been laid and the people seem to have returned to Yahweh, their circumstances will soon change and curse will be replaced by blessing (2:18-19). On the day of the Lord, he will glorify the temple (2:6–9) and reinstate Davidic kingship (2:20-23).[59] This day will also involve God shaking the heavens and the earth (2:6, 21) and overcoming the kings of the nations and their military might (2:22). All of these themes anticipate Zechariah.

59. On this final point, see William T. Koopmans, *Haggai*, HCOT (Leuven: Peeters, 2017), 283–94.

Zechariah

While the opening of Zechariah does not explicitly mention exile, it is very much in view. The disaster that the nation has just endured is explained as resulting from God's great anger (Zech. 1:2), and by implication, punishment for sin. Exile is the time when Yahweh's words and statutes finally overtook the forefathers for their refusal to turn from their evil ways and evil deeds despite the warning of Yahweh through the earlier prophets (1:4-6). Even though many who had been exiled have returned to Jerusalem, Yahweh calls on them to "return to me…and I will return to you" (1:3). This indicates that exile endures as a form of spiritual estrangement.[60]

As the book unfolds, it is clear that the people in Zechariah's day are not experiencing the restoration of blessing that the earlier prophets promised, even though they have returned to the land. The first night vision reveals that the seventy years of Babylonian captivity foretold by Jeremiah are near their end (Zech. 1:12-17; cf. Jer. 25:11-12; 29:10). While non-Israelite nations still hold power over the people of Judah and Jerusalem, God's anger has transferred from his people to the nations with the implication that the nations will be judged (Zech. 1:12, 15). The second night vision looks back to exile with its four horns that "scattered" (זרה) Judah, Israel, and Jerusalem (2:2, 4 [1:19, 21 Eng.]).[61] Yet the vision also looks forward to a time when the horns will be cast down by four craftsmen—hostile nations will be subdued. The third night vision also indicates there is a sense in which exile is ongoing with its call to those who still dwell in Babylon to "Flee from the land of the north… Listen Zion, Escape!" (2:10-11 [2:6-7 Eng.]). The exile is depicted as a time when the Lord "cast" (פרש) his people to the four winds of the heavens on account of their sin, but now he will punish the nations and return to dwell among his people (2:14 [2:10 Eng.]).[62] The fourth night vision refers to the high priest

---

60. Halvorson-Taylor, *Enduring Exile*, 152.

61. Ibid., 185, notes the "vision's expansive notion of exile includes exiles from north and south." For a discussion of the nature of the "scattering," see Mark J. Boda, "Scat! Exilic Motifs in the Book of Zechariah," in Boda et al. (eds), *The Prophets Speak on Forced Migration*, 161–80 (163–4).

62. In Ezekiel, God's glory departed the Jerusalem temple on account of idolatry. This episode seems to be in the background of 2:12 (2:8 Eng.). See Anthony R. Petterson, "The Eschatology of Zechariah's Night Visions," in *"I Lifted My Eyes and Saw": Reading Dream and Vision Reports in the Hebrew Bible*, ed. Lena-Sofia Tiemeyer and Elizabeth R. Hayes, LHBOTS 584 (London: T&T Clark, 2014), 119–34. For a more detailed treatment of the language of exile here, see Boda, "Scat!," 165–6. Boda also suggests the people are the plunder in 2:12 (2:8 Eng.).

Joshua as "a brand plucked from a fire" (3:2), where the fire is most likely a metaphor of exile as God's judgment (cf. Amos 4:11; Zeph. 3:8-9).[63] This vision highlights the need for cleansing from sin for Joshua and the community he represents. The seventh vision does not use the usual vocabulary of exile, but it effectively portrays iniquity and wickedness being exiled from the land (Zech. 5:6-8). An ephah containing a statuette is carried by two women with wings like those of a stork to Shinar, where it is set up in a house (5:9-11). The forced removal (or exile) to Babylon is what is in store for iniquity and wickedness, particularly idolatry.

After the night visions, Zechariah is instructed to take silver and gold from "the exiles" (הגולה) to make a crown that will be placed in the rebuilt temple as a memorial until the coming of Shoot.[64] Like the fourth vision where the priesthood is reinstated for temple service and a stone with seven facets functions as a sign of the coming of Shoot (3:8-9), the sign action seems to set the coming day of the Lord some distance from contemporary events in Yehud.

While Zechariah indicates that many have returned from exile to Jerusalem, there are indications throughout Zechariah 1–8 that exile has not refined the righteous remnant that earlier prophets hoped for. From the outset, the call to "return to me" (1:3) implies that those who have returned to live in Jerusalem are not living in complete obedience to Yahweh. Yet just as the people responded in obedience to the preaching of Haggai, the people are reported as responding positively to the preaching of Zechariah (1:6), initially anyway. However, the fifth vision indicates there are some in the community who "despise the day of small things" (4:10). The sixth vision reveals the persistence of theft and false swearing (5:3-4) along with a corruption of justice since those who commit these crimes are wrongly acquitted (5:3).[65] In the seventh vision, a flying ephah represents the removal of iniquity, wickedness, and idolatry from the land of God's people (5:6-7). These features of the visions indicate that not only has the day of Yahweh's salvation not fully arrived, but also that many of the sins that led to the destruction of Jerusalem and exile still persist among the community in Judah and Jerusalem.

---

63. Alternatively, the emphasis is on Joshua's survival after the destruction of Jerusalem. See Boda, "Scat!," 165.

64. The absence of the article on "Shoot" (צמח) suggests it functions as proper noun. So, A. Wolters, *Zechariah*, HCOT (Leuven: Peeters, 2014), 101. For its metaphorical associations, see Anthony R. Petterson, *Haggai, Zechariah & Malachi*, AOTC 25 (Nottingham: Apollos, 2015), 124–6.

65. See further, Anthony R. Petterson, "The Flying Scroll That Will Not Acquit the Guilty: Exodus 34.7 in Zechariah 5.3," *JSOT* 38 (2014): 347–61.

This sense that the sins that led to exile persist in Zechariah's day continues in Zechariah 7–8, a section that functions as a transition between Zechariah 1–6 and 9–14.[66] In Zechariah's response to a question by a delegation about the need for continued fasting (7:2-3), he uses the opportunity to challenge them about their own covenant faithfulness. Zechariah recounts the words of the earlier prophets in such a way as to address the same issues in his own generation.[67] The failure of the earlier generation to listen to Yahweh meant he "blew" (סער) them over all the nations (7:14; cf. Hos. 13:3; Jon. 1:4, 11, 12, 13; Hab. 3:14).

While the tone of Zechariah 8 is much more positive than Zechariah 7, it is clear that the full realization of Yahweh's salvation purposes lies in the future, even if there were those who thought this to be an impossible miracle (9:6).[68] With echoes of Haggai, Zechariah 8 also acknowledges that the returned exiles suffered adversity on account of neglecting the temple (8:10).[69] Like Zechariah 7, there is a challenge to covenant obedience: "Speak the truth with each other; truth and a judgment of peace render in your gates; and do not devise evil in your heart (against your) neighbour; and do not love a false oath, for all these are what I hate" (8:17; cf. 7:9-10). The implication is that there were some in the community not living this way. Boda summarizes: "the hoped-for restoration is threatened by patterns of behaviour strikingly similar to the behaviour that led to the Exile in the first place."[70] Indeed, that this chapter looks forward to the realization of restoration promises indicates that exile endures.[71]

Zechariah 9–14 consists of two oracles that are generally considered to come from a time after the temple has been completed.[72] One of the features of these chapters is the way that the prophet draws on earlier biblical material to picture the future. Schaefer comments:

66. See Mark J. Boda, "From Fasts to Feasts: The Literary Function of Zechariah 7–8," *CBQ* 65 (2003): 390–407; Yohan Im and Pieter M. Venter, "The Function of Zechariah 7–8 within the book of Zechariah," *HTS Teologiese Studies/Theological Studies* 69 (2013): 1–10.

67. Michael H. Floyd, *Minor Prophets: Part 2*, FOTL 22 (Grand Rapids: Eerdmans, 2000), 415.

68. For a summary of Zechariah's hope for restoration in relation to exile, see Frank R. Ames, "Forced Migration and the Visions of Zechariah 1–8," in Boda et al. (eds), *The Prophets Speak on Forced Migration*, 147–59 (156–9).

69. For the echoes of Haggai here, see Michael R. Stead, *The Intertextuality of Zechariah 1–8*, LHBOTS 506 (New York: T&T Clark, 2009), 238–41.

70. Boda, *A Severe Mercy*, 338.

71. Kenneth A. Ristau, "Rebuilding Jerusalem: Zechariah's Vision within Visions," in Knoppers, Grabbe and Fulton (eds), *Exile and Restoration Revisited*, 195–213 (208).

72. The temple is envisaged as completed in Zech. 11:13.

> The author of Zechariah 9–14…draws from a literary repertoire of phrases and images and interweaves them into his prophecies. As the author refashions his predecessors' material, he recalls past situations, ratifies their message, and renews them for his contemporaries.[73]

This is particularly the case for earlier prophecies which Zechariah renews.[74] There are also instances where Zechariah draws on events in Israel's past, to portray a future salvation event. For instance, the image in Zech. 9:9 of the future king coming to Jerusalem riding on a donkey seems to operate against the backdrop of the return of King David to Jerusalem after he had been exiled by Absalom, an exile in which donkeys feature (2 Sam. 16:2).[75] Similarly, the account of the one who is pierced in a battle which results in a great outpouring of grief (Zech. 12:10-14), seems to draw on the death of Josiah in battle, when he was pierced by a stray arrow, which resulted in national outpouring of grief.[76]

This drawing on the past to picture the future is seen in relation to exile in 9:11-12. On the basis of the national covenant, Yahweh promises to "set free your prisoners from a waterless pit." It is difficult to know if "a waterless pit" (בור) alludes to Joseph (Gen. 27:24), Jeremiah (Jer. 38:6) or the psalmist (Pss 40:3 [40:2 Eng.]; 69:15), or is simply a well understood image. In any case, "a waterless pit" seems to function metaphorically for exile (and death in the Psalms) from which Yahweh "will set free your prisoners" (אסיר), language which echoes the exodus (e.g., Exod. 5:1). Hence a waterless pit is something that imprisons. Those who are freed are to "return (שוב) to the stronghold" (Zech. 9:12), most likely a reference to Jerusalem. Significantly, this passage shows that even though exiles have returned to Jerusalem, a further release and return is envisaged where Yahweh's blessing will be experienced "double"—like the double blessing after the return from "exile" of Joseph (Gen. 48:22) and Job (Job 42:10).[77] Like Amos and Micah, central to this restoration from exile is a future Davidic king (Zech. 9:9-10).

---

73. Konrad R. Schaefer, "Zechariah 14: A Study in Allusion," *CBQ* 57 (1995): 66–91 (72).

74. See Heiko Wenzel, *Reading Zechariah with Zechariah 1:1-6 as the Introduction to the Entire Book*, CBET 59 (Leuven: Peeters, 2011).

75. Pamela J. Scalise, "Zechariah, Malachi," in *Minor Prophets II* (Peabody: Hendrickson, 2009), 177–366 (274).

76. Antti Laato, *Josiah and David Redivivus: The Historical Josiah and the Messianic Expectations of Exilic and Postexilic Times*, ConBOT 33 (Stockholm: Almqvist & Wiksell, 1992), 293.

77. See the discussion of Job in n. 20.

In an extended passage in Zechariah 10, Yahweh promises to bring his people back from the lands to which he had scattered them and bless them (10:6-12). In this passage there is an intriguing focus on the northern kingdom ("the house of Joseph") and extensive use of exodus imagery. The exile is portrayed as a time when Yahweh "rejected them" (10:6) and when he "sowed" them among the nations (10:9). The use of the verb "sow" (זרע) suggests life after burial. Indeed, God promises to bring his people back from the lands of Egypt and Assyria and gather them. Like his actions in the exodus (but with some variation), Yahweh will pass through the sea of distress and smite his enemies with the waves and dry up the depths of the Nile. His people will be redeemed (10:8) and proud and powerful nations will be humbled (10:11). This passage also indicates that the return from exile for the nation as whole is envisaged as still in the future.

Interpretation of Zechariah 11 is complex. Here Zechariah is commanded to perform two sign actions, the first being to break two shepherd's staffs (11:4-14). The interpretative approach that best coheres with the book is to understand the first sign action as reviewing Israel's history and portraying the reason for the division of the kingdom and the devastation of the kingdom of Israel by foreign nations.[78] While "exile" is not mentioned explicitly, the description of God's punishment is consistent with it: "I am delivering each person into the hand of his neighbour, and into the hand of his king, and they will devastate the land, and I will not rescue from their hand" (11:6). The description of people eating the flesh of one another (11:9) corresponds to actions during the siege of a city (cf. Lam. 2:20; 4:10). Along with the instructions for carrying out the sign action, there are reasons given for God's actions. First, the leadership of God's people (the shepherds) have used the flock to serve their own interests, showing them no compassion (Zech. 11:5). Second, Yahweh's people have rejected his shepherding care. Zechariah is called to play the role of a shepherd who represents Yahweh, but the people abhor him (11:8) and they pay him off for thirty pieces of silver (11:12). In these ways, exile is presented as Yahweh's judgment of false leaders, and punishment of his people for rejecting him as shepherd.

The second sign action represents the ill treatment that God's people suffer at the hands of a "foolish shepherd," who represents the foreign rulers the people suffer in exile (11:15-17). The chapter finishes on a note of hope as God's announces woe on the worthless shepherd.

---

78. See Petterson, "Davidic Hope," 229–35. Also Petterson, *Haggai, Zechariah & Malachi*, 239–54.

Zechariah 12–14 forms a second oracle with various events linked by the phrase "on that day," which recurs 17 times. Zechariah 12 does not speak directly of exile, but it does portray a future attack by the nations against Jerusalem to which Zechariah 14 returns. While reminiscent of the Babylonian attack in 587 BCE, on this occasion Yahweh will intervene to strengthen his people to repel their attackers. No reason is given for the attack of the nations, but since it follows directly from the account of Israel's rejection of Yahweh (Zech. 11), and since the outcome of the attack is the opening of a fountain for the house of David and the inhabitants for sin and for impurity (Zech. 13:1), it suggests that this future attack will somehow finally deal with the sin that remained in the post-exilic community. This theme of cleansing continues in 13:2-6, where Yahweh promises that idolatry, false prophecy, and the unclean spirit will be removed from the land (cf. 3:9).

Zechariah 13:7-9 is a short oracle that uses language often associated with exile and punishment to speak of a future refining judgment of God's people that will produce a new covenant relationship. Returning to the shepherd metaphor of Zechariah 9–11, Yahweh commands that an individual leader called "my shepherd…my associate" be struck with the sword so that the sheep "scatter" (פוץ), language often associated with exile (e.g., Gen. 11:8-9; Deut. 28:64; 30:3; Neh. 1:8; Jer. 9:16; Ezek. 34:5). Scattered sheep are endangered by predators. In language reminiscent of Ezekiel's depiction of exile (Ezek. 5:2-4), two thirds will be "cut off" (כרת) and "perish" (גוע) and a third part will be further refined, like silver and gold.[79] This future exile is for the purpose of refining a purified remnant.

Elsewhere I have argued that the one who is pierced in Zech. 12:10 and the stricken shepherd of 13:7 are further descriptions of the coming king of 9:9.[80] Drawing on the suffering servant figure of Isaiah and the suffering David of the Psalms, Zechariah draws again on the past to portray the way that he will finally deal with the problem of sin which the earlier experiences of exile ultimately did not solve. Zechariah envisages a future attack of Jerusalem in which the shepherd-king is killed, the people scattered, and a remnant refined. It is this re-exile of Jerusalem that will ultimately deal with sin and iniquity.

---

79. Boda, "Scat!," 174–5, notes: "it is possible that the two parts include those who are cut off from the community and sent into exile…as opposed to those who perish."

80. Anthony R. Petterson, *Behold Your King: The Hope for the House of David in the Book of Zechariah*, LHBOTS 513 (New York: T&T Clark, 2009), 231–42.

Carol and Eric Meyers argue that "the notion of another destruction and exile that would accompany the ruler's demise does not seem warranted by prophetic evaluations of postexilic society."[81] Yet, following from Zech. 13:1-6 with its indications that idolatry, false prophecy, and impurity remain issues for the post-exilic community, and the indications in Zechariah 1–8 that the exile has not resulted in a righteous remnant, then exile seems entirely appropriate. This re-exile comes as the purifying judgment of God which earlier exiles did not achieve.

Zechariah 14 is essentially a replay of the battle in Zechariah 12, with more detail and a greater emphasis on the agency of Yahweh who strikes the warriors with plague and panic (14:12-13). Once again, language elsewhere associated with the Babylonian campaign against Jerusalem in 587 BCE is employed to speak of the "capture" (לכד) of Jerusalem (cf. Jer. 32:3, 24, 28; 34:22; 37:8; 38:3, 28), its "looting" (שׁסס) (cf. Ps. 89:42 [89:41 Eng.]; Jer. 30:16), and explicit reference to exile: "half the city will go out into the exile (בגולה)" (Zech. 14:2). If these verses are read in relation to Zech. 13:7-9, then the "remainder" may be those who are refined in the process of this attack ("remainder" [יתר] uses the same root as those who "remain" in 13:8).[82] The earthquake in the days of Uzziah recalls another episode from Israel's past, when inhabitants of Jerusalem fled from the city (14:6; cf. Amos 1:1). After all this, Yahweh will come (to Jerusalem?) along with "all the holy ones" (14:5). This expression could refer to the angelic host (cf. 6:1-8), but the context better suits it referring to the inhabitants of Jerusalem who had been driven (or who fled) from the city who now return as "holy ones" to inhabit the city that is "holy to the LORD" (14:20-21).[83]

Zechariah 9–14 therefore marks a development in the Twelve as the prophet draws on the past to speak of another experience of exile which will purify Jerusalem before Yahweh's kingship over the earth is established in all its glory.[84] Central to the presentation in Zechariah 9–14 is a future Davidic king whose death results in cleansing and a renewed covenant relationship between Yahweh and his people, a message inspiring hope.[85]

---

81. Carol L. Meyers and Eric M. Meyers, *Zechariah 9–14: A New Translation with Introduction and Commentary*, AB 25C (New York: Doubleday, 1993), 388.

82. Elizabeth Achtemeier, *Nahum–Malachi* (Atlanta: John Knox, 1986), 165.

83. See Mark J. Boda, *The Book of Zechariah*, NICOT (Grand Rapids: Eerdmans, 2016), 759–60.

84. Note also Boda, "Scat!," 180: "In a final phase Yahweh threatens to return from exile, but this time to bring judgment on Jerusalem, which would experience exile again, even as Yahweh unilaterally purifies the community."

85. See Petterson, *Behold*, 237–45.

While this is a development in the Twelve, there are also many similarities with Ezekiel's portrayal of a battle against Gog of Magog (Ezek. 38–39), which is described before Ezekiel's vision of the new temple, to which Yahweh returns in glory.[86]

Malachi

The book of Malachi begins by contrasting Israel and Edom's experiences after exile. The prophet quotes Edom rhetorically: "we have been demolished, but we will return (שוב) and we will rebuild the ruins" (Mal. 1:4). Yet any hope the Edomites might have of returning and rebuilding what had been destroyed is dashed by Yahweh. Anything Edom builds he will destroy (1:4). Exile as God's punishment or curse on sin is explicit in the case of Edom (1:4) and implicit in the case of Israel. For Malachi, Yahweh's action in restoring Israel and thwarting Edom demonstrates his covenant love for his people. However, even though Jacob/Israel has returned from exile, the people still fail to appreciate Yahweh's love. They fail to honour and fear Yahweh by living out their unique covenant responsibilities amid the nations. The book of Malachi indicates unfaithfulness remains an enduring problem for the remnant who are back in the land after the experience of exile.[87]

Unlike Haggai and Zechariah, Malachi does not portray the coming day of the Lord in military terms and this probably explains why there is no reference to a future exile. However, the themes associated with a future exile in Zechariah 13–14 (refining and cleansing to effect a new covenant relationship between Yahweh and his people), are clearly presented at the end of Malachi where again they are associated with the coming day of Yahweh. Malachi foresees a day when the arrogant and evil doers will be consumed with fire (Mal. 3:19 [4:1 Eng.]) and completely destroyed (3:24 [4:6 Eng.]). Yet it is also a day that will refine God's people like gold and silver and transform their worship (Mal. 3:2–4; cf. Zech. 13:9). It is a day when the righteous will be spared and shown compassion (Mal. 3:17) and blessing (3:20 [4:2 Eng.]). Israel will be Yahweh's treasured possession (3:17; cf. Exod. 19:5). Before that day, God will send the prophet Elijah who will "turn" (שוב) the hearts of God's people so that they might avoid destruction on that day (Mal. 3:24 [4:6 Eng.]).

86. Ezekiel may be the impetus for Zechariah's presentation here as it is elsewhere. See Schaefer, "Zechariah 14: A Study in Allusion," 74.

87. See also Boda, *A Severe Mercy*, 349; James D. Nogalski, "Recurring Themes in the Book of the Twelve: Creating Points of Contact for a Theological Reading," *Int* 61 (2007): 125–36 (127).

Summary and Conclusion

Exile is a theme touched on in one way or another by each of the books of the Twelve. As well as describing geographical displacement from warfare, there are several metaphors in the Twelve that provide additional insight. These include agricultural imagery such as "blowing" chaff (Hos. 13:3; Zech. 7:14) and "scattering" sheep (Zech. 13:7), which emphasize dispersion, loss, and threat. The image of "sowing" seed (Zech. 10:9), seems to indicate exile as burial from which will come life. The metaphor of childbirth portrays exile as a crisis with its associated pain, terror, entrapment, and threat of death (Mic. 4:9-10; Jon. 2), but also the hope of new life (Mic. 5:2 [5:3 Eng.]). Other possible metaphors include: being torn apart by a lion, connoting fear, unstoppable power, savagery, and death (Hos. 5:13; 13:7-8); "fire," which consumes and makes unclean (Zech. 3:2); and the "waterless pit," which imprisons (Zech. 9:11-12).

Exile has several theological associations that are developed in different ways through the Twelve. In relation to theodicy, exile is an expression of Yahweh's justice as punishment for covenantal unfaithfulness, an association found throughout the Twelve and established in the covenant curses of Leviticus 26 and Deuteronomy 28. Exile is being driven from the presence of the Lord. Significantly, exile also serves as punishment for the sins of nations who are not in this covenant relationship (Amos; Obadiah; Nahum; Habakkuk), particularly when those nations themselves have forcibly deported and incarcerated others (Amos 1:6, 9, 11). The God of Israel is the God of all nations and the Book of the Twelve shows that exile only falls after much forbearance (cf. Exod. 34:6-7).

As the Book of the Twelve unfolds, exile also comes to be associated with the refining of a righteous remnant (Amos; Micah; Habakkuk; Zephaniah). The crisis of exile will purify those who emerge from it to serve Yahweh in a renewed covenant relationship. Here hope infuses an otherwise negative theme.

The Book of the Twelve does not detail the Babylonian campaign against Jerusalem but picks up almost 70 years later (the first oracles of Haggai and Zechariah are dated 520 BCE). The problem, evident in Haggai but becoming even clearer in Zechariah and Malachi, is that even though many have returned from Babylon, the exilic experience has not dealt decisively with the problem of sin in the community of Yahweh's people and so there is a sense in which exile endures. Certainly, the glorious restoration has not materialized.

The latter chapters of Zechariah address this problem. The solution is found by reaching back into the past, particularly the hope that exile would refine a righteous remnant, to speak of another exile to come—a re-exile which will bring about the purification of God's people that earlier exiles had clearly failed to do. This will take place on the coming day of Yahweh. While many scholars see the theme of an enduring exile in Second Temple Judaism, this study highlights the way that Zechariah 12–14 presents an attack of Jerusalem by the nations and exile of Jerusalem's inhabitants on the day of Yahweh.[88] Unlike the attack in 587 BCE, Yahweh will deliver his people with a glorious outcome—the people will be refined and purified and return to Jerusalem, which will be made holy, and Yahweh's kingship will be established over all the earth. Crucial to the presentation in Zechariah 9–14 is a future Davidic king whose death results in cleansing and a renewed covenant relationship between Yahweh and his people (cf. Amos, Micah).

While Malachi does not refer to this future exile, the associated themes of refining and cleansing dominate the final chapter (3:1-24 [3:1–4:6 Eng.]), and like Zechariah, are associated with the coming day of Yahweh, when the remnant will be his treasured possession.

---

88. A "re-exile" as background to Jesus's apocalyptic discourses (Mk 13; Lk. 21) and the events of his passion deserves further exploration.

Chapter 3

"HOW CAN I GIVE YOU UP, EPHRAIM?"
(HOSEA 11:8A): THEODICY IN HOSEA

Brittany Kim

Whereas the Judeans who face Babylonian exile repeatedly question YHWH's justice or faithfulness (e.g., Isa. 40:27; 49:14; Ezek. 18:2, 25), the book of Hosea contains no such accusations against YHWH's character. The comparatively stable situation of eighth-century Israel prior to the Assyrian conquest, which provides the primary setting for Hosea, does not present the same need to develop an extensive theodicy.[1] Nevertheless, the sometimes-shocking portraits Hosea paints of Israel's coming judgment implicitly raise questions about the goodness of Israel's God and his faithfulness to his people. Therefore, after examining Hosea's

---

1. While the book does not indicate whether the life and ministry of Hosea continued up to the fall of the northern kingdom, his oracles were undoubtedly compiled and redacted in Judah after the destruction of Samaria (see further J. Andrew Dearman, *The Book of Hosea*, NICOT [Grand Rapids: Eerdmans, 2010], 3–8). Ehud Ben Zvi contends that since the judgment described in the book was "already in the past from [the perspective] of the literati" who were responsible for the book, it was necessary "that the deity be construed...as a punishing deity (and Israel/Judah as highly sinful to the point of 'meriting' such a most severe punishment)" (Ehud Ben Zvi, "Reading Hosea and Imagining YHWH," *HBT* 30 [2008]: 44 n. 5). Yet regardless of how extensively Hosea's words were edited, later redactors did not explicitly challenge YHWH's character in the face of Israel's (or Judah's) destruction. This essay will not seek to trace the composition history of Hosea but will instead examine the book in its final form. Unless otherwise noted, "Hosea" refers to the book rather than the prophet.

descriptions of impending divine judgments, this essay will consider the book's contribution to theodicy. It will argue first that Hosea vindicates YHWH's character by portraying the evil that will befall Israel as just retribution for Israel's sin, emphasizing that the punishment fits the crime. Second, by placing Israel's judgment in the context of metaphorical depictions of YHWH as an aggrieved husband and rejected parent, Hosea generates sympathy for his sufferings. Finally, from beginning to end, Hosea contends that the ultimate aim of YHWH's judgment is to serve as discipline leading the people to repentance and resulting in their restoration to a life of abundant flourishing.

Descriptions of Divine Judgment

Passive Judgments/Rejection

Hosea portrays the divine judgments that are about to befall Israel in both passive and active terms. Although the passive judgments tend to be less problematic for modern readers, they still raise questions about YHWH's failure to care for his people. These passive judgments arise from YHWH's rejection of his people as reflected in the prophetic names given to Hosea's second and third children—"No Compassion" and "Not My People" (1:6, 9)[2]—as well in as the so-called divorce formula applied to the land of Israel,[3] "she is not my wife, and I am not

---

2. All translations are mine unless otherwise noted. In his explanation of this second name, YHWH declares, "for you are not my people, and I am not your 'I AM,'" recalling the revelation of the divine name to Moses in Exod. 3:14 and reversing the covenant formula found in texts like Exod. 6:7 and Lev. 26:12 (see F. C. Fensham, "The Marriage Metaphor in Hosea for the Covenant Relationship between the Lord and His People [Hos. 1:2-9]," *JNSL* 12 [1984]: 74–6).

3. Given the frequent personification of cities as women in the Old Testament (see, e.g., Isa. 47:1-15; 49:14-26; Ezek. 16; 23) and the ancient Near East, some scholars understand Israel's capital city of Samaria as the personified woman in Hos. 2 (e.g., Brad E. Kelle, *Hosea 2: Metaphor and Rhetoric in Historical Perspective*, SBLAB 20 [Leiden: Brill, 2005], 86–94; John J. Schmitt, "The Wife of God in Hosea 2," *BibRes* 34 [1989]: 5–18). However, Hos. 1:2 declares that "the land (הארץ) has committed great sexual immorality by forsaking YHWH." Since Samaria is never mentioned in Hos. 1–3, the feminine singular noun ארץ most likely forms the basis of the female personification, though it should be understood as a metonymy for the people (see also Dearman, *Hosea*, 90–1, 107; idem, "YHWH's House: Gender Roles and Metaphors for Israel in Hosea," *JNSL* 25 [1999]: 97–108; R. Abma, *Bonds of Love: Methodic Studies of Prophetic Texts with Marriage Imagery [Isaiah 50:1-3 and 54:1-10, Hosea 1–3, Jeremiah 2–3]*, SSN [Assen: Van Gorcum, 1999], 141).

her husband" (2:4 [2 Eng.]).[4] Elsewhere, Hosea declares that the people "will go to seek YHWH, but they will not find [him]; he has withdrawn from them" (5:6; cf. 4:6; 9:17).

YHWH's withdrawal entails the removal of his divine protection, leaving his people open to enemy attack. Therefore, ch. 8 warns that "an enemy will pursue" Israel (v. 3) and that "Israel is swallowed up" (v. 8; cf. 10:9-10). Using the Hebrew word שׁוב ("turn" or "return"), which functions as a key word in Hosea and the Book of the Twelve as a whole,[5] the coming judgment is also described as a "return to Egypt" (v. 13; cf. 9:3), in which "Assyria will be his king" (11:5).[6] In 7:9, YHWH proclaims that "foreigners devour [Ephraim's] strength" (cf. 8:7). More disturbingly, 14:1 (13:16 Eng.) declares that "their infants will be dashed in pieces, and their pregnant women ripped open" (cf. 10:14-15). As YHWH warns in 9:12, "woe to them when I depart from them!" When he gives them over to their enemies, they will face all the horrors of the Assyrian army, which was known for its brutal practices.[7]

---

4. Whether these words amount to a formal statement of divorce (so Mayer I. Gruber, *Hosea: A Textual Commentary*, LHBOTS 653 [London: Bloomsbury T&T Clark, 2017], 109–10; Nelly Stienstra, *YHWH Is the Husband of His People: Analysis of a Biblical Metaphor with Special Reference to Translation* [Kampen: Kok Pharos, 1993], 103–4, though she suggests it might simply be a threat) or not (so Kelle, *Hosea 2*, 53–8; Ryan C. Hanley, "The Background and Purpose of Stripping the Adulteress in Hosea 2," *JETS* 60 [2017]: 92), they clearly present a serious rupture in the marital relationship. However, the request that the children plead with their mother to desist from her adulterous behavior suggests that the way is still open for marital reconciliation.

5. See Jason T. LeCureux, *The Thematic Unity of the Book of the Twelve*, HBM 41 (Sheffield: Sheffield Phoenix, 2012), 22, who sees "the call to return" as "a unifying and perhaps controlling theme for the Twelve"; also Aaron Schart, "The First Section of the Book of the Twelve Prophets: Hosea–Joel–Amos," *Int* 61 (2007): 141–4; Brian Gault, "Avenging Husband and Redeeming Lover? Opposing Portraits of God in Hosea," *JETS* 60 (2017): 504–8.

6. Interpreters are divided on whether 11:5 affirms or denies that the Israelites will return to Egypt (compare the NIV with the ESV). Either way, it sees Assyria's coming rule over Israel as analogous to the people's earlier subjection by Egypt and as a "reversal of the exodus" described in v. 1 (Joy Philip Kakkanattu, *God's Enduring Love in the Book of Hosea*, FAT 2/14 [Tübingen: Mohr Siebeck, 2006], 67–8; see also LeCureux, *Thematic Unity*, 71–5).

7. On these practices, see further Charlie Trimm, *Fighting for the King and the Gods: A Survey of Warfare in the Ancient Near East*, SBLRBS 88 (Atlanta: SBL, 2017), 355–64. Note particularly the following description of Tiglath-pileser I: "He slits the wombs of pregnant women; he blinds the infants" (p. 355, citing Mordechai Cogan, "'Ripping Open Pregnant Women' in Light of an Assyrian Analogue," *JAOS*

Not only will an enemy army attack the people of Israel, but judgment will also be expressed through the flora and fauna of Israel's land. Hosea 4:3 declares that "the land mourns, and all who live in it languish; the beasts of the field and the birds of the sky and even the fish of the sea are taken away."[8] The reason that the animal population dwindles may be due to the land expressing its grief in drought, leading to famine.[9] Elsewhere the book refers more explicitly to crop failure, proclaiming that "the standing grain has no head; it will produce no flour" (8:7; cf. 9:2). Although the people will be unable to coax food from the ground, unwanted plants will thrive (10:8; 9:6). As Katherine Hayes observes concerning 4:1-3, the structure of the passage "creates an impression of the land responding directly to the acts done in it."[10] Perhaps in the absence of divine blessing on the land's fertility (cf. Deut. 28:4-5, 11-12), both humans and animals will experience the ground as cursed (cf. Gen. 3:17-19).[11]

Other passive judgments are presented as the natural consequences of Israel's actions. For example, 13:13 offers the unusual image of Ephraim as a child who is about to be birthed, but as "a son without wisdom," he does not emerge from the birth canal at the proper time. The implied result is that both mother (the land?) and child will die.[12] Operating from

---

103 [1983]: 756 [VAT 13833]). See also Corrine L. Patton, "'Should Our Sister Be Treated Like a Whore?': A Response to Feminist Critiques of Ezekiel 23," in *The Book of Ezekiel: Theological and Anthropological Perspectives*, ed. Margaret S. Odell and John T. Strong, SBLSymS 9 (Atlanta: SBL, 2000), 234–5.

8. Comparing this verse to Gen. 1:20-24, Alice Keefe contends that "this listing of the animals in reverse suggests that the whole of creation is to be undone" (Alice A. Keefe, "Hosea's [In]Fertility God," *HBT* 30 [2008]: 38).

9. Katherine M. Hayes, *"The Earth Mourns": Prophetic Metaphor and Oral Aesthetic*, SBLAB 8 (Leiden: Brill, 2002), 44. While some translators take אבל in 4:3 as a separate root meaning "to dry up" (see Roy E. Hayden, "אבל," *NIDOTTE* 1:248), it seems more likely that the uses of the word in the Old Testament all derive from a single root meaning "to mourn" (see also the LXX and Vg.; as well as Joshua N. Moon, *Hosea*, AOTC [Downers Grove: IVP Academic, 2018], 74). Nevertheless, passages where אבל occurs with יבש ("to be dry, wither," e.g., Jer. 12:4; Amos 1:2) may suggest that the land mourns by drying up.

10. Hayes, *"The Earth Mourns,"* 45. Tying Hos. 4:1-3 into a broader theology of creation, she later contends that "human disregard for communal norms and constraints leads to the unraveling of the order that sustains creation itself" (p. 61).

11. Note that "thorn (קוץ) and thistle (דרדר)" appear together only in Gen. 3:18 and Hos. 10:8.

12. See further Laurie J. Braaten, "God Sows: Hosea's Land Theme in the Book of the Twelve," in *Thematic Threads in the Book of the Twelve*, ed. Paul L. Redditt and Aaron Schart (New York: de Gruyter, 2003), 122.

a different metaphorical realm, the wisdom epilogue that concludes the book declares, "the ways of YHWH are right, and the righteous walk in them, but rebels stumble in them" (14:10 [9 Eng.]). Since YHWH has set out good paths for his people to walk in, the image suggests that the rebellious stumble of their own accord, not as a result of YHWH's direct intervention (cf. 4:5; 5:5; 14:2 [1 Eng.]). In other words, their sin brings about its own consequences in the ordered world YHWH has created.

Active Judgments

However, Hosea exhibits some tension between these passive divine judgments and descriptions of YHWH's active participation in the people's coming downfall. With regard to the land's failure to produce, YHWH declares in 2:11 [9 Eng.] that he will "take back" the fruits of their agricultural endeavors (cf. vv. 5 [3 Eng.], 14 [12 Eng.]). Moreover, in 9:12, YHWH speaks of the "woe" that will befall Israel when he "depart[s] from them," which will result in the people being "wanderers among the nations" (v. 17). Yet in that same verse he also contends, "even if they rear their children, *I will bereave* them of every one."[13] Elsewhere, he proclaims, "*I will send* fire on his cities" (8:14), though presumably that fire would come at the hands of enemy invaders. Likewise, in 10:10 YHWH states, "when I desire, I will discipline (אסר) them; peoples will be gathered (אסף) against them," with the similar verbal roots highlighting the concurrence between the actions of YHWH and the nations.[14] Therefore, even if Assyria is the proximate cause of Israel's destruction, Hosea clearly identifies YHWH as the ultimate cause.

YHWH also indicates his active involvement when he declares that he will "punish" (e.g., 2:15 [13 Eng.]; 4:9; 8:13) or even "destroy" (4:5) Israel,[15] and his punishment is depicted with striking metaphors. In ch. 2, where the land of Israel is personified as a woman, YHWH threatens to

---

13. Cf. v. 16, where YHWH states that he will "kill the beloved [children] of their womb," connecting his judgment of infertility (see also v. 11) with an agricultural metaphor that the people of Ephraim will "produce no fruit (פרי)" (see further Gault, "Avenging Husband and Redeeming Lover?" 500; Beth M. Stovell, "'I Will Make Her Like a Desert': Intertextual Allusion and Feminine and Agricultural Metaphors in the Book of the Twelve," in *The Book of the Twelve and the New Form Criticism*, ed. Mark J. Boda, Michael H. Floyd, and Colin M. Toffelmire, SBLANEM 10 [Atlanta: SBL, 2015], 54, 58).

14. Gault, "Avenging Husband and Redeeming Lover?" 500.

15. See also 1:4, where YHWH declares that he will "visit the blood of Jezreel upon the house of Jehu," indicating that Jehu's dynasty will face the same violent

"uncover (*pi'el* גלה) her shame[16] before the eyes of her lovers" (2:12 [10 Eng.]), using a verb that is also connected with going into exile (e.g., 2 Kgs 17:23) and may reflect an intentional double entendre.[17] Elsewhere, the book uses animal imagery to great rhetorical effect. In 5:12 YHWH declares, "I am like a moth to Ephraim," suggesting that he is eating away at the nation as a moth consumes a garment.[18] A couple of verses later he adopts a more terrifying metaphor: "For *I* will be like a lion to Ephraim and like a young lion to the house of Judah. *I, even I*, will tear apart and go away; I will carry off, and no one will deliver" (v. 14; cf. 13:7-8). The threefold repetition of the first-person pronoun serves to emphasize his action in destroying his prey.

As Yisca Zimran points out, the lion could be a royal symbol for Neo-Assyrian kings and sometimes for other gods, and therefore the use of the metaphor "challenges the self-glorification of Assyrian kings or their gods... [These verses] are an attempt to shift the nation's political and religious paradigm, and to redefine whom Israel perceives as the powers that govern them."[19] Even the astonishingly violent portrait of YHWH "tear[ing] open the covering over their heart" like a she-bear who has lost

---

end as the dynasty of Ahab, which Jehu wiped out (see 2 Kgs 9:1–10:17; on this understanding of Hos. 1:4, see Gault, "Avenging Husband and Redeeming Lover?" 491 n. 7).

16. Commentators debate whether the *hapax legomenon* נבלות should be translated as "folly" from the relatively common root נבל (see Dearman, *Hosea*, 116–17) or, given the context, whether it indicates "nakedness" (Gruber, *Hosea*, 135) or "shame," as understood here (see also Sharon Moughtin-Mumby, *Sexual and Marital Metaphors in Hosea, Jeremiah, Isaiah, and Ezekiel* [Oxford: Oxford University Press, 2008], 87, 96; cf. Moon, *Hosea*, 50).

17. See also Moon, *Hosea*, 56; Hanley, "Background and Purpose," 102.

18. Others suggest that עש does not mean "moth" but "maggots" (Yisca Zimran, "The Notion of God Reflected in the Lion Imagery of the Book of Hosea," *VT* 68 [2018]: 150 n. 3; John T. Willis, "Hosea's Unique Figures of Yahweh," *ResQ* 61 [2019]: 168–9), "pus" (see Douglas Stuart, *Hosea–Jonah*, WBC 31 [Waco: Word, 1988], 105), or "emaciating disease" (A. A. Macintosh, *A Critical and Exegetical Commentary on Hosea*, ICC [Edinburgh: T&T Clark, 1997], 207), noting the parallel with רקב ("rot"). However, in Job 13:28, the only other verse where עש and רקב appear together, עש seems to refer to a "moth" (see Dearman, *Hosea*, 185).

19. Zimran, "Notion of God," 163–5, who also observes a wordplay on the word "lurk" in 13:7, which has the same consonants as "Assyria" (אשור) but is vocalized differently (p. 157); see also Göran Eidevall, *Grapes in the Desert: Metaphors, Models, and Themes in Hosea 4–14*, ConBOT 43 (Stockholm: Almqvist & Wiksell, 1996), 87. On the use of the lion image for kings and gods in Mesopotamia, see

her cubs in 13:8 may be to some extent a response to Israel's perceptions of Assyrian dominance and brutality. Charlie Trimm cites an Assyrian letter that "refers to ripping out the hearts of unidentified individuals."[20] Therefore, rather than capitulating to that foreign superpower out of fear of Assyrian reprisal, Hosea challenges the people of Israel to recognize YHWH as the dominant power whom they should fear.[21] Yet these texts still raise the question of how a good God could act with the ferocity of an Assyrian king, especially against his own people.

Judgment as Just Retribution for Israel's Sin

Descriptions of Israel's Sin

Hosea responds to the problem implicitly raised by these violent depictions of YHWH first by presenting Israel's coming judgment as just retribution for the people's sin. Not only does the book employ a rich vocabulary of words from the semantic field of sin,[22] but it also gives considerable space to describing the many ways Israel is at fault. Most significantly, YHWH declares in 8:1 that the people "have transgressed my covenant (ברית) and rebelled against my instruction" (cf. 6:7; 8:12). This covenant breaking is portrayed most poignantly by means of the marriage metaphor. Since YHWH's covenant with Israel is predicated on a relationship of exclusivity, Hosea develops the metaphor of marital infidelity to highlight Israel's rejection of YHWH in the nation's worship of other gods.[23] Within the context of that metaphor, Hosea 2 speaks of the people of Israel using silver and gold received from YHWH in their worship of Baal (v. 10 [8 Eng.]; cf. v. 15 [13 Eng.]), while in 3:1, YHWH

---

further Brent A. Strawn, *What Is Stronger than a Lion? Leonine Image and Metaphor in the Hebrew Bible and the Ancient Near East*, OBO 212 (Göttingen: Vandenhoeck & Ruprecht, 2005), 178–80, 206–8.

20. Trimm, *Fighting for the King and the Gods*, 359 (SAA 11.144).

21. See also Dearman, *Hosea*, 187, concerning YHWH as a lion in 5:14.

22. E.g., חטא ("sin"), עון/און ("iniquity"), רע ("evil"), רשע ("wickedness"), פשע ("rebellion").

23. On the covenant as a significant background for Hosea's use of the marriage metaphor, see Abma, *Bonds of Love*, 23–4; Hanley, "Background and Purpose," 96–101; also Gary Hall, "Origin of the Marriage Metaphor," *HS* 23 (1982): 168–71, though he also views Canaanite mythology as important background. Elaine Adler sees the marriage metaphor as already "present, albeit somewhat latently," within Pentateuchal sources that she sees as pre-dating Hosea (Elaine June Adler, "The Background for the Metaphor of Covenant as Marriage in the Hebrew Bible" [PhD diss., University of California, Berkeley, 1990], 389–90).

laments that the people "turn to other gods" (3:1).[24] Elsewhere, YHWH contends that rather than seeking his guidance, his "people inquire of wood," sacrificing to their idols at a multitude of illicit cultic sites (4:12-13). Hosea even traces Israel's idolatry back to the nation's early years, claiming that when YHWH pursued his people after bringing them out of Egypt, "they sacrificed to the baalim and burned incense to idols" (11:2; cf. 9:10; 13:1).

In a few places, the book refers to calf idol(s), presumably denoting the idols Jeroboam I established in Bethel and Dan (see 1 Kgs 12:28-30), which may have been understood as representations of YHWH.[25] Hosea 8:5 describes YHWH's anger at the people of Samaria concerning their calf idol (cf. v. 11), and the increasing cycle of sin described in 13:2 involves both casting "molten images" and "kiss[ing] calves." Finally, 10:5-6 speaks of the people's fear for "the calf of Beth-aven," which will be taken into exile by the Assyrians. The derogatory name used for the city here reflects its character—rather than "the house of God (בית־אל)," its idol worship has made it "a house of iniquity (בית און)."

With their idolatry, the people have broken the first two covenantal expectations expressed in the Decalogue,[26] but Hos. 4:1-2 also indicts

24. The claim that "Ephraim goes after צו" in 5:11 may also be a disparaging way to denote idolatry, though the precise meaning of צו is debated (see further Dennis T. Olson, "The Lion, the Itch and the Wardrobe: Hosea 5:8–6:6 as a Case Study in the Contemporary Interpretation and Authority of Scripture," *CurTM* 23 [1996]: 173–84 [176]). Similarly, the difficult statement in 7:16 that "they (re)turn (שוב) על לא" may indicate that they turn "not (to) what is above" (so Macintosh, *Hosea*, 285)—i.e., YHWH—or to what is "Not-on-High" (so Duane A. Garrett, *Hosea, Joel*, NAC 19A [Nashville: Broadman & Holman, 1997], 173) or "no-god" (so Francis I. Andersen and David Noel Freedman, *Hosea: A New Translation with Introduction and Commentary*, AB 24 [Garden City: Doubleday, 1980], 477; cf. Moon, *Hosea*, 140)—i.e., idols.

25. Note that in 1 Kgs 12:28 Jeroboam identifies these calf idols as "your gods, O Israel, who brought you up from the land of Egypt" (see further Dearman, *Hosea*, 224–6). However, since the calf was a sacred symbol of Baal, these idols may also have been used in Canaanite worship practices (see Garrett, *Hosea, Joel*, 184).

26. While the dating of YHWH's covenant with Israel and the Pentateuchal legal traditions are hotly contested, some form of the covenant—along with the covenantal expectations that came to written expression in the Decalogue—seems to have pre-dated Hosea and served as a foundation for the prophet's critique of Israel's behavior (Dearman, *Hosea*, 150–2; Gruber, *Hosea*, 187–8; see also Gault, "Avenging Husband and Redeeming Lover?" 506 n. 43; Walter Brueggemann, "The Recovering God of Hosea," *HBT* 30 [2008]: 5–20 [8]).

them for transgressing other decalogic commands. Rather than "faith-fulness," "steadfast love," and "knowledge of God," the land is full of "swearing and lying and murder and stealing and adultery."[27] Working backward, "adultery" (נאף) appears elsewhere in the book in the context of the marriage metaphor to describe Israel's idolatrous worship (see נאפופים in 2:4 [2 Eng.]; also 3:1; 7:4). While 4:13-14 may speak of literal adultery,[28] reading these verses in light of chs. 1–3 makes it more likely that they should be understood metaphorically.[29] Therefore, given the book's emphasis on spiritual adultery, the reference to "adultery" in 4:2 calls to mind primarily the people's idolatrous worship,[30] though the immediate context of violations of the Decalogue also suggests literal transgressions of marital fidelity.

"Stealing" seems to be pervasive, as "the thief breaks in [to houses], and the bandit raids outside" (7:1). Merchants are also culpable—they "love to oppress" with "false scales" (12:8 [7 Eng.]). Moreover, when Ephraim boasts, "I have found wealth for myself (מצאתי און לי); [with] all my property they will not find in me any iniquity (לא ימצאו־לי עון) or sin" (12:9 [8 Eng.]), his claim is clearly disingenuous (or self-deluded), as

---

27. The last three reflect the language of the Decalogue (see Exod. 20:13-15).

28. Most commentators have taken these verses as denoting sacred prostitu-tion connected to the fertility cult of Baal (see, e.g., Hans Walter Wolff, *Hosea: A Commentary on the Book of the Prophet Hosea*, trans. Gary Stansell, Hermeneia [Philadelphia: Fortress, 1974], 86–8; Andersen and Freedman, *Hosea*, 343, 368–70; Garrett, *Hosea, Joel*, 124). However, in the past few decades a growing number of interpreters have argued that the evidence does not support such a practice, though some still see these verses as referring to literal acts of sexual immorality and adultery (see Phyllis Bird, "'To Play the Harlot': An Inquiry into an Old Testament Metaphor," in *Gender and Difference in Ancient Israel*, ed. Peggy L. Day [Minneapolis: Fortress, 1989], 84–6; idem, "Prostitution in the Social World and Religious Rhetoric of Ancient Israel," in *Prostitutes and Courtesans in the Ancient World*, ed. Christopher A. Faraone and Laura K. McClure [Madison: University of Wisconsin Press, 2006], 49–52; Gruber, *Hosea*, 212–26).

29. See Karin Adams, "Metaphor and Dissonance: A Reinterpretation of Hosea 4:13-14," *JBL* 127 (2008): 291–305; Alice A. Keefe, *Woman's Body and the Social Body in Hosea*, JSOTSup 338 (London: Sheffield Academic, 2001), 100–102; Stuart, *Hosea–Jonah*, 82–3.

30. Though not explicitly addressing the sense of the "adultery" in 4:2, Douglas Abel reads the lack of "faithfulness," "steadfast love," and "knowledge of God" (my translation) in v. 1 in light of the marriage metaphor, which he sees as prominent within the chapter as a whole (Douglas Stephen Abel, "The Marriage Metaphor in Hosea 4 and Jeremiah 2: How Prophetic Speech 'Kills Two Birds with One Stone,'" *Proceedings* 29 [2009]: 15–27 [18–19]).

the wordplay connecting "wealth" with "iniquity" highlights the idea of ill-gotten gain.[31] "Murder" is attributed even to priests (6:9), and the city of Gilead is indicted as a city "tracked with blood" (v. 8). Indeed, 10:9 declares, "from the days of Gibeah, you have sinned, O Israel," presumably referring back to the deadly sexual assault and resulting war narrated in Judges 19–20 (see also Hos. 9:9). And the claim that "bloodshed reaches to bloodshed" (4:2) suggests a perpetual cycle of violence.

While "lying" is linked to the ninth commandment, which prohibits giving "false testimony" (Exod. 20:16), it includes a wider range of deceitful activities.[32] Ephraim is condemned for delighting princes "with their lies" (Hos. 7:3) and "surround[ing YHWH] with lies" (12:1 [11:12 Eng.]; cf. 7:1; 10:13). "Swearing (אלה)" can refer to swearing an oath (1 Kgs 8:31) or evoking a curse (1 Sam. 14:24). Hosea 10:4 speaks of "vain oaths (אלות)" in connection with establishing covenants, and improper or fraudulent oaths may also be in view in 4:2.[33]

Aside from breaking the commands of the Decalogue, the people are also condemned for making political decisions without YHWH's consent. For example, in 8:4, YHWH asserts, "they made kings but not from me." Likewise, 7:5-7 speaks of princes with "hearts like an oven" conspiring to "devour their rulers," probably reflecting the tumultuous situation of the monarchy after Jeroboam II, marked by violent revolt. This political upheaval should lead them to turn to YHWH, but he laments, "none of them calls on me" (v. 7).[34] Moreover, 8:14 declares that "Israel has forgotten his Maker and built palaces," seeking its own political and economic advancement while neglecting the God who made it possible.

Israel's foreign policy, like its internal affairs, also reflects a lack of dependence on YHWH, as the people have established political alliances without consulting him. Hosea 7:8-10 states that "Ephraim mixes himself with the peoples," with the result that he "is a cake not turned."[35] In

31. See Moughtin-Mumby, *Sexual and Marital Metaphors*, 58.

32. Dearman, *Hosea*, 148–9.

33. This item offers the least connection with the Decalogue, though some have seen a link with the third commandment concerning the improper use of YHWH's name (see Stuart, *Hosea–Jonah*, 76; Garrett, *Hosea, Joel*, 111).

34. Dearman points out that those who successfully staged a coup would probably have evoked YHWH's name for their own benefit, but YHWH makes it clear that they acted without his approval (*Hosea*, 205).

35. This image could suggest either the unappetizing state of Israel (i.e., that he is burned on one side but raw on the other, so Gary V. Smith, *Hosea, Amos, Micah*, NIVAC [Grand Rapids: Zondervan, 2001], 123) or that the nation will be quickly devoured before it is finished cooking (Gruber, *Hosea*, 321).

particular, YHWH's people appeal to Assyria for help, even though that nation is "not able to heal" Ephraim from his wounds (5:13; cf. 7:11). Not only are Israel's political alliances futile, but they are also viewed as acts of marital unfaithfulness to YHWH, like their idolatrous worship. Indeed, in 8:9 Israel's solicitation of Assyria is portrayed as prostitution. Although marital imagery is not present in 12:2 [1 Eng.], the description of the people "mak[ing] a covenant (ברית) with Assyria" suggests that they are flouting their exclusive covenant with YHWH.[36] Hosea repeatedly empha-sizes the depth and breadth of the people's sin and their failure "to return (שוב)" to YHWH (5:4; 7:10) in order to portray them as clearly deserving of divine judgment.

Punishments that Fit the Crimes

Moreover, the book also contends that Israel's punishments fit the crimes. Hosea 12:3 (2 Eng.) proclaims that YHWH will "punish Jacob according to his ways; he will repay him according to his deeds" (cf. 4:9; 12:15 [14 Eng.]).[37] Elsewhere this point is made by showing how the judgment corresponds to the offense. For example, 10:13-14 states that "because you have trusted in your own way, in your many warriors, the tumult [of war] will arise against your people, and all your fortresses will be destroyed."[38] In other words, if the people are choosing to depend on their warriors rather than YHWH, then he will leave it to their warriors to protect them, though they will be helpless against the Assyrian onslaught.

Sometimes crime and punishment are linked by the use of shared language. For example, in 4:6 YHWH declares, "because you have rejected (מאס) knowledge, I reject (מאס) you as my priest; and [because] you have forgotten (שכח) the instruction of your God, I also will forget (שכח) your children." In 2:10-11 (8-9 Eng.) he contends that the land of Israel "did not know that I gave her the grain (דגן) and the new wine (תירוש) and the oil,...therefore I will return (שוב) and take back my grain (דגן) in its time and my new wine (תירוש) in its season" (cf. v. 14 [12 Eng.]). Moreover, since the people have engaged

---

36. See Dearman, *Hosea*, 298.

37. See further LeCureux, *Thematic Unity*, 66–70.

38. The declaration that Samaria's "pregnant women (הרה) will be ripped open (בקע)" (14:1 [13:16 Eng.]) may also be a punishment that fits the crime since 2 Kgs 15:16 states that Menahem "ripped open (בקע) all the pregnant women (הרה)" of Tiphsah. However, as noted in n. 7, that practice is also attested among Assyrian sources and may simply be an acknowledgment of what will happen when the Assyrian army comes.

in idolatrous worship "on all threshing floors (גרן)," YHWH proclaims
that "threshing floor (גרן)…will not feed them" (9:1-2; see also 10:1-2).
Finally, because the people's "steadfast love is like a morning cloud and
like dew that goes away early (כענן־בקר וכטל משכים הלך)" (6:4), the
people will be "like a morning cloud and like dew that goes away early
(כענן־בקר וכטל משכים הלך)" (13:3). Sharon Moughtin-Mumby contends
that "through such repetition *Hosea* 4–14 implies that Israel's troubling
future is an inevitable, unavoidable, and indeed deserved consequence
of their actions."[39]

In other cases, repeated sounds connect sin and judgment. Hosea 10:13
declares, "you have plowed wickedness (חרשתם־רשע), you have reaped
iniquity, you have eaten the fruit of lies (אכלתם פרי־כחש)" (cf. 8:7). As
Mayer Gruber observes, the repetition of ר, ש, and ח underscores "the
idea that misbehavior and punishment are bound together in a relationship
of logical consequences."[40] Similarly, 12:12 [11 Eng.] uses alliteration
when it contends, "in Gilgal (גלגל) they sacrifice (זבח) bulls; their altars
(מזבח) will be like heaps (גל) [of stones] upon a plowed field." These
poetic devices serve not only literary, but also theodic purposes, offering
a justification for the coming judgments by linking them closely together
with the sins they address. Theodicy in Hosea is grounded first in the idea
that Israel's judgments are deserved and that they fit the offenses.

Judgment in the Context of Metaphorical Depictions of YHWH's Relationship with Israel

The Land of Israel as Adulterous Wife and YHWH as Aggrieved Husband

The book also seeks to generate compassion for YHWH's sufferings
through vivid metaphorical portrayals of his relationship with Israel. Most
famously, it depicts the land of Israel as an adulterous wife and YHWH as
her aggrieved husband (chs. 1–3). Hosea begins with the shocking divine
command to the prophet, "go, take for yourself a wife of promiscuity
(זנונים) and children of promiscuity (זנונים)," with the explanation that "the
land commits sexual immorality (זנה) from [following] after YHWH"
(1:2). Interpreters vary widely in their views on how exactly YHWH's
command should be understood. In my view, YHWH instructs Hosea to
marry a woman whose reputation is tarnished by sexual deviance and who
will continue that behavior after her marriage (see 3:1) as a graphic visual

39. Moughtin-Mumby, *Sexual and Marital Metaphors*, 55, italics original.
40. Gruber, *Hosea*, 443.

display of Israel's behavior toward YHWH.[41] Yet, however the sign act is understood, the primary point of the illustration is clear: the land of Israel has acted like an unfaithful wife, forsaking and even forgetting YHWH to "go after [her] lovers"—primarily other gods like Baal (2:7, 15 [5, 13 Eng.]).

As Phyllis Bird suggests, the preferred use of the זנה root ("to be sexually immoral, promiscuous") in 1:2 and throughout the book, rather than נאף ("to commit adultery"), may be intended "to emphasize promiscuity rather than infidelity, 'wantonness' rather than violation of marriage contract or covenant," and suggest "repeated, habitual, or characteristic behavior."[42] In other words, the land of Israel routinely turns away from YHWH to other gods, a characterization supported by the fivefold reference to her "lovers" in ch. 2 (vv. 7, 9, 12, 14, 15 [5, 7, 10, 12, 13 Eng.]).[43] Hosea 4 reinforces this idea by describing how the people have "forsaken YHWH to *maintain* sexual immorality" (vv. 10-11),[44] as they engage in adulterous worship of other gods at illicit cult sites (4:13-15). Whereas YHWH "loves (אהב) the children of Israel," his people "love" (אהב) sacred cakes used in their idolatrous worship (3:1) and even the "shame" incurred through their deviant behavior (4:18). Elsewhere, the book describes the people as "adulterers, burning like an oven" (7:4), and speaks of the payment they have received from prostituting themselves to other gods (9:1).

41. See, e.g., Gale A. Yee, "Hosea," in *Women's Bible Commentary*, ed. Carol A. Newsom, Sharon H. Ringe, and Jacqueline E. Lapsley, 3rd ed. (Louisville: Westminster John Knox, 2012), 301; Moon, *Hosea*, 41. For a summary of options, see Garrett, *Hosea, Joel*, 44–9; Moughtin-Mumby, *Sexual and Marital Metaphors*, 220–1.

42. Bird, "To Play the Harlot," 80. Following Julie Galambush (*Jerusalem in the Book of Ezekiel: The City as Yahweh's Wife*, SBLDS 130 [Atlanta: Scholars Press, 1992], 29), Karin Adams contends that Hosea adopts a second layer of metaphorical portrayal by depicting adultery (נאף)—which is itself a metaphor for idolatry—as prostitution (זנה; "Metaphor and Dissonance," 298–300). However, the זנה root can be used more broadly for sexual immorality, not just for prostitution (Bird, "To Play the Harlot," 76–80; Yee, "Hosea," 209). Forms of זנה appear 22 times in the book (1:2 [4×]; 2:4 [2 Eng.], 6–7 [4–5 Eng.]; 3:3; 4:10–11; 12 [2×], 13, 14 [2×], 15, 18 [2×]; 5:3–4; 6:10; 9:1), compared to only six occurrences of נאף (2:4 [2 Eng.]; 3:1; 4:2, 13–14; 7:4).

43. Hosea 8:9–10 also counts Assyria and other unnamed nations among Israel's lovers.

44. The phrase uses the verb שמר, which is often associated with "keep[ing]" YHWH's covenant or commandments (e.g., Gen. 17:9-10; Deut. 5:10), making this occurrence highly ironic (see Moughtin-Mumby, *Sexual and Marital Metaphors*, 67). Note also that Hos. 4 contains ten occurrences of the זנה root compressed into seven verses (vv. 10-15, 18).

With this shocking metaphor Hosea cultivates compassion for YHWH's sufferings as a husband who has repeatedly been forsaken by his wife in favor of other lovers. The image evokes not only the anguish of abandonment in this most intimate of human relationships, but also the acute shame of a husband betrayed by his wife, which would be particularly degrading in the male-dominant, honor–shame society of ancient Israel.[45] Moreover, this portrayal invites the people of Israel—not just the women but also the men and even the priests—to identify with YHWH's sexually deviant wife and recognize that his sorrow is the result of their own shameful behavior. Yet despite YHWH's grief and disgrace, he does not ultimately subject his wife to the death penalty, which is the punishment for adultery found in the legal traditions (Lev. 20:10; Deut. 22:22). As Hosea is called to illustrate by redeeming his adulterous wife, YHWH also seeks reconciliation (3:1-5).

Israel as Rebellious Child and YHWH as Rejected Parent

A second metaphorical depiction that serves to vindicate YHWH's character in the face of Israel's coming judgment also derives from the sphere of familial relationships: the image of Israel as rebellious child and YHWH as rejected parent, which dominates Hosea 11. Recalling the nation's early history, YHWH reminisces, "when Israel was a child, I loved him, and out of Egypt I called my son" (v. 1; cf. Exod. 4:22-23). However, the idyllic period of Israel's youth was short-lived. YHWH mourns, "[when] I called them, [thus] they went away from my presence,"[46] abandoning their divine parent to engage in idolatry (Hos. 11:2). Despite this rebellion, YHWH recalls the tender care he took in feeding, caring for, and raising his son (vv. 3-4). Although YHWH has traditionally been identified as Israel's father in this passage, some feminist interpreters argue that the images of child-rearing found here may fit equally well or even better with the role of a mother.[47]

---

45. See Moon, *Hosea*, 40.

46. Like most commentaries, this reading follows the LXX in reading first person singular forms, rather than the third person plural found in the MT: "the more *they* called (קראו) them, the more they went away from *their* presence (מפניהם)" (see Moon, *Hosea*, 181; Kakkanattu, *God's Enduring Love*, 12, 15–17).

47. Yee, "Hosea," 213; Baumann, *Love and Violence*, 101; see also Helen Schüngel-Straumann, "God as Mother in Hosea 11," in *A Feminist Companion to the Latter Prophets*, ed. Athalya Brenner, FCB 8 (Sheffield: Sheffield Academic, 1995), 194–218, who bolsters her position with some non-traditional readings of the difficult Hebrew text. In my view, the passage does not present a gendered role for YHWH but places the emphasis on his parental care (see also Kakkanattu, *God's Enduring Love*, 129; similarly, Marie-Theres Wacker, "Father-God, Mother-God—and Beyond:

Drawing on one of the most unbreakable bonds in human experience, Hosea highlights YHWH's tender love and compassion for his son and therefore his desperate grief when Israel turns his back on his divine parent. Because his people "refuse to return (שוב)" to him and are "bent on waywardness (משובה)," YHWH declares that he will essentially give them over to Assyria, which will result in death by sword (vv. 5-7). However, offering a rare glimpse into his deep internal struggle, he then cries out: "How can I give you up, Ephraim? [How] can I deliver you over, Israel? How can I treat you like Admah? How can I make you like Zeboyim? My heart is overturned (הפך) within me; altogether my compassion grows warm. I will not execute my fierce anger; I will not return (שוב) to destroy Ephraim, for I am God and not a man, the Holy One among you" (vv. 8-9).[48] Anger and compassion, judgment and mercy war within YHWH as he experiences the pain of rejection and betrayal by his beloved son. Certainly parents who have experienced similar filial abandonment can identify with his inner turmoil. However, once again YHWH does not allow judgment to be the final word. Although the law condemns a rebellious son to death (Deut. 21:18-21), YHWH ultimately wills not to abandon his son to that fate.[49] Whereas YHWH "overthrew" (הפך) Admah and Zeboyim (Deut. 29:22 [23 Eng.]), now he "overturn[s]" (הפך) his own heart so as not to execute a similar sentence against Israel. Thus, the marriage and parent–child metaphors contribute to theodicy by giving insight into how YHWH experiences the heartache of Israel's rejection and how he wrestles with the competing claims of anger and compassion.

The Ultimate Aim of YHWH's Judgment

Discipline to Lead Israel to Repentance

Finally, Hosea vindicates YHWH's character by portraying judgment not as an end in itself—or even as an end, as has already been observed in our discussion of the familial metaphors. First, the directives and warnings that are interspersed with images of destruction suggest that the severity of the

Exegetical Constructions and Deconstructions of Hosea 11," *Lectio difficilior* 2 [2012]: 1–21, http://www.lectio.unibe.ch/12_2/wacker_marie_theres_father_god_ mother_god_and_beyond.html#_ednref5. Following the biblical text, however, I will continue to use masculine pronouns for YHWH.

48. LeCureux observes that "the faithfulness of Yhwh is contrasted by his ability to turn from destruction with the unfaithfulness of his people and their inability to turn toward him" (*Thematic Unity*, 82).

49. See Yee, "Hosea," 213.

judgment is intended to shock the people into taking the prophet's words to heart and responding appropriately *before* the announced punishment comes. For example, in 2:4 (2 Eng.) YHWH instructs the children of his adulterous wife (i.e., the inhabitants of the land) to "contend with [their] mother," apprising her of how seriously her marriage has been ruptured and calling her to "put away her sexual immoralities" (v. 4 [2 Eng.]). The "lest" that begins the statement of judgment in v. 5 (3 Eng.) indicates that it is still possible to turn back.

Similarly, 10:12 entreats the people, "sow for yourselves righteousness, reap according to steadfast love, break up for yourselves fallow ground," indicating that when they "seek YHWH," he will "shower righteousness upon" them. Moreover, 12:7 (6 Eng.) urges, "but you, with [the help of] your God,[50] return (שוב), maintain steadfast love and justice, and wait for your God continually," suggesting that in so doing, they may avert disaster. Even more strikingly, the overwhelmingly negative ch. 13 is immediately followed by an exhortation to "return (שוב)...to YHWH" with a prayer of repentance (14:2-4 [1-3 Eng.]).[51] In the final form of the book, the implication is that the full extent of such violent judgment can be avoided if Israel heeds the prophetic summons.[52]

Secondly, some texts indicate that the execution of the judgment either prompts YHWH's people to repent or prevents them from going astray in the first place. This idea may be seen in the image of YHWH as a fowler who casts a net over the flock to prevent them from flying off to Egypt or Assyria (7:11-12). By describing his actions as "discipline" (יסר) (cf. 7:15; 10:10), the passage conveys the idea that they are intended to instruct the people in how they should live, just as parents "discipline" their children to bring about correction (see, e.g., Prov. 19:18).[53] A redemptive arc also appears in 3:4-5, which declares, "the children of Israel will dwell (ישב) many days without king or prince or sacred pillar or ephod or household gods. Afterward the children of Israel will return (שוב) and seek YHWH their God and David their king," with a wordplay that highlights the connection between exile and return to YHWH.[54] As Brian Gault puts it, "whether political, military, or cultic, every possible substitute for their

50. On this understanding of the ב preposition in באלהיך, see LeCureux, *Thematic Unity*, 97; Braaten, "God Sows," 121.

51. See Gloria L. Schaab, "'I Will Love Them Freely': A Metaphorical Theology of Hosea 14," *JBT* 1 (2018): 227–52 (235).

52. See also LeCureux, *Thematic Unity*, 100.

53. See further Dearman, *Hosea*, 211–12.

54. Gault, "Avenging Husband and Redeeming Lover?" 494. A similar pun may be found in 9:3.

dependence on YHWH will be stripped away."[55] In 5:15 after attacking his people like a lion, YHWH states, "I will go [and] I will return (שׁוּב) to my place until…they seek my face."[56]

The aim to bring about repentance is evident even in YHWH's judgment of stripping his unfaithful wife in Hosea 2.[57] In v. 5 (3 Eng.) the stripping of the woman is linked to the devastation of the land by drought: "otherwise I will strip her naked and make her like the day of her birth, and I will make her like a desert and turn her into a dry land and kill her with thirst." Similarly, in v. 11 (9 Eng.) YHWH declares, "I will take away my wool and my linen to cover her nakedness," exposing her before her lovers (v. 12 [10 Eng.]). Again, the images of woman and land merge as the seizure of materials to make clothing form part of a broader agricultural collapse so that the removal of the woman's clothes signifies the stripping of the land's produce.[58] Within the rhetoric of the chapter, the stripping of YHWH's wife is not a gratuitous punishment intended merely to shame her but an object lesson designed to teach her that her lovers

---

55. Ibid. Kakkanattu contends, however, that "the hope of Israel's return in 3,5 is not to be understood as the result of the punishment mentioned in 3,4 but much more as the consequence of the love of Yahweh, that waits for Israel's return [see v. 1]…for Hosea, return to Yahweh is not a precondition for Yahweh's healing and pardon, rather it is Yahweh's healing that makes the return possible" (*God's Enduring Love*, 136).

56. Göran Eidevall contends that YHWH's retreat produces a change of heart in the people because "it is not the presence, but the absence of God that is the problem" (*Grapes in the Desert*, 89; similarly, LeCureux, *Thematic Unity*, 77).

57. Some feminist interpreters see this passage as depicting sexual abuse and argue that it legitimates abuse on the part of human husbands (see, e.g., J. Cheryl Exum, "Prophetic Pornography," in *Plotted, Shot, and Painted: Cultural Represen-tations of Biblical Women*, JSOTSup 215 [Sheffield: Sheffield Academic, 1996], 104–5, 112–14; Gerlinde Baumann, *Love and Violence: Marriage as Metaphor for the Relationship between YHWH and Israel in the Prophetic Books*, trans. Linda M. Maloney [Collegeville: Liturgical, 2003], 98–9). However, the Old Testament does not condone sexual abuse, not even as a punishment for marital infidelity (see further Brittany Kim, "Yhwh as Jealous Husband: Abusive Authoritarian or Passionate Protector? A Reexamination of a Prophetic Image," in *Daughter Zion: Her Portrait, Her Response*, ed. Mark J. Boda, Carol J. Dempsey, and LeAnn Snow Flesher, SBLAIL 13 [Atlanta: SBL, 2012], 127–47 [140–1]). The judgment here probably derives from the sphere of the covenantal curses, not from the marital image (see further Hanley, "Background and Purpose," 99–100; similarly, Peggy L. Day, "Adulterous Jerusalem's Imagined Demise: Death of a Metaphor in Ezekiel XVI," *VT* 50 [2000]: 285–309, with regard to Ezek. 16).

58. See further Hayes, *"The Earth Mourns,"* 51–4; Keefe, *Woman's Body*, 214–16; Stienstra, *YHWH is the Husband of His People*, 106–9.

are not providing her with fruitfulness like she thought (vv. 7, 10, 14 [5, 8, 12 Eng.]).[59] Similarly, YHWH's act of hedging her in seeks to prevent her from reaching her lovers (vv. 8-9a [6-7a Eng.]). While the imagery in this chapter is troubling, it serves the rhetorical aim of startling the people to produce a response. Indeed, v. 9b (7b Eng.) declares that these judgments will prompt the land to decide, "I will go and return (שׁוב) to my first husband, for it was better for me then than now" (v. 9b).

The Restoration of Israel

Finally, while some individual passages conclude with what sounds like total destruction (see esp. 13:14-16),[60] interspersed throughout the book are promises of renewal, indicating that YHWH's ultimate aim is to bring about a complete restoration.[61] Soon after Hosea's third child is given the name "Not My People" (1:8-9), that symbolic name is reversed: "in the place where it was said to them, 'You are not my people,' it will be said to them, 'children of the living God'" (2:1 [1:10 Eng.];[62] cf. 2:3 [2:1 Eng.]). That pattern of judgment being overturned to express a promise of renewal continues throughout the book. For example, Jezreel, the name of Hosea's oldest son, at first signifies YHWH's judgment on the house of Jehu (1:4-5) but is later tied to a promise of the reunification of Israel and Judah (2:2 [1:11 Eng.]). It also comes to symbolize the re-fructification of the ground, reflecting the name's meaning: "God plants" (2:23–25 [21-23 Eng.]).

---

59. Stienstra also points out that if he divorced his wife, he is no longer required to provide for her: "this verse therefore shows YHWH treating His wife as if He has in fact repudiated her," with the hope that it "may bring her to her senses" (*YHWH is the Husband of His People*, 116).

60. Some interpreters take 13:14 as a positive statement that YHWH "will ransom [the people] from the hand of Sheol" and "redeem them from death," in line with Paul's use of the verse in 1 Cor. 15:55 (e.g., Moon, *Hosea*, 213–14). However, in light of the concluding statement, "compassion is hidden from my eyes," it seems more likely that the verse begins with rhetorical questions that assume a negative answer: "Shall I ransom [the people] from the hand of Sheol? Shall I redeem them from death?" (see Stuart, *Hosea–Jonah*, 207; Dearman, *Hosea*, 328–9).

61. John Barton observes that the prophets tend to see YHWH's plan as traversing "through the necessity of judgment before restoration can be contemplated" (John Barton, "Prophecy and Theodicy," in *Thus Says the Lord: Essays on the Former and Latter Prophets in Honor of Robert R. Wilson*, ed. John J. Ahn and Stephen L. Cook [New York: T&T Clark, 2009], 81; see also LeCureux, *Thematic Unity*, 89–90).

62. The first part of this verse also recalls YHWH's promises to Abraham in Gen. 22:17.

This new planting forms part of a marriage renewal, in which YHWH will "allure" his wife and "bring her into the wilderness," where their relationship first began after the exodus (2:16-17 [14-15 Eng.]), thereby reversing the pronouncement, "I am not her husband" (v. 4 [2 Eng.]). Assuaging any concerns about a future disruption in his relationship with the land, YHWH promises, "I will betroth you to myself forever, and I will betroth you to myself in righteousness and in justice and in steadfast love and in compassion. I will betroth you to myself in faithfulness, and you will know YHWH" (vv. 21-22 [19-20 Eng.]). As Walter Brueggemann points out, YHWH's "'wedding vow'…reiterates five of the fundamental terms of covenant fidelity" in a promise that "is unilateral on YHWH's part, without requiring from Israel a comparable pledge of fidelity."[63] Moreover, this engagement is marked by a covenant of peace with all living things (v. 20 [18 Eng.]), suggesting a renewal of creation.[64]

Glimpses of restoration also appear in later chapters. When the prophet pleads with his people to "return (שוב) to YHWH" in 6:1-2,[65] he expresses the assurance that though YHWH had "torn" his people, he would also "heal," "bind," "revive," and "raise [them] up." Indeed, he contends that YHWH's coming is as certain as the rising of the sun and as refreshing as the rains in their seasons (v. 3). Similarly, the words of repentance that the prophet provides as a model in 14:2-4 (1-3 Eng.) conclude with confidence that "in [YHWH] the orphan finds compassion."[66] YHWH's desire to "restore the fortunes of [his] people" and bring healing is also expressed in 6:11b–7:1a, though commentators debate whether that desire is thwarted by the people's sin (see 7:1b; cf. 7:13) or whether it reflects hope for a future divine intervention.[67]

In some cases, images associated with Israel's sin or divine judgment are rehabilitated and used to portray a promised redemption. For example, the

63. Brueggemann, "The Recovering God of Hosea," 15.

64. Note the connections to the creation (Gen. 1:28-30) and flood accounts (6:20; 8:17-19), and particularly the covenant YHWH establishes after the flood (9:8-17; Dearman, *Hosea*, 126).

65. While some commentators take these verses as the words of the people, perhaps reflecting a deficient repentance (so Gruber, *Hosea*, 281–7; Olson, "The Lion, the Itch and the Wardrobe," 178–9), it seems more likely that they present the prophet's attempt to elicit repentance (so Smith, *Hosea, Amos, Micah*, 110; Moon, *Hosea*, 114–15; Garrett, *Hosea, Joel*, 156–7).

66. The "orphan" here evokes the image of Israel as YHWH's rejected son (ch. 11; Dearman, *Hosea*, 339), though the use of the root רחם ("compassion") also points to Hosea's daughter, "No Compassion" (לא רחמה, 1:6); Braaten, "God Sows," 123.

67. For the former, see Macintosh, *Hosea*, 250–51; for the latter, see Stuart, *Hosea*, 112–13; Garrett, *Hosea, Joel*, 166.

violent image of YHWH as an attacking lion (5:14; 13:7-8) is transformed in 11:10 to depict the thunderous roar of the lion calling his children home from exile. In v. 11 the returning exiles are portrayed as doves, reversing the image of Ephraim as a senseless dove flitting toward Egypt and Assyria in 7:11.[68] Likewise, whereas Hosea highlights the transience of dew when using it as an image of the people's inconstancy toward YHWH (6:4) or their impending demise (13:3), 14:6 [5 Eng.] adapts it as a picture of YHWH nourishing Israel.[69] In Moughtin-Mumby's view, such reversals suggest that the people's "punishment holds the key to their future."[70] For those who raise the question of theodicy, Hosea implies not only that the path to Israel's well-being leads through judgment, but also that even the judgments themselves may be transformed by YHWH into agents of blessing.

The image of YHWH as life-giving dew forms part of the astonishing portrait of restoration that concludes the book. Here YHWH promises not only to heal Israel (as in 6:1; 7:1; cf. 11:3) but also to "heal their waywardness (משובת)," using a form of the key root שוב. This will enable the people to finally return to their God, who will "love them freely" now that his "anger has turned away (שוב) from them" (v. 5 [4 Eng.]). Israel's flourishing will reflect both the delicate beauty of the lily and the majesty and strength of the famed cedars of Lebanon, with roots stretching deep into the ground (vv. 6b-7 [5b-6 Eng.]). Rather than seeking shelter from other nations, Israel will become a source of shelter himself as people "return (שוב) [and] dwell in his shade" (v. 8a [7a Eng.]).[71] In contrast to the dispute over grain, wine, and oil in ch. 2, now the people will "flourish like grain" and "blossom like the vine," with "fame like the wine of Lebanon" (v. 8 [7 Eng.]) and "splendor like the olive" (v. 7 [6 Eng.]).[72] Moreover, YHWH promises to "answer" and "take notice of" Ephraim, unlike the idols who failed to provide (v. 9a [8a Eng.]). And in

---

68. See further Göran Eidevall, "Lions and Birds as Literature: Some Notes on Isaiah 31 and Hosea 11," *SJOT* 7 [1993]: 78–87 [83]; Willis, "Hosea's Unique Figures of Yahweh," 178–80.

69. See further Olson, "The Lion, The Itch, and the Wardrobe," 181; Willis, "Hosea's Unique Figures of Yahweh," 175–7.

70. Moughtin-Mumby, *Sexual and Marital Metaphors*, 56.

71. Some commentators emend the third person suffix on בצלו ("in his shade") to first person, reading it as a reference to the people of Israel dwelling in YHWH's shade (e.g., Wolff, *Hosea*, 232; LeCureux, *Thematic Unity*, 83 n. 66). However, the LXX and Vg. support the MT (see also Dearman, *Hosea*, 342).

72. On the connection to Hos. 2, see further Schaab, "I Will Love Them Freely," 246.

a picture that is unique within the Old Testament, YHWH is portrayed as an evergreen cypress, a faithful and dependable tree of life, which, in a wordplay on Ephraim's name, provides the nation with "fruit" (פרי, v. 9b [8b Eng.]).[73] As the people finally realize that the fruitfulness of their land derives from YHWH, not their idols, they will bloom like a well-tended garden.[74]

Conclusion

While the book of Hosea never explicitly questions YHWH's goodness or justice, it nevertheless "offers to readers various ways to identify and to explain why Israel fell to the Assyrians."[75] For later postexilic readers of the Book of the Twelve, those explanations may be applied to the Babylonian exile as well. Moreover, Hosea suggests a way forward for postexilic Jewish communities, prompting them to heed Hosea's prophetic warnings so that they may experience the promised restoration.

Placed at the head of the Twelve Prophets, Hosea sets a couple of major trajectories for how theodicy is approached. First, it emphasizes that the judgments Israel receives are just retribution for the people's sins. That idea may be found throughout the Book of the Twelve, as, for example, in Mic. 2:1-5, which declares that those who take land from the poor will lose their land to an enemy (cf. 6:9-16). Similarly, Amos 3:13-15 contends that Israel's idolatrous altars will be torn down and the mansions built on the backs of the poor will be destroyed.

Second, as James Crenshaw observes, "caught in the tension between justice and compassion, [the Twelve Prophets] refused to relinquish either one. Hosea's terrible announcement that compassion is hidden from Yahweh's eyes (13:14) alternates with a proclamation of divine courtship (2:14-15 [2:16-17])."[76] However, the trajectory of both Hosea and the Twelve as a whole suggests that ultimately this tension between justice and compassion finds some resolution in the idea that judgment is

---

73. Brueggemann speaks of "Hosea's capacity to use 'fertility' language but to transpose it into images of faithful, life-giving relatedness" ("The Recovering God of Hosea," 10; similarly, Keefe, "Hosea's [In]Fertility God," 22, concerning Hos. 2).

74. Moughtin-Mumby suggests parallels between Hos. 14 and the Song of Songs (*Sexual and Marital Metaphors*, 76–7).

75. Dearman, *Hosea*, 14.

76. Crenshaw, "Theodicy in the Book of the Twelve," in Redditt and Schart (eds), *Thematic Threads in the Book of the Twelve*, 191. Schaab also discusses these opposing tendencies in YHWH's personhood, emphasizing divine mystery ("I Will Love them Freely," 250–2).

executed in the service of restoration. For example, in Joel 2:1–3:5 [2:1-32 Eng.], the coming of an enemy army prompts a call to "return" (שוב) to YHWH (2:12-13), which results in a stunning promise of renewal, and Zephaniah 3; Zech. 13:1-9; and Mal. 3:1-5, 19-24 (4:1-6 Eng.) depict judgment as a means of purification.[77] Gault's words about Hosea apply to the Book of the Twelve as a whole: YHWH's "justice and mercy work together to serve one purpose—*bringing his unfaithful people back into a faithful relationship with him.*"[78]

However, what sets Hosea's contribution to theodicy apart from the rest of the Twelve Prophets is his developed metaphorical portrayal of YHWH as aggrieved husband and rejected parent.[79] These familial metaphors provide readers with a glimpse of YHWH's passion for his people, his profound grief at how they have spurned him, and his inner struggle between anger and love. While the Book of the Twelve offers many depictions of restoration (e.g., Amos 9:11-15; Mic. 4:1–5:9 [8 Eng.]; Zech. 14), Hosea offers a distinctive vision by setting Israel's future flourishing in the framework of renewed familial relationship with YHWH. By presenting YHWH's judgments as just retribution for Israel's sin, expressing their ultimate aim to bring about restoration, and placing them in the context of the familial metaphors, the book affirms the testimony of the epilogue that "the ways of YHWH are right" (14:10 [9 Eng.]).

---

77. James Crenshaw says concerning Amos 4, "The prophet offers a theodicy in which misfortune is viewed instrumentally; suffering comes from God to stimulate repentance" (Crenshaw, "Theodicy in the Book of the Twelve," 190), though there Israel's persistent failure to repent prevents them from experiencing restoration.

78. Gault, "Avenging Husband and Redeeming Lover?" 508, italics original; similarly, Moughtin-Mumby, *Sexual and Marital Metaphors*, 61, who sees Hosea as asserting that "Israel's punishment is utterly deserved and, indeed, [is] the very act that will bring about the nation's renewal."

79. Malachi also makes some use of the parent–child metaphor (see 1:6; 2:10; 3:17), but he does not significantly develop the image.

Chapter 4

HOPE THROUGH HUMAN TRAFFICKING?
THEODICY IN JOEL 4:4-8

Heath A. Thomas

Introduction

In his classic *Sin and Judgment in the Prophets* (1982), Patrick Miller
states of Joel 4:4-8: "In this passage...we encounter one of the most
complete examples of correspondence between crime and punishment
in the prophets."[1] This statement is indicative of the perceived correspondence between crime and divine punishment in later scholarship on
this passage. Miller's assertion about Joel 4:4-8 fits within his monograph,
in which he identifies the correspondences between sin and judgment
found in prophetic literature and describes how they create a pattern of
"poetic justice." Poetic justice comprises the judgment/punishment of
human sin as fitting to the crime(s) committed by the perpetrator. In its
hallmark forms, "poetic justice" is talionic—it follows the law of equal
measure.

But Miller's work reveals poetic justice as not talionic in theory only. He
demonstrates how poetic justice emerges in poetry itself: through artistic
balance of terms, phrases, and lineation in divine judgment speeches,
YHWH renders just judgment in which punishment fits the crime. In this
way, the sensuous flesh of poetry becomes the medium by which readers

---

1. Patrick D. Miller, Jr., *Sin and Judgment in the Prophets: A Stylistic and
Theological Analysis*, SBLMS 27 (Chico: Scholars Press, 1982), 131 (see also pp.
75–6).

perceive divine justice in the prophets. As it relates to Joel 4:4-8, it is no wonder why Miller highlights this text as one of the most complete examples of poetic justice in the prophets, as shall be demonstrated below. The balance of the lineation and poetics creates the impression of smooth balance between human sin and divine punishment. However, upon closer inspection, an irregularity in the verses creates turbulence in presentation of poetic justice depicted therein.

The purpose of this chapter is to reexamine Joel 4:4-8 and the purported theodicy it espouses. I shall demonstrate that the hope on display in these verses emerges in divine punishment of human trafficking *through* human trafficking, in a retributive move. However, I shall also demonstrate that hope in Joel 4:4-8 is deferred through a disruption in poetic justice in Joel 4:5. This deferral of hope creates space for a future restoration of God's temple in God's land, which finds its fulfilment in a later book within the Twelve.

The argument advances in four basic steps. I shall (a) survey research to establish how Joel 4:4-8 has been read as a deployment of retribution in the prophets. I shall then (b) provide a literary analysis of the passage to expose and explain the text's cohesiveness and artistry, to (c) expose how retributive justice emerges in Joel 4:4-8. After laying this foundation, I will (d) expose the disruption of retribution in Joel 4:5 by noting the oddity of the verse in the balance of the pericope. After these four steps, I offer some conclusions regarding the hope on display in Joel 4:4-8 and how this text relates to the Book of the Twelve.

Survey of Recent Research

Many consider Joel 4:4-8 (Hebrew) a late addition to the book.[2] When viewed in this manner, scholarly interest has to do with when this passage was added to the book and why. The verses provide specificity to trafficking language offered in Joel 4:3, and the verses remain talionic, as Miller describes. They reveal retributive justice—God is vindicated

---

2. For instance, see Hans Walter Wolff, *Joel and Amos*, Hermeneia (Philadelphia: Fortress, 1977), 77–8; Karl Elliger, "Ein Zeugnis aus der jüdischen Gemeinde im Alexanderjahr 322 v. Chr," *ZAW* 62 (1950): 63–115. See also John Barton, *Joel and Obadiah*, OTL (Louisville: Westminster John Knox, 2001), 101. By contrast, Assis believes the verses (and the book) belong to the exilic period in Judah, sometime between 587–538 BCE. See Elie Assis, *The Book of Joel: A Prophet between Calamity and Hope*, LHBOTS 581 (London: Bloomsbury T&T Clark, 2013), 3–24, 212–24.

in divine punishment because of the supposed wickedness of human trafficking. The verses encourage oppressed Judahites who suffer under adverse circumstances, admonishing them to hope in YHWH for his sure-to-come vindication and judgment: as the trafficking nations have done, it shall be done to them at the hand of YHWH. Special attention comes with the historical placement of the "Ionians" in v. 6 and "Sabeans" in v. 8 as clues that might shed light on the date of the book. The central claim of the needfulness of the addition is that vv. 4-8 provide further specificity to the general claims about human trafficking mentioned in Joel 4:3, drawing attention to Phoenicia and Philistia.

For example, Prinsloo agrees the passage is a later insertion that has been carefully interwoven into the corpus of Joel 4:1-17. He argues that this prose account

> is no mere arbitrary insertion, but a piece of competent, deliberate editing, apparently aimed at concretizing and specifying the vague, general assertions of the preceding pericope section (1-3a). Proclaiming Yahweh's wrathful treatment of the gojim would have been a fitting message for the catastrophic period after the exile.[3]

Not much more is said beyond this. If one looks for theological comment, one finds virtually nothing. Other than its historical placement and its clarifying role in Joel 4, what is most interesting about Joel 4:4-8 is the paucity of comment regarding its presentation of divine justice, or in some cases, a lack of comment at all.

Prinsloo's quote above introduces a pattern of under-explanation on the verses. For instance, Barton's able commentary glides over the verses in a historicist emphasis, helpfully elucidating how and when these verses plausibly could be placed on a historical timeline. But as to its theological significance, he offers nothing more than saying that the text presents a "tit-for-tat" form of punishment.[4] A recent theological commentary by Christopher Seitz does little more than Barton on these verses, arguing the verses provide a "theme of tit-for-tat, or retributive logic."[5]

This chapter is not primarily concerned about Joel 4:4-8 within the development of the book, whether or when it was added and why. With Prinsloo and Barker, I am reading the book of Joel as a unity (even if it

---

3. Willem S. Prinsloo, *The Theology of the Book of Joel*, BZAW 163 (Berlin: de Gruyter, 1985), 110;

4. Barton, *Joel and Obadiah*, 100–102, esp. 101.

5. Christopher Seitz, *Joel*, ITC (London: Bloomsbury T&T Clark, 2016), 205.

is a complex unity), with coherence in terms of structure and messages.[6] Rather, the focus of my argument is how the section's cohesion and artistry fits within the complex of Joel 4 (Hebrew) and how Joel 4:5 disrupts this cohesion.

More recent scholarship attends more closely to the text in the argument advanced in Joel 3–4. For instance, Joel Barker's rhetorical analysis of Joel indicates that 4:4-8 specifies the logic of God's judgment and the hope that comes for Israel because of it:

> The genre reflected in this subunit is judicial, focusing on the crimes of these specific nations while also detailing their punishment. The effect of using judicial speech in this subunit is interesting when one considers the nature of the text's audiences. Joel 4:4-8 is constructed as divine speech directed at Tyre, Sidon, and Philistia, detailing YHWH's grievances against them. While YHWH announces judgment, it is also helpful to consider the implied Judahite audience who hears YHWH's declarations. For this audience, YHWH's dialogue with the nations reinforces YHWH's commitment to act on their behalf that has been active since Joel 2:18. Thus, the judicial rhetoric in Joel 4:4-8 also strengthens the case for the implied audience to have confidence in YHWH.[7]

Barker correctly identifies the judicial overtones of the section. As in the prophets, when YHWH enacts judgment, he often does so in the role of a judge (and sometimes as a prosecutor also).[8]

In our verses (and in the complex of Joel 4:1-18), YHWH is the judge who renders a judgment against the nations that have committed crimes against both himself and his people. The immediate context of the Valley of Vision (or Jehoshaphat) in Joel 4 makes this apparent. The punishment is designed to instill *hope* in the rhetorical audience of Joel, leaving to the side the question of the book's provenance or originating audience (or the provenance of the section under investigation). For the readers of the vision, God's people can have confidence, even hope, in YHWH because the *divine judge* will render just judgment. The logic is advanced through literary artistry that builds cohesion and a retributive logic in Joel 4:4-8. It is to the literary cohesion of the passage that we now turn.

---

6. Prinsloo, *The Theology*, 110; Joel Barker, *From the Depths of Despair to the Promise of Presence: A Rhetorical Reading of the Book of Joel*, Siphrut 11 (Winona Lake: Eisenbrauns, 2014), 227–8.

7. Barker, *From the Depths*, 227–8.

8. Kirsten Nielsen, *Yahweh as Prosecutor and Judge: An Investigation of the Prophetic Lawsuit (Rîb-Pattern)*, JSOTSup 9 (Sheffield: Sheffield Academic, 1978).

Literary Analysis of Joel 4:4-8

The text in question breaks down into three basic units: (1) divine questions (v. 4a-b); (2) human crimes (vv. 5-6); (3) divine verdict (vv. 7-8). With these three basic units in view, the text reads as follows:

Divine Questions (v. 4):

הגמול אתם משלמים עלי

v. 4a: "Are you repaying vengeance against me?[9]"

ואם־גמלים אתם עלי קל מהרה אשיב גמלכם בראשכם

v. 4b: "Or you are paying me back? Very quickly I will turn your vengeance upon your head."

Human Crimes (vv. 5-6)

אשר־כספי וזהבי לקחתם ומחמדי הטבים הבאתם להיכליכם

v. 5: "For my silver and my gold—you took them; and my beautiful precious things—you brought them out to your temples."

ובני יהודה ובני ירושלם מכרתם לבני היונים למען הרחיקם מעל גבולם

v. 6: "And the people of Judah and Jerusalem you sold to the people of the Ionians (Greeks), in order to remove them from their territory."

Divine Verdict (vv. 7-8):

הנני מעירם מן־המקום אשר־מכרתם אתם שמה והשבתי גמלכם בראשכם

v. 7: "I am rousing them from the place where you sold them. And I will return your vengeance upon your head."

ומכרתי את־בניכם ואת־בנותיכם ביד בני יהודה ומכרום לשבאים אל־גוי רחוק כי יהוה דבר

v. 8: "And I will sell your sons and your daughters into the hand of the people of Judah. And they will sell them to the Sabeans, to a distant nation. For YHWH has spoken"

Literary Cohesion and Artistry

Miller introduces us to the artistry and cohesion of the poetry, as mentioned above. I would take his analysis further to highlight three poetic devices that appear in vv. 4-8. These devices also recur in other poetic texts in the

---

9. Unless otherwise noted, all translations are mine.

Hebrew Bible—namely, root repetition ("rootplay"), object fronting, and terseness in some of the lines. Despite these hallmarks of poetry at work within it, the section is not poetry but prose. *BHS* and various translations concur based upon their formatting. Although it uses other devices found in Hebrew poetry, the passage does not easily divide into parallel lines, regardless of how one attempts to discover caesuras, which normally demarcate lineation. Nor does one easily discern kinds of parallelism that are normally in play in Hebrew poetry: semantic, syntactic, grammatical, etc.

Thus, the text is prose, but it coheres with a high degree of literary artistry, tightly woven together with rootplay, clausal repetition, and a play on geographical balance. To understand its cohesion and artistry, one notes the following features. *Rootplay* emerges in the re-use of roots throughout the verses: גמל, vv. 4 (3×), 7; מכר, vv. 6, 7, 8 (2×); רחק, vv. 6, 8; שוב, vv. 4, 7. Combined with rootplay, one notes carefully placed repetition of phrases throughout the pericope:

(v. 4) אשיב גמלכם בראשכם

(v. 7) והשבתי גמלכם בראשכם

(v. 6) ובני יהודה ובני ירושלם מכרתם לבני היונים

(v. 8) ומכרתי את־בניכם ואת־בנותיכם ביד בני יהודה

This clausal repetition gives a sense of balance to the crime and punishment, as shall be demonstrated, below. Finally, geographical balance emerges between crime and punishment. Judah and Jerusalem are sold to a distant country in the northwest (Greeks); *Judahites "roused" from a distant country to come back home to Jerusalem* (v. 6). Phoenicians (northwest) and Philistines (southwest) are sold to a distant country in the southeast (Sabeans): *Phoenicians and Philistines do not come back to their homes* (v. 8).

All three features stand out to indicate the cohesion and artistry present in the verses.[10] As to the third aspect identified above, Nogalski rightly recognizes the use of geographical displacement as a form of poetic justice in Joel 4:4-8, and land is significant in the construction of these verses.[11] The homeland of Judah, particularly Jerusalem, lay at the center.

10. See Miller's discussion of the literary cohesion of the passage in *Sin and Judgment*, 75–6, 131–2.

11. James D. Nogalski, *Redactional Processes in the Book of the Twelve*, BZAW 218 (Berlin: de Gruyter, 1993), 29.

The reason for the trafficking of Judahites and Jerusalemites is to remove them from their territory (לְמַעַן הרחיקם מעל גבולם, v. 6). The displacement of peoples to various locations exposes an imbalance that YHWH rectifies through judgment: north to south and west to east, from home to exile to back home again. YHWH brings a trafficked people from their displacement and settles them back home. YHWH brings the trafficker from their homeland to a foreign land. Traffickers become the trafficked, and the trafficked becomes the trafficker. Geographical balance reinforces a notion of fair judgment.

Poetic Pattern of Judgment in Joel 4:4-8

Rootplay, repetition, and geographic balance generates cohesion and symmetry in the verses, and these features are not mere artifice. Rather, the passage's literary cohesion and artistry open the reader to the patterning of equitable divine punishment for human crimes. Especially in the pattern of repeated phrases and geographic balance, divine retributive judgment emerges. One notes this even more clearly when the passage is schematized:

Figure 1. Pattern of Repeated Phrases in Joel 4:4-8

v. 4:   אשיב גמלכם בראשכם

    v. 6:   ובני יהודה ובני ירושלם מכרתם לבני היונים

    v. 6:   הרחיקם מעל גבולם

v. 7:   והשבתי גמלכם בראשכם

    v. 8:   ומכרתי את־בניכם ואת־בנותיכם ביד בני יהודה

    v. 8:   אל־גוי רחוק

Or, put another way:

Actions of Phoenicia and Philistia	Divine Response
Vengeance (גמל), v. 4	Vengeance on your head (גמלכם בראשכם), vv. 4, 7
You sold them (מכרתם), v. 6	I will sell your sons and daughters (ומכרתי), v. 8
Sending Judah to a "far off nation," v. 6	Sending enemies to a "far off nation," v. 8

The clauses in vv. 4 and 7 parallel one another with the idea of YHWH returning vengeance upon the perpetrators' heads. The clauses in vv. 6

and 8 parallel one another regarding the selling of YHWH's peoples to another people group.

YHWH will return the enemies' "vengeance" upon their own heads (vv. 4, 7) using the same terminology. Joel 4:4 likely borrows from Obad. 15b, as has long been recognized.[12] And because they "sold" (מכרתם) the people of Judah and Jerusalem to the people of the Greeks in v. 6, YHWH will sell (ומכרתי) the sons and daughters of the enemies by the hand of the children of Judah (v. 8). In both verses, YHWH is the supreme actor who enacts judgment against the Philistines and Phoenicians. And although he "sells" (ומכרתי) the people of Philistia and Phoenicia in v. 8, he does so through the agency (ביד) of the children of Judah. In this way, one finds a balance to the injustice enacted against the people of YHWH.

David Baker mentions the problem of human trafficking in Joel 4:4-8 (see his comments on 3:4-8 in English), ably showing how Israelite law forbids kidnapping (Exod. 21:16; Deut. 24:7) and this interpretation of enemy nations *kidnapping* and selling Judahites may well be in view in Joel 4:4-8. Baker states, "Whether the issue is the concept of slavery itself (and that of Israelites in particular by their enemies) or the deprivation of basic human dignity, God is upset at Israel's neighbors for their actions."[13]

Clausal repetition in the verses exposes what most have rightly identified as a juridical image of YHWH judging the Philistines and the Phoenicians. Phoenicia and Philistia have trafficked Judahites and Jerusalemites away from their homeland (v. 5). And in whatever way these nations conceive their attempted "vengeance (גמל)," YHWH envisions it as a fundamental affront. Instead of the action fulfilling its end, it ends up turning back on the "heads" of those nations (v. 4). YHWH responds swiftly and terribly. He turns the violation back upon the violators.

Joel 4:4-8 and Theodicy

Scholarship reveals retribution and poetic justice lie at the heart of our text, but does it advance retributive theodicy? Other options are possible, and Laato and de Moor provide a helpful taxonomy of theodicy in the Hebrew Bible/Old Testament. They identify six kinds of theodicy in the biblical material:

12. Obad. 15b reads, "Your vengeance will return on your head" (גְּמֻלְךָ יָשׁוּב בְּרֹאשֶׁךָ). For full discussion, see Siefgried Bergler, *Joel als Schriftinterpret*, BEATAJ 16 (Frankfurt am Main: Peter Lang, 1988), 301–10; Marvin Sweeney, *The Twelve Prophets: Volume One*, Berit Olam (Collegeville: Liturgical, 2000), 175–7, 179–80.

13. David W. Baker, *Joel, Obadiah, Malachi*, NIVAC (Downers Grove: Zondervan, 2009), 128.

1. *Retribution theodicy*: faithful life leads to blessing, but disobedient life leads to judgment.
2. *Educative theodicy*: suffering can be borne because God uses it to teach some virtue.
3. *Eschatological (or recompense) theodicy*: suffering can be borne because God will set things to rights in a future time of judgment and vindication.
4. *The mystery of theodicy*: humans cannot understand or conceive the relationship between God and human suffering.
5. *Communion theodicy*: suffering is productive in that it brings humans closer to God.
6. *Human determinism theodicy*: humans cannot escape their fate ordained by God.[14]

Where does Joel 4:4-8 fit into this taxonomy? Some of the options fall away almost immediately. Joel 4:4-8 does not offer a kind of education in suffering for either the Phoenicians, the Philistines, or the Judahites. Thus, educative theodicy is eliminated. Furthermore, the text does not indicate human determinism. Judah's demise is not due to their sin, nor is it "fate" that they experience trafficking. It is not the "fate" of the Phoenicians/ Philistines to be trafficked either, and their action against Judahites and Judeans is never attributed to something like original sin, or God or "the devil" making them do it. Their action is entirely their own, and the text does not indicate what motive propels it.

A further note deserves mention at this point in our discussion. It is unlikely that one can advance a deterministic explanation of crime and punishment to explain our verses. I have in mind Klaus Koch's now quite famous theory that there is no retribution in ancient Hebrew literature. Koch argued that an act–consequence relationship (*Tat–Ergehen Zusammenhang*) determines human action and its natural outcomes. If one sins, then that action will necessarily come back on one's head. After a survey of selected texts, Koch argues that there is no concept of retribution, if by that one means that God directly punishes sinful activity as a demonstration of justice. Rather, he argues, one's sin naturally brings about its own negative consequences.[15]

---

14. A. Laato and J. C. de Moor, "Introduction," in *Theodicy in the World of the Bible*, ed. A. Laato and J. C. de Moor (Leiden: Brill, 2003), xxx–liv.

15. Klaus Koch, "Gibt es ein Vergeltungsdogma im Alten Testament?" *ZTK* 52 (1955): 1–42. Koch uses the language "Tat-Ergehen Zusammenhang" (p. 8). For a helpful discussion on Koch's view and its reception, see Peter Hatton, "A Cautionary Tale: The Acts–Consequence 'Construct'," *JSOT* 35 (2011): 375–84.

Although it may appear that Joel 4:4-8 affirms Koch's act–consequence nexus, this text simply does support such a view. The first-person verbs in vv. 4, 7-8 clearly indicate YHWH's direct involvement in divine punishment for crimes. This is neither a deterministic nor a passive execution of justice. Rather, what we see here is a judicial enactment in which YHWH pronounces and enacts divine punishment against crimes. This is not an act–consequence relationship with no divine involvement. Nor can one say that this is an example of act–consequence built into the fabric of creation order in a mechanistic explanation. Clearly, YHWH enacts judgment against the criminals as they are identified.

Mystery theodicy is not invoked in our passage either, because the text makes clear that judgment comes because of Phoenicia's and Philistia's crimes. The rationale for divine judgment is not mysterious or confusing. Furthermore, the idea that the suffering on view in Joel 4:4-8 provides a closer communion with God is interesting, but the text does not explicitly advocate this or even raise it as a possibility.

While portions of Habakkuk might exhibit a communion theodicy, Joel 4:3-4 does not.[16] The former depicts a spiritual transformation from questioning faith that leads to a deeper, fuller faithfulness to God; Joel does not depict theodicy along these lines. Rather, the verses studied in this chapter focus upon human sin and divine punishment. Thus, theodicy in Joel 4 does not lie on the spiritual development or deeper communion between God and the people through suffering but rather on the way that God will punish wrongdoers for their sin.

According to Laato and de Moor, "Eschatological or recompense theodicy is the usual way to comfort and exhort the righteous ones to live according to the will of God in the Second Temple Judaism and this form of theodicy is regarded as self-evident in the New Testament writings."[17] Eschatological theodicy helps sufferers understand that at the end of all things, God will vindicate the righteous sufferers and punish the wicked. It may be that the Twelve's concept of the "the last days" (באחרית הימים) provides a vision of future hope, as I have argued elsewhere.[18] However, the presentation of Joel 4:4-8 depicts a clear balanced retribution that is

---

16. For a reading of Habakkuk that argues it presents a theodicy in which greater communion with God comes as a result, see Heath A. Thomas, *Habakkuk*, THOTC (Grand Rapids: Eerdmans, 2018), 169–211.

17. Laato and de Moor, "Introduction," xlv.

18. Hos. 3:5; Mic. 4:1. Cf. Zech. 8:6, 10. See Heath A. Thomas, "Hearing the Minor Prophets: The Book of the Twelve and God's Address," in *Hearing the Old Testament: Listening for God's Address*, ed. Craig G. Bartholomew and David J. H. Beldman (Grand Rapids: Eerdmans, 2012), 366–8.

coming in the near future rather than being reserved for some eschato-logical horizon in the last days. Though this may fit Joel 4:9-21 more broadly, the description cannot fit Joel 4:4-8.

The final option that is most viable is a retribution theodicy. Crenshaw, like most, posits that Joel 4:4-8 advances *retributive* theodicy. "Joel envisions an exact measure for measure when Yhwh will finally avenge Israel and Judah, a retribution replete with irony for seafaring peoples driven into the desert and semi-nomads forced to venture forth on dangerous waters."[19] His words "exact measure" and "retribution" reveal his view that YHWH will enact a tit-for-tat kind of punishment for the crime—the very heart of retribution. As Laato and de Moor affirm, "[R]etribution is the prevailing type of theodicy in the Hebrew Scriptures" especially in the prophets.[20] Or, as Chisholm argues, since YHWH is just, he rewards people according to their actions, whether good or bad, whether individually or communally.[21] As these nations have trafficked God's people, their actions will come back upon their heads. As covenant-enforcers, the prophets explained the actions of God for good or ill along the lines of covenant fidelity: either YHWH's blessing is due to Israel's covenant faithfulness or YHWH's punishment is due to Israel's covenant breach.

But in Joel 4:4-8, the object of divine retribution is not Israel but the coastal nations. Thus, the Israelite covenant is not the origin of the retributive form of justice. Rather, it is a category in which to demonstrate his "imperial" justice (Peterson's language).[22] YHWH enacts judgment in equal measure against Phoenicia and Philistia because YHWH is the imperial deity over *all* nations in the Judahite perspective. Miller still reckons this retribution within a category of talionic correspondence, or the punishment exactly fits the crime. He says, "In legal talion formulations the general relationship of punishment to crime becomes very precise and exact. The punishment will be the same as the crime. The wrongdoer will suffer the same injury as his victim did."[23] Crenshaw, following Miller and

---

19. James L. Crenshaw, "Theodicy and Prophetic Literature," in Laato and de Moor (eds), *Theodicy in the World of the Bible* (Leiden: Brill, 2003), 236–55 (248).

20. Laato and de Moor, "Introduction," xxxii.

21. So R. B. Chisholm Jr., "Retribution," in *Dictionary of the Old Testament Prophets*, ed. J. G. McConville and M. J. Boda (Downers Grove: InterVarsity, 2012), 671.

22. "Imperial" is David L. Peterson's language in *The Prophetic Literature: An Introduction* (Louisville: Westminster John Knox, 2002), 38.

23. Miller, *Sin and Judgment*, 105. Miller goes on to say that this works for crimes against people, but it is not as helpful when it comes to other crimes, which is important.

others, summarizes: "Joel envisions an exact measure for measure when Yhwh will finally avenge Israel and Judah, a retribution replete with irony for seafaring peoples driven into the desert and semi-nomads forced to venture forth on dangerous waters."[24]

The retributive principle finds its place not only in Joel 4:4-8, but also in the remainder of the chapter. Nogalski plausibly sees Joel 4 as chiastic, highlighting in perfect symmetry the property of poetic justice:

A　The coming restoration of Judah and Jerusalem (4:1)

　　B　Judgment against the nations in the valley of Jehoshaphat (4:2)

　　　　C　Slavery of YHWH's people (4:3)

　　　　C'　Slavery of YHWH's people (4:4-8)

　　B'　Judgment against the nations in the valley of Jehoshaphat (4:9-17)

A'　The coming restoration of Judah and Jerusalem (4:18-21)[25]

The balance is exact, and Joel 4:4-8 is the second half of the center of the chiasm: slavery of YHWH's people. As they have been enslaved, they will be liberated, or so the retributive logic of both our verses and the entirety of the chapter goes. In Nogalski's rendering, Joel 4:4-8 appears theodic and retributive. The retributive construction, so clearly elucidated in the chiasm above, is complicated by the text. Verse 5 complicates the balanced lineation and supposed retributive logic advanced in vv. 4-8.

Disruption of Retributive Theodicy: Verse 5

The problem of Joel 4:4-8 lies in the fact that the great retributive principle at work in this passage is inexact. One witnesses a significant disruption in this pattern, which most scholars overlook. If the retribution theodicy demands punishment of equal measure, then Joel 4:4-8 does not embody such balance fully. Whether we call it "retributive justice" (Laato and de Moor) or "poetic justice" (Miller), if it is a form of equal measure, then what is *omitted* from the balance of the verses remains significant.

The plundered riches mentioned in v. 5 do not find a counterpart in the divine verdict of vv. 7-8. Miller neglects v. 5 in his foundational work, likely because v. 5 speaks to a crime not specifically directed against

---

24. Crenshaw, "Theodicy and Prophetic Literature," 248.
25. Nogalski, *Redactional Processes*, 5.

human persons.[26] This is a curious omission because v. 5 belongs clearly with the remainder of the section syntactically.

Coherence within vv. 4-8 is apparent from its close relationship with vv. 4 and 6. The relative clause introducing the crimes section in vv. 5-6 is followed by verbs whose action in v. 5 is coordinated by a conjunctive *waw* at the beginning of v. 6 (ובני יהודה ובני ירושלם, v. 6). This conjunction links the action of the verses, highlighting their fit. Further, the syntax of vv. 5-6 is parallel: fronted objects + verbs + prepositional phrases. The verbs are all second person plural.

Prepositional Phrase	Verbs in vv. 5-6	Fronted Objects vv. 5-6
None[27]	לקחתם	אשר־כספי וזהבי
להיכליכם	הבאתם	ומחמדי הטבים
לבני היונים	מכרתם	ובני יהודה ובני ירושלם

In both crimes that have been elucidated, the objects that have been taken are fronted in the clauses, followed by the verb with a third masculine plural suffixed pronoun, followed by a prepositional phrase. Furthermore, v. 5 fits not only with v. 6 but also v. 4. Repetition of the first common singular suffixed pronouns connects vv. 4 (2×) and 5 (3×). The perpetrators have attempted to work against YHWH ("against me," v. 4) by looting his temple ("my silver, my gold, and my precious things," v. 5). The combination of first-person pronouns in vv. 4-5 indicate YHWH's ownership over the entirety of the set that the nations have looted.[28] Nowhere else does this concentration of the first-person suffixed pronouns occur in the verses. So, v. 5 is syntactically connected to vv. 4 and 6, enabling us to recognize its fit in the verses.

26. Miller, *Sin and Judgment*, 105: "Obviously such a formulation has only limited applicability in this precise sense. If functions primarily with regard to crimes against the body or persons… It does not work as well for other sorts of crimes or illegal acts."

27. No prepositional phrase is given, but presumably "to your temples/palaces" (להיכליכם) in v. 5 serves double duty and for both verbs. This omission of the prepositional phrase in the first clause and deferring it to the second clause of v. 5 may highlight the connection between "silver and gold" and "precious things" as physical treasures taken to "their temples/palaces." In this way, a literary distinction is made between the treasures (v. 5) and the people (v. 6).

28. Barker, *From the Depths of Despair*, 231.

But v. 5 clearly disrupts the poetic justice at play in vv. 4-8. What is the purpose of its presence? Leslie Allen is one of the few who make mention of the oddity of v. 5 and give an explanation. He argues (rightly) that vv. 5-6 belong together, and that the conjunction of crimes represents an increasing scale of wickedness. Stealing from the temple is bad, but Allen says that trafficking humans is worse. Such action "represents a climax of wickedness, worthy of more censure even than the misappropriation of temple property… [T]he announcement of punishment takes up a reversal of this second charge and passes over the first. People matter more than things."[29] In Allen's view, v. 5 is explainable with v. 6 in terms of the second crime being greater: people over things!

One cannot make such an assertion without some explanation or rationale for its validity. Is it true that "things" are of relatively less value than "people"? Perhaps, but the argument only works if the temple implements are recognized as being of lesser value than people. While this may be possible, I do not believe this point has been proved. Furthermore, Allen's explanation only highlights the fact that the crime of the nations' looting "temple property" is left unanswered by divine punishment. For poetic justice to be fully established in these verses, the crime of theft in v. 5 naturally would find a counterbalancing punishment. Such punishment is, however, absent.

Another way to tackle the oddity of v. 5 in conjunction with v. 6 is to argue that v. 5 closely relates to v. 6 in terms of a metonymical relationship. That is, the gold, silver, and precious things mentioned in v. 5 are *metaphorical*, serving as a metonomy of the people of Israel.[30] Like "the crown" represents the royal line, or "the sword" represents an army, "gold," "silver," and "precious things" represents the people of Judah and Jerusalem. Elie Assis helpfully elucidates that possibility in his exploration of Joel: "It is possible to interpret the verses as referring to people who were taken as slaves to work in the temples or palaces of the Philistines."[31]

On this reading, YHWH enacts equitable retribution because people have been spirited away and he punishes the perpetrators of their crime: "my silver and my gold" and "beautiful precious things" of v. 5 equates to the people taken away; "the people of Judah and Jerusalem" of v. 6 parallel the displaced and trafficked people described in v. 5. In this understanding, vv. 5-6 describe one crime: trafficking people. Verse 5 is

29. Leslie C. Allen, *The Books of Joel, Obadiah, Jonah, and Micah*, NICOT (Grand Rapids: Eerdmans, 1976), 113.
30. Assis uses the language of "metaphorical" in *The Book of Joel*, 219.
31. Assis, *The Book of Joel*, 218–19.

metaphorical and v. 6 is more literal, but both verses indicate the same crime: violating the people of Jerusalem and Judah and trafficking them to a faraway place. This reading obviates the problem of two crimes, collapsing them into one, and maintaining the poetic justice put forth in vv. 4-8.

While this reading is possible, it is unlikely for four reasons. First, in the Hebrew Bible, "gold and silver" most often indicate physical substances, wealth and riches. The phrase indicates the precious metals used to beautify or adorn temples or palaces, sometimes YHWH's palace/temple. The phrase "gold and silver" does not occur again in Joel. And in our closest literary context (the book of the Twelve) the terminology of "silver" and "gold" occurs in close proximity in the following texts: Hos. 2:8; 8:4; Joel 4:5; Nah. 2:10; Hab. 2:19; Zeph. 1:18; Hag. 2:8; Zech. 6:10-11; 9:3; 13:9; 14:14; Mal. 3:3.

In both Hosea texts, the terminology indicates the silver and gold Israel used to fashion idols, recalling Exodus 32–34. In Joel, the terminology indicates riches, likely temple riches, that have been looted and spirited away. In Nahum, the terms appear in parallel and they indicate wealth. In Hab. 2:19, silver and gold is the substance that covers impotent idols. In Zeph 1:18, "neither their silver nor their gold" will save Jerusalem and Judah from YHWH's wrath. "Their silver" and "their gold" indicates wealth rather than people. In Hag. 2:8, the silver and gold mentioned comprises the wealth of the Jerusalem temple that has been evacuated and brought into foreign temples, but YHWH brings it back because the silver and gold belong to him (לי הכסף ולי הזהב). The first personal pronoun, "my," in both Joel 4:5 and Hag. 2:8 reinforces the point that the enemy nations have committed theft of YHWH's possessions; they have dishonored YHWH, as Assis notes.[32] In Zechariah, silver and gold is used to create a crown on Joshua's head (Zech. 6:10-11). In these texts, the silver and gold are precious metals used to forge the crown rather than people. Zechariah 9:3 depicts the silver and gold as the building materials of a rampart constructed in Tyre. In Zech. 13:9, God's people will be tested and refined like silver and gold. In this text, the people's refining process is compared with the refinement of precious metals. In Zech. 14:14, the vast riches ("silver, gold, and clothing") of the nations will be gathered back to Jerusalem. And finally, in Mal. 3:3, the priests are refined like gold and silver until they present appropriate sacrifices. As in Zech. 13:9, the refining of silver and gold comprises the metaphor for Judah's refinement through suffering.

---

32. Elie Assis, "A Disputed Temple (Haggai 2,1-9)," *ZAW* 120 (2008): 582–96 (585–6).

Taken together, these texts from the Minor Prophets employ the terminology silver and gold in three primary ways. Silver and gold depicts: (1) the physical substance that depict wealth for trust or for idol creation (Hos. 2:8; 8:4; Nah. 2:10; Hab. 2:19; Zeph. 1:18; Zech. 6:10-11; 9:3; 14:14); (2) temple riches (Joel 4:5; Hag. 2:8); or (3) a metaphor to depict refinement through suffering (Zech. 13:9; Mal. 3:3).[33] It is unlikely, at least from the immediate usage in the Twelve, that "silver and gold" is a metonym for the people of Judah and Jerusalem.

Joel 4:5 is closest to Hag. 2:8 as the collocation silver and gold appears alongside the first person singular suffixed pronoun. In both of these texts, YHWH is the owner of the silver and gold; in no other text where silver and gold emerges in the Twelve does the first person singular suffixed pronoun appear with YHWH as the speaker. Thus, Joel 4:5 and Hag. 2:8 share a common notion of YHWH's silver and gold stolen by the nations (Joel) and YHWH's silver and gold gathered from the nations (Haggai). The first reason why silver and gold likely does not metaphorically depict human beings in Joel 4:5 is because it would fall outside the normal scope of how the phrase is used in the Twelve. It is possible, but unlikely.

The second reason derives from the first. If they trafficked human beings and looted the temple or palace of YHWH, then Phoenicia and Philistia committed two crimes, not one. And the theft of YHWH's riches and the trafficking of human beings comprises the most sensible reading of the text.[34] Although Assis provides the possibility of a metaphorical reading of the silver and gold of v. 5, collapsing two crimes (theft and human trafficking) into one (human trafficking), he demurs, "I am doubtful as to whether this interpretation is correct."[35] After all, two crimes are apparent in the syntax of vv. 5-6, as I have argued above. This makes one crime less than convincing.

---

33. One other text deserves mention. Zech. 9:16 does not use the language "silver and gold" but it does depict the people as jewels in the crown. The difference between Joel 4:5 and Zech. 9:16 is that the latter avoids the terminology silver/gold and instead uses "jewels in a crown shining upon his land" (כי אבני־נזר מתנוססות על־אדמתו). In this latter case, "silver and gold" is absent and the metaphorical depiction of the people in the crown emerges with the comparative *kaph* governing the depiction. The people are *like* a flock; and the people are *indeed* jewels in a crown shining on the land. Zech. 9:16 deploys different language and imagery than Joel 4:5.

34. Two crimes have been attested in ancient commentary as well. See, for instance, Theodoret of Cyrus, *Commentaries on the Prophets, Volume 3: Commentary on the Twelve Prophets*, trans. R. C. Hill (Brookline: Holy Cross Orthodox Press, 2006), 99.

35. Assis, *The Book of Joel*, 219.

Third, although the term מחמד in v. 5 can possibly intend the people of Jerusalem, the evidence is not conclusive. For instance, the term מחמד appears in Lam. 1:10, but I argue elsewhere that it is intentionally ambiguous.[36] The combination of מחמד with gold and silver most likely intends the precious treasures of the temple. The actual referent of these treasures remains unspecified. Whatever the substance of the silver and gold, it belongs to YHWH and in Joel 4:4-8 we find no punishment for the theft.

And finally, such a reading does not do well with the geography mentioned in vv. 5-6. If the silver and gold are people, v. 5 would indicate that the people were taken to the temples of the Phoenicians and Philistines, and v. 6 would indicate that they were taken away to the land of the Greeks. This reading unduly creates confusion between the verses. It is better to interpret that the temple riches went to the temples of the Phoenicians/Philistines and the people went to the Greeks.

For these reasons, I argue that two crimes emerge in vv. 5-6, not one: theft of YHWH's riches and the trafficking of YHWH's people. In this I agree with Assis, who rightly thinks v. 5 demarcates a despoliation of the temple and the spiriting away of some of its treasures.[37] This crime is matched by spiriting away of people and the selling of them to the Greeks, explained in v. 6.

The crime in v. 5 is that of spiriting away temple treasures to foreign palaces. The verse reads:

v. 5: אשר־כספי וזהבי לקחתם ומחמדי הטבים הבאתם להיכליכם

If retribution is an account of just punishment, then retribution does not apply to Joel 4:5, at least not in the context of Joel. Although he has been plundered, YHWH enacts *no* punishment for the theft of "my silver, and

36. Heath A. Thomas, *Poetry and Theology in the Book of Lamentations: The Aesthetics of an Open Text*, HBM 47 (Sheffield: Sheffield Phoenix, 2013), 108, 114–16.

37. Elie Assis, *The Book of Joel*, 218–19. Assis is clear that the despoliation of the temple in view equates the invasion of the Neo-Babylonian forces in the sixth century BCE. Whilst this view perhaps is sensible, it is not determinative. The text leaves underdetermined the specific historical referent of despoliation, in my view. Crenshaw, amongst others, is not convinced (Crenshaw, *Joel*, 181). But the lack of historical reference does little to detract from the argument advanced here. It is not necessary to be overly specific as to which treasures were taken by the nations or to explicitly link the plundering of the treasures with the Neo-Babylonian invasion; it is possible to speak in general terms about temple treasures, which the nations looted, and still recognize that treasures were returned for the temple.

my gold, and my beautiful precious things" (v. 5). There is no counterbalancing judgment from YHWH to address the offense. The verses from
4-8, then, do not find perfect symmetry, as scholars have argued:

v. 4:	אשיב גמלכם בראשכם
v. 5:	אשר־כספי וזהבי לקחתם ומחמדי הטבים הבאתם להיכליכם
v. 6:	ובני יהודה ובני ירושלם מכרתם לבני היונים
v. 6:	הרחיקם מעל גבולם
v. 7:	והשבתי גמלכם בראשכם
v. 8:	ומכרתי את־בניכם ואת־בנותיכם ביד בני יהודה
v. 8:	אל־גוי רחוק

Divine punishment against Philistia and Phoenicia only corresponds to
their abuse of God's *people*. YHWH, then, passes over the justice owed
him for the despoiling of his temple riches. In this way, the Phoenicians
and Philistines, in fact, do *not* receive their *full* just deserts—at least in
Joel. They are guilty before God for their actions against his people and
receive poetic justice as a result. However, no counterbalancing judgment
for the crime of theft appears in Joel. The insertion of v. 5 creates a
deferral of hope concerning God's punishment against the nations for this
crime against YHWH.

Although he enacts poetic justice in part (vv. 4, 6-8), the oddity of v. 5
creates space for *future* retribution, in which God takes his temple implements back to their place. I ground this claim on repetition of language
in the Twelve. Scholars have long noted connections between the Twelve,
which unify the entirety of the corpus.[38] I argue something similar here,

---

38. This is true from a variety of methodological approaches: historical and
redactional, literary and rhetorical, or canonical approaches. For the historical and
redactional approach, see, e.g., James D. Nogalski, *Literary Precursors to the Book of
the Twelve*, BZAW 217 (Berlin: de Gruyter, 1993); Nogalski, *Redactional Processes*;
Aaron Schart, *Die Entstehung des Zwölfprophetenbuchs: Neubearbeitungen von
Amos im Rahmen schriftenübergreifender Redaktionsprozesse*, BZAW 260 (Berlin:
de Gruyter, 1998); Martin Beck, *Der "Tag YHWHs" im Dodekapropheton: Studien
im Spannungsfeld von Traditions- und Redaktionsgeschichte*, BZAW 356 (Berlin:
de Gruyter, 2005); Rainer Albertz, James D. Nogalski, and Jakob Wöhrle (eds),
*Perspectives on the Formation of the Book of the Twelve: Methodological Founda-
tions—Reactional Processes—Historical Insights*, BZAW 433 (Berlin: de Gruyter,
2012). For the literary and thematic approach, see, e.g., Paul House, *The Unity of the*

without asserting a full redactional process in the fashion of Nogalski or Schart. Rather, a tacit lexical connection between Joel 4:5 and another text in the Twelve emerges. Other than Joel 4:5, the only other instance in the Twelve where silver and gold is used with the first-person pronoun (referring to God as the speaker) appears in Hag. 2:8, as noted above. Assis explores this verse to reconstruct historical perspectives on the temple in the restoration period.[39] My concern is different. I am interested in how Hag. 2:8 "answers" the retributive expectation of Joel 4:5.

The Haggai text reads:

לי הכסף ולי הזהב נאם יהוה צבאות

> The silver belongs to me, and the gold belongs to me: utterance of YHWH of Armies. (Hag. 2:8)

In terms of background, Haggai 2 is especially concerned with the restoration of the temple, along with the re-establishment of YHWH's glory and peace in his place (Hag. 2:6-9). In Haggai's text, YHWH announces the restoration of the temple, in which the glory of the latter temple will exceed that of the former temple (Hag. 2:9). "All the nations" will bring their wealth (חמדת כל־הגוים), and YHWH will fill his *house* with glory (Hag. 2:7).

Reading the passages in the light of one another through the repetition of the language silver and gold belonging to YHWH, Joel 4:5 creates a hope that God would vindicate the theft of his temple, bringing justice to his place just as he has done for his people. This hope has to do with the restoration of place and worship just as much as it does a restoration of his people. But Joel does not provide an answer to that hope. Rather, YHWH's retributive justice is deferred, and hope is deferred. The

---

Twelve, JSOTSup 97 (Sheffield: Almond, 1990); Rolf Rendtorff, "Alas for the Day! The 'Day of the LORD' in the Book of the Twelve," in *God in the Fray: A Tribute to Walter Brueggemann*, ed. T. Linafelt and T. K. Beal (Minneapolis: Fortress, 1998), 186–97. For the canonical approach, see, e.g., Christopher R. Seitz, *Prophecy and Hermeneutics: Toward a New Introduction to the Prophets*, STI (Grand Rapids: Baker Academic, 2007); Michael B. Shepherd, "Compositional Analysis of the Twelve," *ZAW* 120 (2008): 184–93; Donald C. Collett, "Prophetic Intentionality and the Book of the Twelve: A Study in the Hermeneutics of Prophecy" (PhD diss., University of St. Andrews, 2007). Note the variety of approaches on display in Paul L. Redditt and Aaron Schart (eds), *Thematic Threads in the Book of the Twelve*, BZAW 325 (Berlin: de Gruyter, 2003).

39. Assis, "A Disputed Temple (Haggai 2,1-9)," 585–6.

despoiling of the holy place by Philistia and Phoenicia creates a forward momentum to the passage, despite the retributive balance displayed in the other verses, indeed the rest of the chapter.

Although the traffickers will be trafficked, and those who were taken from their place and trafficked will be resettled, and they will traffic those who trafficked them, the crime of stealing from YHWH's temple and re-appropriating his riches is left unanswered.

One way to understand the apparent association between Joel and Haggai is in terms of earlier and later use of tradition: Haggai uses the earlier Joel text to provide an answer to hope deferred in Joel 4:5. This turns on the possibility that Joel is an exilic text and Haggai, as a post-exilic text, utilizes the former tradition. Assis advances this logic in his reading of the hope on display in Haggai: "Joel [4:5] describes the looting of the Lord's treasures at the time of the destruction of the Temple; at the stage of redemption, Haggai describes the restoration of the Temple to its former state."[40]

I agree with Assis in general terms but am non-committal to linking the referent to the Neo-Babylonian sacking of the temple in the sixth century BCE. The text of Joel leaves the historical referent underdetermined. However, Assis has correctly made the connection to develop a despoliation–restoration motif regarding the temple between texts.

Another possibility is that the linkage between Joel 4:5 and Hag. 2:8 reveals scribal activity in the post-exilic period. Scribes have created the text of Joel with the remainder of the Twelve in view; Joel, then, serves as a kind of large-scale guide for the Book of the Twelve, giving insights on how the entirety should be read. As Nogalski states of Joel: "Recurring vocabulary takes place in Joel's reinterpretation of images and phrases from neighboring writings, and in the use of Joel's reinterpreted images in subsequent writings. This use of Joel in other contexts provides the

---

40. Ibid. Haggai, then, receives and responds to Joel's deferral of hope. However, the logic of Joel opening a horizon that Haggai fills works as well from a scribal perspective. If Joel is later than Haggai (which Bergler, Prinsloo, Nogalski, Sweeney, and others affirm), then Joel's placement before the remainder of the Twelve prophets enables the reader to expect the theft of YHWH's riches to be answered by another prophet in the collection. In this way, Joel 4:5 sets an expectation of retribution yet to be filled until Hag. 2:8. This nuances the argument of James D. Nogalski that Joel serves as a "literary anchor" to the Twelve prophets and extends it. See Nogalski, "Joel as 'Literary Anchor" for the Book of the Twelve," in *Reading and Hearing the Book of the Twelve*, ed. James D. Nogalski and Marvin A. Sweeney, SBLSymS 15 (Atlanta: SBL, 2000), 91–109.

clues for determining the transcended 'historical' paradigm which shapes the Twelve."[41]

In this way of seeing things, lexical correspondence between Joel 4:5 and Hag. 2:8 is intentional and scribal, as Haggai's use of silver and gold opens a conversation between the two texts and establishes YHWH's vindication, a theological point rather than a purely historical connection between the texts. The "silver and gold" housed in these foreign nations clearly is not their own. The strong use of the possessive construction, not once but twice, indicates that the "silver and gold" taken away now has been restored to its rightful owner. The possessive construction with the *waw* conjunction in Hag. 2:8 is a variation on Joel 4:5, creating a definitive response from the former to the latter. Although silver and gold were stolen and spirited away in Joel, now in Haggai "all nations" bring their treasures to fill YHWH's temple, defining a bit more clearly the lines of divine justice in the Twelve as a whole. This reading would remain sensible even if Joel is late, as the scribal move and placement of Joel early in the collection creates a reading expectation and a message of divine justice in the reading of the Twelve as a whole.

In either reading, hope that YHWH would restore his treasures is deferred in Joel, but that hope is realized at the construction of the temple and the return of the temple treasures. In Haggai, YHWH restores his place as he has done for his people in Joel 4:4-8. Schematically arranged, it looks like this:

Hope Deferred in Joel	//	*Hope Realized in Haggai*
כספי וזהבי	//	לי הכסף ולי הזהב
הבאתם להיכליכם	//	ובאו חמדת כל־הגוים ומלאתי את־הבית הזה כבוד

Resonance between the texts reinforce the intertextual conversation between Joel 4:5 and Hag 2:8. The first common singular pronoun appears in both texts. Also, the root בוא recurs in both texts, establishing a broad retributive logic: Philistia and Phoenicia brought (הבאתם) the treasures to their temples (Joel 4:5) but YHWH shakes the nations so that they will bring (ובאו) their "treasures" (חמדת) and YHWH will fill his house with glory (Hag. 2:8).

---

41. Nogalski, "Joel as 'Literary Anchor'," 92. In a different vein, note the approach of Jörg Jeremias, "The Function of the Book of Joel for Reading the Twelve," in Albertz, Nogalski, and Wöhrle (eds), *Perspectives on the Formation of the Book of the Twelve*, 77–87. He disputes Nogalski's understanding, but not his general approach of viewing Joel as late and scribal activity generating the function of Joel in the Twelve.

Full retributive theodicy advanced in Joel 4:4-8 is deferred in the book but finds its fulfilment in Hag. 2:8 when read in the context of the Twelve. Hope in the justice of YHWH is partially fulfilled in Joel 4:4-8 as the second crime (human trafficking) finds poetic justice in vv. 7-8. But the hope that YHWH would vindicate his temple is deferred in this passage, generating a future hope in Joel 4:5. It is a hope that YHWH *would* restore his temple in accordance with his justice and retribution.

Conclusion

If I am correct in my analysis, several implications emerge in the study of Joel and theodicy. One cannot identify the theodicy in Joel 4:4-8 as purely retributive. It is retributive only if one omits v. 5 from consideration. This study has demonstrated that Joel 4:4, 6-8 is theodic and reinforces the justice of YHWH as he restores his people in a kind of "poetic justice" that Miller identifies. The hope on display in Joel 4:4, 6-8 is a hope that YHWH will restore his people in accordance with his divine sense of equal measure: divine punishment justly meets human offense.

Still, one cannot define poetic justice as fitting *fully* to this passage. Verse 5 has been overlooked for its contribution to theodicy in vv. 4-8 as well as the chapter. One must allow v. 5 to speak to the structure of the chapter as a whole. I have in mind here Nogalski's seminal work and his construction of symmetry in the verses, as discussed above.[42] Nogalski's construction collapses the distinctive perspective of v. 5 in the complex of 4:4-8, conflating the two crimes of Phoenicia and Philistia into *one*: human trafficking. He comes to this *despite* the fact that he recognizes two crimes in vv. 4-5 rather than one.[43] Joel 4:5 disrupts conventional poetic justice to open a horizon on future hope beyond immediate retribution. Thus, the text presents inexact retribution theodicy wherein YHWH absorbs the offense of theft by the Phoenicians and Philistines and v. 5 with no counterbalancing punishment.

In light of this imbalance, v. 5 opens an expectation of hope beyond Joel. Hope is deferred to a future time and a future restoration of the temple, where the YHWH's riches might be returned from the nations. In its restoration vision, Haggai 2 depicts the balancing restoration anticipated in Joel 4:5. Haggai 2:8 presents an intertextual link between

---

42. Nogalski, *Redactional Processes*, 5.

43. "The actual crimes committed, delineated in 4:5f, are two-fold. The oracle accuses these western neighbors of pillaging the temple…and of selling Judeans and Jerusalemites as slaves to the Greeks" (ibid., 28–9).

Joel 4:5. The nations' return of temple riches in the restoration of the temple are fitting because the nations have spirited YHWH's temple riches away in the first place. In this way, Joel 4:5 provides hope beyond human trafficking in Joel 4:4-8 and depicts a robust, if complex, presentation of divine retribution.

Chapter 5

THE LAWLESSNESS OF THE LION-GOD:
THEODICY IN THE BOOK OF AMOS

Chelsea D. Mak

Introduction

Classic formulations of theodicy are concerned with the character of God
in light of present evil and suffering. As a result, one might ask whether it
is possible for God to be good or just if evil persists in the world. Such a
question is predicated on the viability of human interrogation of the divine
and implies a concern with the reliability of God. Thus, one might also
ask whether God is worthy of human dedication. While both questions
are important considerations for contemporary communities of faith and
practice, the book of Amos suggests that such questioning is neither of
primary importance nor an appropriate human response. Instead, Amos
presents the divine as the ultimate Other, entirely outside of human
structural governance and control. Given God's positionality as radically
other-than-human, it is not the place of human beings to question the
character of God. To this end, even Amos' voice of protest is silenced as
God's commitment to destroy Israel is solidified (7:1-9; cf. 8:3).

This presentation of the Divine is illustrated by what has frequently
been called the book's motto: "Yhwh roars from Zion" (1:2).[1] Drawing

---

1. See, e.g., James D. Nogalski, *The Book of the Twelve: Hosea–Jonah*, SHBC
(Macon: Smyth & Helwys, 2011), 275; and Göran Eidevall, *Amos: A New Translation
with Introduction and Commentary*, AYB 24G (New Haven: Yale University Press,
2017), 96. Unless otherwise indicated, all translations are my own.

on recent work at the intersection of animality and biblical studies, together with the now classic work of Jacques Derrida, *The Beast and the Sovereign*, I propose that the presentation of Yhwh as lion suggests a radical othering of the divine sovereign—by aligning Yhwh with the animal other—that absolves Yhwh of culpability concerning any evil or injustice associated with Yhwh's action or inaction.[2] Thus, the appropriate question is not whether God is good or just but rather, where does one stand in relation to the lion-God? After all, as Hugh Pyper has aptly noted, "to follow a lion is rather different from facing one..."[3] Indeed, it is the positionality of the community before or behind the roar of Yhwh that emerges as the primary concern of Amos in its final form, which brings forward Judah, rather than Israel as its target audience. In this reading, the book's opening verses, the oracles against Judah (2:4-5), and the hope of restoration for the Davidic monarchy (9:11-15)—all of which are additions to the text—highlight that a decision of positionality is being presented to Judah. From the perspective of history, the Northern Kingdom lies defeated before Yhwh, making the lion's roar "the boast of the predator after he has made his kill."[4] In contrast, Judah may still choose to follow the Lion and live. Finally, contemporary reading communities are also presented with a choice of positionality, both with regard to the God of the text and with regard to Amos's negation of the premise of theodicy itself.

Constructing Thresholds:
Theodicy, History, and Animality in Amos

Theodicy as Problem in the Hebrew Bible

Coined by Gottfried Willhelm Leibniz in 1710, the term "theodicy" is a compound word derived from the Greek nouns θεός (God) and δίκη (justice). Despite this, however, the term remained largely undefined by Leibniz—in fact, it first appeared only in the title, *Essais de Théodicée*. The book, while leaving its title to speak for itself, covered topics including the goodness of God, evil, and free will, thus paving the way for what soon became an important concept within Christian

---

2. Jacques Derrida, *The Beast and the Sovereign*, 2 vols (Chicago: University of Chicago Press, 2009 and 2011).

3. Hugh S. Pyper, "The Lion King: Yahweh as Sovereign Beast in Israel's Imaginary," in *The Bible and Posthumanism*, ed. Jennifer L. Koosed, SemeiaSt 74 (Atlanta: SBL, 2014), 59–74 (73).

4. Francis I. Anderson and David Noel Freedman, *Amos: A New Translation with Introduction and Commentary*, AB 24A (New York: Doubleday, 1989), 221.

theology.[5] In its most formal expression, the term came to represent a logical problem, what Ronald Green has called a "trilemma," within Christianity. Green writes,

> The "problem of theodicy" arises when the experienced reality of suffering is juxtaposed with two sets of beliefs traditionally associated with ethical monotheism. One is the belief that God is absolutely good and compassionate. The other is the belief that he controls all events in history, that he is both all-powerful (omnipotent) and all-knowing (omniscient). When combined with some other implicit beliefs—for example, the belief that a good being would try to prevent suffering insofar as he is able—these various ideas seem contradictory. They appear to form a logical trilemma, in the sense that, while any two of these sets of ideas can be accepted, the addition of the third renders the whole logically inconsistent... Theodicy may be thought of as the effort to resist the conclusion that such a logical trilemma exists. It aims to show that traditional ideas about God's power and goodness are compatible with the fact of suffering.[6]

This formulation of the "problem of theodicy," carefully articulated by Green, is dependent upon the Christian tradition of philosophical theology, especially as it emerged in modernity.[7] Posing the question of theodicy to the literature of the Hebrew Bible (HB), then, ought not be a simple or straightforward task. Indeed, two additional "problems" must be raised prior to considering the Bible and theodicy—or, here, the book of Amos and theodicy: modernity and Christianity.

Marcel Sarot has already articulated the changes in philosophical thought that emerged in modernity, giving rise to the concept of theodicy as stated above, namely: (1) the problem of evil as internal or external to Christianity; (2) doubt in the character of human beings versus doubt of the character of the divine; (3) a shift from practical orientation to theoretical orientation; and, related to the first, (4) an audience comprised of Christians versus one comprised of so-called non-believers.[8] However, Sarot's focus on modernity—a problem he finds surmountable, so long as definitions of theodicy remain flexible—leads him to miss the significance of the problem of Christianity.

5. Marcel Sarot, "Theodicy and Modernity: An Inquiry into the Historicity of Theodicy," in *Theodicy in the World of the Bible*, ed. Antti Laato and Johannes C. de Moor (Leiden: Brill, 2003), 1–26 (2).

6. Ronald M. Green, "Theodicy," in *The Encyclopedia of Religion*, ed. M. Eliade (New York: Macmillan, 1987), 431.

7. See Sarot, "Theodicy," for a thorough discussion of the origins of theodicy in modernity and the consequences thereof.

8. Ibid., 6.

Concomitant with the intellectual shifts arising from the impact of modernity upon Christianity was the rise of anthropology and, with it, the development of universalizing definitions of religion.[9] Such definitions, as has been robustly demonstrated by scholars associated with the Material Turn in religious studies,[10] evidence a distinctly Protestant bias—one that has profoundly impacted the study of religion. Such bias has produced scholarship on religion that is (1) heavily focused on texts and textual interpretation, and (2) unduly weighted towards "belief" over and above "practice."[11] Classically articulated by Clifford Geertz, this understanding of religion enshrines "meaning-making" through a system of symbols that cohere to create a sense of order and wellbeing for the "believer."[12] Within Geertz's definition, three elements of "chaos" can disrupt the coherence of the religious system: (1) bafflement, a state that emerges when empirical observation is in itself unexplainable or contradicts one's understanding of the world; (2) suffering, which poses an intrinsic challenge to the meaningfulness of life; and (3) intractable ethical paradox.[13] While Geertz is not expressly attempting to deal with the problem of theodicy, one can no doubt see how religion is, in a sense, theodical in his definition.

Although he does not cite Geertz, the influence of this definition of religion is clearly evident in James Crenshaw's introduction to theodicy in the edited volume, *Theodicy in the Old Testament*.[14] In his contribution to the volume, Crenshaw highlights that the questions posed by

9. Talal Asad, *Genealogies of Religion: Discipline and Reasons of Power in Christianity and Islam* (Baltimore: The Johns Hopkins University Press, 1993), 19, 29.

10. See, e.g., Birgit Meyer, "An Author Meets Her Critics: Around Birgit Meyer's 'Mediation and the Genesis of Presence: Toward a Material Approach to Religion'," *RelSoc* 5 (2014): 205–54; Robert A. Orsi, *Between Heaven and Earth: The Religious Worlds People Make and the Scholars Who Study Them* (Princeton: Princeton University Press, 2005), 175–204; and Manuel A. Vásquez, *More Than Belief: A Materialist Theory of Religion* (New York: Oxford University Press, 2011).

11. Meyer, "An Author Meets Her Critics," 207.

12. Geertz defines religion as "(1) a system of symbols which acts to (2) establish powerful, pervasive, and long-lasting moods and motivations in men by (3) formulating conceptions of a general order of existence and (4) clothing these in conceptions with such an aura of factuality that (5) the moods and motivations seem uniquely realistic" (Clifford Geertz, *The Interpretation of Cultures: Selected Essays* [London: Fontana, 1993], 90).

13. Ibid., 101–8.

14. James L. Crenshaw (ed.), *Theodicy in the Old Testament*, IRT 4 (Philadelphia: Fortress Press, 1983).

theodicy are inherently a quest for meaning, arguing that disruptions to understood patterns of an ordered cosmos and society threatened what he calls the Israelite "belief system." Thus, an account had to be made for disturbances such as "evil, suffering, and death."[15] Crenshaw argues that such challenges to the religion's coherence occasionally led to questions about God's character (theodicy), but more often produced answers located in the character of human beings (anthropodicy).[16] Inherent to both Crenshaw's question and the answers he finds in the HB is the assumption that meaning and coherence are of primary importance within Israelite religion.

I do not intend to deny that the religions of Israel had cognitive content—they certainly did. However, the critique of the Protestant bias in the study of religion suggests that other aspects of the embodied, subjective experiences of what we term "religious" may have been (and may continue to be) more integral to the fabric of those religions in their various forms. Of these, practice and materiality, together with mediations of power, may emerge as more significant than rightly oriented beliefs about god and human. Thus, studying the "problem of theodicy" in the book of Amos, and the HB, should not only begin with the broadening of definitions,[17] but by holding open the possibility that there may be no problem of theodicy at all; something "otherwise than meaning" may be at stake.[18] In order to consider the stakes involved, however, one must have an idea of the community of reception and the circumstances governing their response to and participation in the divine. Thus, a consideration of Amos's early addressees is in order.

15. James L. Crenshaw, "Introduction: The Shift from Theodicy to Anthropodicy," in Crenshaw (ed.), *Theodicy in the Old Testament*, 2.

16. Ibid., 5.

17. On definitions, see Dalit Rom-Shiloni, "Theodical Discourse: Theodicy and Protest in Sixth Century BCE Hebrew Bible Theology," in *Theodicy and Protest: Jewish and Christian Perspectives*, ed. Beate Ego (Leipzig: Evangelische Veragsanstalt, 2018), vii–liv; and Antti Laato and Johannes C. de Moor, "Introduction," in Laato and de Moor (eds), *Theodicy in the World of the Bible*, vii–liv. On various approaches to the question of theodicy in the prophetic literature, see Paul L. Redditt, "Theodicy," in *Oxford Encyclopedia of the Bible and Ethics*, ed. Robert L. Brawley (Oxford: Oxford University Press, 2014), 348–53; and James L. Crenshaw, "Theodicy and Prophetic Literature," in Laato and de Moor (eds), *Theodicy in the World of the Bible*, 236–55.

18. For an extended critique of Geertz's definition of religion *vis-à-vis* the meaninglessness of suffering, see Don Seeman, "Otherwise Than Meaning: On the Generosity of Ritual," *Social Analysis: The International Journal of Social and Cultural Practice* 48 (2004): 55–71.

Amos Among the Judahites

According to the book of Amos, the man Amos acted as prophet in Samaria during the reigns of King Jeroboam son of Joash in the north and King Uzziah in the south (1:1), this despite Amos's stated vocation as a sheep breeder (1:1; cf. 7:14), his denial of the office of prophet (7:14), and his origin in Tekoa of Judah. The book's superscription further states that Amos's prophetic activity took place two years before *the* earthquake, implying, as numerous scholars have pointed out, an event occupying the living memory of the book's addressees. Taken together, these data suggest a possible date of composition in the middle of the eighth century BCE—and some argue that the book in its entirety can be dated to this period.[19] Still, additional data culled from the book push against such a conclusion, especially the book's closing—and only—oracle of hope addressed to Judah (9:11-15), and the southern orientation of the book's "motto" in 1:2.

The opening and concluding lines of the book further create tension in its content, which would otherwise be almost entirely negative in orientation. In its final form, the book now presents a message of "no hope" throughout chs 1–6; "perhaps hope," with the glimmer of divine repentance in ch. 7; and "hope for Judah" in ch. 9.[20] Given this, a more recent consensus has emerged that the book has a more complex redactional history than some would assume.[21] While detailed discussions of the redaction history of the book can be found within the scholarly literature,[22] my aim here is only to detail what is perceived in the present essay to be the community (or communities) that received the final form of Amos and what circumstances shaped their reception of the book's message.

With Jason Radine, I take the relevant historical time period for the book's redaction to be between the eighth and mid-fifth centuries, dating the final form of the book to the Persian period.[23] Within that context,

19. Douglas Stuart, *Hosea–Jonah*, WBC 31 (Grand Rapids: Zondervan, 1988), 285.

20. Eidevall, *Amos*, 16.

21. See, e.g., Eidevall, *Amos*, 18; Jörg Jeremias, *The Book of Amos: A Commentary*, OTL (Louisville: Westminster John Knox, 1995), 5–9; James Luther Mays, *Amos: A Commentary*, OTL (Philadelphia: Westminster, 1969), 13–14; and Nogalski, *The Book of the Twelve*, 261–3.

22. Of these, Eidevall's recent commentary for Anchor Bible and Jason Radine's monograph are especially helpful (Eidevall, *Amos*, 24–6; Jason Radine, *The Book of Amos in Emergent Judah*, FAT 2 [Tübingen: Mohr Siebeck, 2010]).

23. Radine, *The Book of Amos*, 216–18. Amos, and especially the opening and closing verses of the book, has enjoyed prominence of place in recent reconstructions

the early reception community for Amos's re-worked oracles of doom over the northern kingdom was likely comprised of refugees and/or repatriated Judahites. Such an interpretation takes seriously the book's "otherwise total fatalism"[24] and suggests that, for those who survived the siege warfare and forced migrations imposed on Judah by the Babylonian imperial powers, the book conveyed a message of mitigated hope. That is, from a Judahite perspective of history, Israel lay defeated before Yhwh. Further, under present circumstances, the community of Judah is keenly aware that it is always possible that Yhwh may lash out against Yhwh's own people in such a way again. Given this, the book both explains the fall of the northern kingdom and presents an alternative future for Judah— should they follow Yhwh and live.[25]

of the Book of the Twelve as an intentional, coherent literary unit. In such recon-structions, Amos features as one of the writings that comprised a precursor to the Book of the Twelve, one which likely began with the mutual development of Hosea–Amos as a literary unit. Given this, it may strike some as odd to speak of Amos's development as a "book" rather than a "writing" on its way to inclusion in "The Book of the Twelve." However, it remains disputed whether the evidence supports a reading of the Twelve Prophets as a literary unity or as a collection best likened to an anthology. Indeed, with Ehud Ben Zvi and David L. Peterson, I take the latter option as more probable (Ehud Ben Zvi, "Twelve Prophetic Books or 'the Twelve': A Few Preliminary Considerations," in *Forming Prophetic Literature Essays on Isaiah and the Twelve in Honor of John D.W. Watts*, ed. Paul R. House and James W. Watts, JSOTSup 235 [Sheffield: Sheffield Academic, 1996], 125–56; and David L. Peterson, "A Book of the Twelve?" in *Reading and Hearing the Book of the Twelve*, ed. James D. Nogalski and Marvin A. Sweeney, SBLSymS 15 [Atlanta: SBL, 2000], 3–10). This position is better supported by, especially, the individual superscriptions of the books, the fluidity of the ordering of the books between the Hebrew and Greek manuscripts, and the individual commentaries on Hosea, Micah, Nahum, and Habakkuk at Qumran (as opposed to a commentary on the Book of the Twelve, which suggests that some of the earliest readers of the books did not read them as part of a larger whole). By no means does this preclude the possibility that earlier writings influenced later writings; rather, such influence ought to be expected given "the common repertoire of a relatively small social group consisting of educated writers and readers within which and for which prophetic—and other 'biblical'—books were written" (Ben Zvi, "Twelve Prophetic Books," 155). Still, each of the Twelve Prophets can and should be read as a unit unto itself, as well as a part of a larger collection, one which would include not only the twelve Minor Prophets, but potentially also Isaiah, Jeremiah, and Ezekiel.

24. Radine, *The Book of Amos*, 41.
25. Ibid., 212.

Key to the rhetoric of the final form of the book, then, are the late additions of 1:2 and 9:11-15, since these directly address a Judahite audience and serve to frame the rest of the book. Further, though brief, 1:2's allusion to the roaring lion in the figure of the divine, has implications for the way the book presents Yhwh's sovereignty—illustrated immediately following the motto in the oracles against the nations—and serves as an important site for extended reflection. The verse, however, does not stand alone but connects to a thematic thread in Amos that Eidevall calls "the roaring lion and other dangerous animals."[26] Read together with other occurrences of this theme (3:4, 8, 12; and 5:18-20), the reader comes to view Yhwh as a predator on the hunt with Israel as prey.[27] Indeed, this beastly portrayal of Yhwh suggests a rather unlikely conversation partner for a discussion of theodicy and the Book of the Twelve: Jacques Derrida.

The Beast and the Sovereign

Jacques Derrida's late seminars, entitled *The Beast and the Sovereign*,[28] take up the question of animality already posed in *The Animal That Therefore I Am*.[29] In that early essay, later compiled with other such reflections into a book-length volume, Derrida finds his own animality exposed through the subjectivity revealed in the gaze of his cat. The volume thus takes up the sharply driven wedge between the animal and the human, especially in western philosophy. Derrida, then, as one would expect, commences the task of deconstructing the human–animal binary, not merely by "demonstrating how each term of the opposition is joined to its companion by an invisible network of arteries"—which, by now, has been aptly demonstrated in the biological sciences—but by further

---

26. Eidevall, *Amos*, 12.

27. An element of the book that picks up what Mary Mills has identified as the most significant and challenging theme of the book, divine violence. See Mary Mills, "Divine Violence in the Book of Amos," in *The Aesthetics of Violence in the Prophets*, ed. Julia M. O'Brien and Chris Franke, LHBOTS 517 (New York: T&T Clark, 2010), 153–79.

28. Jacques Derrida, *The Beast and the Sovereign*, vol. 1 (Chicago: University of Chicago Press, 2009); and Jacques Derrida, *The Beast and the Sovereign*, trans. Geoffrey Bennington, vol. 2 (Chicago: University of Chicago Press, 2011). For a critical summary of and introduction to Derrida's work, see David Farrell Krell, *Derrida and Our Animal Others: Derrida's Final Seminar, "The Beast and Sovereign"* (Bloomington: Indiana University Press, 2013).

29. Jacques Derrida, *The Animal That Therefore I Am*, trans. David Wills (New York: Fordham University Press, 2008).

troubling the singularity posited by "the animal."[30] Derrida demonstrates how this reduction of the great multiplicity of animal life, the equating of moth and ibex or giraffe and raven, has further permitted unmitigated human consumption—of animal as meat, but also of animal as instrument for human gain.[31]

This treatise leads to what Hannah Strømmen identifies as the three main calls to action of Derrida's work on animality:

> (1) greater vigilance in philosophical thought over the supposedly distinct difference between humans and animals; (2) compassion and an awakening to the animal other as a condition of ethics—an awakening that is linked to Derrida's dream for an unconditional hospitality; and (3) responsibility in the face of a horizon of justice that will always be to some extent excessive, incalculable, and impossible but that nonetheless demands our interminable response with respect to the other as any other.[32]

Strømmen thus highlights the ways in which Derrida demonstrates how the erasure of difference among animals serves human interests by radically othering the monolithic "animal." Derrida and Strømmen thus argue that it is only in "awakening" to the other that ethics can be pursued. To do such work is to identify the threshold between human and animal, to see who is "inside" and who is "outside," to critically consider on what terms the threshold is constructed, and to do the work of dismantling such systems of power in order to welcome the other, "who is both potentially threatening and loving, never determined (or determinable) in advance as one or the other."[33] That is, to act in hospitality. Such work requires pathos—compassion—to come to bear on "law, ethics, and politics."[34]

Then, in *The Beast and the Sovereign*, Derrida returns to animality, this time a particular type of animality: "that [which] is called the 'beast' or that is represented as bestiality, on the one hand, and on the other a sovereignty that is most often represented as human or divine, in truth anthropo-theological."[35] Through an extended series of seminars, Derrida

---

30. Stephen D. Moore, "Introduction: From Animal Theory to Creaturely Theology," in *Divinanimality: Animal Theory, Creaturely Theology*, ed. Stephen D. Moore, Transdiciplinary Theological Colloquia (New York: Fordham University Press, 2014), 7.

31. Derrida, *The Animal*, 34.

32. Hannah M. Strømmen, *Biblical Animality after Jacques Derrida*, SemeiaSt 91 (Atlanta: SBL, 2018), 26.

33. Ibid., 28.

34. Derrida, *The Animal*, 26.

35. Derrida, *The Beast*, 14.

demonstrates how the image of the beast—most often the wolf, but also the lion and the great sea monster, Leviathan—and that of the sovereign simultaneously oppose each other and collapse in on each other, so that the sovereign becomes the beast. This is at work in the word play of the French title, *et* and *est*, indistinguishable in spoken French. So it is that Derrida discusses both, "The Beast *and* (*et*) The Sovereign" and also, "The Beast [who] *is* (*est*) The Sovereign."[36]

This merging and diverging is illustrated by Derrida through a survey of western literature and political-philosophical treatise, and can perhaps be summarized in a quote of La Fontaine: "The reason of the strongest is always best; as we shall shortly show."[37] The quotation, which circles and permeates Derrida's reflections, highlights an essential aspect of the merging of beast and sovereign, that of strength or power. Such power is illustrated in two important ways: (1) the idea of devouring as expression of sovereign might; and (2) the creation of law in the othering of the sovereign.

The might of the sovereign, and thus the sovereign's power to govern, especially through fear, is frequently expressed in the language of devouring: "it's about the mouth, teeth, tongue, and the violent rush to bite, engulf, swallow the other, to take the other into oneself too, to kill it, or mourn it."[38] In such language, the image of the "maw of the untamable beast"[39] and the mouth of the sovereign—which is also the source of speech and "therefore, of obeying in receiving"—come together in the rule of might.[40] Further, in as much as the beast, in all its ferocity and its ability to consume its prey (human and animal), is imaged as the one "who respects nothing, scorns the law" and, thus, "immediately situates himself above the law, at a distance from the law," so too the sovereign structures the law precisely by locating himself outside of it.[41] Like the criminal, then, beast and sovereign share the status of "being-outside-the-law"— they are other-than-the-law and, as a result, other-than-human. Beast and sovereign, together, become an ultimate Other to the human masses.[42]

That the beast—and the lion in particular—is a ubiquitous image in the ancient world from which the HB emerges is well known and easily

---

36. Ibid., 32.

37. Derrida quotes La Fontaine, *The Wolf and the Lamb*, in *The Beast and the Sovereign*, 11.

38. Derrida, *The Beast*, 23.

39. Ibid., 18.

40. Ibid., 23.

41. Ibid., 17, 49.

42. Ibid., 17.

demonstrated, whether through text or image. One need not look much farther than Brent Strawn's monograph, *What Is Stronger than a Lion?*, to verify such a claim.[43] Strawn's survey of the biblical and ancient Near Eastern material demonstrates the importance of the lion in the social imaginary—and, indeed, the ecosystem—of ancient Israel. Lions are expressly mentioned in the HB more than 150 times, not including possible allusions.[44] Of these, and despite the polyvalence of the lion as symbol in the HB, Strawn shows that the lion's roar and its predation— "the maw of the untamable beast"[45]—are its most frequently referenced traits. Such an emphasis accords with the image's more common symbolic values, "*threat* and *power*."[46]

In contrast to its ancient Near Eastern context, where the image of the lion and the human sovereign frequently merge in literature and, especially, iconography, the HB contains few references to leonine kingship in Israel.[47] Rather, the image of the lion appears to be reserved for the divine sovereign, Yhwh. Such imagery is especially common in the Hebrew prophets—such as Amos. Further, while Strawn is hesitant to push too hard towards claims about origins, that the use of leonine imagery in depictions of royal rulers was especially prominent in the Neo-Assyrian empire at least suggests such external influence. The imagery thus carries the implication that its use was "socio-politically oriented."[48] Thus, Derrida's insight, limited as it is to the modern, western intellectual tradition, may also illuminate the image of Yhwh in the book of Amos. In the context of this chapter, given how issues of justice, lawlessness, and power coalesce in Derrida's work on beastly sovereignty, this insight may further shed light on the issue of theodicy, particularly theodicy as a defense of God's justice. Accordingly, I turn now to consider the image of the lion in Amos 1:2; 3:4, 8, 12; and 5:18-20, before taking up the issue of justice and the sovereignty of Yhwh as a "being-outside-the-law" in 1:3–2:16.[49] In conclusion, I will return to the question of Amos among the Judahites by briefly considering 9:11-15 as these verses relate to the lion-God of the preceding chapters of the book.

43. Brent A. Strawn, *What Is Stronger Than a Lion? Leonine Image and Metaphor in the Hebrew Bible and the Ancient Near East*, OBO 212 (Göttingen: Vandenhoeck & Ruprecht, 2005).

44. Strawn, *What Is Stronger?*, 25–6.

45. Derrida, *The Beast*, 18.

46. Strawn, *What Is Stronger?*, 45, 27.

47. Ibid., 250.

48. Ibid., 268, 69.

49. Derrida, *The Beast*, 17.

Beastly Sovereignty: Yhwh as Lion in the Book of Amos

Amos 1:1-2

The two opening verses of the book of Amos, while differing in style and form, constitute a single unit within the first chapter of the book. Verse 1, written in prose, assigns the prophetic activity of Amos, the נקד, "shepherd" or "sheep-breeder," to the middle of the eighth century.[50] Verse 2, composed of two lines of balanced poetry, introduces the main themes of Amos in what is frequently called the "motto" of the book.[51] The two verses are linked syntactically by the dependence of v. 2's unspecified pronoun in "then he said" (ויאמר), which points back to v. 1 for its antecedent. Thus, the two verses should be read together as part of the book's frame.

Verse 2 is thus best read as an editorial addition intended to frame the content of the entire book of Amos, rather than merely an introduction to the oracles against the nations that begin in v. 3, culminating in the oracle against Israel in 2:6-16. This is further illustrated by the verse's emphasis on the Northern Kingdom—the desiccation of Mount Carmel.[52] The verse, then, is significant for considering the message of the final form of the book, as well as for the present discussion, as it also includes the first—albeit veiled—leonine depiction of Yhwh.

ויאמר
יהוה מציון ישאג
ומירושלם יתן קולו
ואבלו נאות הרעים
ויבש ראש הכרמל

² Then he said:
From Zion, Yhwh roars
    And from Jerusalem, he gives his voice.
Then the shepherd's pastures wither,
    And the peak of Carmel dries up.

---

50. The noun, נקדים, occurs only twice in the HB, here and in 2 Kgs 3:4, where it refers to Moab's King Mesha, who provided Israel with lambs and wool. Its occurrence there supports the reading of shepherd or sheep-breeder, given the context. Further evidence is provided by the Ugaritic *nqd*, "head shepherd, chief shepherd" (*DULAT*, 630), and Akkadian *nāqidu*, "herdsman" (*CAD*, 11:333).

51. See, e.g., Nogalski, *The Book of the Twelve*, 275, and Eidevall, *Amos*, 96.

52. Indeed, references to Carmel frame the book of Amos. The mountain is identified as the target of Yhwh's wrath here and named as an inadequate hiding place for those fleeing said wrath in Amos 9:3.

The translation, "Yhwh roars," in some ways removes the ambiguity of the reference to Yhwh as lion in the verse. However, the parallel phrase in the second half of the line, יתן קולו, "he gives his voice," demonstrates the problem, since this phrase is used elsewhere to describe the sound of thunder. Taken together, then, the two half-lines lead to the question, does Yhwh roar as lion or does Yhwh thunder as in a storm? Given this, the semantic range of שאג and the word pair נתן and קול is crucial to the present discussion.

With 20 occurrences in the HB, the verb שאג, "to roar" is most frequently used with an animal lion as its subject (e.g., Amos 3:4, 8; but also, Judg. 14:5; Isa. 5:29; Jer. 2:15; 51:38; Ezek. 22:25; and Zeph. 3:3)—although the lion in these cases may also refer metaphorically to an approaching enemy (Isa. 5:29). However, as here, it is also used with reference to Yhwh. This usage is primarily employed in the prophetic literature (see, Jer. 25:30; Hos. 11:10; and Joel 4:16). Otherwise, the verb is used in the Psalms, referring to both a lion (Pss 22:14; 104:21) and the cry of a human (Ps. 38:9). Its one occurrence in Job may refer to the sound of thunder or YHWH or, more likely, both (37:4).

In its noun form, שאגה, occurs seven times: Isa. 5:29; Ezek. 19:7; Zech. 11:3; Pss 22:2; 32:3; Job 2:24, and 4:10. The range of usage is similar when the root is used nominally. It is clustered together with the animal lion in Isaiah, Ezekiel, Zechariah, and Job 4:10—with the first two referring metaphorically to nations at war or training for war and the last referring to the lions that roam the desolate places; Job's reference refers to the animal.[53] Thus, although it remains possible that שאג means thunder in this case, its usage elsewhere is more heavily weighted towards the roar of the lion. Still, what of its pairing with נתן and קול?

The combination of נתן and קול is quite common, occurring 47 times. People, the heavens, the deep, and other creatures can all "give voice / sound." Of these, 15 are particularly relevant. On 12 occasions, the words are paired together with Yhwh as subject. When this occurs, the context suggests participation in a broader social and cultural context that includes the storm-god motif and, especially, that of the Cloud-rider, Baal from Ugaritic mythology.[54] Each of these describe theophanies, or theophany-like events, that include stormy elements. There are some texts where theophany is in view, but storm elements are lacking (e.g., Jer. 25:20;

53. The two occurrences in the Psalms and Job 2:24 have human subjects, who are in physical and emotional turmoil. In these cases, the noun expresses a sound of groaning, screaming, or crying out in suffering.
54. See, e.g., 2 Sam. 22:14; Pss 18:14; 46:7 (6 Eng.); and 68:34 (33 Eng.).

Joel 2:11; 4:16), and still others have a cosmogenic and hymn-like quality (e.g., Jer. 10:13 and 51:16), with a distinct blending of the two in the Psalms (e.g., Pss 18 and 68). In the Prophets, the phrase is frequently militaristic in tone and, in contrast to the Psalms, often oriented against Israel or Judah. In such contexts, the phrase is fear inspiring, rather than a declaration of Yhwh's redemptive power. Still elsewhere, primarily in the Deuteronomistic history, the usage clearly describes Yhwh as the one who can and does bring rain or hailstorm.[55] This survey indicates that the phrase is most often theophanic in nature, frequently calling on the Storm-god motif, though not always.

However, there are also three occurrences, all in the prophets, where the phrase refers to lions.[56] And, of those listed above, three occur with the root שאג, as in Amos 1:2. When the phrase occurs in the prophetic literature, it is almost always militaristic in nature, and more frequently brings an adverse effect for Israel or Judah.[57] In this case, then, the connection with the storm-god motif in Amos 1 weakens, at least if one reads this motif as primarily about rain and fertility. Here we do not have Yhwh giving voice as one who rides the clouds with thunder and brings life-sustaining rain, but Yhwh issuing a roar that causes withering and desolation. However, if the storm-god motif is read alongside the associated Ugaritic texts, an alternative, distinctly political reading emerges.[58]

This reading still calls on the Ugaritic mythology, but not in the way it is often invoked in the literature. The Ugaritic text in question is that of the Baal Cycle, and especially *KTU* 1.4 VII 13-42—the installment of a window in Baal's palace. The verbal links between this text and Amos 1:2 demonstrate the relevance of the Ugaritic text here. However, while it remains common to interpret the Baal Cycle at this point as being primarily concerned with the coming of the rain and the fertility of the land, Smith and Pitard have convincingly demonstrated the important

---

55. So, Exod. 9:23 and 1 Sam. 12:17; notably in both these cases, קול occurs in the plural form.

56. Jer. 2:15; 12:8; and Amos 3:4. Joel 4:16 (3:16 Eng.) constitutes a possible fourth, but is dependent in large part on the interpretation here.

57. For example, Joel 2:11, where Yhwh speaks as head of the army that has ravaged the land with fire, further paralleled in Amos 1 and 2's description of Yhwh's fiery destruction of the nations.

58. See, especially, *KTU* 1.4 VII 13-42, the section the Baal Cycle wherein Baal installs a window in his palace abode. Line 29 reads, *qâla-hǔ qadiša ba'lu yatina* / Baal gave forth his holy voice. Note the occurrence of the Ugaritic cognates for קול and נתן, *ql* and *ytn*, used here to describe Baal's speech.

political elements of this moment in the narrative.[59] Preceded by Baal's tour of the earthly kingdoms and followed by his decision to challenge Mot for dominion of the underworld, the installment of Baal's window—and the issuance of his voice—take on decidedly political connotations.[60] The completion of Baal's palace through the installation of the window is therefore a demonstration of Baal's successful garnering of political authority in the divine and earthly realm, success that leads to his audacious attempt to gain such sovereignty in the realm of the dead. The issuance of Baal's voice, then, is not only a promise of fertility, but also a claim to political dominion. The collocation of political power in the Baal Cycle is also present in Amos 1:2, as is clearly demonstrated in oracles against the nations that follow directly on the declaration of Yhwh's voice.

So Yhwh roars from his palace abode, Zion, as Baal does in the Ugaritic mythology. The giving of Baal's voice seems to mean the coming rain, and, as a result, the fertility of the land;[61] but here, if Yhwh's voice is to be associated with fertility at all, it is a reversal of the land's fecundity—Yhwh's voice is not that which brings the rain, but drought and desolation. Such an irony is possible here, especially given that irony and surprising reversal play a role elsewhere in Amos. Indeed, there may be a double irony in the verse, given that van Hecke has shown how the appearance of Yhwh as lion preying on Yhwh's own people is frequently paired with the reversal of pastoral images.[62] So Yhwh refuses to shepherd Yhwh's own flock, instead devouring the sheep. Further, the roaring lion also features in texts that discuss the desolation of the land,

---

59. Mark S. Smith and Wayne T. Pitard, *The Ugaritic Baal Cycle: Volume 2, Introduction with Text, Translation and Commentary of KTU/CAT 1.3–1.4*, VTSup 114 (Leiden: Brill, 2009), 608–10. See also Wayne T. Pitard, "The Combat Myth as a Succession Story at Ugarit," in *Creation and Chaos: A Reconsideration of Hermann Gunkel's Chaoskampf Hypothesis*, ed. JoAnn Scurlock and Richard H. Beal (Winona Lake: Eisenbrauns, 2013), 199–205; and Aaron Tugendhaft, "Politics and Time in the Baal Cycle," *JANER* 12 (2012): 147–57.

60. This is not to claim that rainfall and fertility are not an issue here; instead, I seek only to highlight that both are marks of Baal's, albeit limited, political sovereignty.

61. Although only implied in *KTU* 1.4 VII 13–42, in *KTU* 1.4 IV 6 Anat makes a direct link between the building of Baal's palace with his ability to send forth the rains for the benefit of the earth and "give for his voice in the clouds" (again, *ql* and *ytn*).

62. P. van Hecke, "'For I Will Be Like a Lion to Ephraim': Leonine Metaphors in the Twelve Prophets," in *The Books of the Twelve Prophets: Minor Prophets—Major Theologies*, ed. Heinz-Josef Fabry, BETL 295 (Leuven: Peeters, 2018), 387–402.

resulting from divine punishment through the forced migrations enacted by contemporary political powers. That is, when the people go into exile, the roaring lion roams the desolate land (e.g., Zech. 11:3). Taken together, then, the use of שאג together with קול and נתן creates what Eidevall has called a "kind of double exposure," so that the image of the roaring lion merges with that of the storm-god.[63] Key, however, is that Yhwh appears as political sovereign, asserting dominion over Israel, Judah, and, as the reader soon finds out, the surrounding nations.

Amos 3:1-15

With Yhwh's political sovereignty asserted in 1:2 and demonstrated in 1:3–2:16, Amos 3 opens with the plural imperative, שמעו, "hear!"[64] Those indicted by the final oracle of ch. 2, Israel, are directly addressed in the exhortation to attend to the words of Yhwh—an exhortation that also picks up the themes of Exodus and covenant that featured in 2:9-11. While the two opening verses of ch. 3 are sometimes taken as a unit,[65] distinct from what follows, the use of the root שמע in ch. 3, together with the repetition of the phrase "children of Israel" (vv. 1 and 12); the root ידע (vv. 2 and 10); the root פקד (vv. 2 and 14); and of particular interest for the present conversation, words designating the lion (v. 4, אריה and כפיר; v. 8, ארדה; and v. 12, ארי),[66] suggest that, in its final form, the chapter should be taken as a whole.

Internally, then, the chapter has three parts, each marked by an introductory use of the verb שמע: (1) vv. 1-8; (2) vv. 9-12; (3) vv. 13-15. With

---

63. Eidevall, *Amos*, 97. Alternatively, the appearance of both leonine and storm-god imagery here may be understood as a blended metaphor. For a detailed discussion of metaphor and conceptual blending with specific reference to the Book of the Twelve, see Beth M. Stovell, "'I Will Make Her Like a Desert': Intertextual Allusion and Feminine and Agricultural Metaphors in the Book of the Twelve," in *The Book of the Twelve and the New Form Criticism*, ed. Mark J. Boda, Michael H. Floyd, and Colin M. Toffelmire, ANEM 10 (Atlanta: SBL, 2015), 37–61.

64. See also 4:1 and 5:1, where the opening verb can be considered a structural marker in the final organization of the oracles attributed to Amos.

65. For example, Shalom M. Paul, "Amos 3:3-8: The Irresistible Sequence of Cause and Effect," *HAR* 7 (1983): 203–20 (204); and Sara J. Milstein, "'Who Would Not Write?': The Prophet as Yhwh's Prey in Amos 3:3-8," *CBQ* 75 (2013): 429–45 (434).

66. For more detailed discussion of leonine vocabulary in the HB, see Strawn, *What Is Stronger?*, 293–326; and David J. A. Clines, "Misapprehensions, Ancient and Modern, About Lions (Nahum 2:13)," in *Poets, Prophets, and Texts in Play: Studies in Biblical Poetry and Prophecy in Honour of Francis Landy*, ed. Ehud Ben Zvi et al., LHBOTS 597 (London: Bloomsbury T&T Clark, 2015), 70–6.

each use of the verb, there is a shift in both audience and emphasis, as the addressees of the verb change. So, in part one, Israel is addressed directly and exhorted to hear the voice of Yhwh and its charge against them. The audience is then led through a series of rhetorical questions, which lead to the inevitable conclusion that the initial speech of Yhwh has resulted in the proclamation of guilt and punishment beginning in v. 9.

Verse 9's opening command, השמיעו (Hiphil, plural imperative; "make known"), thus introduces a new section of the chapter, one which builds on the first. In response to the inevitability of prophecy when Yhwh speaks (v. 8), an unknown collective must "make known" Israel's inability to do what is right and the consequential punishment of Yhwh.[67] Thus, the inhabitants of Ashdod and Egypt are called to look upon the affliction (מהומת רבות and עשוקים) brought upon Samaria by Yhwh.[68] This state of panic within Israel, according to v. 10, results from their failure to know

---

67. Several attempts have been made to argue that the series of questions in vv. 3-8 build to a climactic moment in v. 8, with the declaration of the inevitability of the prophetic office resulting from Yhwh's speech. Of these, Sara Milstein ("'Who Would Not Write?,'" 429–45) makes the strongest claim, arguing that the verses form a call narrative that can be likened to that of Isaiah, Jeremiah, or Ezekiel. Amos, who is nowhere called a prophet in the book, thus validates the oracles that follow by locating their origin in Yhwh. Such a position, however, is only possible if the following verse, and its plural imperative—"proclaim!"—is ignored. The passage is better understood as building to the indictment of Israel that follows (see also van Hecke, "Leonine Metaphors," 393–4). In this sense, Yhwh's speech propels anyone who hears to prophesy and thus bypasses the silencing of Yhwh's prophets detailed in 2:12. See also Jack R. Lundbom, "The Lion Has Roared: Rhetorical Structure in Amos 1:2–3:8," in *Milk and Honey: Essays on Ancient Israel and the Bible in Appreciation of the Judaic Studies Program at the University of California, San Diego*, ed. S. Malina and D. Miano (Winona Lake: Eisenbrauns, 2007), 73; Paul, "Amos 3:3-8," 203–4; James R. Linville, "Amos among the 'Dead Prophets Society'; Re-Reading the Lion's Roar," *JSOT* 25 (2000): 55–77 (73).

68. Derived from הום, possibly, "to confuse," מהומת occurs twelve times in the HB and in every case is associated with Yhwh's activity among groups of people, usually for harm. Some examples from the prophetic literature include: (1) Isa. 22:5, where Yhwh's day is said to be a day of מהומה with the "battering down of walls" and "a cry for help"—possibly in the context of siege warfare; (2) Ezek. 7:7, where a day of מהומה is coming when the Yhwh will punish Yhwh's people; (3) Zech. 14:13, where a day is coming when Yhwh will punish Jerusalem's enemies and includes מהומה that causes everyone to fight against one another; and in a close parallel to Amos 3:10 (4) Ezek. 22:5, where the punishment of Yhwh comes upon Judah as one who is seen, mocked, and called "full of great מהומה." Taken together, the occurrences of the word indicate a state in Israel brought on by Yhwh's punishment, one of panic or confusion like that of a raging battlefield. While it is possible to take the

how to do what is right, instead storing up "violence (חמס) and devastation (שד) in their citadels." Israel's lack of knowledge contrasts Yhwh's own in v. 2—whereas Yhwh has only known Israel among the nations, Israel does not know how to do right and, as a result, does not know Yhwh. Therefore, vv. 11-12, articulate the means of Yhwh's punishment, the attack of an enemy, and its totality, with reference to the lion (more below).

Finally, v. 13 opens with the last repetition of שמע, another plural imperative, as in v. 1, "hear!"—but now addresses an unknown collective, instead of the nation of Israel. These addressees, most likely those addressed in v. 9, have heard and witnessed the crimes of Israel, *vis-à-vis* the message of vv. 9-12, and are now called to testify against the nation, which Yhwh is calling to account (פקד, v. 2 and twice in v. 14). Further, the final line of v. 15, "I will destroy the houses of ivory and sweep away (ספה) the great houses," closes the chapter with an allusion to Israel's covenant relationship with Yhwh—the root, ספה, used only in situations of divine punishment, is used to describe the consequences of covenant violation in Deut. 29:18 and 32:23.[69] Within this matrix of divine entrapment and vengeance, there are three references to the figure of the lion that, together, shape how Amos 1:2 and, indeed, the book of Amos is read with regard to the question of theodicy. The first is found in Amos 3:4.

הישאג אריה ביער וטעף אין לו

היתן כפיר קולו ממענתו בלתי אם-לכד

> [4] Will a lion roar in the thicket if it has no prey?
> Will a [young] lion give its voice[70] from its hiding place if it has caught nothing?

verse as a call to look upon the injustices committed in Israel (and so, justification for their punishment), the source of this state elsewhere instead suggests it is God's punishment that Ashdod and Egypt witness.

69. In Deut. 29:18, in the context of Israel's covenant renewal with Yhwh, those who go their own way (i.e., do not follow the law of Yhwh), while telling themselves that they are safe from Yhwh's judgment (cf. Amos 9:10) bring ספה on themselves. And, in Deut. 32:23 and 24, Yhwh is said to ספה a nation that has rebelled. Notably, Yhwh will also send the teeth of beasts and the venom of crawling creatures against them (cf. Amos 5:19).

70. I have chosen the wooden translation, "give its voice" in this case to facilitate comparison with the parallel construction in Amos 1:2. For an alternative translation of the verse based on the hunting habits of lions, see Edward R. Hope, "Problems of Interpretation in Amos 3:4," *BT* 42 (1991): 201–5.

While the blending of the leonine and storm-god imagery in 1:2 remains, the use of both שאג and the word pair נתן / קול here highlights Yhwh as lion and encourages the reader to re-frame their understanding of the book in light of the leonine characteristics of the lion-God given in this chapter. The two questions here belong to a longer series of questions running through vv. 3-8, each one garnering a negative response from Amos's implied audience and leading to their entrapment by the final question in v. 8 and, thus, the reception of the subsequent prophetic words as sourced in Yhwh's speech.[71]

The verse not only sheds light on Amos's introduction, but also introduces a new element that is important for understanding both the book and what follows in ch. 3—that is, the lion roars because it has caught (לכד) its prey (טרף). The use of both words is localized in Amos to this chapter and further heightens the sense of entrapment already created through the flow of questions in these verses. The root לכד typically denotes the trapping of animals as prey or food, but it can also refer to the trapping of people (Judg. 7:25) and military conquest or siege warfare. Here, however, with טרף, which is most commonly used to describe something that is consumed (rather than an animal of prey being stalked; see, e.g., Gen. 49:4; Num. 23:24; and Isa. 5:29), the context is that of the hunt's end. Thus, the image is of a lion that has had success in the hunt, brought down its prey, and is ready to devour its flesh. Accordingly, given the ways in which this verse exposes the rhetoric of Amos 1:2, the reader may begin to wonder whether drought on Mount Carmel is the only implication of Yhwh's roar.

אריה שאג מי לא יירא
אדני יהוה דבר מי לא ינבא

[8] A lion roars, who does not fear?
 The Lord Yhwh speaks, who does not prophesy?

In the words of Derrida, "it is as though, through the maw of the untamable beast, a figure of the sovereign were to appear."[72] In Amos 3:8, the ambiguity of 1:2 and 3:4 briefly dissipates as the prophet brings the figures of lion and deity together in two lines of well-balanced prophetic poetry. The root שאג is repeated once more, this time paired with דבר and, as a result, harkens back to 3:1: "Hear this word (דבר) that Yhwh has spoken (דבר) against you, O children of Israel." While the comparison

---

71. Lundbom, "The Lion," 73.
72. Derrida, *The Beast*, 18.

here is most obviously between the two responses to the utterances of the lion and Yhwh (i.e., when a lion roars the response is fear and when Yhwh speaks the response is prophecy), the verse also creates a connection between שאג and ירא. In 3:4, the lion's roar was an indication of its triumph over its prey—one imagines its bloodied teeth opening to release the chilling sound. This is the image of the lion as predator, it is one that evokes both power and threat, rightly inspiring fear in the hearer, animal and human-animal alike.

Perhaps, by force of lexical collocation, the pairing of the two verbs in this case also implies the rightfulness of fear in response to the sound of שאג elsewhere in the book, namely in 1:2, where it is Yhwh that roars. If so, it is interesting that this verse is the only place in Amos where the root ירא occurs, particularly since Amos is a book filled with the threat of Yhwh's vengeance and little hope of escape. The rhetorical force of the questions in this chapter pushes to the conclusion that it is impossible not to fear the lion's roar and at least suggests that such a reaction is appropriate for Yhwh's roar as well; why, then, does Israel not fear the beastly sovereign that emerges here? Perhaps, as 9:10 claims, the people of Israel have become complacent in the presence of Yhwh and have thus lost the fear that ought to have kept them within the bounds of Yhwh's law. As a result, the reader is perhaps no longer surprised to find that the emergent question of 3:4—is Yhwh also devouring Yhwh's prey?—is answered in the affirmative by 3:12.

כה אמר יהוה
כאשר יציל הרעה מפי הארי שתי כרעים או בדל־אזן
כן ינצלו בני ישראל הישבים בשמרון בפאת מטה ובדמשק ערש

12 Thus Yhwh says:
Just as the shepherd pulls from the mouth of a lion two legs or the lobe of an ear,
so shall the children of Israel escape, those who sit in Samaria on the edge of a bed[73] and on the silk[74] of a couch.

73. The word פאה only occurs here in the book of Amos. In this context, *HALOT* suggests the meaning (for the whole phrase), "the splendor of a couch" (3:908). However, the word more commonly means an edge or a corner, occurring 85 times elsewhere in the HB. If it has a different meaning in this case, it would only carry that sense here. Thus, the weight of the evidence pushes against such a reading. In contrast, BDB suggests, "the corner of a divan" (802).

74. For the *hapax* דמשק, *HALOT* suggests "damask, fine silk fabric," with the possible Arabic cognate, *dimaqs*. In contrast, the LXX has Damascus, which could be achieved here with a simple repointing. However, there are enough differences

Here is the final reference to the lion in ch. 3, and a conclusive answer to any question about Yhwh's prey. While aspects of the verse are notoriously difficult to translate (see the notes), the sense of v. 12b is sufficiently illuminated by v. 12a, providing confidence in interpretation. The verse opens with a new image of the lion, this time with its mouth full, rather than open in full roar. This lion, too, has caught its prey (compare with 3:4), identified as having been among a shepherd's flock. The picture is a vivid one, illustrating the impossibility of escaping the lion's jaws. For, despite the possibility of translating נצל as "to save," it is obvious that what is rescued from the lion's mouth is not the life of the lamb—only dismembered parts of its lifeless body remain.

With horror, then, the following line reveals the identity of Yhwh's prey: the people of Samaria. Here the verb נצל is used a second time, ironically, to describe what will be left of Israel when Yhwh is finished Yhwh's meal—like the lamb, the people of Samaria will not escape with their lives. Notably, the repeated ב of the final line in the verse is frequently translated "with," so the NRSV: "so shall the people who live in Samaria be rescued, *with* the corner of a couch and part of a bed."[75] However, this misses the point of the preceding image—it is not that the lamb escapes with a piece of its ear and two of its legs, but that the lamb does not escape at all. Instead, the repeated use of ב indicates location, where those who sit in Samaria are to be found. Perhaps these are the wealthy of Amos 6:4, who rest easy on beds of ivory and recline on couches. Regardless of precise identity, the point here is that Israel will not escape being consumed by Yhwh—not that some will flee carrying parts of a bed and couch.[76] This impossibility of escape is further illustrated by the final reference to a lion in the book of Amos, 5:19-20's description of the Day of Yhwh.

---

between the LXX and the MT in this case to suggest a different *Vorlage* or a very free translation. Further, the repetition of ערש in 6:4 pushes against following the LXX, which does not share the link between the verses. With as much confidence as the limited evidence allows, I have followed *HALOT* in translating "silk," perhaps reflecting the opulence of the wealthy of Samaria also highlighted in ch. 6. Ultimately, however, this word does not dramatically impact the sense of the passage.

75. My emphasis.

76. Further, it makes little sense to think that, in the face of utter destruction, the people of Israel would choose to take with them the items described here (the edge of a couch or the silk from a bed); rather, we might expect other things to be a priority, such as provisions and loved ones. Thus, in both cases the ב is locative, indicating the locations in which the Samarians are sitting (so, see Duane A. Garrett, *Amos: A Handbook on the Hebrew Text*, Baylor Handbook on the Hebrew Bible [Waco: Baylor University Press, 2008], 98–9).

Amos 5:18-20

Amos 5:18-20 directly follows the funeral dirge at the center of the book of Amos (5:1-17).[77] Introduced by the particle, הוי ("woe"), the verses comprise a distinct unit within the rest of the chapter, as is further illustrated by the inclusio created by the repetition of יום יהוה and the nouns חשך and אור. Despite its brevity, the passage is one of the most debated in the book, in large part due to disagreements concerning the significance and origin of the Day of Yhwh motif in the HB broadly.[78] Such conversations are further incited by the possibility that this oracle in Amos dates to the eighth century BCE, suggesting that other references to the Day of the Lord in the prophetic literature may be dependent on it.[79] Despite this, the rhetorical impact of the verses within the book of Amos can be ascertained, especially as it picks up on thematic elements present elsewhere, such as a day of judgment, dramatic reversals, entrapment, and animal imagery, notably, the lion.

הוי המתאום את־יום יהוה
למה־זה לכם יום יהוה הוא־חשך ולא־אור
כאשר ינוס איש מפני הארי ופנעו הדב
ובא הבית וסמך ידו על־הקיר ונשכו הנחש
הלא־חשך יום יהוה
ולא־אור ואפל ולא־נגה לו

[5:18] Woe to those who wish for the Day of Yhwh
    Why do you want the Day of Yhwh for yourselves? It is darkness
    and not light.
[19] As though someone fled from the lion and the bear met him
Or entered the house and laid his hand on the wall and the snake bit him.
[20] Is not the Day of Yhwh darkness and no light?
    And gloom without brightness in it?

Within book of Amos, the phrase, יום יהוה is used only here, in vv. 18 and 20. However, a marked day is discussed in 2:16; 8:3, 9, 13; and 9:11.[80] In each case, the phrase "in that day," ביום־ההוא, is used. Further, a day of accounting is mentioned in 3:14 and an evil day in 6:3 (cf. 3:6).

---

77. Eidevall, *Amos*, 152.

78. Anderson and Freedman, *Amos*, 521–2; Shalom M. Paul, *Amos*, Hermeneia (Minneapolis: Fortress, 1991), 183–6; and Eidevall, *Amos*, 164.

79. Eidevall, *Amos*, 163.

80. The day mentioned in ch. 8 of Amos has the strongest connections to the Day of Yhwh in Amos 5, given its assertion that such a day will be one when light will be darkened.

All, except 9:11, refer to a day of Yhwh's visitation for violence and punishment. The frequency of such a day, named explicitly here at the center of the book and at the end of Israel's funeral dirge, suggests that the book can be understood as being structured around a day of Yhwh's visitation for vengeance, named here as the Day of Yhwh.[81]

Despite the consistency with which the book refers to a day of impending demise, the rhetoric of the Amos 5 suggests Amos's earliest audience may have anticipated the opposite. The oracle thus picks up a theme by now common in Amos: reversed expectations. This theme was already illustrated in 1:2 and 3:12's inversion of pastoral depictions of Yhwh, where Yhwh hunts the people as lion rather than acting as shepherd. Eidevall points to the question in v. 18b as "decidedly contextual and relational," asking not only what the Day of Yhwh will be like in general, but what it will be like for *you*—Amos's addressees.[82] Given this, it seems likely that those who received the oracle thought that the day would be positive (light), not negative (darkness and gloom), as Amos emphasizes. This does not preclude, however, the possibility that others may experience the day differently depending on their position in relation to Yhwh and Yhwh's day (so, 9:11).

Still, given Israel's current position—in front of the lion-God and hunted as prey—v. 19's depiction of the inevitability of their being trapped by Yhwh's vengeance accords with the rest of the book. This sense of entrapment, not dissimilar to that evoked in Amos 3:3-8's set of rhetorical questions (although, by different literary means), is especially evident in that the protagonist is attacked just as he "begins to relax, since he feels secure in his home."[83] So, miraculously, the man has outrun a lion and dodged a bear, only to fall victim to a snake bite at home. The verse contains, then, not merely a sequence of horrifying events, but a set of encounters that successively escalate the implied terror.[84]

Finally, and to conclude our tour through Amos's beastly images of the divine sovereign, v. 19 includes a final lion figure. Unlike previous examples, the short story included in Amos 5:19 is not typically understood to have metaphorical undertones—that is, the lion here is not

---

81. Though, of course, the book's addition at the end of ch. 9, allows for the possibility of an alternative kind of day; see below.

82. Eidevall, *Amos*, 164.

83. Ibid., 165.

84. Aulikki Nahkola, "Amos Animalizing: Lion, Bear and Snake in Amos 5:19," in *Aspects of Amos: Exegesis and Interpretation*, ed. Anselm C. Hagedorn and Andrew Mein, LHBOTS 536 (London: Bloomsbury T&T Clark, 2011), 83–104 (84).

thought to refer to Yhwh.[85] Rather, the images in question are considered naturalistic, drawn from the life of the Israelite pastoralist, even if representing less common occurrences than their usage in Israelite literature may suggest.[86] Still, the framing of the book as a whole, with its evocative images of Yhwh roaring, and the direct connection between Yhwh and the lion in 3:8, allows for at least the possibility that Yhwh could be in view here. So too the use of the definite article in this case, הארי, "the lion," rather than the indefinite, "a lion," points backward in the text, urging the reader to consider which lion is in question. Perhaps, together with ch. 3, we may read here, "so an Israelite tries to flee the lion-God, he will only meet the bear.[87] Has he still managed to escape? No matter, the snake will find him.[88] For, "not one of them will flee a runaway; not one of them will escape a survivor" (לא־ינוס להם נס ולא־ימלט להם פליט, Amos 9:1).

The Lawlessness of God:
An Illustration in Amos 1:3–2:16

Amos's presentation of Yhwh as the lion-God, and the beastly depiction of sovereignty contained therein, does not, on its own, necessitate the conclusion that the book presents an image of Yhwh that is outside

85. For example, Eidevall, *Amos*, 165; and Paul, *Amos*, 185–6.

86. As Aulikki Nahkola states, based on the combined evidence of zooarchaeology and contemporary zoology, "such incidents loomed large in Israel's experience, but actual encounters with lions or bears, or fatal encounters with snakes, were very rare and exceptional" (Nahkola, "Amos Animalizing," 103).

87. The figure of the bear, and especially the she-bear robbed of her young, is nearly always a threatening image in the HB—for example, David must protect the flock from bears and lions, just as Yhwh must protect David (1 Sam. 17:34, 37); warriors may be enraged like a bear (1 Sam. 17:8); bears may kill human children (2 Kgs 2:24); and a wicked ruler may be like a roaring lion or charging bear coming against the poor (Prov. 28:15). Though less common than the lion, Yhwh may also be depicted as a bear in punishing Israel. So in Hos. 13:8 Yhwh will, "fall upon them like a bear robbed of her cubs and tear open the covering of their hearts" (NRSV) and in Lam. 3:10 God is "a bear lying in wait for me, a lion in hiding" (NRSV). Only in Isaiah does the bear take on a positive connotation, as a symbol of peace in Isa. 11:7 and as an image of those who long for justice in 59:11.

88. The word pair, נשך and נחש occurs twice in Amos, here and in 9:3, where the snake is a Sea Serpent and the implication is that, even if Israel tries to flee and hide at the bottom of the sea, Yhwh will see them and tell the Sea Serpent to bite them. While, unlike with the bear and lion, Yhwh is not depicted as a snake in the HB, the two words also come together in the description of Israel's punishment during the wilderness wanderings (Num. 21:6, 9) and in Jer. 8:1.

the bounds of the law—and, thus, whose justice cannot be questioned. While the image does push in this direction, especially given hints of the lawlessness of lions elsewhere in the HB, it is better demonstrated by a final illustration in Amos 1:3–2:16.[89]

Directly following the lion-God's roar in 1:2, Amos 1:3–2:16 consists of a series of oracles against the nations, building to a climactic finish in the oracle against Israel, that demonstrate Yhwh's political sovereignty. The section is carefully constructed, organized by the refrain "Thus says Yhwh: Concerning the three crimes[90] of [insert nation], and concerning four, I will not remove it," and other leitmotif, such as fire (אש) and, fortifications (such as the city wall, חומה, and citadel, ארמון). Each unit within the whole contains: (1) the opening declaration of Yhwh's speech; (2) the fixed refrain (see above); (3) the accusation, always initially constructed with an infinitive construct and pronominal suffix following the preposition, על; (4) the punishment, usually Yhwh's sending of fire against the city's fortifications; and (5) the colophon, "Yhwh says."

Still, the symmetry is not perfect. The oracles vary in length, with some extending the charges and others lengthening the explanation of punishment.[91] The oracle against Israel is the most distinct of the eight units, and lacks both the fire motif and the colophon; it is also the longest unit. Further, while the first six units are primarily concerned with the brutalities of warfare in the ancient world (for example, the forced migrations of

---

89. See, e.g., Zeph. 3:3, where the officials of Jerusalem are described as lion-like in their rebellious behavior—they are like lions who listen to no one. In this case, the lion is outside the law, unrestrained even by the divine command.

90. The noun פשע suggests a crime, rebellion, or violation, one which may concern people or property and creates a breach between the offender and God or the community (*HALOT* 3:981). The noun occurs ten times in Amos (1:3, 6, 9, 11, 13; 2:1, 4, 6; 3:14; 5:12) and the root twice in its verbal form (both in 4:4). Its concentration in chs. 1 and 2, paired with its formulaic use, is one feature that ties these two chapters together as a unit. The root occurs elsewhere in the Twelve at Hos. 7:13; 8:1; 14:9; Mic. 1:5 (×2), 13; 3:8; 6:7; 7:18; and Zeph. 3:11. In each case, the one who commits the crime is Israel or Judah. In Hos 8:1, Torah and covenant violation are mentioned specifically. In the Twelve, then, the usage with reference to other nations is unique. Indeed, its usage elsewhere in the HB is overwhelmingly with reference to Israel or Judah's transgressions against YHWH. It rarely refers to a people other than YHWH's own; where it does, it occurs within the context of political relationships between nations. So, for example, in 2 Kgs 3:7, Moab, who has been paying tribute to Israel, revolts and King Jehoram of Israel musters troops and summons Judah to go into battle and subdue Moab.

91. Eidevall, *Amos*, 101.

people groups or the slaughtering of pregnant women), the oracles against Judah and Israel are concerned with Torah obedience and mistreatment of the vulnerable, respectively.

The passage is perhaps best described as heightened direct speech, where the repetition of formulaic elements may even be reflective of an early, oral history (although there can be no doubt that the passage has since been redacted for literary presentation).[92] Thus, the two chapters blend features of prose and poetry, where the repetition and thematic elements lend the text a rhythm akin to poetry, but the limited use of parallelism and the consistent inclusion of prose particles lend it affinity with prose texts. As the passage progresses, and the units get longer, the features of poetry become more pronounced so that the final lines of the oracle against Israel are marked by terseness and a proliferation of parallelism. This, together with the length and thematic shifts of the final oracle suggest that the interpretive weight ought to be placed there. Further, the placement of these features at the end of the passage, together with their thematic ties to the remainder of the book, indicate that they also serve to bridge from the oracles against the nations to the proclamations against Israel in chs 3 and 4.

Still, 1:3–2:3 is significant in its placement before the oracles against Judah and Israel. Their focus is on the violations of Israel's neighbors' conduct in war, leading some scholars to call them war crimes.[93] However, as Nili Wazana has demonstrated, no such standard has been preserved from the ancient Near East.[94] Indeed, little to no explanation of the motive behind these acts is given—with the only exception being that of Ammon, who is said to have split in two pregnant women in order to expand their territory (1:13). Given this, it is difficult to claim that Amos's audience would have recognized these acts as the heinous crimes implied by some commentators—indeed, several can be shown to be common practices of ancient warfare.[95]

Taken together, the lack of a clear historical referent suggests that the answer to the question of what law the nations violate must be found

---

92. On the passage's oral features, see Anderson and Freedman, *Amos*, 214; on its redactional layers, see Eidevall, *Amos*, 91–120.

93. For example, see Nili Wazana, "'War Crimes' in Amos's Oracles against the Nations (Amos 1:3–2:3)," in *Literature as Politics, Politics as Literature: Essays on the Ancient Near East in Honor of Peter Machinist*, ed. D. S. Vanderhooft and A. Winitzer (Winona Lake: Eisenbrauns, 2013), 479–501 (480–1).

94. Wazana, "'War Crimes'"

95. Ibid., 480.

within the rhetorical pulse of the passage. For this, we might consider the refrain opening each oracle. On first reading, the pattern, "concerning the three crimes of [insert nation], and concerning four, I will not remove it," appears to mirror the so-called staircase parallelism found in Israel's wisdom tradition (so, Prov. 30:18). However, closer inspection reveals that the literary trope is not fully employed here, since the accusations listed following the refrain rarely, if ever, contain three or four crimes. Most frequently, only one is provided—the oracle against Israel comes the closest, with at least four accusations (although some have argued for as many as ten).[96] In this case, then, rather than referring to a specific set of crimes, the phrase seems to highlight that Yhwh has run out of patience and will no longer refrain from meting out punishment—so, with Anderson, it is possible to read the significance in the total of the two numbers, $3 + 4 = 7$, a symbolic wholeness.[97]

Accordingly, the crimes of the nations should be understood as completely or utterly in violation of the standard by which they are measured. Notably, however, the only standard that the reader has available is that of Yhwh. These are laws set by the divine sovereign, to which all are expected to comply. But what about the lion-God? Must the sovereign operate within the bounds of the law? A careful consideration of the accusations made against the nations demands an answer in the negative.

There are six oracles directed at nations other than Judah and Israel, those against Damascus (1:3-5), Gaza (1:6-8), Tyre (1:9-10), Edom (1:11-12), Ammon (1:13-15), and Moab (2:1-3). Of these, five of the six accusations made by Yhwh against the nation are elsewhere "crimes" committed by Yhwh. These include: (1) threshing a nation, of Gilead in 1:3, of Yhwh in Hab. 3:12; (2) and (3) taking into exile (גלה) and handing over (סגר), of Edom in 1:6 and Tyre in 1:9, of Yhwh in Amos 5:5, 27; 6:7; 7:11, 17 (גלה) and Amos 6:8 (סגר);[98] (4) pursuit with the sword, of Edom in Amos 1:11, of Yhwh in Jer. 29:18, cf. Amos 7:17; and (5) cleaving open pregnant women, of Ammon in 1:13, of Yhwh in Hos. 13:16. In the list, only Moab's crime of burning the king of Edom's bones to lime is not also, elsewhere, an activity of Yhwh. Whatever standard Yhwh holds the nations to here, it does not apply to Yhwh the lion-God, who is, evidently, lawless.

---

96. Eidevall, *Amos*, 102.
97. Anderson and Freedman, *Amos*, 207.
98. And on numerous other occasions in the HB.

Given this, the rhetorical pull of the passage may not be the kind of entrapment commonly described by scholars—namely, that Amos condemns Israel's neighbors for obviously heinous war crimes in order to gain their compliance and to trap them into acknowledging their own guilt.[99] Rather, in recognizing that the crimes of the nation are unknown as legal violations in the ancient world, the prophet's goal may be that of surprise and horror. Amos's audience may find the claims of the oracles against the nations shocking—Yhwh holds other nations accountable even for those practices common to warfare. In comparison, then, the claims of the oracles against Israel are horrifying—how much more will Yhwh punish for violations of covenant agreements known among Yhwh's people? As a result, Amos demonstrates two claims: (1) Yhwh's leonine sovereignty places Yhwh outside the law, so Yhwh cannot be questioned; and (2) Israel (later, Judah) is in the opposite position. Amos's audience must abide by Yhwh's law or risk being consumed—by fire, as in the oracles against the nations, or as prey in the mouth of the lion (3:12).

Facing Lions:
Amos Among the Judahites and Amos in Reception

In the redactional history of the book of Amos, the late additions of 1:2 and 9:11-15 function to frame the content of an earlier collection of oracles, attributed to Amos and originating (in some form) in eighth-century Israel. Further, these additions re-frame Amos's rhetoric of Israel's demise, resulting from Yhwh's predation, for a Judahite audience. For this audience, situated in near proximity to the fall of Jerusalem and subsequent forced migrations imposed by the Babylonian imperial powers, Amos's message became one of potential hope, for the possibility remained that Yhwh would replant them in the land, where they would cultivate and build anew (Amos 9:13-14). Still, such an audience had the perspective of history as a demonstration of Yhwh's voracious appetite. Even more than that, they also knew what it meant to face the lion-God Yhwh, as the use of the image in Lam. 3:10-11 suggests.[100]

Thus, the book of Amos presents its Judahite audience with a choice: face the Lion as prey, or follow the Lion and live. Such an ultimatum is a matter of position, one which Hugh Pyper describes well:

99. Lundbom, "The Lion," 70.
100. "He is a bear lying in wait for me, a lion in hiding; he led me off my way and tore me to pieces; he has made me desolate" (Lam. 3:10-11, NRSV).

> The lion is consistent, the difference depends on where we are standing. Lion
> statues are used across the ancient Near East and beyond as the guardians
> of thresholds, for the very good reason that there is a world of difference in
> being face-to-face with a lion and standing behind it. Once allowed past the
> threat of the lion, one moves into its protection. The lion does not move, the
> spectator moves; but its symbolic force changes.[101]

Amos's rhetoric compels the Judahite audience into action, urging them
to reposition themselves on the safe side of the Lion through social and
religious practices within the bounds determined by, but not restrictive of,
Yhwh alone. Indeed, the use of such imagery within the Twelve Prophets
implies that the Judahite community did understand themselves to be
on the safe side of the threshold—while Yhwh as lion is predator of the
Northern Kingdom in Hosea and Amos, Yhwh as lion is refuge in Joel
4:16's reworking of Amos 1:2.[102]

Notably, Yhwh's character and Yhwh's justice are not in question—nor
is this a matter of right *belief*. Rather, Yhwh as leonine sovereign is a
being-outside-the-law, the ultimate Other and not to be challenged. Given
this, theodicy is not the right problem to pose to the book of Amos. In
fact, both theodicy as the effort to resist the trilemma of divine justice,
goodness, and human suffering and theodicy as defense of the divine may
well be inappropriate responses to the deity presented by Amos.[103] If there
is a theodicy here, it is the dismantling of theodicy altogether. Amos has
constructed a threshold, modelled on the leonine guardians of city gates
in the ancient world. In so doing, the lion-God imaged within the book
has been modeled as a "being-outside-the-law," just like the lion, who is
respecter of no law.[104] Amos's threshold others both Yhwh and the lion.

Still, what of those who continue to seek the Divine in the book of
Amos? I would like to suggest that another turn to Derrida may well prove
a fruitful source of illumination. Derrida alerts us that the beginning of
ethics is often a task of deconstruction, an awakening to the other, both
divine and animal, in order to welcome them with hospitality. Both will
remain "potentially threatening and loving, never determined (or determinable) in advance as one or the other," a reality that implies we may yet
be surprised. In fact, the embeddedness of Amos's vision of the divine
within the systems of power and violence of its time demands the task of

101. Pyper, "The Lion King," 64.

102. See Hos. 5:14 and 13:7-8.

103. Definitions proposed by Dalit Rom-Shiloni ("Theodical Discourse," 57) and
James Crenshaw ("Introduction," 12), respectively.

104. Derrida, *The Beast*, 17, 49.

deconstruction—both of the text and our own systems of oppression.[105] In the end, then, theodicy—as an interrogation of the divine character—may be an inquiry closed off for Amos's implied audience, but questioning the imaging of the Divine remains ever the task of the book's receptive readers.

---

105. S. Tamar Kamionkowski, "The Problem of Violence in Prophetic Literature: Definitions as the Real Problem," in *Religion and Violence: The Biblical Heritage*, ed. David A. Bernat and Jonathan Klawans (Sheffield: Sheffield Phoenix, 2007), 45.

Chapter 6

Theodicy in Micah

Rainer Kessler

Theodicy is a central theme in the prophetic books of the Hebrew Bible. According to the biblical tradition, prophets in the eighth and seventh centuries BCE announced doom to Israel and Judah. They even expected the total destruction of these kingdoms and the decimation and deportation of their populations. It suffices to give some examples. Amos hears YHWH saying to him, "The end has come upon my people Israel" (Amos 8:2).[1] When Isaiah asks how long he has to preach to the people, YHWH answers, "Until cities lie waste without inhabitant, and houses without people, and the land is utterly desolate" (Isa. 6:11). Micah, the third and last example, expects that "Zion shall be ploughed as a field; Jerusalem shall become a heap of ruins, and the mountain of the house a wooded height" (Mic. 3:12).

These announcements provoke questions. Does God's punishment fit the crime denounced by the same prophets? Amos, Isaiah, and Micah in the eighth century, and Jeremiah and Zephaniah in the seventh, tend to think that the offenses that God will punish are committed mainly by the members of the ruling classes in Israel and Judah. Why then does God bring punishment on the whole nation? How can he accept that all are going to perish, including those whom the rulers and the wealthy have been oppressing and exploiting? Is there not a gross disproportion between the sins of the people and God's punishment? All these are questions of theodicy.

---

1. If not indicated otherwise, quotations of biblical texts follow the NRSV. Instead of the traditional translation "the Lord," I write "YHWH."

The prophetic books of the Hebrew Bible in their final form were certainly written down and finished after the destructions of Samaria and Jerusalem in the years 722 and 586 BCE, respectively. Theodicy no longer is a question of announcement and expectation. The prophetic books in their final form have to do with a disaster that is already past. They have to explain why the God who has brought the catastrophe (or at least has not averted it) remains a just and righteous God. This also is the question of theodicy.[2]

When we speak about theodicy in the books of the prophets we must be aware that we are using an anachronism. The word "theodicy" was coined by Gottfried Wilhelm Leibniz in his "Essais de Théodicée," published in 1710. For the philosophical tradition, the "justification of God" was a theoretical problem caused by the existence of evil and suffering on the one hand and the idea of God as a morally good and omnipotent being on the other hand. Philosophers searched for the resolution of the problem by human reason. This is not the approach of ancient extra-biblical and biblical texts. For them, suffering and evil are not an intellectual problem but a crisis of faith that can only be solved from revelation. However, though the ancient authors did not know the term, "theodicy is…an undertaking that did not begin with modern man…"[3] In this broader sense of the word—and knowing that it is an anachronism—we now turn to the problem of theodicy as it is seen in the book of Micah.

1. *Theodicy in Micah 1–3**

For many scholars who follow the historical-critical approach to the biblical literature, the nucleus of the book of Micah is to be found in Micah 1–3 (minus some verses within these chapters, indicated by the

---

2. On theodicy in the prophets in general cf. John Barton, *Ethics in Ancient Israel* (Oxford: Oxford University Press, 2014), 246–56. For some contemporary scholars who deny the existence of prophets of doom in the eighth century BCE the idea of a deity bringing an end to his own people was first conceptualized after the fall of Samaria and Jerusalem, respectively. Theodicy then would stand at the cradle of prophecy as we find it in the biblical books; cf. Uwe Becker, *Jesaja—von der Botschaft zum Buch*, FRLANT 178 (Göttingen: Vandenhoeck & Ruprecht, 1997); Reinhard Gregor Kratz, "Die Worte des Amos von Tekoa," in *Prophetenstudien: Kleine Schriften II*, ed. Reinhard Gregor Kratz (Tübingen: Mohr Siebeck, 2011), 310–43; Björn Corzilius, *Michas Rätsel: Eine Untersuchung zur Kompositionsgeschichte des Michabuches*, BZAW 483 (Berlin: de Gruyter, 2016).

3. James Crenshaw, "Popular Questioning of the Justice of God in Ancient Israel," *ZAW* 82 (1970): 380.

convention to write Mic. 1–3*). The composition includes a theophany directed against Samaria and a poem on the destruction of cities in the Judaean lowlands (ch. 1), oracles directed against the wealthy landowners (ch. 2) and the ruling class of Jerusalem (ch. 3), and the announcement of the total destruction of Jerusalem (3:12). Scholars generally agree that the composition has to do with the campaign of the Assyrian king Sennacherib in 701 BCE against the kingdom of Judah.[4] The Assyrian army conquered the landscape of Judah including all strong cities, walled forts, and smaller villages, and besieged Jerusalem. However, the Assyrians failed to take the city and withdrew for reasons we do not know.

a. *The Function of Micah 1–3**

The function and meaning of the composition of Micah 1–3* depends on when it is dated. Many agree that chs 1–3* are to be assigned to the eighth-century prophet Micah of Moresheth, leaving aside the disputed question whether these chapters are the only text going back to Micah,[5] or whether other parts or even the whole book must be ascribed to the eighth-century prophet.[6] As Micah 1–3* refers to the Assyrian campaign of 701 BCE, it should have been written "about 700 B.C."[7] This dating raises two questions that are crucial for the theme of theodicy. First: When exactly is "about 700 B.C."? Is it before Sennacherib's withdrawal from the siege, or after? The answer has immediate impact on the second question: What is the function and meaning of this collection of sayings?

Weingart's dating is, perhaps, the most precise date in the scholarly literature. According to her, Mic. 1:5–3:12* was written "shortly before the withdrawal of the Assyrians from Jerusalem in the year 701."[8] The function of the text was "to motivate the Jerusalemites to repent."[9] In this case, the text has nothing to do with theodicy. If the text was written as a warning and call to repentance, we must ask, however, how it was read a

4. Cf. Ralph L. Smith, *Micah–Malachi*, WBC 32 (Waco: Word, 1984), 20–1; Rainer Kessler, *Micha*, 2nd ed., HThKAT (Freiburg: Herder, 2000), 102–3; Bruce K. Waltke, *A Commentary on Micah* (Grand Rapids: Eerdmans, 2007), 64, 87.

5. So William McKane, *The Book of Micah: Introduction and Commentary* (Edinburgh: T. & T. Clark, 1998), 7.

6. So Waltke, *A Commentary on Micah*, 8–13.

7. Smith, *Micah–Malachi*, 9.

8. Kristin Weingart, "Wie Samaria so auch Jerusalem: Umfang und Pragmatik einer frühen Micha-Komposition," *VT* 69 (2019): 477 ("kurz vor dem Abzug der Assyrer von Jerusalem im Jahr 701"). Cf. Smith, *Micah–Malachi*, 35 who dates the oracle of 3:12 "probably around 711 B.C. or 701 B.C. at the latest."

9. Ibid. ("die Jerusalemer zur Umkehr zu bewegen").

few months later when Jerusalem was saved and Zion not at all "ploughed as a field" as Micah had announced (Mic. 3:12). Was Micah a false prophet because his prediction did not take place? Or did people believe that the Jerusalemites or at least the king had indeed repented? This understanding would be in line with the words of the elders according to Jer. 26:19 who refer to Mic. 3:12 asking: "Did he (i.e. King Hezekiah) not fear YHWH and entreat the favor of YHWH, and did not YHWH change his mind about the disaster that he had pronounced against them?" But is the call to repentance indeed the original meaning of Micah 1–3*? Is this not, rather, a later interpretation of the author of Jeremiah 26?

The tradition of Micah 1–3* as well as that of Jeremiah 26 is correct in attributing a threat against Jerusalem in the context of the Assyrian campaign of 701 BCE to Micah of Moresheth. This, however, does not necessarily mean that Micah himself wrote these oracles down and brought them in a harmonious composition as we find it in Micah 1–3*. Micah and those who collected and edited his words were in the same position as Isaiah and those who handed down his oracles. Isaiah's message as well as that of Micah were rejected. The king did not follow Isaiah's counsel in the crisis of 734/33 BCE (Isa. 7). The situation of 701 BCE was interpreted as a triumph and not as an ongoing threat to Jerusalem. That is why Isaiah's words were written down to save them as a warning for the future (cf. Isa. 8:16-18). The so-called memoir of Isaiah (Isa. 6–8*) is "the archive of the hidden God" as Friedhelm Hartenstein has named it.[10] The same is true with Micah. Micah's warnings were not heard. Jerusalem was saved but, for those who followed Micah's message, the threat was still hanging over the city. Micah 1–3* is a "memoir" to save Micah's message for the future written by his followers after the events of 701 BCE.[11]

The purpose of such a memoir is justification. In the first place, this is the justification of the prophet. Although he had proclaimed a catastrophe for Jerusalem which had not come, he is not a false prophet. The threat is still present. Another aspect of justification is that of God, that is, theodicy in a literal sense: when the end will come to Zion, in spite of Sennacherib's withdrawal and in accordance with Micah's prediction, it is not because God is unjust or too weak to protect his people and city, but because the people had not listened to the prophet's message.

10. Friedhelm Hartenstein, *Das Archiv des verborgenen Gottes: Studien zur Unheilsprophetie Jesajas und zur Zionstheologie der Psalmen in assyrischer Zeit*, BthSt 74 (Neukirchen-Vluyn: Neukirchener Theologie, 2011).
11. My interpretation in Kessler, *Micha*, 94–7.

b. *The Justification of the Prophet as Justification of YHWH (Micah 2:6-11 and 3:1-12)*

Within the memoir of Micah 1–3*, two texts are dedicated to the justification of the prophet. The first, Mic. 2:6-11, begins with the words of Micah's opponents, probably the greedy land-grabbers of vv. 1-5 to whom he had said that God was devising evil against them. They are convinced that God does not punish his people: "'Do not preach'—thus they preach—'one should not preach of such things; disgrace will not overtake us.'" They ask the prophet: "Is YHWH's patience exhausted? Are these his doings?" (2:6-7a). "The opponents of Micah are questioning the premisses of doom prophecy."[12] The prophet confirms his position by denouncing new offenses of his hearers: not only "householder and house" are their victims (v. 2) but also "the women of my people" and "their young children" (v. 9). Consequently, God's announcement of "evil" for the wealthy wicked (v. 3) is justified. In defending himself against his opponents, the prophet defends God's justice.[13]

Whereas Mic. 2:1-11 is directed against the wealthy land-grabbers, Mic. 3:1-12 turns to the prophets (vv. 5-8) and the ruling class ("the rulers and chiefs," vv. 1, 9) including their ideologists ("the priests and prophets," v. 11). Like the wicked rich, they are convinced that God will not bring any punishment on them; they say, "Surely YHWH is with us! No harm shall come upon us" (3:11). However, according to the prophet, they are not right. Micah is the one who is "filled with power, with the spirit of YHWH, and with justice and might" (Mic. 3:8), and not the rulers and their propagandists. Again, the prophet (or those who formulated the memoir) defends God's justice by defending himself.

c. *"Because of You" (Micah 3:12)*

For the memoir of Micah 1–3*, Micah is the prophet who announces doom in the name of YHWH. Judgment is justified because of the sins of the wealthy land-grabbers, the ruling class of Jerusalem and Judah, including the priests and prophets. However, the catastrophe of Jerusalem will not only touch these perpetrators. Ralph Smith writes: "Micah's description of Jerusalem's fate is a vivid picture of a defeated city. The inhabitants were killed or enslaved and the city was destroyed to prevent future uprisings. The city wall was broken down into rubble, along with the palace and temple, and the entire city was burned. Anything left of value was taken as

12. McKane, *The Book of Micah*, 81.
13. Cf. Crenshaw, "Popular Questioning of the Justice of God in Ancient Israel," 394.

spoil…"[14] This means that YHWH's doom will not only hit those who are responsible but also the victims of their exploitation and oppression. At this point we reach the core of prophetic theodicy. What John Barton says about Amos is also true for Micah: the judgment seems "out of proportion to the sin"; "the moral failings of a small group, those in positions of power, is [*sic*] to bring judgement not simply on them but on the entire nation"; "the rulers were offending God by oppressing the poor," but "the whole nation, including those very same poor people, was about to perish by the hand of God."[15] How can God be justified?

The answer of the memoir consists in only one word (in Hebrew): "*because of you*—Zion shall be ploughed as a field; Jerusalem shall become a heap of ruins, and the mountain of the house a wooded height" (Mic. 3:12). The behavior and actions of the wealthy and powerful are the reason why a foreign conqueror will come and destroy Jerusalem and kill her inhabitants. Is this God's fault? God's punishment—in the words of John Barton, "by the hand of God"—does not mean that he will come like a superman or an extra-terrestrial power who could punish only the guilty and spare their victims. God's punishment according to biblical thinking comes either in the form of natural disaster (earthquake, drought, locusts, etc.) or military defeat with its consequences (destruction, deportation, foreign domination, etc.). In both cases, there is no distinction between culprits and their victims. The biblical prophets thus articulate a position not dissimilar from some modern people. The bombing of German towns at the end of World War II might be interpreted as a punishment of the German people who in their majority had followed Hitler. However, the bombs of the allied forces also killed Jews who were hidden in some attic or back room. The bombing of the isle of Wangerooge in April 1945 cost the lives of 131 German soldiers together with the lives of 121 slave laborers from the Netherlands, Belgium, Poland, France, and Morocco. Perpetrators and victims alike were killed. Is God to blame for this?

Possibly Micah's accusations and announcements were uttered before the events of 701 BCE. Probably the memoir was formulated after the withdrawal of the Assyrian army from Jerusalem. In any case, Micah's words were handed down to the times of Jeremiah and quoted around the events of 586 BCE. During a trial against Jeremiah who had pronounced disaster against the city of Jerusalem and the temple, some of the elders of the land quote the prophet: "Micah of Moresheth, who prophesied during the days of King Hezekiah of Judah, said to all the people of Judah: 'Thus

14. Smith, *Micah–Malachi*, 35.
15. Barton, *Ethics in Ancient Israel*, 248.

says YHWH of hosts, Zion shall be ploughed as a field; Jerusalem shall become a heap of ruins, and the mountain of the house a wooded height'" (Jer. 26:18). After the fall of Jerusalem, the end of the temple and the Davidic dynasty the oracles of Micah and Jeremiah against Jerusalem and the temple had proven right.

Was it enough in this situation to say that God was not responsible for the deeds of the Babylonians who had conquered the city? Could this be the last word? No, it could not. The book of Micah develops two strategies to further deal with the question of theodicy. In the first, the focus is on God's side: oracles of salvation are added to those of judgment. The second throws light on human activities; it has to do with the question of repentance.

2. *Judgment and Salvation in the Book of Micah*

The structure of the book of Micah is characterized by abrupt changes between sections of doom and sections of hope. The memoir of Micah 1–3* is interrupted by words of hope in 2:12-13; chs 1–3* are followed by chs 4–5, which form a close composition of visions and words of salvation. Chapters 6–7 lead from new accusations to the final hope and can be seen as a unit that can be separated into a section of doom (6:1–7:6) and one of hope (7:7-20). Two studies published in 2001 find the overall structure and coherence of the book of Micah in the concepts of "judgment" and "hope"[16] or "judgement" and "salvation."[17]

The majority of scholars understand chs 4–5 as younger than the earliest text of Micah. Micah 4–5 likely were added to the memoir in chs 1–3* after the fall of Jerusalem in 586 BCE. The composition in 4:9–5:3 (4:9–5:4 Eng.) already speaks of the deportation to Babylon and alludes to the end of the Judean kingdom (4:14 [5:1 Eng.]). At the same time, it shifts from catastrophe to new hope: "There (in Babylon) you shall be rescued" (4:10); "I will make your horn iron and your hoofs bronze" (4:13); "from you (Bethlehem) shall come forth for me one who is to rule in Israel" (5:1 [5:2 Eng.]). Whereas this composition may date to the Babylonian epoch, the vision of the nations' pilgrimage to Mount Zion (4:1-5) reflects the Persian ideology of the peoples coming to the king, hewn in stone in the Persepolis reliefs.[18]

---

16. Mignon R. Jacobs, *The Conceptual Coherence of the Book of Micah*, JSOTSup 233 (Sheffield: Sheffield Academic, 2001).

17. Jan A. Wagenaar, *Judgement and Salvation: The Composition and Redaction of Micah 2–5*, VTSup 85 (Leiden: Brill, 2001).

18. See also the post-exilic texts Isa. 60 and Hag. 2.

Reading the book as it stands, however, one must conclude that "judgment or hope," the dominant themes of chs 1–3 and 4–5 respectively, are not alternatives but that both together form the most prominent theme of the book of Micah.[19] The function of the juxtaposition of these chapters is the consolation of the people and the justification of God (the theodicy) after the judgment. YHWH's judgment is directed against the two capitals of the kingdoms of Israel and Judah. The fact that the foundations of Samaria, the capital of the northern state of Israel, will be uncovered (1:6) means that the city has come to a permanent end. Though the judgment against Jerusalem is formulated in similar words (3:12), it is not definitive. After the general pause between 3:12 and 4:1, we can perceive Zion as the highest of the mountains and Jerusalem as the center of the world.

In the case of Jerusalem, punishment is not God's last word. This is a theological concept because, in fact, Samaria was rebuilt soon after its destruction. However, for the book of Micah and even the book of the Twelve, where Samaria will never again be mentioned after Mic. 1:6, the former Northern capital has come to an end. Only Jerusalem has a bright future. Marvin Sweeney writes that:

> Micah 4–5 is joined to 3:9–12…by the concern to demonstrate that the previously announced punishment of Jerusalem will lead ultimately to its restoration and exaltation in the midst of the nations as the process of Jerusalem's punishment and purification together with the manifestation of YHWH's sovereignty over the nations takes place.[20]

This quotation contains two elements of theodicy. The second is purification and will be treated in the next section. To grasp the first, we have to look at Sweeney's wording and grammar: he uses future forms, saying that "punishment…*will* lead ultimately to…restoration."

What Micah 4–5 has to say about Jerusalem is not a description of Persian-period reality. "The writer longs for the world to be different than it is and provides a powerful portrait of an alternative reality… The imagery of these chapters serves to create an attractive alternative reality."[21] In prophetic literature, this is one of the most important attitudes

---

19. Cf. Jacobs, *The Conceptual Coherence of the Book of Micah*, 222–3.

20. Marvin A. Sweeney, *The Twelve Prophets: Volume Two*, Berit Olam (Collegeville: Liturgical, 2000), 376.

21. Julia M. O'Brien, *Micah*, Wisdom Commentary 37 (Collegeville: Liturgical, 2015), 39–40.

towards theodicy. According to prophecies of doom, there is a strict correlation between conduct and punishment. This strict correlation is broken
when prophets affirm the grace of God despite the sins and rebellion of
the people. God is a just deity not only in that he punishes trespasses, but
also in that he opens new perspectives after the punishment. In the end,
God's will to forgive triumphs over his will to punish. One might criticize
this as "escaping to the safe position of expectancy,"[22] as "the surrender of
the present moment in favor of future rectification... The further into the
future...this expected deliverance is projected, the safer the theodicy..."[23]
However, it has its foundation in the central confession of the Torah that
YHWH is "a God merciful and gracious, slow to anger, and abounding in
steadfast love and faithfulness, keeping steadfast love for the thousandth
generation, forgiving iniquity and transgression and sin, yet by no means
clearing the guilty..." (Exod. 34:6-7). It is not by chance that the last
words of the book of Micah allude to this confession (Mic. 7:18-20).

This form of theodicy is "hoping against hope" in much the same way
that Paul characterizes Abraham's faith (Rom. 4:18). But it is not the only
form of theodicy in the second half of the book of Micah.

3. *Purification, Repentance, and Theodicy*

To give hope a foundation and so to bring God's history with Zion to a
successful conclusion, two actions were necessary in the eyes of those
who crafted the final form of the book of Micah in the Persian period. The
first is an action by God: he will purify his people. The second must be
fulfilled by the people themselves: repentance.

a. *Israel's Purification (Mic. 5:9-14 [Eng. 5:10-15])*

Micah 4–5 as it stands now points to the distant future. The chapters are
framed by two units that deal with this future, introduced by "And it will
come about, in the end of the days" (4:1) and by "And it will happen in that
day" (5:9 [5:10 Eng.]).[24] The second of these units (5:9-14 [5:10-15 Eng.])

---

22. Crenshaw, "Popular Questioning of the Justice of God in Ancient Israel," 384.

23. James L. Crenshaw, "Introduction: The Shift from Theodicy to Anthropodicy," in *Theodicy in the Old Testament*, ed. James L. Crenshaw, IRT 4 (Philadelphia:
Fortress; London: SPCK, 1983), 7.

24. Translation by Francis I. Andersen and David Noel Freedman, *Micah: A
New Translation with Introduction and Commentar*, AB 24E (New York: Doubleday,
2000), 395, 488.

is about Israel's purification. The one who speaks is YHWH, the addressee is Jacob/Israel in the form of the masculine plural suffix ("your"). "The oracle is essentially an inventory of things that will be 'cut off'."[25] YHWH will "cut off your horses" "and destroy your chariots," he will "cut off the cities of your land and throw down all your strongholds," he will "cut off sorceries from your hand," he will "cut off your images and your pillars," and will "uproot your sacred poles" and "destroy your towns." The objects mentioned stand for the military strength and idolatrous installations and practices of Israel. These are "things that fracture its covenantal relation" with God.[26]

The oracle can be understood as "threat" and "punishment against Judah."[27] It threatens, however, only things that separate Israel from YHWH. When these things have disappeared, Israel will have new access to God. The way will be paved for new hope. Seen in this perspective, the oracle is "a promise in the form of a threat."[28] "…[T]he focus of this unit is the cleansing of the nation."[29] Purification is the prerequisite for Israel's salvation.

According to the book of Micah, God is justified when he punishes his people because of the trespasses of the people. The responsibility for the death of innocent people is not on God's side, it is on the side of the ruling class ("because of you," Mic. 3:12) and, of course, of the military juggernaut of the imperial armies. But this is not the last word: God gives new hope to his people. Hope, however, can only be fulfilled when Israel is purified. It is God himself who cleanses his people by cutting off everything which separates them from him. What now is needed for full restoration is Israel's response: repentance.

b. *Israel's Repentance*

The last chapters of the book of Micah, chs 6–7, are formed by four units. In the center, in units two and three, we find new accusations (Mic. 6:9-16 and 7:1-7). A frame is formed by units one (6:1-8) and four (7:8-20). They have to do with repentance amongst other things. In the first unit, it is repentance in an inadequate form. The last unit begins with true repentance and ends in the hope of God's final forgiving.

25. Andersen and Freedman, *Micah*, 489.
26. Waltke, *A Commentary on Micah*, 331.
27. Cf. O'Brien, *Micah*, 68–70.
28. McKane, *The Book of Micah*, 173.
29. Jacobs, *The Conceptual Coherence of the Book of Micah*, 155.

(1) *False Repentance (Micah 6:1-8)*

The first unit of chs 6–7 begins as a lawsuit. "YHWH has a controversy with his people, and he will contend with Israel" (v. 2). God asks them: "O my people, what have I done to you? In what have I wearied you? Answer me!" (v. 3). The people's answer sounds like repentance. However, what they understand by repentance is absurd, exaggerated, and not corresponding to God's will: "Shall I come before him with burnt-offerings, with calves a year old? Will YHWH be pleased with thousands of rams, with tens of thousands of rivers of oil? Shall I give my firstborn for my transgression, the fruit of my body for the sin of my soul?" (vv. 6-7). This is not repentance; this is a caricature of true repentance.

The prophet's answer to what the people offer is a little theodicy in itself. He says: "He has told you, O mortal, what is good; and what does YHWH require of you but to do justice, and to love kindness, and to walk humbly with your God?" (v. 8). God's will is known to the people and obvious not only to the Israelites but to all humankind (in Hebrew: *'ādām*). God has spoken through the prophets,[30] but also in the Torah and in sapiential tradition.[31] Humans do not have any excuse when they do not follow what God requires from them. They have heard God's instructions. His will is quite simple: doing justice, loving kindness, and walking humbly with God. When the world lacks justice, kindness, and fear of God, this is not God's fault.

As mentioned above, the following units bring new accusations. They are directed against "the city" (6:9), likely Jerusalem,[32] where the wicked collect "treasures of wickedness" and the "wealthy are full of violence" (vv. 10-12). The next pericope is directed in its first part against the ruling class ("the official, the judge, and the powerful," 7:3), but then warns against corruption of all relationships of friends and family: "put no trust in a friend, have no confidence in a loved one" (v. 5); son stands against father, daughter against mother, daughter-in-law against mother-in-law (v. 6). What is missing in society is, in the words of 6:8, justice and kindness. Because humans know how they should live, God is responsible neither for their situation not for the consequences. There remains only one chance: true repentance.

---

30. Andersen and Freedman, *Micah*, 526.
31. Cf. Kessler, *Micha*, 269–70.
32. Cf. O'Brien, *Micah*, 94.

(2) *True Repentance (Micah 7:8-20)*

The last unit of the book of Micah is a composition created for its present position in the book. It alludes to many themes and key words within the whole book. Its main function is theodicy by confession of sin and trust in God's will to pardon and to be faithful and loyal to Israel.[33]

Micah 7:7 is the end of the preceding unit, but in a certain sense the verse is also transitional.[34] The prophet who speaks in the verse already waits "for the God of my salvation," and is sure that "my God will hear me," thus introducing the theme of 7:8-20; v. 7 opens the path for the last section. Micah 7:8-20 is made up of four distinct parts. The first is a confession of sin and trust (vv. 8-10), followed by a prophetic oracle (vv. 11-13) and a prayer (vv. 14-17). The last section is an indirect confession of sin and a hymn praising God for his forgiveness and loyalty. The first and last units are crucial for the question of theodicy.

In vv. 8-10 an unidentified "I" is addressing an enemy. Who is the "I"? Commentators sometimes speak of "the nation"[35] or "Israel."[36] However, the feminine suffix in the enemy's words in v. 10—"Where is YHWH your (fem.) God?"—clearly indicate that it is Zion[37] or (Daughter/Lady) Jerusalem[38] who speaks. She addresses an unnamed enemy who is also personified as a woman ("enemy" in v. 8 is feminine) and whose identity is not revealed. Zion/Jerusalem forbids her enemy to rejoice over her. She has fallen, indeed, and sits in darkness. However, she is convinced that she shall rise, that YHWH will be a light to her and bring her out to the light.

This conviction is grounded in her confession: "I must bear the indignation of YHWH, because I have sinned against him" (v. 9). The Hebrew root for the verb and noun "(to) sin" is a leitmotif in the book of Micah. It appears in prophetic accusations (1:5, 13; 6:13), and the prophet himself is portrayed as the one "to declare to Jacob his transgression and to Israel

---

33. Cf. Kessler, *Micha*, 296–9; Yair Hoffman, "Theodicy and Protest in Micah 7," in *Theodicy and Protest: Jewish and Christian Perspectives*, ed. Beate Ego et al. (Leipzig: Evangelische Verlagsanstalt, 2018), 49.

34. Cf. Smith, *Micah–Malachi*, 58; Mark S. Gignilliat, *Micah*, ITC (London: Bloomsbury T&T Clark, 2019), 221–2.

35. Smith, *Micah–Malachi*, 58.

36. McKane, *The Book of Micah*, 220.

37. Andersen and Freedman, *Micah*, 578.

38. Sweeney, *The Twelve Prophets*, 409; Waltke, *A Commentary on Micah*, 449; O'Brien, *Micah*, 106.

his sin" (3:8). The people themselves also use the word in their inadequate proposal for repentance: "Shall I give my firstborn for my transgression, the fruit of my body for the sin of my soul?" (6:7). But Jacob/Israel were never ready to repent. For the first time in the book it is Zion/Jerusalem who is able openly to confess her sin.[39] By doing this she makes it possible that God's will to forgive and the people's hope of future vindication by YHWH come together.

The indissoluble unity of confession and hope is demonstrated in the last section of Mic. 7:8-20, namely, vv. 18-20, the last words of the whole book. The speaker still is anonymous. It is no longer a feminine personification but a group speaking in the first person plural ("show us mercy," "our iniquities," "our ancestors," vv. 19-20). The last verse identifies them as descendants of Jacob and Abraham; they are the people of Israel represented by those who speak these words in congregation.[40] Their words begin and end with direct address to God, the central verse, however, switches to third-person narrative.

Zion's confession of sin is not repeated, but taken for granted when the people speak of "our iniquities" and "their" or "our sins."[41] They are able to mention their iniquities and sins frankly because they trust in the God who is "pardoning iniquity and passing over the transgressions" (7:18). As mentioned above, 7:18-20 is full of allusions to the creedal affirmation of Exod. 34:5-6.[42] At Mount Sinai God presented himself as "a God (Hebrew: *'ēl*) merciful and gracious, slow to anger and abounding in steadfast love and faithfulness, keeping steadfast love for the thousandth generation, forgiving iniquity and transgression and sin…" The speaker of Mic. 7:18-20 works with this vocabulary, sometimes quoting it directly and sometimes integrating it into the new context (identical words in italics): "Who is a *God* (Hebrew: *'ēl*) like you, *forgiving iniquity* and passing over *the transgression* of the remnant of your possession? He does not retain *his anger* forever, because he delights in showing *steadfast love*. He will show us *mercy* again; he will tread our *iniquities* under foot. You will cast

---

39. Cf. Smith, *Micah–Malachi*, 58.

40. Cf. ibid., 59.

41. The Hebrew suffix is "their," but the ancient versions and some manuscripts have "our"; see the discussion in McKane, *The Book of Micah*, 235, and Andersen and Freedman, *Micah*, 599.

42. Cf. Sweeney, *The Twelve Prophets*, 413; James L. Crenshaw, "Theodicy in the Book of the Twelve," in *Thematic Threads in the Book of the Twelve*, ed. Paul L. Redditt and Aaron Schart, BZAW 325 (Berlin: de Gruyter, 2003), 189–90; Waltke, *A Commentary on Micah*, 462; Gignilliat, *Micah*, 231.

all our *sins* into the depths of the sea. You will show *faithfulness* to Jacob and *steadfast love* to Abraham…"[43]

In Mic. 7:18-20, confession of sin and trust in God's steadfast love and faithfulness are closely joined together. It would be one-sided to say that repentance is the prerequisite for the final reconciliation.[44] It is true that Jerusalem must confess her sins so that YHWH may forgive her. However, it is also true that Jerusalem is only able to repent because she believes in a God who is willing to forgive. Seen this way, God's faithfulness is the prerequisite for the confession of sin. Both are joined together and mutually dependent on each other.[45]

Theodicy in the last unit of Micah has two aspects. The first consists in the confession of the speaker that "he bears YHWH's wrath on account of having sinned against YHWH."[46] By this confession, God is "justified." The other side is the speaker's "confidence that once YHWH hears the facts of the case, justice will be done."[47] God is "justified" because in the end he will bring salvation.

4. *Giving Profile to Theodicy in Micah*

It is worth looking at other prophetic books to better understand the unique profile of theodicy in Micah. It is evident that one strategy of theodicy used in other books is absent in Micah. It can be found, for example, in Amos 9:10, "where a distinction is made between the guilty and innocent and only the former punished."[48] "All the sinners of my people shall die by the sword, who say, 'Evil shall not overtake or meet us'" (Amos 9:10). This is not a distinction made in the original judgment, but an expectation for the future. The original doom makes no difference between sinners and innocent victims. Amos says, "The end has come to my people Israel" (Amos 8:2). This includes all, both perpetrators

43. The translation of Mic. 7:18-20 is mine because the translation of Mic. 7:18-20 in NRSV is not congruent with that of Exod. 34:5-6.

44. This is the interpretation of Hoffman, "Theodicy and Protest in Micah 7," 48: "The idea is that a deep and sincere conviction of the nation that it deserves its punishment, an honest confession justifying God's wrath, will turn the God of Justice into the God of Mercy."

45. To use the words of Hoffman (ibid., quoted in the preceding footnote), "the God of Justice" needs not to "turn into the God of Mercy," he has always been the God of Mercy.

46. Sweeney, *The Twelve Prophets*, 410.

47. Ibid.

48. Crenshaw, "Popular Questioning of the Justice of God in Ancient Israel," 385.

and their victims. However, the end of the book of Amos discusses new perspectives, and here the prerequisite for hope is the distinction between the guilty and innocent. God is justified because, in the future, he will punish only the guilty.

The same strategy is found in the book of Zephaniah. The future according to this book will bring the elimination of the perpetrators; God says, "then I will remove from your midst your proudly exultant ones... I will leave in the midst of you a people humble and lowly...[they] shall do no wrong and utter no lies..." (Zeph. 3:11-13). Obviously, this strategy has no need of confession of sin by the collective Israel/Jacob or Zion/ Jerusalem as we find it in Micah.

What we have in Micah is the idea of purification (5:9-14 [5:10-15 Eng.]). This, however, is the purification of the whole nation and must not be confused with the distinction between the guilty and innocent and the elimination only of the evildoers. Because Micah does not know this distinction, it needs a collective confession of sin. Otherwise God would not be "justified."

5. *Conclusion*

Generally speaking, we find several attitudes towards theodicy in the prophetic literature. The accusations underline that God's punishment is just. The fact that also the innocent must suffer from judgment is not God's fault, but lies in the responsibility of the ruling class and is also due to the cruelty of the foreign armies who execute judgment. Concerning the future, one can distinguish between three devices. The first is the juxtaposition of judgment and salvation in the sense that the future is dominated by hope. The second consists in two acts, one by God and one by the people; God will purify his people, and the people shall answer him by true repentance. The third strategy is the distinction between the guilty and their victims in a future intervention by God.

As mentioned above the third strategy is absent in Micah. The first and second are combined in several ways. The hope of salvation is expressed independently from the motif of repentance; it appears already in chs 4–5 whereas the motif of repentance is restricted to chs 6–7. The motif of purification of the collective stands at the end of the hope-section in chs 4–5, thus introducing the theme of false and true repentance framing chs 6–7. Within the last unit (7:8-20), the aspect of repentance and that of salvation are joined together in a new way. Because of Zion's confession of sin, God's wrath will not last for ever; it is temporary. Zion's confession includes this aspect, saying "I must bear YHWH's indignation, because I have sinned against him, *until* he takes my side and executes judgment for me" (7:9). And the confession of trust by the congregation praises God as the one who "does not retain his anger *for ever*" (7:18). The wrath of God is understood "to be remedial and so temporary, and not penal and so final."[49]

Through all these strategies, God is "justified." However, one has to write the word "justified" with quotation marks. "Justification of God" is a theological and philosophical undertaking to find a rational solution to the problem of the coexistence of evil and an omnipotent God of justice. The biblical texts do not discuss the question on a theoretical level; in the words of Yair Hoffman, in the prophetic literature and the Psalms, the problem is "national and personal rather than theoretical-philosophical."[50] For the prophets, the question is whether judgment on Israel and Judah is justified and whether God's people have a future beyond destruction and exile. Their answer is affirmative, but not on a rational level. Nearly ninety years ago, Walther Eichrodt wrote, "prophecy's answer…is not to formulate a theory…but to point still more earnestly to the decisive deed of the divine judge and redeemer."[51]

Purification, confession of sin, and above all the hope of salvation are the main elements of theodicy in Micah. They are no theoretical concepts. Micah's approach to theodicy is pragmatic, not philosophic or theological.[52]

---

49. Waltke, *A Commentary on Micah*, 453.

50. Hoffman, "Theodicy and Protest in Micah 7," 48.

51. Walther Eichrodt, "Faith in Providence and Theodicy in the Old Testament," trans. Laurence L. Welborn, in Crenshaw (ed.), *Theodicy in the Old Testament*, 28. Originally Walther Eichrodt, "Vorsehungsglaube und Theodizee im Alten Testament," in *Festschrift Otto Procksch zum sechzigssten Geburtstag am 9. August 1934*, ed. Albrecht Alt (Leipzig: A. Deichert'sche Verlangsbuchhandlung/J. C. Hinrich'sche Buchhandlung, 1934), 58: "So ist die Antwort des Prophetismus…nicht die Ausbildung einer Theorie…sondern der umso ernstere Hinweis auf die entscheidende Tat des göttlichen Richters und Erlösers."

52. Cf. Hoffman, "Theodicy and Protest in Micah 7," 51.

Chapter 7

"AH, ASSYRIA IS NO MORE!"
RETRIBUTION, THEODICY, AND HOPE IN NAHUM*

Daniel C. Timmer

Despite the clear reasons it gives for YHWH's punishment of Assyria, the book of Nahum presents several challenges for theodicy, especially the potentially inconsistent punishment of violence with more violence and the apparently blunt punishment of an entire empire for offenses committed by a part of its population. This chapter develops an inductive theodicy of Nahum by exploring the book's characterizations and condemnations of the empire, the moral bases it gives for YHWH's response to her imperialism, and the presuppositions that support its affirmation that divine violence against Assyria is both morally acceptable and desirable.

At first glance, Nahum might not seem fertile territory for a study of theodicy. After all, who (apart from an Assyrian in the seventh century) would object to its message that YHWH will soon do away with an empire that violently, relentlessly, and successfully subjugated the entire ancient Near East for its own benefit? Upon reflection, however, Nahum's message contains several elements that repay closer examination. In particular, readers may wonder how God can justifiably punish violence with more violence,[1] or how punishing an

* I am thankful for the generous support of the Priscilla and Stanford Reid Trust, which made possible the presentation of an earlier draft of this study at the 2016 Institute for Biblical Research session in San Antonio.
  1. Posed by Edward Ball, "'When the Towers Fall': Interpreting Nahum as Christian Scripture," in *In Search of True Wisdom: Essays in Old Testament Interpretation in Honour of Ronald E. Clements*, ed. E. Ball, JSOTSup 300 (Sheffield: Sheffield Academic, 1999), 211–30 (229).

entire empire for the beliefs and actions of its leaders and elites is consistent with justice.[2]

In this study, I will explore these two questions in relation to theodicy, tracing the theme of divine justice first in the book's presentation of Judah, then at more length in its extended critique of the Neo-Assyrian Empire.[3] Since my approach is descriptive, the study will analyze the beliefs and reasoning that the Book of Nahum uses to present God's retributive justice as both just and good news for those who trust in him. This will be done with an eye to the two questions evoked above, but will occasionally consider other challenges to Nahum's theodicy, or consider how Nahum's perspective compares with those found in other writings of the Hebrew Bible/Old Testament. I will conclude by reflecting briefly on some epistemological and theological aspects of developing a theodicy of Nahum.

For the purposes of our discussion, theodicy involves several key elements: belief in one God, who is all-powerful and absolutely good, and belief that evil and human suffering are real but not (at least not necessarily and intrinsically) good.[4] I also assume the significance, as well as

---

2. Francisco O. Garcia-Treto, "The Book of Nahum," *NIB* 7:592–617 (596–7).

3. The question of why Nineveh is not called to repent in Nahum seems to be answered, especially in the context of the Book of the Twelve, by Jonah, which presents its repentance as real but short-lived. This makes clear that YHWH's destruction of Assyria in Nahum is not impulsive. See Daniel C. Timmer, *A Compassionate and Gracious God: Mission, Salvation, and Spirituality in Jonah*, NSBT 26 (Leicester: Apollos, 2011), 115, 131; Jerome F. D. Creach, *Violence in Scripture*, Interpretation (Louisville: Westminster John Knox, 2013), 171–3; and Aaron Schart, "The Jonah-Narrative within the Book of the Twelve," in *Perspectives on the Formation of the Book of the Twelve: Methodological Foundations—Redactional Processes—Historical Insights*, ed. R. Albertz, J. Nogalski, and J. Wöhrle, BZAW 433 (Berlin: de Gruyter, 2012), 109–28.

4. Following Ronald M. Green, "Theodicy," in *The Encyclopedia of Religion*, ed. M. Eliade, 16 vols (New York: Macmillan, 1987), 14:431, cited in A. Laato and J. C. de Moor, "Introduction," in *Theodicy in the World of the Bible*, ed. A. Laato and J. C. de Moor (Leiden: Brill, 2003), x. Nahum's message is consistent with the assumption that God is the source and standard of good; cf. Dennis P. McCann, "Good, The," in *Dictionary of Scripture and Ethics*, ed. J. B. Green (Grand Rapids: Baker Academic, 2011), 333. As to whether human suffering is "good," various distinctions (extrinsic or intrinsic, teleological or absolute, whole versus part, etc.) must be considered, and I cannot settle the question here; cf. Nicholas Dent, "Good," in *The Oxford Companion to Philosophy*, ed. T. Honderich (Oxford: Oxford University Press, 1995), 322. One should note, amid the biblical data, Micah's explanation of human good as including both justice and merciful faithfulness (Mic. 6:8) and the psalmist's confession that at

the limits, of human agency[5] and the determinative nature of God's will and actions. Likewise, I take for granted that human beings can and do sin, but that there is not necessarily an immediate, observable punishment for such behavior.[6] These points are important facets of a biblical theodicy in their own right, and they are either assumed or affirmed by the author of Nahum.[7]

Finally, I will approach the book of Nahum as a unified work not because it presents no conceptual, literary, or historical quandaries or tensions, but because these features are outweighed by others that hold the book together.[8] The presupposition of a literary work's possible unity is an indispensable starting point for diachronic/compositional approaches as well as others.[9] The elements of Nahum that contribute to its theodicy interrelate to such a degree that, for our purposes, the work can be treated as a whole.[10] Issues of its composition, such as there are, do not affect the following discussion.

least the outcome of his suffering was good (Ps. 119:71); cf. also, in the New Testament, Rom. 8:35-37. Nahum uses the term טוב twice, once as descriptive of God (1:7) and once to express the perceived attractiveness of the Assyrian Empire as an economic partner (3:4).

5. Daniel Castelo, *Theological Theodicy*, Cascade Companions 14 (Cascade: Wipf & Stock, 2012), 60.

6. Human beings consistently fail to conform perfectly to the divine will from Gen. 3 onward; cf. Rolf Rendtorff, *The Canonical Hebrew Bible: A Theology of the Old Testament*, trans. D. E. Orton, Tools for Biblical Studies 7 (Leiderdorp: Deo, 2005), 15–16.

7. Laato and de Moor, "Introduction," xxix–xxx, identify six distinct theodicies that all accept these four basic premises (one good, all-powerful God and the reality of human suffering and evil).

8. Francis Landy, "Three Sides of a Coin: In Conversation with Ben Zvi and Nogalski, *Two Sides of a Coin*," *JHS* 10 (2010): 14, argues that a text is coherent as long as its "centripetal tendencies overwhelm centrifugal ones."

9. Robert A. Dooley and Stephen H. Levinsohn, *Analyzing Discourse: A Manual of Basic Concepts* (Dallas: SIL International, 2001), 11; John Barton, "Reading Texts Holistically: The Foundation of Biblical Criticism," in *Congress Volume Ljubljana 2007*, ed. André Lemaire, VTSup 133 (Leiden: Brill, 2010), 367–80, esp. 371.

10. Representative arguments in favor of separating the hymn in 1:2-8 from the rest of the book can be found in Anselm Hagedorn, *Die Anderen im Spiegel: Israels Auseinandersetzung mit den Völkern in den Büchern Nahum, Zefanja, Obadja und Joel*, BZAW 414 (Berlin: de Gruyter, 2011), 72–80.

Theodicy and Judah

Before turning to our main focus, it is worth noting that Nahum explains Assyria's mistreatment of Judah in terms of YHWH's "affliction" of his people. In 1:12-13, in his first address to Judah, YHWH announces a paradigm shift from punishment to deliverance: "although I have afflicted you, I will no longer afflict you. Now I will break his yoke-bar off you, and I will remove his shackles."[11] The contrast between the past and future is apparent in the shift from a perfective to an imperfective verb in 1:12 and further emphasized by the adverb "no longer" and the transitional "now" that separates the era of servitude and oppression under Assyria from one of liberty and freedom from its yoke (1:13).[12]

Here it is the assertion that YHWH has "afflicted" Judah in the past, with the Piel of עָנָה, that interests us. This root is used frequently (but not exclusively) to correlate YHWH's covenantal discipline with Israel's behavior (cf. 1 Kgs 11:39; Pss 88:7; 90:15; 107:17; Isa. 64:12; Lam. 3:33), and the punitive sense is required by the immediate and larger contexts of Nahum. The Sinai covenant clearly connected Judah's behavior to its weal or woe, and Assyria's suzerainty over Israel and then Judah is nearly a paraphrase of various covenant curses (cf. Deut. 28:25, 30, 32-33, 45-52). The book of Kings corroborates this interpretation, so we can conclude that Nah. 1:12 implicitly affirms YHWH's determinative role in punishing Judah for covenantal infractions.

If we define violence as "action producing bodily or psychological harm,"[13] it is immediately clear that YHWH's punishment of Israel and Judah by means of Assyria was violent. To note only one example, the fall of the Judean city of Lachish in 701 was part of a far-ranging Assyrian

---

11. All translations are my own.

12. On the frequent use of imperfective forms for future tense in discourse, see Christo H. J. van der Merwe, Jacobus A. Naudé, and Jan H. Kroeze, *A Biblical Hebrew Reference Grammar*, 2nd ed. (London: Bloomsbury T&T Clark, 2017), 161. On the aspectual features of imperfective forms, see Tania Notarius, "Aspectual Markers," in *Encyclopedia of Hebrew Language and Linguistics*, ed. G. Khan, 4 vols (Leiden: Brill, 2013), 1:218–20.

13. Ziony Zevit limits the referent to physical harm, "The Search for Violence in Israelite Culture and in the Bible," in *Religion and Violence: The Biblical Heritage*, ed. D. A. Bernat and J. Klawans (Sheffield: Sheffield Phoenix, 2007), 16. Contrariwise, James K. Wellman and Kyoko Tokuno see harm as including emotional injury, and therefore include non-physical (e.g., verbal) acts; "Is Religious Violence Inevitable?" *JSSR* 43 (2004): 291–6 (295).

campaign that destroyed the entire southern portion of Judah.[14] The Assyrian reliefs of the attack on Lachish, while surely using common tropes to display the siege and conquest of the city, probably represent quite faithfully the scope and degree of the violence that accompanied the Assyrian victory, including the flaying and impalement of captured Judeans.[15]

It is therefore striking that Nahum nowhere alleges that YHWH has mistreated Judah by punishing her by means of Assyria.[16] Even though the book presents deliverance from final judgment by YHWH as a manifestation of his "goodness" (1:7), nowhere does it imply that Judah's punishment by YHWH was therefore not "good" or was on par with Assyria's "evil." The diametrically opposed understandings of Assyria's and YHWH's involvement in the same historical events suggests that, for the book's author(s), violence can be morally good or evil depending on who exercises it, and how and why it is exercised.

The situation is quite different with respect to Assyria, the immediate agent of YHWH's punishment of Judah. Nahum affirms repeatedly that Assyria is morally culpable, most pointedly by describing its treatment of the surrounding nations as "evil" (3:19). We will now turn to this issue of Nahum's theodicy with respect to Assyria.

Theodicy and Assyria

Nahum presents most of YHWH's interventions against Assyria as primarily retributive, giving the guilty offender a proportionate punishment

---

14. Ephraim Stern, *Archaeology of the Land of the Bible: Vol. 2, The Assyrian, Babylonian, and Persian Periods (732–332 B.C.E.)*, ABRL (New York: Doubleday, 2001), 130.

15. Cf. David Ussishkin, "The 'Lachish Reliefs' and the City of Lachish," *IEJ* 30 (1980): 174–95. Part of the relief can be seen on the website of the British Museum, https://www.britishmuseum.org/collection/object/W_1856-0909-14_2.

16. The assumption that only God can exercise violence in a way that is good without qualification, and the implication that make divine justice and goodness are consistent with one another, accord with the Hebrew Bible/Old Testament's consistent affirmation that divine goodness and justice are linked and compatible, and so are suitable hermeneutical presuppositions for understanding Nahum's treatment of violence. Patrick D. Miller concludes similarly: "Judgment is to be understood as an outcome of God's justice, righteousness, and steadfast love (see Jer 9:24)" ("'Slow to Anger': The God of the Prophets," in *The Way of the Lord: Essays in Old Testament Theology* [Grand Rapids: Eerdmans, 2004], 269–85 [278]). See also the discussions in Creach, *Violence*, 217–39, and Bernat and Klawans (eds), *Religion and Violence*.

that expresses the just consequences of its behavior.[17] This sort of punishment is strongly emphasized from the very beginning of the book, where YHWH's "vengeance" (expressed by various forms of נקם) is central (1:2-3). It is subsequently developed in the destruction of those who plotted against YHWH (1:9) and of the boastful Assyrian monarch's reputation, gods, and legacy (1:14), to note only two examples (see also 2:12-14 [11-13 Eng.]; 3:1-3, 19).

A significant modification of this pattern of retribution appears in the shaming of the metaphorical prostitute in 3:4-7. That context highlights the Assyrian Empire's deceitful abuse and exploitation of its client states, with an undertone of divination that probably associates or even identifies Nineveh with Ishtar of Nineveh, its patron deity.[18] Here the punishment for these wrongs is "communicative," involving exposure of the metaphorical prostitute's nudity to those whom she has misused.[19] This exposure symbolizes the deconstruction of the empire's ideology, the uncovering of its false promises, and the shame that accompanied its fall.[20]

17. "As a justification for inflicting punishment, retributive justice requires that the recipient must be *guilty* of wrongdoing (the principle of deserts) and that the pain of the penalty must be *proportionate* to the seriousness of the crime (the principle of equivalence). In these circumstances the imposition of punishment is not only appropriate, it is morally *necessary* in order to satisfy the objective standards of justice (the principle of justice)" (Chris Marshall, "Divine Justice as Restorative Justice," in *Christian Reflection: Prison* [Waco: Baylor University Press, 2012], 11–19 [13]).

18. Assurbanipal's close relation to the goddess is especially interesting given the book's seventh-century setting, on which see Barbara N. Porter, "Ishtar of Nineveh and Her Collaborator, Ishtar of Arbela, in the Reign of Assurbanipal," *Iraq* 66 (2004): 41–4. Note also the seventh-century appellations "Lady of Nineveh" for Ishtar (ibid., 41) and "the noble metropolis, the city beloved of Ishtar" for Nineveh; see D. D. Luckenbill, *Ancient Records of Assyria and Babylonia: Vol. 2, Historical Records from Assyria from Sargon to the End* (Chicago: University of Chicago Press, 1927), 160.

19. Cf. R. Antony Duff, "Punishment," in *Oxford Handbook of Practical Ethics*, ed. H. LaFollette (Oxford: Oxford University Press, 2003), 331–57 (343).

20. The personification of Nineveh (which stands *pars pro toto* for the empire, cf. 1:1) raises some difficult questions, especially concerning sexual violence against a female figure and the negative characterization of the same. On the first point, clear language for sexual violence such as that in Jer. 13:22 (נחמסו עקביך, literally "your heels suffered violence"; cf. also Gen. 34:2; Deut. 22:28; 2 Sam. 13:12, 14) is absent from Nah. 3, while its וגליתי שוליך ("I will uncover your skirts") is less likely an act of sexual violence than exposure as public shaming; cf. Georg Fischer, *Jeremia 1–25*, HThKAT (Freiburg: Herder, 2005), 460–1. The shaming of a prostitute is referred to as a well-known practice in "The Inscriptions of Bar-Ga'yah and Mati'el from

This communicative punishment also reasserts the victims' full humanity by having them witness the punishment of Neo-Assyria's dehumanizing violence. Still, the punishment includes a retributive element, since the sentence does not have Assyria's correction or rehabilitation in view.

When it comes to the grounds for YHWH's varied punishments of Assyria, Nahum offers an impressive array of condemnations. Plotting against YHWH is condemned as subversive of his moral order and authority in 1:9. In 1:14 the Assyrian monarch has failed to appreciate his insignificance and has instead glorified himself while honoring his gods as those who enabled his success. The empire's excessive appetite for destruction and expansion involved predatory violence against other human beings and extreme self-interest, both condemned in 2:12-14 (11-13 Eng.) and 3:1-3. Finally, 3:4-7 charges that Assyria's diplomatic and economic relationships with other nations involved extensive divination

---

Sefire," trans. Joseph A. Fitzmeyer, *COS* 2.82:214. This punishment was to be applied to both men and women for various offenses per Middle Assyrian law collections; cf. Martha T. Roth, *Law Collections from Mesopotamia and Asia Minor*, SBLWAW 6, 2nd ed. (Atlanta: Scholars Press, 1997), 168–9, 206. Humiliation is also required by the rest of the verse, which speaks of showing (Hiphil ראה) Nineveh's nakedness and shame to the nations. See the related discussion of these issues in Majella Franzmann, "The City as Woman: The Case of Babylon in Isaiah 47," *ABR* 43 (1995): 1–19, esp. 12–15.

As to the second point, Karolien Vermeulen, "The Body of Nineveh: The Conceptual Image of the City in Nahum 2–3," *JHS* 17 (2017): 1–17, treats personification as a subset of metaphor. Notably, the metaphor transmits the actions involving the personified female city in 3:4 to the empire as an ideological complex created and enacted by its elite male population, especially the king (cf. 1:14; 3:18; note also "officer," 2:6 [5 Eng.]; commanders, 2:9 [8 Eng.]; "troops," 3:13; "princes" and "scribes," 3:17; "shepherds," "nobles," 3:18, and the [male] lion metaphor in 2:12-13 [11-12 Eng.]).

The likelihood that the "uncovering" in 3:4 involves shame rather than sexual violence, the conceptual distance between a literal woman and the city of Nineveh upon which the personification depends, and the prominence of male elites as the literal victims of the attacker's violence do not remove every difficulty from the image in 3:4, but do resist interpretations that would legitimize sexual violence or favor misogynist attitudes. See further Julia M. O'Brien, *Nahum*, 2nd ed., Readings (Sheffield: Sheffield Phoenix, 2009), 61–3, 80–99; Cynthia R. Chapman, *The Gendered Language of Warfare in the Israelite–Assyrian Encounter*, HSM 62 (Winona Lake: Eisenbrauns, 2004), esp. 103–10; Laurel Lanner, *"Who Will Lament Her?" The Feminine and the Fantastic in the Book of Nahum*, LHBOTS 434 (New York: T&T Clark, 2006); Heinz-Josef Fabry, *Nahum*, HThKAT (Freiburg im Breisgau: Herder, 2006), 109–11.

(especially during Esarhaddon's reign),[21] deceit, and a utilitarian approach to whole "nations and clans." Assuming the validity of these accusations is essential to a sympathetic rather than "against the grain" reading of the book,[22] and will help us as we take up the two questions articulated at the outset. Even without this assumption, however, it is beyond doubt that Nahum presents YHWH's punishments of Assyria as well-justified and far from being arbitrary or impulsive.[23]

Punishing Assyrian Violence with (Medo-Babylonian) Violence

The necessary correlation of God's violent punishment with sin

We are now prepared to take up a question of crucial importance for this study: Can violence justly punish violence? The following elements of the theodicy equation noted earlier are preeminent here: (1) who?—God as the one exercising justice by inflicting violent punishment;[24] (2) how?—destruction of an empire, including significant loss of life through human violence; and (3) why?—mainly as retribution for Assyria's sinful behaviors and attitudes toward God and other nations, and secondarily as deliverance for its victims, Judah in particular.

While presupposing God's absolute justice would constitute an important argument that his punishment of Assyria is necessarily just, here I pose the question without that presupposition in order to better understand the theology and theodicy that support such a conclusion. Thus, the *who* does not solve our problem, since we may not circumvent the question by simply affirming that all God's actions are just. Nor does the *why*. No one would disagree that Nahum presents the fall of the Assyrian Empire as a

---

21. On the relevance of divination for Neo-Assyrian warcraft, see Andreas Fuchs, "Assyria at War: Strategy and Conduct," in *The Oxford Handbook of Cuneiform Culture*, ed. K. Radner and E. Robson (Oxford: Oxford University Press, 2011), 380–401 (386). Beaulieu's observation that Esarhaddon's reign provides "the most extensive evidence for the excessive popularity of divination, especially astrology, at the court" is particularly relevant. Paul-Alain Beaulieu, "Mesopotamia," in *Religions of the Ancient World*, ed. S. I. Johnston (Cambridge: Belknap Press of Harvard University Press, 2004), 171.

22. I have argued for this hermeneutic in Daniel C. Timmer, "The Use and Abuse of Power in Amos: Identity and Ideology," *JSOT* 39 (2014): 101–18, esp. 116–18.

23. *Pace* Eryl W. Davies, "The Morally Dubious Passages of the Hebrew Bible: An Examination of Some Proposed Solutions," *CBR* 3 (2005): 197–228, it is not necessary to dilute or balance biblical presentations of God's wrath with affirmation of his mercy in order to render the former morally acceptable (pp. 212–13).

24. The agent-role concerns hierarchy and prerogative/responsibility, among other things.

consequence for its violent, non-YHWHistic, exploitative imperialism. But that still does not establish that YHWH's *violent* response is fitting, that is, morally good. The nub of the problem is thus *how* YHWH's punishment is applied.

While some have argued that all divine justice must be restorative,[25] this does not square with the biblical data. While YHWH often attenuates his punishment of Israelites and non-Israelites alike,[26] the consequences of sin from the very beginning of the biblical narrative are nothing less than death, a quite insuperable consequence that does violence to the whole human being and is destructive rather than restorative.[27] Further, death is violent regardless of how it comes about. In the Hebrew Bible/ Old Testament, God is the only, universal king, and as the source of life and of all good his character demands that evil be punished and ultimately destroyed. As creator he thus imposes the gravest of consequences for human actions that deny his sovereign right to his image bearers' undivided love, obedience, and service. At the same time, the violent realization of the punishment is well suited to Assyria given its legendary violence across the ancient Near East.[28] "God's actions against Nineveh are intended to stop violence and correct it, not perpetuate it."[29]

25. E.g., Thomas Talbott, "Punishment, Forgiveness, and Divine Justice," *RelS* 29 (1993): 151–68, who argues that God's "justice requires exactly the same thing his love requires: the absolute destruction of sin; it requires that sinners repent of any wrong they have done to others and that they be reconciled one to another" (p. 168).

26. Mark J. Boda, *A Severe Mercy: Sin and Its Remedy in the Old Testament*, Siphrut 1 (Winona Lake: Eisenbrauns, 2009), 520: "The fact that full punishment is rarely exacted but rather more often a punishment is mitigated reveals its disciplinary design."

27. Even in the Hebrew Bible/Old Testament it is permissible to speak of death as a punishment that separates one's body from one's "spirit" (avoiding the anachronistic "soul") in light of bodily burial on the one hand and the prominence of one's presence in Sheol (or, occasionally, in God's presence; cf. Pss 16:10; 49:15; 73:24; Isa. 26:19; Dan. 12:2) on the other.

28. As Carroll R. observes, "divine punishment is vitally connected and corresponds to the transgression." See M. Daniel Carroll R., "'I Will Send Fire': Reflections on the Violence of God in Amos," in *Wrestling with the Violence of God: Soundings in the Old Testament*, ed. M. Daniel Carroll R. and J. B. Wilgus, BBRSup 10 (Winona Lake: Eisenbrauns, 2015), 113–32 (122). On Neo-Assyrian violence, see Frederick M. Fales, *Guerre et paix en Assyrie: Religion et impérialisme*, Les conférences de l'École Pratique des Hautes Études (Paris: Cerf, 2010), 9–25.

29. Creach, *Violence*, 173.

The correlation of God's punishment of sin with restoration

We should note in passing that YHWH's violent intervention *against Assyria* (which is retributive and destructive in that respect) is also restorative and gracious *for the other nations* that it affects. It is restorative because it frees them from the yoke (and, not infrequently, the sword) of their Assyrian overlord. For the nations other than Judah, none of whom worshipped YHWH, his deliverance was clearly unmerited. It was especially gracious for Judah because YHWH delivered her despite her sins that violate his unique covenant relationship with her and despite the apparent absence of any significant repentance.

Although we will not explore it here, the link between these negative and positive elements of YHWH's actions in Nahum is important. Negatively, the destruction of Assyria demonstrates YHWH's power and justice while granting his people political freedom. Positively, several passages in Nahum sketch a trajectory of restoration that culminates in the promise in 2:3 (2 Eng.) that "YHWH will restore the majesty of Jacob like the majesty of Israel" (cf. also 2:1 [1:15 Eng.]). The terminus of the trajectory on which divine wrath against Assyria is a single point is God's glory in and through the deliverance of his people, resulting in universal justice and peace.[30]

Medo-Babylonian involvement and multiple causation

The fact that God is the ultimate cause of Assyria's fall should not cause us to overlook the importance of human agency as a secondary cause.[31] This introduces the distinct possibility that the violence executed against Assyria by the Medo-Babylonian coalition[32] would include wrongs at the level of their motivations for it, their accomplishment of it, and their understanding of its significance within their worldview. The consistency with which the Hebrew Bible/Old Testament condemns the violence, arrogance, and religion of the various nations that punished Israel and Judah implies that human agents (especially empires) simply cannot be instrumental in the application of divine justice without adding various

---

30. Rainer Kessler notes how these two facets of theodicy are interrelated in Micah in his essay in Chapter 7 of this volume.

31. Here I take "cause" to be "that which necessitates the events that are their effects"; cf. Penelope J. Mackie, "Causality," in Honderich (ed.), *The Oxford Companion to Philosophy*, 127, while allowing for multiple or complex causation.

32. Median participation in the Babylonian campaign was "formalised by a treaty perhaps cemented by dynastic marriage." See Amélie Kuhrt, *The Ancient Near East c. 3000–330 BC*, Routledge History of the Ancient World, 2 vols (London: Routledge, 1995), 590.

objectionable elements to its realization (e.g., Isa. 10:5-19; Hab. 2:5-19). Yet in all such cases, the biblical texts also affirm that the judgment comes from God, and that it fits the crime (e.g., Isa. 10:1-4; Hab. 1:6). We must therefore take account of dual agency whenever YHWH employs human means to accomplish his will, whether punitive or not.[33]

On this basis we can suggest that Nahum's affirmation of God's justice in violently punishing a violent empire is both comprehensible and defensible, for it does not imply that the *humanly executed* divine sentence will accord with divine justice or the divine will in every respect.[34] "The fusion of the two, divine and human action, does not diminish the reality of either. Both are fully operative. That does not mean that they are equal, for the divine and human are never equal in the Bible, but both are fully present as what they are."[35] The Hebrew Bible/Old Testament and extant Babylonian records alike agree that Babylon's conquest of Assyria was not motivated by, or even consistent with, respect for YHWH's uniqueness and will or by benevolent concern for Judeans.[36] On the contrary, it was an imperialism in which might was right,[37] the Babylonian gods were essentially sovereign,[38] and the glory of the empire and of the

33. Similarly, see Carly Crouch, *War and Ethics in the Ancient Near East: Military Violence in Light of Cosmology and History*, BZAW 407 (Berlin: de Gruyter, 2009), 166–7.

34. Eleonore Stump, "The Problem of Evil and the History of Peoples: Think of Amalek," in *Divine Evil? The Moral Character of the God of Abraham*, ed. M. Bergmann, M. J. Murray, and M. C. Rea (Oxford: Oxford University Press, 2010), 179–97, helpfully explores the analogous case of human punishment of sin within ancient Israel's legal system (pp. 187–9). Her observation that the other side of the "messiness" of (sinful) human involvement is the potential goodness of just human actions merits reflection (p. 189).

35. Dan Via, *Divine Justice, Divine Judgment: Rethinking the Judgment of Nations*, Facets (Minneapolis: Fortress, 2007), 21.

36. Contrast Nebuchadnezzar's claim that "Marduk sublimely commanded me to lead the land aright, to shepherd the people, to provide for cult centers, (and) to renew temples." VAB 4 72, cited in David S. Vanderhooft, *The Neo-Babylonian Empire and Babylon in the Latter Prophets*, HSM 59 (Atlanta: Scholars, 1999), 35.

37. Per the Babylonian Chronicle (Chronicle 3), the Babylonian army "marched along the bank of the Tigris. [... they encamp]ed against Nineveh. From the month Sivan until the month Ab—for three [months--...]...they subjected the city to a heavy siege. [On the Nth day] of the month Ab [...] they inflicted a major [defeat upon a g]reat [*people*]... They carried off the vast booty of the city and the temple (and) [turned] the city into a ruin heap." A. Kirk Grayson, *Assyrian and Babylonian Chronicles* (Winona Lake: Eisenbrauns, 2000), 94.

38. Nabopolassar characteristically "appeals to the gods, to his piety and his deeds to justify his dominion. And the pious attitude of this *homo novus* is rewarded

king were central.[39] The involvement of the Medo-Babylonian coalition in God's punishment of Assyria removes neither the grounds for its justice nor the moral responsibility of Assyria's destroyers. As Dan Via observes, "God succeeds in carrying out God's purposes by acting through—not by negating—the agency of semi-autonomous human beings."[40] M. Daniel Carroll R.'s conclusion that "the judgments that the prophetic books announce...cannot be tidy" is true precisely because God sees fit to accomplish them (outside any eschatological scenario; see below) through *sinful* human agents.[41] Thus while the judgments *in themselves* are God's, their historical *realization* is also, in Carroll R.'s words, "a harrowing window into the darkness" of the souls of those who effect them.[42]

Punishing All in Connection with the Sins of Some

What groups does Nahum construct in Assyria?

We now take up our second question: what of the fact that the attacker's violence will affect all Assyrians, not merely those who embody, in their actions and attitudes, the empire's arrogance, inhumane violence, and claims to divine prerogative? Nahum's focus on Judah as a state makes the Assyrian Empire the most natural context in which to address Judah, but the book does not present Assyria as a monochrome and homogeneous political entity, characterized primarily by empirical features like population, borders, and gross domestic product. Assyria is above all an empire with an ideology in which the king was the gods' instrument by which to extend their realm worldwide through military conquest.[43] The

by the gods: the destruction of the enemy is always made possible through divine intervention." Rocio Da Riva, *The Neo-Babylonian Royal Inscriptions: An Introduction*, Guides to the Mesopotamian Textual Record 4 (Münster: Ugarit-Verlag, 2008), 5.

39. The goal was "to throw off their [the Assyrians'] yoke." See Paul-Alain Beaulieu (trans.), "Nabopolassar's Restoration of Imgur-Enlil: The Inner Defensive Wall of Babylon (2.121)," *COS* 2:307–8 (307).

40. Via, *Divine Justice*, 7; *pace* James Crenshaw, "Theodicy and Prophetic Literature," in Laato and de Moor (eds), *Theodicy in the World of the Bible*, 236–55 (255). It is thus unhelpful to develop dichotomies like that offered by Duane Christiansen, "Nahum," in *Harper's Bible Commentary*, ed. J. L. Mays (San Francisco: Harper & Row, 1988), 736: "Nahum is primarily a book about God's justice, not about human vengeance, hatred, and military conquest."

41. Carroll R., "I Will Send Fire," 125.

42. Ibid., 123.

43. See Bustaney Oded, *War, Peace and Empire: Justifications for War in Assyrian Royal Inscriptions* (Wiesbaden: Dr Ludwig Reichert Verlag, 1992); Crouch, *War and Ethics*; Daniel C. Timmer, "Nahum's Representation of and Response to

empire's approach to the states and people groups around it (including their gods) was thus dominating and utilitarian.[44] As a result, Assyria thus appears in very distinctive garb in Nahum, almost invariably wearing royal robes (1:14; 3:18-19) or a military uniform (1:9, 11; 2:12-14 [11-13 Eng.]; 3:1-3, 12-15), with the pinstripe suit of a wolfish trader appearing less frequently (3:4-7, 16).

Only after the empire has proleptically fallen do we see "ordinary" Assyrians, disheveled, vanquished, and anguished amid Nineveh's rubble (2:11 [10 Eng.]) and scattered across a crumbling empire (3:18). Their survival corresponds to Nahum's prediction of the empire's fall, and not of the annihilation of the entire population (which would have included all Judeans if Judah was an Assyrian vassal when Nahum was composed). The presence of Assyrian survivors in Nahum's descriptions of Assyria's fall is consistent with the fall of the empire *as an ideological and political entity*, distinct from its population as a whole, although the latter could not escape varying degrees of suffering and hardship produced by the empire's fall.

How does divine judgment correlate with these groups?

How then does divine judgment correlate with these two groups, i.e., the elites and the rest of the population? The sins that Nahum attributes to the empire are punished in the destruction of the empire and the elimination (and probable death) of its elite, the king in particular. Without asserting that the general population was sinless, Nahum does not associate them directly with the empire's imperialism, so their fate must be understood (at least partially) on other grounds.[45] The elites thus experience divine punishment as the Medo-Babylonian coalition destroys

Neo-Assyria: Imperialism as a Multifaceted Point of Contact in Nahum," *BBR* 24.3 (2014): 349–62; Fales, *Guerre et paix*, 9–94, 207–30.

44. See esp. Markus Zehnder, *Umgang mit Fremden in Israel und Assyrien: Ein Beitrag zur Anthropologie des 'Fremden' im Licht antiker Quellen*, BWANT 168 (Stuttgart: Kohlhammer, 2005), 63–74, 546, 554; Meghan Cifarelli, "Gesture and Alterity in the Art of Ashurnasirpal II of Assyria," *The Art Bulletin* 80 (1998): 210–28; and Fales, *Guerre et paix*.

45. "Wars...and many other afflictions are...not very discriminating. Therefore if we see them only as retaliation or retribution for specific sins, we shall be terribly confused when people who have not indulged in such sins suffer along with those who have. But if instead we see such sufferings as, in the first place, the effluent of the fall, the result of a fallen world, the consequence of evil that is really evil and in which we ourselves all too frequently indulge, then...we will not be taken by surprise" (D. A. Carson, *How Long, O Lord? Reflections on Suffering and Evil*, 2nd ed. [Grand Rapids: Baker Academic, 2006], 45).

their empire, while the rest of the population suffers incidental violence but is not *destroyed* as such, nor even punished for particular sins in the same way or to the same degree as the empire.

Nuanced or graded retribution

Still, on the Hebrew Bible/Old Testament's terms, *all* Assyrians, as bearers of the divine image living in rebellion against their creator, merited death—and indeed all died.[46] But they did not all die during the decade or so in which the Assyrian Empire fell apart as part of the judgment Nahum announced. Their eventual death, like the hardships the Assyrian populace suffered at the hands of their opponent, can be understood as *general* consequences of sins not directly linked to Assyria's imperialism, or even as the inevitable consequences of living in a fallen world, without any reference to a particular moral fault on their part.

However, there are reasons for seeing the general population as justly being caught up in the punishment of the empire even though the empire is largely defined by the elite. As Carroll R. observes, "There can be multiple kinds of participation by the wider population" in the projects of the elite.[47] Some connection to Assyria's imperial project on the part of the general populace surely existed, whether in profiting from security from external threats, benefitting from royal roads and irrigation projects, or mere complicity.

In light of these complexities, we might best describe the fall of Assyria *as a whole* as involving graded or proportional retribution, in which those most directly responsible for the empire's violence and ideology receive the most severe punishment, while the non-elites are less catastrophically deprived of their Assyrian Empire-home and presumably continue life as citizens of the Babylonian Empire. Without denying that a corporate view of Assyrian guilt contributes to a theodicy of Nahum, a focus on the different groups that Nahum constructs within Assyria is necessary given the prominence of the elite throughout the book. Consequently, a nuanced or graded theodicy best describes Nahum's explanation of God's actions against Assyria.

46. The idea of any population or individual, Israelite or not, being entirely without sin is foreign to the Hebrew Bible/Old Testament; cf. 1 Kgs 8:46; Ps. 51:7 (5 Eng.), etc. "The worldview of the Hebrew Bible does not set out from the image of the undisturbed creation described in the first two chapters but from the situation after the 'Fall'" (Rendtorff, *The Canonical Hebrew Bible*, 430).

47. Carroll R., "I Will Send Fire," 124. See Howard McGary, "Groups, Moral Status of," in *Encyclopedia of Ethics*, ed. L. C Becker and C. B. Becker (London: Routledge, 2001), 635–9. My thanks to Dr. Jay Sklar for helping me think through some of these issues.

Moving beyond Nahum and Assyria

Nahum and Worldwide Judgment (1:2-8)

God renders justice to Assyria as recompense for its evils against him and against many nearby states, and this entails the empire's destruction by earthly powers. The fall of Assyria is not God's full program of justice, however, and the book of Nahum itself makes clear that the end of the empire is a foretaste of the global, final resolution of all sin and injustice that YHWH will one day realize himself, without any human agent (1:2-8). The violence against Assyria, even if that violence is justifiable, and even if God's involvement in it does not implicate him in wrong, should be seen against the ultimate horizon and goal of the book: the righteous world order that Assyria's fall contributes to and prefigures.[48]

This is most evident in the opening oracle of 1:2-8, which mentions neither Judah nor Assyria and which associates individuals, rather than groups, with contrasting *ultimate* fates (deliverance or destruction by God himself) rather than with political restoration or dissolution, repatriation or deportation, and so on.[49] God's *unmediated* vengeance against his enemies brings about their "complete end" (1:8), while his being slow to anger and "good" makes possible deliverance from his final judgment for those who have committed moral wrongs but seek refuge in him (1:7). Because this definitive divine punishment and deliverance is not mediated through or executed by a human agent, it is untarnished by human excesses and hubris.

The Progressive Revelation of God's Justice

These considerations show that 1:2-8 anchors the book's later exploration of divine justice with respect to Neo-Assyria in a theme that culminates in YHWH's full and final victory over all evil and his gracious deliverance

---

48. Cf. H. H. Schmid, *Gerechtigkeit als Weltordnung: Hintergrund und Geschichte der alttestamentliche Gerechtigkeitsbegriffes* (Tübingen: Mohr Siebeck, 1968); the "peaceable kingdom" that Stephen B. Chapman sees as the "consistent goal of God's activity in the world," in his "Martial Memory, Peaceable Vision: Divine War in the Old Testament," in *Holy War in the Bible: Christian Morality and an Old Testament Problem*, ed. H. A. Thomas, J. Evans, and P. Copan (Downers Grove: IVP Academic, 2013), 47–67 (61–7); and Carroll R., "I Will Send Fire," 129–30.

49. Hagedorn, *Die Anderen im Spiegel*, 80, and others likewise recognize that 1:2-8 (in Hagedorn's case, 1:2-10) function as a *Leseanleitung* (instruction for reading), although it need not be later than or rather at odds with most of the rest of the book as Hagedorn argues (p. 46).

of those who seek refuge in him.[50] As Angelika Berlejung has noted, "The final divine judgment over all mortals is a theological necessity, because it is the only way to prove the…justice of God."[51] This conviction appears frequently in the HB (Isa. 66; Joel 4 [3 Eng.]; Hab. 3; Zeph. 1; Zech. 14; Mal. 4), and is often connected with the full establishment of YHWH's kingship over the world (e.g., Pss 96–99; Isa. 24–27). The destruction of the "evil empire" in the New Testament book of Revelation, characterized (like Assyria) in military, religious, and economic terms, shows significant dependence upon the characterization and theological evaluation of earthly empires that previously instantiated it in the Hebrew Bible/Old Testament.[52]

Conclusions

In this chapter, I have tried to articulate a few aspects of a theodicy of Nahum that are faithful to the book and its author's presuppositions. Nahum's arguments depend on several foundational claims that can be summed up as follows: human guilt (although varying in degree) is pandemic, and God as the absolutely good and just Creator must punish sin and so can impose death upon all immediately. However, while all deserve death, not all receive it right away, and God can extend mercy in varying degrees, even making possible ultimate deliverance from death for those who take refuge in him, while leaving those who continue to oppose him to the inevitable consequences of their actions. These claims allow the affirmation of God's justice in the various scenarios Nahum describes, even if lesser or subsequent questions remain.[53] God can be vindicated even if we are not able to fully understand him and his ways, and this trust makes possible the hope Nahum holds out to its readers.[54]

---

50. This point in developed in more detail in Daniel C. Timmer, *The Non-Israelite Nations in the Book of the Twelve: Thematic Coherence and the Diachronic–Synchronic Relationship in the Minor Prophets*, BibInt 135 (Leiden: Brill, 2015), 119–35.

51. Berlejung, "Sin and punishment," 281.

52. Richard J. Bauckham, *The Theology of the Book of Revelation*, NTT (Cambridge: Cambridge University Press, 1993), 17, 35–6, and passim.

53. These claims are also present in a recent Jewish interpretation of Nahum; see Aron Pinker, "Nahum's Theological Perspectives," *JBQ* 32 (2004): 148–57, especially points 1, 2, 4, and 10.

54. Jean Lévêque, "L'interprétation des discours de YHWH (Job 38,1–42,6)," in *The Book of Job*, ed. W. M. Beuken, BETL 114 (Leuven: Leuven University Press, 1994), 203–22 (222).

Chapter 8

The Triumph of Hope in Habakkuk

David J. Fuller

Introduction

From the Second Temple period onwards, it is evident that the collection called the "Book of the Twelve"[1] was considered to be a source of comfort and hope, as attested in Sir. 49:10.[2] Although there have been a number of

---

1. The present study adopts a final-form reading of the Book of the Twelve, although without disputing the possibility of earlier forms of this collection. It thus follows the approach described by Heath A. Thomas, *Habakkuk*, THOTC (Grand Rapids: Eerdmans, 2018), 19–24. Thomas argues that even if the manuscript evidence (particularly from Qumran) or redactional arguments for the Twelve being intentionally shaped as a singular collection are unconvincing, one can nonetheless still profitably read "Habakkuk as presenting a set of messages that can then be understood in the larger literary presentation of the Twelve" (p. 22). That this framework is chiefly "literary" in its orientation, however, does not make it historically disengaged. Only by paying close attention to the historical situations being addressed in the individual books can the modern interpreter extract the future hope and multifaceted picture of YHWH's dealings with his people expressed by this collection as a whole (p. 23).

2. Heath A. Thomas, "Hearing the Minor Prophets: The Book of the Twelve and God's Address," in *Hearing the Old Testament: Listening for God's Address*, ed. Craig G. Bartholomew and David J. H. Beldman (Grand Rapids: Eerdmans, 2012), 356–82 (360). Sirach 49:10 reads, "May the bones of the Twelve Prophets send forth new life from where they lie, for they comforted the people of Jacob and delivered them with confident hope" (NRSV). For further discussion of the reception of the Minor Prophets in early Judaism, see Jutta Leonhardt-Balzer, "The Minor Prophets in the

different suggestions made regarding the unifying theme of this corpus,[3] there is a general consensus that it contains a number of indicators of hope.[4] While Habakkuk itself has a darker tone than the other books,[5] it is not lacking in an ultimately hopeful posture, despite the situation it describes. It is the intention of the present study to examine the two key moments of hope in Habakkuk (2:1 and 3:18) in the context of the Book of the Twelve, paying attention to context and the ways in which these and similar expressions are used elsewhere in this corpus. This study contends that Hab. 3:18 is a unique expression of rejoicing within the Twelve, as although the motifs of agricultural infertility (Hab. 3:17) and rejoicing (3:18) appear elsewhere in the Twelve, the outright act of praise during a time of infertility is only found in Habakkuk. Additionally, Hab. 2:1 functions as an embryonic manifestation of this hope, pointing towards this final address of Habakkuk and reinforcing the prophet's trust in YHWH, even as he wrestles with YHWH's plan.

Habakkuk 3: Overview

Structurally, Habakkuk 3 is enclosed by a superscription (v. 1) and closing performance instructions (v. 19b), containing three scenes. In scene one (v. 2), the prophet testifies to YHWH's past deeds and asks that similar great works will happen again. In scene two (vv. 3-15), YHWH's glory is said to fill the heavens and his mere movements shake creation (vv. 3-6),

Judaism of the Second Temple Period," in *The Minor Prophets in the New Testament*, ed. Maarten J. J. Menken and Steve Moyise, LNTS 377 (New York: T&T Clark, 2009), 7–25.

    3. Anthony R. Petterson, "The Shape of the Davidic Hope across the Book of the Twelve," *JSOT* 35 (2010): 225–46. Petterson examines the theme of the "restoration of the Davidic monarchy" across the Twelve, a concept that is at best hinted at in Hab. 3:13 (p. 242). Knud Jeppesen, "'Because of You!': An Essay about the Centre of the Book of the Twelve," in *In Search of True Wisdom: Essays in Old Testament Interpretation in Honour of Ronald E. Clements*, ed. Edward Ball, JSOTSup 300 (Sheffield: Sheffield Academic, 1999), 196–210. For Jeppesen, the center of the Twelve is Mic. 3:12, thus highlighting the departure of YHWH and hope of his return. Rolf Rendtorff, "How to Read the Book of the Twelve as a Theological Unity," in *Society of Biblical Literature 1997 Seminar Papers*, SBLSPS 36 (Atlanta: SBL, 1997), 420–32. Rendtorff identifies the "main line" of the day of the Lord (p. 423).

    4. Thomas, "Hearing the Minor Prophets," 366–8.

    5. Julia M. O'Brien, *Nahum, Habakkuk, Zephaniah, Haggai, Zechariah, Malachi*, AOTC (Nashville: Abingdon, 2004), 58. Remarking on the transition from Nahum to Habakkuk, O'Brien states, "The tone is no longer one of bold confidence that God will destroy the wicked, but one of pointed skepticism about God's justice and care."

the prophet testifies that the nations quake (v. 7), and the prophet interrogates YHWH concerning his battle with the sea, and ultimately his defeat of the enemies of his people (vv. 8-15). In scene three (vv. 16-19a), the prophet testifies to his terror, but ultimately makes a proclamation of faith in the salvific work of his God.[6]

A number of issues complicate the study of Habakkuk 3: extensive textual corruption, the possibility that it was a separate composition from the rest of the book, the unity of the chapter itself, the identification of its genre(s), and supposed parallels with "archaic" biblical and ancient Near Eastern poetry and imagery.[7] However, for the purposes of the present study, none of the relevant sections requires extensive emendation, and the unity of Habakkuk 3 with the rest of Habakkuk remains a defensible position in the absence of concrete textual evidence to the contrary.[8]

It is widely recognized that the final section of Habakkuk 3 is a resounding cry of hope in a book that is largely otherwise quite desolate and oriented towards judgment. Nogalski notes that this "hope" in Hab. 3:16-20 is specifically in the context of the anticipation of Babylon conquering Judah, followed by Babylon itself being destroyed; thus, "the hope they offer is directed only to the remnant that survives the coming

---

6. Jeanette Mathews, *Performing Habakkuk: Faithful Re-enactment in the Midst of Crisis* (Eugene: Pickwick, 2012), 142.

7. Oskar Dangl, "Habakkuk in Recent Research," *CBR* 9 (2001): 131–68 (144–51). For further discussion, see Yitzhak Avishur, *Studies in Hebrew and Ugaritic Psalms* (Jerusalem: Magnes, 1994), 111–205.

8. Joshua L. Harper, *Responding to a Puzzled Scribe: The Barberini Version of Habakkuk 3 Analysed in the Light of the Other Greek Versions*, LHBOTS 608 (London: Bloomsbury T&T Clark, 2015), 27. Despite the absence of Hab. 3 in the Qumran Habakkuk pesher (1QpHab) and the existence of the Greek "Barberini" variant edition of Hab. 3 alone, Harper argues that it is more likely that these were "excerpted" versions of the book for liturgical use, and that the canonical book of Habakkuk is a literary unity. Grace Ko, *Theodicy in Habakkuk*, Paternoster Theological Monographs (Milton Keynes: Paternoster, 2014), 16–20, summarizes and responds to the various arguments against the original unity of Hab. 3 and the rest of the book. She ultimately notes that the rest of Habakkuk would be incoherent without the final climactic expressions of lament and hope, pointing to a thematic parallel in Job and Ps. 77, "where arguments over theodicy also conclude with a theophany" (p. 19). It is also notable that the redactional scheme of Jakob Wöhrle, *Der Abschluss des Zwölfprophetenbuches: Buchübergreifende Redaktionsprozesse in den späten Sammlungen*, BZAW 389 (Berlin: de Gruyter, 2008), 317–19, includes the majority of ch. 3 in the original (pre-Babylonian) compositional layer of Habakkuk, along with the opening laments (1:2-4, 12a, 13-14), the promise of the vision (2:1-5), and portions of the woe oracles.

judgement."[9] Habakkuk's attitude is one of "resignation...which sees hope, but only after devastation."[10] Reading Habakkuk in concert with Nahum, O'Brien observes that just as Nahum proclaimed the destruction of Assyria with an opening theophanic hymn, so Habakkuk closes with a similar literary construction to teach that Babylon's dominance is only temporary. By emphasizing parallels in how YHWH works, Habakkuk communicates to his audience that YHWH will likewise deal with the Babylonians.[11] Crenshaw instead focuses on the relative inconstancy of the situation at hand and the resultant resilience of Habakkuk himself. For him, Habakkuk 3 communicates, "the prophet's determination to remain faithful in unpromising circumstances. These sentiments usher the reader into the company of others who cherish divine presence above presents."[12] House concurs with this assessment, viewing Habakkuk 3 as a celebration of God's constancy.[13] Everson explicitly places the message of Habakkuk in the context of the death of Josiah, and with this lens reads Hab. 3:17-18 as "words of encouragement for the faithful."[14]

9. James D. Nogalski, "Recurring Themes in the Book of the Twelve: Creating Points of Contact for a Theological Reading," *Int* 61 (2007): 125–36 (132).

10. Ibid., 136.

11. Julia M. O'Brien, "Nahum–Habakkuk—Zephaniah: Reading the 'Former Prophets' in the Persian Period," *Int* 61 (2007): 168–83 (177). O'Brien states, "In sequential literary form, Habakkuk looks back to Divine Warrior images such as Nahum as precedent for belief that YHWH will also stand up against the Babylonians."

12. James L. Crenshaw, "Theodicy in the Book of the Twelve," in *Thematic Threads in the Book of the Twelve*, ed. Paul L. Redditt and Aaron Schart, BZAW 325 (Berlin: de Gruyter, 2003), 175–91 (187).

13. Paul R. House, *The Unity of the Twelve*, JSOTSup 97 (Sheffield: Sheffield Academic, 1990), 93. House states, "Regardless of how bleak the national situation becomes, Habakkuk promises to watch, wait, and hope for Yahweh to act." Also see his "The Character of God in the Book of the Twelve," in *Reading and Hearing the Book of the Twelve*, ed. James D. Nogalski and Marvin A. Sweeney, SBLSymS 15 (Atlanta: SBL, 2000), 125–45 (139). Here, House states, "For this sort of miracle the prophet is willing to wait (3:16). By faith he will wait, though everything around him seems bleak (3:17-19). He will live by faith despite the fact that Israel and Babylon must fall before his faith is vindicated. God's word alone is enough to fuel this belief."

14. Joseph A. Everson, "The Canonical Location of Habakkuk," in Redditt and Schart (eds), *Thematic Threads in the Book of the Twelve*, 165–74 (172). He further states, "The words are remembered as encouragement to people, urging patience and trust in the promises that God had given, even when the world does not make sense." Also see Paul R. House, "Endings as New Beginnings: Returning to the Lord, the Day of the Lord, and Renewal in the Book of the Twelve," in Redditt and Schart (eds), *Thematic Threads in the Book of the Twelve*, 313–38 (332).

Infertility in Habakkuk 3:17 and the Rest of the Twelve

With this partial consensus established, it is now profitable to examine the text of Hab. 3:17 more closely. The chart below will present the individual clauses along with the translation of the NRSV, with some modifications.

Table 1. Habakkuk 3:17

clause 1	כִּי־תְאֵנָה לֹא־תִפְרָח	Though the fig tree does not blossom
clause 2	וְאֵין יְבוּל בַּגְּפָנִים	and no fruit is on the vines
clause 3	כִּחֵשׁ מַעֲשֵׂה־זַיִת	[though] the produce of the olive fails
clause 4	וּשְׁדֵמוֹת לֹא־עָשָׂה אֹכֶל	and the fields yield no food
clause 5	גָּזַר מִמִּכְלָה צֹאן	[though] the flock is cut off from the fold
clause 6	וְאֵין בָּקָר בָּרְפָתִים	and there is no herd in the stalls

The six clauses comprising Hab. 3:17 separate neatly into three parallel pairs. Aside from the כִּי conjunction at the beginning of clause 1 that places the entire verse into a subordinate relationship with 3:18, each A-line is devoid of introductory conjunctions, while each B-line (clauses 2, 4, 6) begins with a וְ conjunction. The frequent use of the negative particles לֹא (clauses 1, 4) and אֵין (clauses 2, 6) indicates that the text is deliberately pointing out what is not the case to rhetorically highlight its absence. Regarding word order, the first two clauses have a parallel subject–predicate structure,[15] while the second and third couplets utilize a chiastic arrangement of predicate–subject–subject–predicate. The first and third couplets have a verbal clause followed by a verbless clause, while the middle couplet has two verbal clauses. The verbal type shifts from a *yiqtol* form in clause 1 to *qatal* forms in clauses 3 and 5. The *yiqtol* in the first clause likely governs the "conditional" nature of the rest

15. Contra Walter Dietrich, *Nahum Habakkuk Zephaniah*, IECOT, trans. Peter Altmann (Stuttgart: Kohlhammer, 2016), 176, who instead diagnoses the second line of the first bicolon as predicate–subject. This error is likely due to a hasty use of his translation ("Not do bear the vines") for the analysis, mistaking the noun יְבוּל ("produce of the soil") for a verbal form. This error is not present in his main translation of the clause, "and there is no yield on the vines" (160). The present study would also disagree with the semantic chiastic structure proposed by Francis I. Andersen, *Habakkuk*, AB 25 (New Haven: Yale University Press, 2001), 347, as it curiously mismatches parts of speech. For example, in the second couplet, he writes, "work [/] OLIVE: FIELDS [/] work," which implies a parallel between the noun מַעֲשֵׂה and the verb עָשָׂה merely on the basis of their frequently being glossed "work" in English (while acknowledging their consonantal similarity).

of the verse,[16] while the *qatal* verbs express confidence that this situation concretely exists.[17] Semantically, there is a movement from items that grow in the ground and crops to animals, a kind of development from least to greatest.[18] Within the book of Habakkuk as a whole, this expression indicates a crisis point, drawing all of the previous laments together. As Bratcher states, "The prophet had complained of a disruption of society brought about by the wicked which affected law and justice and led him to a challenge of God. But now he is speaking of a disruption of nature which does not affect justice but life itself."[19] Bratcher's point remains valid whether this is an isolated agricultural catastrophe,[20] the direct result of the Babylonian invasion,[21] or the aftermath of YHWH's theophany.[22]

These data regarding Hab. 3:17 are necessary for the comparison with the contexts of the theme of infertility in the rest of the Book of the Twelve. Other usages of agricultural disaster in the Twelve will be examined below, with a particular emphasis on the purpose of the given instance, its evaluation, and response, if any.

Hosea 2:11, 14, 24, (vv. 9, 12, 22 in English translations) all directly speak of the theme of fertility in the context of God's relationship with Israel. After Hosea marries the adulterous woman and she bears children in 1:2–2:3, 2:4-25 provides in poetic form a description of how this image of nation unfaithfulness will play out.[23] Verses 4-15 focus on the

16. Bill T. Arnold and John H. Choi, *A Guide to Biblical Hebrew Syntax* (New York: Cambridge University Press, 2003), 59.

17. This holds whether one adopts a temporal, aspectual, or modal understanding of the Biblical Hebrew verbal system.

18. Ben Y. Leigh, "A Rhetorical and Structural Study of the Book of Habakkuk" (PhD diss., Golden Gate Baptist Seminary, 1992), 181. Leigh states, "The figure anabasis, *incrementum*, is used in the present verse. The six cola are arranged according to an increasing monetary value: figs < wine < olive (oil) < field crops < flock < cattle. The first three cola concern fruit raising, colon d concerns field cropping, and the last two cola concern herding. Three forms of agriculture are exhausted."

19. Dennis Ray Bratcher, "The Theological Message of Habakkuk: A Literary-Rhetorical Analysis" (PhD diss., Union Theological Seminary in Virginia, 1984), 276.

20. Andersen, *Habakkuk*, 345.

21. Ko, *Theodicy in Habakkuk*, 96; G. Michael O'Neal, *Interpreting Habakkuk as Scripture: An Application of the Canonical Approach of Brevard S. Childs*, StBibLit 9 (New York: Peter Lang, 2007), 133.

22. Dietrich, *Nahum*, 176.

23. Francis I. Andersen and David Noel Freedman, *Hosea* (AB 24; New York: Doubleday, 1980), 218.

character of the woman, whom YHWH will rebuke, and whose children will go unloved. This woman is depicted as chasing after lovers, who she imagines provide her with good things, and as being shamed and punished by YHWH for participating in the worship of false gods. Verses 16-25 more directly address Israel, introducing the hope of future restoration based on the memory of the intimate relationship between God and Israel in the wilderness. False idols will be abolished, and the terror of warfare will be taken away. A significant part of this state of restoration to come will be the reinstatement of the fertility of the ground. After v. 10, in which YHWH notes his provision was not acknowledged,[24] v. 11 records the punishment:

Table 2. Hosea 2:11

לָכֵן אָשׁוּב וְלָקַחְתִּי דְגָנִי בְּעִתּוֹ וְתִירוֹשִׁי בְּמוֹעֲדוֹ וְהִצַּלְתִּי צַמְרִי וּפִשְׁתִּי לְכַסּוֹת אֶת־עֶרְוָתָהּ	Therefore I will take back my grain in its time, and my wine in its season; and I will take away my wool and my flax, which were to cover her nakedness.

Next, YHWH will humiliate Israel by making her naked (v. 12), and all religious celebrations will be terminated (v. 13). Israel has surrendered to false worship, and her resources will likewise be revoked (v. 14):[25]

Table 3. Hosea 2:14

וַהֲשִׁמֹּתִי גַּפְנָהּ וּתְאֵנָתָהּ אֲשֶׁר אָמְרָה אֶתְנָה הֵמָּה לִי אֲשֶׁר נָתְנוּ־לִי מְאַהֲבָי וְשַׂמְתִּים לְיַעַר וַאֲכָלָתַם חַיַּת הַשָּׂדֶה	I will lay waste her vines and her fig trees, of which she said, "These are my pay, which my lovers have given me." I will make them a forest, and the wild animals shall devour them.

If this were not clear enough, v. 15 explicitly describes this activity as punishment. The use of infertility imagery in Hosea 2 is clearly as punishment for disobedience, although the restoration of fertility (v. 24) seems to be initiated by YHWH's goodness and redeeming love (v. 16).

---

24. Ibid., 245. Andersen and Freedman state, "The emphasis, however, is on Yahweh's ownership of such things... Yahweh never ceases to own his gifts. This is why he can take them back without doing wrong (Job 1:21). In Hosea's case, where the woman wrongfully claims ownership (doubly, for she attributes the items first to Baal and then to herself) it is also a question of recovering stolen property."

25. Ibid., 241. These verses must also be read in the context of v. 7, as it also relates to the fact that Israel understood her lovers to be the givers of resources.

The locust invasion of Joel 1 also heavily features the destruction of the fertility of the land. The drinkers of wine are commanded to mourn (1:5), because the locusts have ruined the vines (גֶּפֶן) and fig trees (תְּאֵנָה) (1:7).[26] The cultic leaders are instructed to mourn and declare fasting (1:13-14). An extensive list of entities ruined by this scourge is given, including fields, ground, grain, new wine, and olive oil (1:10); wheat, barley, and harvest of the fields (1:11); and seeds, storehouses, granaries, and grain (1:17). Just as in Hab. 3:17, there is a movement towards animals at the end of this section, with the suffering of cattle, herds, and flocks, and the destruction of their grazing areas described in 1:18-20.[27] The context of this ruin is clearly one of judgment and a call to repent, as is evident in Joel 2:12-14.[28] In the midst of this devastation, in 1:19, the prophet calls (קָרָא) to YHWH, but this is certainly an act of desperation, not rejoicing.[29]

Thematically, Amos 4 is very similar to Joel 1 in that it speaks of ecological disharmony in the context of a call to return. Beginning with a description of the looming exile (4:2-3), the passage describes a multitude of differing judgments, all punctuated with the refrain "you have not returned to me" (וְלֹא־שַׁבְתֶּם עָדַי) (4:6, 8, 9, 10, 11). In vv. 6-9, the diminished fertility of the land is described in detail. People go hungry and do

---

26. John Barton, *Joel and Obadiah: A Commentary* (Louisville: Westminster John Knox, 2001), 51. Barton notes that vines and fig trees are generally connected with "peace and prosperity," so the revoking of "divine blessing" is signaled by their wasting away.

27. Laurie J. Braaten, "Earth Community in Joel 1–2: A Call to Identify with the Rest of Creation," *HBT* 28 (2006): 113–29 (116–21). Braaten emphasizes that the earth itself is mourning in this crisis.

28. Jason T. LeCureux, *The Thematic Unity of the Book of the Twelve*, HBM 41 (Sheffield: Sheffield Phoenix, 2012), 120–8. For LeCureux, disaster can still be avoided through repentance, which is part of his understanding of the concept of the Day of the Lord (2:1, 11) in Joel. Willem S. Prinsloo, *The Theology of the Book of Joel*, BZAW 163 (Berlin: de Gruyter, 1985), 26–7. Prinsloo states, "But the plague of locusts is not interpreted purely as a natural disaster, but as an event calling men to repentance... Men have been deprived of their staple foods, but normal cultic life has also been suspended. Farming and religion are intimately linked... The national lament about the crisis achieves its climax and true purpose in the cry of distress to Yahweh."

29. Hans Walter Wolff, *Joel and Amos*, trans. Waldemar Janzen, S. Dean McBride Jr., and Charles A. Muenchow, Hermeneia (Philadelphia: Fortress, 1977), 36. Wolff states, "For the time being, the present situation of distress leads to the conclusion to cry to Yahweh (vv. 14b, 19a), and that in the customary forms of the cultus. In the course of listening to the older prophetic oracles, the extraordinary contemporary happening becomes the occasion for turning to Yahweh as the lord of the present calamity as well as of the approaching day."

not have bread (v. 6), and the fields are denied rain (v. 7). YHWH has directly attacked the gardens (גַּנָּה), vineyards (כֶּרֶם), and let the locusts ravage the fig trees (תְּאֵנָה) and olive trees (זַיִת) (v. 9).[30] In case it was not obvious enough, the chapter ends with a reminder that YHWH is the direct cause of these punishments (4:12-13).[31] At the end of the book, this agricultural language is again referenced with the restoration of fertility accompanying Israel's return to YHWH (Amos 9:11-15).

Micah 6:14–7:1 uses the theme of infertility as part of a larger discourse pronouncing judgment on Israel for its sins. Earlier in the chapter YHWH announces he has a case against the people (6:2), and announces that, despite his repeated salvation of the people (6:3-5), they are dishonest (6:11) and violent (6:12), and as result must receive punishment (vv. 13, 15). The voice shifts to the prophet at 7:1,[32] but the theme of infertility is retained. The relevant verses are thus 6:15[33] and 7:1.[34] In 6:15, despite their best efforts to the contrary, the Israelites will fail to reap (קָצַר), be anointed (סוּךְ) with oil, and drink (שָׁתָה) wine.[35] These failures are the result of disobedience. In 7:1, the prophet mourns due to the lack of clusters (אֶשְׁכּוֹל) of grapes and early figs (בִּכּוּרָה), an image for the dearth of "fruitful" righteousness in the land.[36] Nonetheless, this is still all ultimately in the context of the hope of restoration (7:19),[37] as YHWH's attitude towards his people will turn back to compassion.

30. Jörg Jeremias, *The Book of Amos: A Commentary*, OTL (Philadelphia: Westminster John Knox, 1998), 72–3. Jeremias observes that the descriptions of agricultural failure utilize a pattern of "increasing severity."

31. LeCureux, *The Thematic Unity of the Book of the Twelve*, 148–9. LeCureux notes that, in its larger context, this is still ultimately an expression of God's desire for Israel to be restored (Amos 5:4-5).

32. James D. Nogalski, *The Book of the Twelve: Micah–Malachi*, SHBC (Macon: Smith & Helwys, 2011), 577. Some believe it is the voice of Lady Zion.

33. "You shall eat, but not be satisfied, and there shall be a gnawing hunger within you; you shall put away, but not save, and what you save, I will hand over to the sword" (NRSV).

34. "Woe is me! For I have become like one who, after the summer fruit has been gathered, after the vintage has been gleaned, finds no cluster to eat; there is no first-ripe fig for which I hunger" (NRSV).

35. Marvin A. Sweeney, *The Twelve Prophets: Volume Two*, Berit Olam (Collegeville: Liturgical Press, 2000), 403. Sweeney notes this repeated use of the "but not" formula is reminiscent of ancient Near Eastern curses from treaty formulas.

36. Ibid., 407, alternatively views this verse as literally describing the desperately impoverished conditions during the siege of Sennacherib (2 Kgs 18:27 // Isa. 36:12).

37. LeCureux, *The Thematic Unity of the Book of the Twelve*, 156–7. It is YHWH who will initiate this restoration.

The post-exilic book of Haggai also contributes to the theme of infertility in the Twelve. Throughout the first chapter, the people are criticized for failing to rebuild the temple in Jerusalem, and thus have lacked adequate food (1:6, 10-11). Because the heavens have not produced dew (טַל), produce (יְבוּל) has not come forth from the earth (1:10). Thus, the people are deprived of grain (דָּגָן), new wine (תִּירוֹשׁ), oil (יִצְהָר), and there are negative effects on the cattle (בְּהֵמָה) (1:11). Following this word, Zerubbabel and Joshua repent and begin the work (1:12-15). Achtemeier hears Deuteronomic themes undergirding this expression of crop failure as a result of neglect of the temple.[38] These themes are reiterated in 2:15-19 with the declaration that these conditions of want will be overturned, with the concept of the Israelite's return implied in 2:17.[39]

The final occurrence of the theme of infertility in the Book of the Twelve is in Mal. 3:10-11. As YHWH accuses his people (3:10) of "neglecting the provisions necessary for the ongoing operation of the temple cult,"[40] he asks them to test him by faithfully bringing tithes and offerings, in order that he may bless them by opening the "windows of heaven" (אֲרֻבּוֹת הַשָּׁמַיִם) and pour out a "blessing" (בְּרָכָה).[41] Additionally, such obedience means that YHWH will restrain the "devourer" (אֹכֵל with a prefixed בְּ preposition), best understood as an "insect infestation."[42] This rebuking action of YHWH will guarantee the security of the "fruits of the ground" (פְּרִי הָאֲדָמָה) and will prevent the vine in the field (הַגֶּפֶן בַּשָּׂדֶה) from "casting" (תְשַׁכֵּל). As a result of the happy state of the land, other nations will pronounce blessings on Israel (3:12).[43]

---

38. Elizabeth Achtemeier, *Nahum–Malachi*, IBC (Atlanta: John Knox, 1986), 98–9. Also see Nogalski, *The Book of the Twelve*, 776.

39. LeCureux, *The Thematic Unity of the Book of the Twelve*, 167.

40. David W. Baker, *Joel, Obadiah, Malachi*, NIVAC (Grand Rapids: Zondervan, 2006), 284.

41. Karl William Weyde, *Prophecy and Teaching: Prophetic Authority, Form Problems, and the Use of Traditions in the Book of Malachi*, BZAW 288 (Berlin: de Gruyter, 2000), 335, connects this promise of blessing to the idiom of rain making the soil fertile, which occurs in, among other places, "Joel 2:23f."

42. Baker, *Joel*, 287. Baker additionally notes that some have instead identified the "devourer" with greedy priests (p. 286).

43. Laurie J. Braaten, "God Sows: Hosea's Land Theme in the Book of the Twelve," in Redditt and Schart (eds), *Thematic Threads in the Book of the Twelve*, 104–32 (128) connects this passage to its canonical neighbors, stating "The repentance sought in Hosea and Joel (and throughout the Twelve) is still required."

With this survey of infertility in the Twelve in mind, a couple of observations can be made. In every case the infertility is said to be the direct result of God's judgment for disobedience. Even if this is carried out through an intermediary (such as the locusts in Joel), the solution involves a renewal of the relationship between God and Israel, following the pattern of judgment, then restoration. In some cases, it seems that reconciliation is exclusively initiated by YHWH (Hosea and Micah), while in others the people's repentance and return is stressed (Joel, Amos, Haggai, Malachi).[44] Compared to the occurrence of this imagery in Hab. 3:17,[45] the contrast is quite striking. While in the most global context of the book, the infertility can be understood as part of the results of Israel's sin,[46] there is no mention of Israel and God coming back into fellowship, nor of which party will initiate this reconciliation.[47] There is no call to repent, nor indeed any acknowledgment of the need for it at any point in the book.[48] Furthermore, in the expected relational response in these other contexts of infertility is at best a hope of YHWH reversing the circumstances in the distant but indeterminate future. None of these other occurrences quite match the outright rejoicing of Habakkuk (Hab. 3:18). This act of rejoicing, and its occurrence in the rest of the Twelve, will be examined below.

44. Nogalski, "Recurring Themes," 128. Of course, further delineation is possible. Nogalski notes that, while repentance is prescribed in Joel and possible in Hosea, it is no longer an option in Amos.

45. James Nogalski, *Redactional Processes in the Book of the Twelve*, BZAW 218 (Berlin: de Gruyter, 1993), 176–8, 180. Nogalski highlights the lexical parallels between Joel 1–2 and Hab. 3:18, arguing that the latter is a redactional insertion based on the former, for the purpose of better connecting Habakkuk to the larger context of the book of the Twelve, specifically linking the invasion of the Babylonians to the devastation caused by locusts in Joel.

46. This is implied through the lament over social injustice in Judea in 1:2-4, which is answered by the notice of the imminent Babylonian invasion in 1:5-11. The propriety of using the Babylonians to mend the ills of Judah—the cure seemingly worse than the disease—is pondered throughout the rest of the book.

47. The autobiographical framework of Habakkuk provides at least a partial reason for this glaring silence. The book begins and ends with a focus on the personal faith experience of the prophet rather than on the nation as a whole. Conceivably, as the book was used didactically, the community was encouraged to learn from the experience of the prophet and place its trust in YHWH.

48. Ko, *Theodicy in Habakkuk*, 1.

Rejoicing in Habakkuk 3:18 and the Rest of the Twelve

The chart below provides the text of Hab. 3:18,[49] with some discussion to follow.

Table 4. Habakkuk 3:18

וַאֲנִי בַּיהוָה אֶעְלוֹזָה	Yet I will rejoice in the LORD
אָגִילָה בֵּאלֹהֵי יִשְׁעִי	I will exult in the God of my salvation.

Collectively, these two clauses function as the apodosis for which the protasis is Hab. 3:17, and the unit they form is introduced with a וֹ conjunction.[50] The word order of the clauses creates an A–B–C–C–B structure in which an independent pronoun functions as subject in the A-line,[51] followed by a prepositional phrase functioning as the indirect object, and finally a finite verb. The B-line opens with a finite verb, followed by a prepositional phrase functioning as the indirect object. Both clauses use cohortative verbs and are semantically parallel. Both express in the first person the thought of rejoicing in YHWH, who is more specifically described as the "God of my salvation" in the second

---

49. Some readers may wonder why the first three clauses of Hab. 3:19 were not included in this analysis and comparison, since they continue the note of praise begun in 3:18, with: יְהוָה אֲדֹנָי חֵילִי וַיָּשֶׂם רַגְלַי כָּאַיָּלוֹת וְעַל בָּמוֹתַי יַדְרִכֵנִי, "The Lord God is my strength, And He has made my feet like hinds' *feet*, And makes me walk on my high places" (NASB).

There are two reasons why 3:19 was not included in this study. First, while it is functioning to express praise, it is properly an assertion about YHWH, not self-description on the part of the prophet (note that the grammatical subject in all three clauses is YHWH). Second, this kind of reflection on what YHWH has personally done for a prophet is relatively rare in the Book of the Twelve, as the most direct parallels to these lines lie outside this corpus (see Deut. 32:13; 33:29; Ps. 18:34 // 2 Sam. 22:34; Isa. 58:14).

50. Arnold and Choi, *A Guide to Biblical Hebrew Syntax*, 147. Arnold and Choi provide a "conditional" category for the use of the conjunction to introduce apodoses. A monosemic bias would cast doubt on so much meaning being assigned to the conjunction itself, and instead note that it is used to indicate co-ordination in a specific larger context. Structurally, it is useful to note that a break from the previous verse can be clearly identified, as in Hab. 3:17 the conjunction was consistently used to introduce the B-lines of the poetic couplets, while here in 3:18 it initiates the A-line and the B-line has no introductory conjunctions.

51. Andersen, *Habakkuk*, 347. Andersen comments on this redundant declaration of the subject, stating, "The use of the personal pronoun is very emphatic and indicates a tremendous assertion of faith. The response is intensely individual."

line.[52] Compared to the protasis in Hab. 3:17, the entities involved could not be any more different; the focus on the cast of agricultural entities has been replaced by the prophet and YHWH.[53] Also, the predominant use of *qatal* verbs in 3:17 expressing the concrete situation of infertility gives way to cohortative verbs in 3:18, as the prophet pledges to rejoice despite the present circumstances.

With this groundwork in place, it is now necessary to survey the theme of Israel's (and the prophets') rejoicing in the Book of the Twelve. Hosea 9:1 directly commands Israel not to rejoice (אַל־תִּשְׂמַח), the reason being that Israel has been unfaithful to God ("for you have played the whore, departing from your God. You have loved a prostitute's pay on all threshing floors").[54] This follows Hosea 8, in which Israel's rebellion through idolatry is detailed, along with their trust in other nations instead of YHWH and consequent ineffectiveness of their cultus. Further explication of the termination of the cultus and impending judgment are given in 9:2-9.[55]

In Joel 1:12, 16, which occur in the context of the declaration of infertility (see above), the prophet observes that joy and gladness have disappeared from among the people along with food. Verse 16 even places food and joy in an elliptical construction that implies that the verb for food being cut off in the first clause applies to joy (שִׂמְחָה) and gladness (גִּיל) as well. However, this cloud passes quickly and not long afterwards both the land (2:21)[56] and the people (2:23)[57] are directly

---

52. Bratcher, "The Theological Message of Habakkuk," 280–1. Bratcher sees this usage of the possessive pronominal suffix as emphasizing "the prophet's degree of confidence."

53. Leigh, "A Rhetorical and Structural Study of the Book of Habakkuk," 182. Leigh states, "It is remarkable that the prophet's confession of faith in the Lord is articulated when he is reduced to the most disastrous condition. The prophet calls Him salvation in a situation which is usually regarded as the judgement of the Lord, the opposite of salvation."

54. Douglas Stuart, *Hosea–Jonah*, WBC 31 (Waco: Word, 1987), 142. This prohibition involved a reversal of expectations: "The people obviously considered their celebration of Yahweh's blessing in harvest a proper act of devotion. Hosea accuses them, however, of being covenant breakers whose celebration is evidence of their infidelity to Yahweh!"

55. Andersen and Freedman, *Hosea*, 522. Andersen and Freedman understand this to be a Canaanite form of worship the Israelites are participating in.

56. Stuart, *Hosea–Jonah*, 259. This command for the land to rejoice was both a sign of "a dramatic reversal of fortunes" as well as a reference back to the implication that the land was mourning in Joel 1.

57. Ibid. Stuart further observes that this provision from YHWH is due to his righteousness, which here implies generosity as well.

commanded to be glad and rejoice (using the appropriate imperative forms of גִּיל and שָׂמַח).[58] This change of tone comes after the prescription for fasting and repentance in 2:12-17, as well as YHWH's turn to mercy (2:18), provision of fertility (2:19), and destruction of the locusts (2:20). This blessing for which they are to rejoice is largely described in terms of the return of fertility (2:23-26).

Another negative occurrence of the theme of rejoicing occurs in Amos 6:13, where the Israelites are chided for rejoicing in dubious military victories. After Amos 6:1-7, in which the Israelites live in luxury, oblivious to impending judgment, 6:8 and 6:11 record YHWH's anger towards Israel and plans to topple the city. The reason for this punishment is identified in 6:12: the Israelites have perverted justice and righteousness. Amos 6:13 expresses this rejoicing with the substantival participle הַשְּׂמֵחִים. The object of this rejoicing is the wordplay "Lo-debar" (לֹא דָבָר), which, while referencing military victories of Jeroboam II (2 Kgs 14:28),[59] literally means "nothing," thus making this assertion an expose of "false security."[60] As a result, God will raise a nation against Israel (Amos 6:15).

In Jonah 2, Jonah's desperate prayer in the belly of the fish turns to praise and thanksgiving in its final moments. Jonah begins by crying out to God (v. 3) and reflecting with dramatic descriptions of how he was hopelessly drowning (v. 4, 6), when he looked toward the temple (v. 5). Although he was sinking to the "roots of the mountains," God saved him (v. 7), and he prayed in his moment of greatest distress (v. 8). Significantly, this expression of thanksgiving in 2:10 (2:9 in English translations) is in the context of cultic observance:

Table 5. Jonah 2:10

וַאֲנִי בְּקוֹל תּוֹדָה אֶזְבְּחָה־לָּךְ אֲשֶׁר נָדַרְתִּי אֲשַׁלֵּמָה יְשׁוּעָתָה לַיהוָה	But I with the voice of thanksgiving will sacrifice to you; what I have vowed I will pay. Deliverance belongs to the LORD!

---

58. James L. Crenshaw, *Joel*, AB 24C (New York: Doubleday, 1995), 153. Crenshaw identifies a pattern that moves from the land, to creatures, to the people, which is reminiscent of the movement from land to animals in the infertility passages surveyed above.

59. Stuart, *Hosea–Jonah*, 365. Israel wrongly saw itself as responsible for a victory that was given by YHWH.

60. David Allan Hubbard, *Joel and Amos*, TOTC (Downers Grove: InterVarsity, 1989), 199.

This expression "voice of thanksgiving" occurs in a prepositional phrase functioning adverbially to modify the cohortative verbal action of sacrificing.[61] Two clauses with cohortative verbs function in parallel to express the actions of sacrificing and paying vows,[62] and a final verbless clause expresses that salvation is from YHWH. Jonah's direct expression of deliverance ("yet you brought up my life from the Pit, O LORD my God") is back in v. 7, and directly preceding this cry of thanks in v. 10 is a polemic against idolaters in v. 9.

Another expression of celebration in a cultic context occurs in Nah. 2:1 (1:15 in English translations). Nahum 1, which some identify as an intentional parallel hymn to Habakkuk 3,[63] begins with a description of YHWH's jealous and righteous character (1:2-3), and that he can vanquish both the sea and the mountains (1:4-6). Following this there is a description of how YHWH will destroy Nineveh (1:8-14). In 2:1, the positive consequences of this action for Judah are spelled out with a description of a messenger on the mountains bringing peace and good tidings. This is followed by an imperatival summons to worship: חָגִּי יְהוּדָה חַגַּיִךְ שַׁלְּמִי נְדָרָיִךְ ("Celebrate your festivals, O Judah, fulfill your vows"). The verse ends with a reminder that Judah will no longer be invaded by the Assyrians. Clines gives the verb חָגַג a gloss of "celebrate festival."[64] Significantly, the verb שָׁלֵם, used for the paying of vows, was also used in Jon. 2:10. The context of Nahum is national instead of individual deliverance, the end result is still cultic observance in response to YHWH's saving action.

At the climax of the book of Zephaniah, Israel rejoices that their time of punishment is over. After the time in which YHWH's wrath is unleashed on Jerusalem (3:6-8), YHWH will make Israel pure (3:9), and they will worship in humility (3:10-11). The new Israel will be pure in heart and character (3:12-13), and will rejoice (3:14), as YHWH has taken away their punishment and now rejoices in them (3:15-17). In the key passage (3:14), a string of imperatives summons Israel to celebrate. They are to "sing aloud" (רָנַן), "shout" (רוּעַ), "rejoice" (שָׂמַח), and "exult" (עָלַז).

---

61. Jerome T. Walsh, "Jonah 2:3-10: A Rhetorical Critical Study," *Bib* 63 (1982): 219–29 (226). Walsh observes that this mirrors the "cry" of v. 3.

62. Stuart, *Hosea–Jonah*, 478. Jonah promises to carry out these cultic actions on subsequent occasions. Also, the final verbless clause suggests that "Yahweh is in charge of salvation." So Jack M. Sasson, *Jonah*, AB 24B (New York: Doubleday, 1990), 199. Sasson likewise emphasizes the projective nature of Jonah's desire, as his present circumstances prohibit him from carrying it out.

63. Dietrich, *Nahum*, 18.

64. David J. A. Clines (ed.), *The Dictionary of Classical Hebrew*, 9 vols (Sheffield: Sheffield Academic, 1993–2014), 3:158.

Finally, at several different places in Zechariah, the Israelites are described as rejoicing in times of renewal. The first is in 2:14 (Eng. 2:10), which occurs in the context of Jerusalem being measured for the large population that will reside in it in the time of its restoration.[65] Daughter Zion is commanded to "shout" (רָנַן) and "be glad" (שָׂמַח), due to the fact that YHWH is dwelling with her. In Zechariah 8, the blessing of the remnant is described, and part of this is the cultic celebrations they will enact with "joy" (שָׂשׂוֹן) and "gladness" (8:19) (שִׂמְחָה). In Zech. 9:9, immediately after a description of how YHWH will defeat the nations that oppressed Israel, Israel is commanded to "rejoice greatly"[66] (גִּיל modified with the adverb מְאֹד) and to "shout aloud (רוּעַ) as its king comes to make peace."[67] In Zechariah 10, in the midst of a description of YHWH's restoration of Judah (10:6, 8), it states (10:7) that the Ephraimites will be like warriors, that their hearts will be glad (שָׂמַח), as will their children,[68] who will also rejoice (גִּיל) in YHWH.

Some recurring patterns can be identified when these passages are synthesized. Negations of rejoicing, in the forms of commands not to rejoice (Hos. 9:1), observations that rejoicing has vanished from the land (Joel 1:12, 16), and the condemnation of rejoicing over falsely perceived success (Amos 6:13) all occur in the context of either impending or actual judgment that is coming as a result of disobedience. Another visible theme is the use of imperatives to command Israel's people to rejoice. These occur in Joel 2:21, 23, due to the return of fertility by YHWH's mercy, in Zeph. 3:17, in a time of restoration with all enemies vanquished and YHWH's punishment out of sight, in Zech. 2:14, in anticipation of dwelling with YHWH in safety, and in Zech. 9:9, in welcoming the victorious king who brings peace. A third recurring concept is the tying of joy to cultic observance. This happens in Jon. 2:10, where Jonah vows to sacrifice and pay vows to YHWH while in the fish, Nah. 2:1, where there is an order to celebrate festivals with the defeat of the Assyrians, and Zech. 8:18, where in the time of restoration,

---

65. Carol L. Meyers and Eric M. Meyers, *Haggai, Zechariah 1–8*, AB 25B (New York: Doubleday, 1987), 167. This vocabulary is often used for "the announcement of God's coming."

66. Carol L. Meyers and Eric M. Meyers, *Zechariah 9–14*, AB 25C (New York: Doubleday, 1993), 121. They state, "The term probably refers to the spontaneous shouting, without specific sung or spoken words, that expresses great joy."

67. Ibid., 122.

68. Ibid., 212. The children are indicative of times to come. Note the repetition of the word "heart."

the various fasts will be occasions of joy. The only text that does not
fit the above categories is Zech. 10:7, which predicts the Ephraimites
becoming joyful.

Habakkuk 3:18 is something of an outlier when placed in the context
of these passages. It does not directly mention cultic observation,[69] and
describes rejoicing in the first person in a time of infertility, instead of as
a response to fertility (such as Joel 2). In these respects (of volition and
hardship) it is most like Jon. 2:9, although lacking in the cultic element.
The vocabulary of the experience of nature is another thread tying together
Jonah 2 and Habakkuk 3.[70] However, Jonah rejoices when he has already
experienced a deliverance (albeit a deliverance to the belly of a fish),
whereas Habakkuk rejoices despite a time of outright infertility—a circum-
stance in which many of the other texts in the Twelve either commanded
the people not to rejoice, or observed that all celebration had vanished from
the land. In terms of direct lexical connections, there are no other verses in
the Old Testament that use the verbs עָלַז and גִּיל together, as does Hab. 3:18.
However, when the search parameters are broadened by a distance of up to
three verses, these verbs are used for nature rejoicing (Ps. 96:11-12), and
YHWH's people praising him (Ps. 145:2, 5), and most notably, Zeph. 3:14,
17, where daughter Zion first rejoices in v. 14 (see above), and then YHWH
rejoices in v. 17. Thus, Hab. 3:18 is a unique expression in the Twelve
of rejoicing in a time of infertility. Habakkuk expresses a level of trust
that includes praise even in the bleakest of times. As the prophet pleads
for YHWH to perform his work and show mercy (3:2) he remembers
YHWH's primeval power over not just the nations, but even nature itself
and the cosmos as a whole. This memory of past deliverance moves him to
cry out in praise even while he is still requesting salvation from suffering.

Addendum: Hope in Habakkuk 2:1

While Hab. 3:18 is unquestionably the climactic expression of trust in
YHWH at the very end of the book, one more moment of hope in a
dark time deserves to be examined, as it functions as a sort of proleptic

---

69. This is a separate matter from the question of whether or not Hab. 3 was used
liturgically in the cultus.

70. Another shared feature of Jonah and Habakkuk is that they both make use
of the first person. House, *The Unity of the Twelve*, 232, states, "Probably the most
significant point about first-person narration is that it allows the reader to identify with
the emotions of the prophets. Otherwise they can become almost god-like themselves
instead of the reader's fellow struggler."

occurrence of this theme. Habakkuk 2:1 occurs at the end of Habakkuk's second speech, stretching from 1:12–2:1. In 1:12, Habakkuk rhetorically questions the eternality of YHWH, requests his people not die, and acknowledges that indeed the Babylonians have been appointed by YHWH to execute judgment. While YHWH is compelled by his nature to destroy evil (here likely the social problems of Judah), he seems at this time to be lenient toward it (1:13). Humans are like fish that the Babylonians easily catch *ad infinitum* (1:14-17), a way of expressing the danger posed by the Babylonians. With the stage set—a context where YHWH is apparently turning a blind eye to evil and his appointed saviors are brutal and ruthless—Habakkuk expresses an openness to hear further from YHWH and places himself in a receptive posture. The chart below displays 2:1, with some formatting to aid in the recognition of the clausal structuring:

Table 6. Habakkuk 2:1

עַל־מִשְׁמַרְתִּי אֶעֱמֹדָה	I will stand at my watch-post
וְאֶתְיַצְּבָה עַל־מָצוֹר	and station myself on the rampart
וַאֲצַפֶּה לִרְאוֹת	[and] I will keep watch to see
מַה־יְדַבֶּר־בִּי וּמָה	what he will say to me
וּמָה אָשִׁיב עַל־תּוֹכַחְתִּי	and what I will answer concerning my complaint.

From the above chart, it is clear that the first two clauses exist in a parallel structure that utilizes a chiastic word order of prepositional phrase–verb–verb–prepositional phrase. Both of these verbs are cohortatives; the only other two cohortatives in form in the book are in 3:18 (see above). Habakkuk thus expresses volitional desire to be at his post. The third clause contains two additional embedded clauses beginning with indefinite pronouns modifying the verbal action "to see."[71] Habakkuk is watching for what YHWH will speak to him, and what he (Habakkuk) may return regarding his complaint.[72] While some find cultic overtones

71. Christo H. J. van der Merwe, Jackie A. Naudé and Jan H. Kroeze, *A Biblical Hebrew Reference Grammar*, Biblical Languages: Hebrew 3 (Sheffield: Sheffield Academic, 1999), 323. *BHRG* describes this use of particles that are usually interrogatives.

72. David J. Fuller, *A Discourse Analysis of Habakkuk*, SSN 72 (Leiden: Brill, 2019), 131–2, identifies links to previous parts of the book that suggest that the prophet's posture was one of trust, rather than one of desperation or manipulation. First, the prophet is still willing to "look" despite his complaints earlier about YHWH's passive observance of evil (1:3, 13). Second, Habakkuk's "looking" is an act of direct obedience to the divine commands to "watch" in 1:5.

in מִשְׁמֶרֶת,[73] Clines instead believes the military connotations are in play here, glossing this usage as a "place of watching, (sentry) post."[74] He additionally glosses מָצוֹר here as "watchtower."[75]

A significant lexical link to similar expressions in the Twelve is found with the use here of the verb צָפָה.[76] Hosea 9:8 uses a participial form functioning as a noun to express "The prophet is a sentinel for my God over Ephraim," in a context of the imminent punishment of Israel (9:7a), a nation who despises YHWH's messengers (9:7b).[77] The rest of 9:8 further describes the contempt Israel has for prophets: "a fowler's snare is on all his ways, and hostility in the house of his God." Although Hosea and Habakkuk share in this characterization of the prophet's role as one who watches, Habakkuk does not describe the kind of hostility faced by Hosea. Also relevant is Mic. 7:7, in which Micah uses the same Piel form of צָפָה in the phrase "I will look to the LORD," in the context of a land devastated by the consequences of sin (compare to Hab. 3:18, although Mic. 7:7 does not quite rise to the level of outright rejoicing).[78] Despite the circumstances, both Micah and Habakkuk resolutely look towards YHWH in expectation. This use in Micah strengthens the case that Hab. 2:1 is an expression of hope.

A final connection can tentatively be identified with Jon. 2:5 (Eng. 2:4). Although it has no direct lexical links with Hab. 2:1, there is a conceptual parallel with the usage of the verb נָבַט to express Jonah's choice to look to YHWH's temple as he is in the belly of the fish.[79] As explored above, this anticipates the cultic language in Jonah's final expression of thanksgiving in 2:10 (regardless of whether or not Jonah was truly repentant). Like Habakkuk, Jonah chooses to look to YHWH (or his temple) in a time of distress.

LeCureux (for whom returning is the main theme of the Twelve) focuses on the use of שׁוּב in the final part of Hab. 2:1. This is the only place it is used for "answering" in the Twelve, although it has this function

73. Andersen, *Habakkuk*, 192.

74. Clines (ed), *Dictionary of Classical Hebrew*, 5:547.

75. Ibid., 5:450.

76. Ibid., 7:144, glosses this usage of צָפָה in Hab. 2:1 as "look, wait (in expectation)," and the usage in Mic. 7:7 as "look with expectation (to), look with hope (to)."

77. Andersen and Freedman, *Hosea*, 533–4. Andersen and Freedman state that this, "places the prophet over against the people…he is in danger from the people, whose welfare he seeks."

78. Nogalski, *The Book of the Twelve*, 578–80. Nogalski finds further parallels between Mic. 7:1-7 and the book of Habakkuk as a whole.

79. Interestingly, נָבַט is used a number of times in Habakkuk. Of its seven other occurrences in the Twelve, four of them are in Habakkuk.

elsewhere.[80] He further observes that since it is YHWH who speaks for the remainder of Habakkuk 2, it is the hymn of Habakkuk 3 that fills the role of what Habakkuk "will answer" as described at the end of 2:1.[81] Habakkuk is anticipating that YHWH's response will result in him having a significant mood change. Thus, Hab. 2:1 serves as a pivotal point in the structure of the book as a whole. While LeCureux's insistence on connecting the occurrence of this lexeme with other calls to return in the Twelve are not convincing, his key interpretive point that this verse has the effect of involving the audience in the posing of the question of theodicy is still compelling.[82] Thus, when examined in the light of thematically similar passages in the Twelve, Hab. 2:1 is definitely an expression of hope, as the prophet's role of being a watchman in harsh times is being carried out with a watchful eye towards what YHWH is doing.

Conclusion

This study has started with the expressions of hope found in Hab. 3:18 and 2:1, and accordingly, has looked at how these assertions function in their contexts. For the case of Hab. 3:18, this necessitated investigating the theme of infertility in the Twelve and its usage, as well as the theme of rejoicing in the Twelve and its usage. This process of comparison yielded the insights that infertility generally commands a response of grieving or repentance with an expectation of a future time of restoration. In Habakkuk 3, neither of these responses are given, and there is no immediate description of a reversal of the circumstances. This observation dovetails with the study of the theme of rejoicing in the Twelve, which revealed that rejoicing is often forbidden or noted as lacking during times of judgment, that it is commanded in times of restoration, and that it is often tied to cultic observance. Habakkuk 3:18 significantly contrasts with these texts, as it explicitly has the prophet rejoicing with no immediate deliverance in sight. While the book's silence on the matter of repentance can be confusing for modern interpreters, a Babylonian- or Persian-period reading audience would doubtless have been moved to confession of sin and obedience by the prophet's example of steadfast trust even while wrestling with YHWH. As a supplementary thought, while the resolve of the prophet to stand and look to YHWH in 2:1 is comparable to other

---

80. LeCureux, *The Thematic Unity of the Book of the Twelve*, 161. Most notable are a string of appearances in Job, where it is "used as a way to answer a contentious conversation."

81. Ibid., 162.

82. Ibid., 163.

such phrasings in the Twelve, it deserves recognition as playing a key linking role in anticipating the final response of Habakkuk in Habakkuk 3. This posture of faith—rejoicing in the darkest times while recalling YHWH's past work of deliverance—is not only unique within the Twelve, but provides a valuable counterpoint to the multitude of other canonical voices that address periods of deprivation by moving immediately to expression of guilt and penitence.

Chapter 9

The Hope of Habakkuk
in the Anthropocene Age

Michael H. Floyd

Introduction

As I write this article, the novel COVID-19 virus is raging outside. By the time you read it, who knows how the pandemic may have progressed? Whether it continues unabated, or becomes somewhat manageable, or is completely contained by a vaccine, it will mark a turning point in how we think of such threats. Here I would like to suggest that this pandemic is presently the most palpable among several signs of the dawning of a new epoch in world history: the Anthropocene Age.

The defining characteristic of this new age is the extent to which human beings are affecting the ecology of the planet. Like each of earth's previous developmental stages defined by geologists, the Anthropocene Age is characterized by a different deposit layer. In this case, the earth's surface has been covered by an accumulation of never before existing chemical compounds with a distinctively human origin—plastics, for example.[1]

This accumulation of a new geological stratum goes hand in hand with the phenomenon of global warming. The age we are leaving behind, the Holocene Epoch, was characterized by the stabilization of earth's climate. For the past 11,700 years, the annual average global temperature has not

---

1. Shannon Hall, "Found: Thousands of Man-Made Minerals—Another Argument for the Anthropocene," *Scientific American*, March 1, 2017.

varied more than one degree Celsius, making possible the transition from hunter-gathering to urban civilization based on agriculture.[2] The global warming that we are currently experiencing thus portends the destabilization of long-existing ecological systems, resulting in disasters on a massive, if not global scale.[3]

Because earth's ecological systems are so deeply interrelated, no aspect of human life and no segment of the population will be unaffected. Some effects of the breakdown of these ecological systems will be sketched out below, but here at the outset, in view of the current situation, I would like to call attention to only one: the ecology of diseases. In the Anthropocene, plagues promise to become more common if not normal. The present COVID-19 pandemic is but one aspect of an overall global transformation, signaling that the many different effects of global warming, most of which have until now seemed remote from common experience, have begun hitting close to home.

With all this in the back of my mind, as I was wondering about what the future might hold for my grandchildren, I was working on several different studies of Habakkuk. It occurred to me that in the theophanic description of YHWH in ch. 3, his advent is explicitly accompanied by plague and pestilence, and it results in an earth-wide chaotic and cataclysmic eruption of earthquake and flood. Although the references to plague and pestilence are peculiar to Habakkuk 3, this same general scenario is found in other texts commonly called theophanies of YHWH.[4] As I explored the secondary literature, I found to my surprise that there was little if any sustained reflection on this theme, theological or otherwise. The thunderstorm theophany in Psalm 29, for example, has evoked a good deal of scholarly comment, but its implications are often reduced to some general remarks about the power of God in nature. The idea that the same divine power that brings salvation could also be revealed in a terrifying storm is sometimes treated as a primitive superstition arising from the fact that the ancients did not know much

---

2. Frank Oldfield, "Introduction: The Holocene, A Special Time," in *Global Change in the Holocene*, ed. Anson McKay, Rick Batarbee, John Birks, and Frank Oldfield (London: Arnold, 2005), 1–9; Neil Roberts, *The Holocene: An Environmental History*, 3rd ed. (Malden: Wiley-Blackwell, 2014), 83–177.

3. Ian Angus, *Facing the Anthropocene: Fossil Capitalism and the Crisis of the Earth System* (New York: Monthly Review Press, 2016), 27–77.

4. E.g., Exod. 19:16-20 (volcanic tremors); Judg. 5:19-22 (flood); Deut. 32:21-22 (wildfire); Pss 18:8-16 [7-15 Eng.] (earthquake and thunderstorm); Ps. 29 (thunderstorm, wildfire, and earthquake); Ps. 68:8-9 (earthquake); and Ps. 97:4-5 (thunderstorm and earthquake); Ps. 114 (earthquake).

about meteorology. One prominent writer even denies any theological significance to the thunderstorm theophany as such, characterizing it as a purely incidental metaphor for expressing a doxological intention.[5]

The main exception to the foregoing generalizations is Job's theophany in the whirlwind (Job 38:1–42:6), which has received a great deal of scholarly attention, particularly in relation to the problem of theodicy posed by the book as a whole. The complexities of Joban scholarship lie beyond the scope of this study. Suffice it to note here that the theophanies in Habakkuk 3 and Job have similarities and differences that would reward comparative analysis.[6]

In the case of Habakkuk 3, the description of YHWH's advent as cosmically chaotic is at least partly the basis for the hope that is expressed, even though this might also seem to exacerbate the problem of theodicy, which the book poses with radical frankness. Moreover, because of the way Habakkuk 3 regards YHWH's being accompanied by plague and pestilence as revelatory, it speaks to the situation in which we now find ourselves, beset by the COVID-19 pandemic here at the dawn of the Anthropocene Age. In what follows, I propose looking at Habakkuk 3 in this particular light.

A Sketch of the Anthropocene: Trends and Challenges

Global warming is the central fact of the transition to the Anthropocene. We do not yet know what will happen when human interference simultaneously stresses several global ecological cycles up to or beyond the limits of their sustainability.[7] However, it is only reasonable to suppose that such stressed ecological cycles could well reach "tipping points" at which they suddenly collapse in unpredictable ways.[8]

---

5. James L. Mays, "Psalm 29," *Int* 39 (1985): 60–4. I cannot help but suspect Karl Barth's rejection of natural theology lurking behind this view (e.g., *Church Dogmatics* 2, trans. and ed. Geoffrey W. Bromiley and Thomas F. Torrance [Edinburgh: T. & T. Clark, 1957], 168–70).

6. See, e.g., Kathryn Schifferdecker, *Out of the Whirlwind: Creation Theology in the Book of Job*, HTS 61 (Cambridge, MA: Harvard University Press, 2004); Paul Wallace, *Stars Beneath Us: Finding God in the Evolving Cosmos* (Minneapolis: Fortress, 2015).

7. Paul J. Crutzen, John R. McNeill, and Will Steffen, "The Anthropocene: Are Humans Now Overwhelming the Great Forces of Nature?" *AMBIO: A Journal of the Human Environment* 36 (2007): 614–21.

8. National Research Council, *Abrupt Impacts of Climate Change: Anticipating Surprises* (Washington, DC: National Academies, 2013).

Attempts to mitigate the warming trend by lowering carbon dioxide emissions have thus far failed, and there is no reason to expect any substantial improvement.[9] The Paris Climate Accord of 2015 established a goal of reducing emissions enough to limit warming to 2 degrees Celsius by 2100. If this goal were to be achieved, such a global temperature rise would still wreak havoc on the earth's ecosystem. Given that even this modest goal will not be met, and that greenhouse emissions will at best be minimally reduced, it is virtually certain that by 2100 there will be a rise of at least 4 degrees Celsius. A 4-degree rise will bring with it a whole new climate regime, a global environment with a completely different array of climate possibilities.[10]

All forms of life on earth will be challenged to adapt not only to higher average temperatures, but also to unpredictable and increasingly intensive above-average spikes of extreme heat. By 2100 unprecedented heat waves will affect over half the earth, and the people in these areas will live in conditions too extreme for the human body to maintain its heat balance during physical activity. Agricultural workers will face both reduced hours of work and lowered production of the crops they depend on for food and income.[11]

As arable land dries up and becomes scarce, and at the same time becomes less productive, there will be an impetus to convert more and more presently unused land to cultivation. Given current agricultural practices, this will entail ever greater use of fertilizers, resulting in greater nitrogen and phosphorous pollution. Excess nitrogen and phosphorous go from fields into streams and rivers, and eventually into the ocean, resulting in severe oxygen losses in sea water. The huge "dead zone" in the Gulf of Mexico is just the beginning of what this process portends.[12]

9. Dale Jamieson, *Reason in a Dark Time: Why the Struggle against Climate Change Failed—and What It Means for Our Future* (New York: Oxford University Press, 2014); *Emissions Gap Report 2019* (Nairobi: United Nations Environment Programme, 2019).

10. The Intergovernmental Panel on Climate Change (IPCC), which is pretty conservative in its findings, cites studies which predict that average global temperatures could rise as much as 7.8 degrees Celsius by 2100. See "Summary for Policy Makers," in *Climate Change 2014: Mitigation of Climate Change* (Cambridge: Cambridge University Press, 2014), 8.

11. Alistair Woodward et al., "Climate Change and Health: On the Latest IPCC Report," *The Lancet* 383 (2014): 1187; Potsdam Institute for Climate Impact Research and Climate Analytics, *Turn Down the Heat: Confronting the New Climate Normal* (Washington, DC: World Bank, 2014), 16.

12. Robert J. Diaz and Rutger Rosenberg, "Spreading Dead Zones and Consequences for Marine Ecosystems," *Science* 321, no. 5891 (2008): 926–9.

Human modification of the environment is perhaps most evident in what has been done to the earth's waterways, water supply, and oceans. Rivers have been so dammed, diverted, and drained for irrigation that only twelve per cent of them now run freely from source to sea. Humans control two-thirds of the world's fresh water, and are re-distributing and using it at an ever-increasing rate, mainly for expanding agricultural and industrial purposes. Humanity's present use of fresh water from sources that are regularly replenished is only barely within the limits of sustainability, and underground aquifers are being depleted much faster than their capacity to refill. Global warming will increase the need for fresh water, particularly for agriculture, at the same time when the supply begins to run lower.[13]

As fresh water sources are being diminished, carbon dioxide emissions are being dissolved in the oceans, making them too acidic for corals, many shellfish, and plankton, causing the collapse of various food webs with consequent reduction in fish and marine mammal populations. Over 75% of marine fisheries are already exhausted or pressed to the limit of their sustainability.[14] Sea levels are rising because of glacial melt, radically altering coastal habitats including many of the world's great cities.

With regard to the atmosphere, we have in the past century used up most of the fossil fuel reserves that were generated over several hundred million years, raising sulfur dioxide emissions to twice their previously existing natural level. Fluorocarbons in refrigerants and aerosols nearly depleted the stratospheric ozone layer over the Arctic and Antarctic Circles. This trend has been reversed by finding less-polluting substitutes, but it will take at least a century for the ozone layer to recover enough to once again offer protection against cancer from ultraviolet radiation.[15] Air pollution in general, even at present levels, causes about 7.2 million deaths per year.[16]

Such stresses on the ecosystems of the land, the waters, and the air will challenge all forms of life on earth, including human beings, to adapt to the changing conditions. It is not only a question of a species' capacity to

13. Johan Rockström et al., "The Unfolding Water Drama in the Anthropocene: Toward a Resilience-Based Perspective on Water for Global Sustainability," *Hydrology* 7 (2014): 1249–61.

14. United Nations Food and Agriculture Organization, "General Situation of World Fish Stocks," http://www.fao.org/newsroom/common/ecg/1000505/en/stocks.pdf.

15. Angus, *Facing the Anthropocene*, 78–88.

16. World Health Organization, http://www.who.int/phe/health_topics/outdoorair/databases/en/.

adapt, but also a question of whether it can do so quickly enough. Present experience suggests that many may not be able to do so. If current trends of habitat loss and overexploitation continue, 75% of species could die out in the next few centuries. This would be earth's sixth mass extinction event.[17]

In line with our particular concern with plagues, it is noteworthy that global warming will bring great shifts in the ecology of diseases. Climate change allows disease-causing bacteria, viruses, and fungi to move into new areas where they may harm various species, including humans. The climatic boundaries that previously limited pathogens—particularly insect-borne pathogens—to specific regions are retreating, leaving new areas open to epidemic infections for which there are no natural defenses.[18]

The growing threat of infection is a multi-dimensional and complex process in which rising temperatures are one major direct cause among other interrelated and variable factors. For example, if a species that has served as a buffer, to prevent a particular pathogen from jumping from its host to human beings, goes extinct, humans are left more vulnerable to the disease. In areas where the higher heat level is not in itself problematic, it can nevertheless converge with spikes in higher than average humidity to affect bacteria that are normally harmless to an organism, turning them lethal.[19]

Thus, the COVID-19 pandemic is not a singularity. It is an early symptom of the approaching breakdown of earth's interrelated ecological systems that will affect every aspect of human life everywhere, not only health in the narrow sense of the word. It is an integral part of the evolutionary process in reaction to human intervention. If we succeed in containing it, there will only be more mass epidemics because they will be a common if not normal part of the global transformation that is now under way.

The challenge of adaptation would be daunting enough if humanity could be expected to work together cooperatively toward a common strategy that would aim for the maximum possible wellbeing of all. However, climate change will be reaching an unprecedented crisis

17. Elizabeth Kolbert, *The Sixth Extinction: An Unnatural History* (New York: Henry Holt, 2014).

18. C. Drew Harvell et al., "Climate Warming and Disease Risks for Terrestrial and Marine Biota," *Science* 296, no. 5576 (2002): 2158–62; Felicia Keesing et al., "Impacts of Biodiversity on the Emergence and Transmission of Infectious Diseases," *Nature* 648 (December 2010): 647–62.

19. David Wallace-Wells, *The Uninhabitable Earth: Life After Warming* (New York: Tim Duggan, 2019), 109–14.

point just as the inequality between rich and poor is also reaching an unprecedented extreme.[20] Climate change will have significantly unequal impacts across regions, social groups, and economic classes, inflicting the greatest damage on poor countries with the fewest resources for effective adaptation.

> Instead of galvanizing heroic innovation and international cooperation, growing environmental and socio-economic turbulence may simply drive elite publics into more frenzied attempts to wall themselves off from the rest of humanity. Global mitigation, in this unexplored but not improbable scenario, would be tacitly abandoned—as, to some extent it already has been—in favor of accelerated investment in selective adaptation for Earth's first-class passengers. The goal would be the creation of green and gated oases of permanent affluence on an otherwise stricken planet.[21]

Archbishop Desmond Tutu has called such a policy stance "adaptation apartheid,"[22] and it has been further described as *exterminism*, defined as follows:

> the tacit or open acceptance of the necessity of mass exterminations or die-offs...as the price for continued accumulation and the political dominance of a ruling class...frequently accomplished by calculated neglect—the instruments of which are poverty, disease, and "natural" disasters...and frequently facilitated by economic isolation and the mass displacement of populations.[23]

The environmental crisis brought on by the Anthropocene thus poses for the world community an acute political and ethical question: Will we react to the coming changes defensively so as to protect our own narrowly conceived interests, continuing the same economic and social policies that have brought us to this pass, relegating the rest of the world and many of the earth's ecosystems to the global garbage heap?

---

20. Ricardo Fuentes-Nieva and Nick Galasso, "Working for the Few: Political Capture and Economic Inequality," *Oxfam International Briefing Paper* (January 2014): 2.

21. Mike Davis, "Who Will Build the Ark?" *New Left Review* 61 (2010): 38.

22. United Nations Development Program, *Human Development Report 2007/2008: Fighting Climate Change, Human Solidarity in a Divided World* (New York: Palgrave McMillan, 2007), 166.

23. Stan Goff, "Exterminism and the World in the Wake of Katrina," *From the Wilderness*, http://www.fromthewilderness.com/free/ww3/102305_exterminism_katrina.shtml, quoted in Angus, *Facing the Anthropocene*, 180.

Or will we proactively accept our responsibility to shape the world for the common good of all, changing economic and social policies so as to promote a healthy relationship between the human community and the life-sustaining global ecosystem? This is also a profoundly spiritual question, because the outcome depends in large part on our vision of the natural world and our place in it.[24] For communities of faith, the issue is the more specifically theological question of how we view God in relation to creation.[25] With this question in mind, let us now turn to consider the theophanic description of YHWH in Habakkuk 3.

God and Creation in Habakkuk 3

Habakkuk is unique among the prophetic books because it includes, as its third concluding chapter, a poem marked off at its beginning and end with annotations of a sort that are elsewhere found only in the Psalter. Many theories have been proposed concerning the origins of this poem and how it came to be associated with the main body of the book in chs 1–2.[26] I doubt whether these questions can be conclusively answered, given the limitations of the information and methods at our disposal. In any case, in this essay I am making only the minimal historical assumption that within the world of the text the setting is the Babylonian intervention in Judah in the late sixth century BCE, although the book itself may well have been written at a later date. References to "Habakkuk" or "the prophet" describe a character within the book without making any claims about a historical person.

For present purposes I propose that we consider two interpretive questions that are key points in view of the angle from which we are approaching the text, looking for what it might suggest about a theological response to the dawn of the Anthropocene Age. First, we will ask how ch. 3 is related to chs 1–2, not historically but intertextually, using the only explicit clues that we have, namely, the psalm-like annotations. Here these create inner-biblical links with the main body of the book in much the same way that similar annotations in the Psalms create inner-biblical links with passages from the narrative and prophetic books. Second, we will draw out the implications of the genre of ch. 3 for how its main sections

24. See, e.g., Jedediah Purdy, *After Nature: A Politics for the Anthropocene* (Cambridge, MA: Belknap/Harvard University Press, 2015).

25. See, e.g., David Toolan, *At Home in the Cosmos* (Maryknoll: Orbis, 2001), esp. 9–40 and 193–240.

26. See, e.g., Theodore Hiebert, *God of My Victory: The Ancient Hymn in Habakkuk 3*, HSM 38 (Atlanta: Scholars Press, 1986), 127–49.

are interrelated. Although ch. 3 is often described as a hymn, it is actually a complaint psalm, a genre that combines in a distinctive way the lamentation of adversity with trust in YHWH. Consideration of these two points will shed light on the theological basis for Habakkuk's hope for salvation, which he affirms despite the lack of a conclusive explanation for YHWH's apparent complicity with evil and injustice.

I am focusing on annotations that link psalms with particular persons. There are other sorts of information in the psalm headings, identifying the type of poem that follows, how it is to be liturgically performed, the name of the tune to which it is to be sung, etc. In addition, the obscure term *śelâ* punctuates the text of many psalms.[27] We also have these other sorts of information in the annotations to Habakkuk 3. In v. 1 the poem is identified as a "prayer" (*təpillâ*) and associated with the category of *šigyonôt* (cf. Ps. 7:1). In v. 19b the expression *lamnaṣṣēaḥ* indicates that this, like many psalms, is assigned "to the conductor," and the expression *binĝînôt* indicates that it is to be performed with string accompaniment (cf. Ps. 4:1). Also, *śelâ* appears at the conclusion of vv. 3, 9, and 13. These distinct similarities with the way poems are presented in the Psalter show that the poem in Habakkuk 3 is being presented in much the same way, although it is outside the Psalter.

We should therefore expect that the identification with Habakkuk in the heading of the poem would function in much the same way as the identification of various other persons in the headings of psalms.[28] David is the one most frequently mentioned, sometimes with a biographical reference to an incident involving him, but others are mentioned too: Jeduthun (Pss 39; 62; 77), the sons of Korah (Pss 42; 44; 47–49; 84–85; 87–88), Asaph (Pss 50; 73–83), Solomon (Pss 72; 127), Ethan the Ezrahite (Ps. 89), and Moses (Ps. 90). The LXX psalm headings also mention prophetic figures: Jeremiah and Ezekiel (Ps. 64 [65 MT]), and Haggai and Zechariah (Pss 146–148 [145–148 MT]).[29] In such cases the reference to a person in the headings serves to create a link between the psalm and how that person is characterized in historical narratives from the Pentateuch

27. Sigmund Mowinckel, *The Psalms in Israel's Worship*, trans. D. R. Ap-Thomas, 2 vols (New York and Nashville: Abingdon, 1967), 2:207–17; Eliezer Slomovic, "Toward an Understanding of the Formation of the Historical Titles in the Book of Psalms," *ZAW* 91 (1979): 350–80.

28. Brevard S. Childs, "Psalm Titles and Midrashic Exegesis," *JSS* 16 (1971): 137–50.

29. Albert Pietersma, "Septuagintal Exegesis and the Superscriptions of the Greek Psalter," in *The Book of Psalms*, ed. Peter W. Flint and Patrick D. Miller, VTSup 99 (Leiden: Brill, 2005), 443–75.

or the Former Prophets, or, particularly in the case of prophetic figures, how they are characterized in the prophetic books named for them. These inner-biblical links often create complementary connotations between the linked texts. The psalms are self-standing poems that need to be imagined in some context in order to make good sense of them, and, by being linked with a character in a narrative or prophetic book, the reader gains an awareness of context that would otherwise be lacking. Conversely, the characters in biblical narrative and prophetic books often have little attention paid to their inner thoughts and feelings,[30] and, by their being linked with a psalm that fits their situation, the reader often gains a "window into the soul" that would otherwise be lacking.

For example, the heading of Psalm 51 associates it with David, "when Nathan the prophet came to him, after he had gone into Bathsheba." Without this link, Psalm 51 would have to be read as a general confession with no particular sin in view. Now, however, it smacks specifically of adultery. And conversely, over in 2 Samuel 12, upon being confronted by Nathan, David matter-of-factly confesses his guilt, saying "I have sinned against the LORD" (2 Sam. 12:13). Without the link to Psalm 51, the reader would have to leave it at that, but in view of the connection the reader can imagine via the psalm something of David's inner grief and guilty turmoil. Similarly, when Psalm 147 is linked with the descriptions of Haggai and Zechariah's temple-restoration efforts in the books named for them, as well as in Ezra 5:1-3 and 6:13-15, the reference to YHWH "building up Jerusalem and gathering the outcasts of Israel" (v. 2) is no longer just a generally praiseworthy attribute, but the reflection of the particular project of temple restoration with which these prophets were associated. Conversely, the theological motivation of these prophets remains somewhat obscure until one imagines via the psalm the thoughts and feelings that would have driven them to serve YHWH in this way.

If we similarly construe the relationship between Habakkuk 3 and the main body of the book in chs 1–2, these two parts of the book likewise gain complementary connotations in relation to one another. The poem gains a specific historical context, which it would otherwise not have by virtue of its own internal references to its setting. The poem says only that YHWH "tramples the nations" in order to save his people (vv. 12-13). Read in light of chs 1–2, where the prophet complains about the oppressive domination of the Babylonians and

---

30. Erich Auerbach famously observed that little attention is typically given to the inner thoughts and feeling of the characters in biblical narrative (*Mimesis: The Representation of Reality in Western Literature* [Princeton: Princeton University Press, 1953], 1–23).

YHWH promises eventual deliverance, the poem can be read as envisioning the defeat of Babylon in a cataclysmic transformation of the world order.

When read in light of the poem, chs 1–2 gain a similar specificity. There the defeat of Babylon is described only as the consequence of its overly exploitative and finally self-defeating imperialism. When chs 1–2 are read in light of the poem, the reader can see something of the theological motivation that underlies the prophet's life-affirming and steadfast faith in YHWH's promise of deliverance, despite all outward appearances to the contrary. Habakkuk's confidence is rooted in the constancy of YHWH's character as Creator. The author of the world order, including the natural as well as the social order, is always breaking down whatever power structures thwart his desire for a just world, and always reconstituting new ones that have the potential for better fulfilling this desire.

Assuming this view of the book as a whole, let us look more closely at the poem in ch. 3. It has the basic elements of the complaint genre:

1. invocation of YHWH (v. 2a)
2. petition for deliverance (v. 2b)
3. hymnic description of YHWH's deliverance (vv. 3-15)
4. description of the supplicant's distress (v. 16) and
5. an affirmation of confidence (vv. 17-19a).[31]

Habakkuk 3 resembles several other examples of the complaint genre in which YHWH's deliverance is described in terms of mythic events. In this and several other cases, YHWH's action is portrayed as a re-actualization of mythic reports that the prophet has heard about a primeval battle between YHWH and the chaos monster—Israel's variation on a common ancient Near Eastern creation myth pattern.[32] Habakkuk 3 is distinctive because in v. 7 the prophet gives a first-person report of having witnessed the onset of the kind of cosmic shake-up that is implied in such a retelling of the combat myth.

By this interpretation of the fall of Babylon as a re-actualization of the combat myth, the text does not imply that the fantastic exploits described in Hab. 3:3-15 were literally witnessed by the prophet as events that

---

31. Erhard S. Gerstenberger, *Psalms: Part I with an Introduction to Cultic Poetry*, FOTL 14 (Grand Rapids: Eerdmans, 1988), 11–14; Michael H. Floyd, *Minor Prophets: Part 2*, FOTL 22 (Grand Rapids: Eerdmans, 2000), 152–7.

32. E.g., Pss 74, 77, and 89. See John Day, *God's Conflict with the Dragon and the Sea: Echoes of a Canaanite Myth in the Old Testament* (Cambridge: Cambridge University Press, 1985).

actually happened. The intent is to draw a figurative analogy between the mythic narrative of the creation and the fall of Babylon. In both cases, violent struggle transforms a world dominated by the oppressive forces of chaos into a world ordered in a new and more just way. The mythic events in the narrative did not actually happen, but they provide a symbolic pattern in terms of which the prophet can understand the significance of events that are actually happening. The prophet's report in v. 7 of his having seen seismic tremors in the south is not a claim that YHWH's battle with chaos is literally unfolding before his eyes. It is the prophet's observation of a sign that Babylon's fall, which is currently under way, is actually happening in a way that portends what the comparison with the myth suggests. An oppressive and unjust world order is disintegrating, making possible the establishment of a new and more just world order.

Despite this evidence of YHWH's activity, the poem ends with the supplicant still waiting for deliverance, affirming that he will continue to hope even if no further signs of YHWH's salvific intentions appear (vv. 16-19a). The description of YHWH's victory in vv. 3-15 should thus be understood in terms of the convention that is found in some complaints: the supplicant affirms that YHWH has accepted his petition, that YHWH has already begun to respond to the supplicant's petition, and in effect achieved it, whether this is in the supplicant's favor or not.[33]

In what follows, our focus is on the theophany described in vv. 3-15, but it should be noted that the function of such hymnic description within the complaint genre is to provide a basis for the affirmation of confidence. This means that the kind of affirmation of confidence that we find in vv. 17-19a—expressing hope despite the lack of conclusive evidence— is based on the kind of theophanic description that we find in vv. 3-15. Moreover, in view of the relationship of ch. 3 to chs 1–2, this theophanic description also provides the theological underpinnings for the kind of faith that YHWH commends in 2:4b, in response to the prophet's oracular inquiry concerning the duration of Babylonian domination. Thus, we now turn to take a closer look at vv. 3-15.

Habakkuk 3:3-12 describes the advent of YHWH. He is portrayed as the divine warrior, marching from the south to Judah (v. 3).[34] He appears

33. E.g., Pss 6:10 [9 Eng.]; 22:25b [24b Eng.]; 28:6; 54:9 [7 Eng.]; 56:14 [13 Eng.]; 71:24b; and Jon. 2:6b; etc. Cf. the anticipatory thanksgiving in Pss 13:7 [6 Eng.]; 22:25-24 [24–25 Eng.]; 31:22 [21 Eng.]; 40:2-4 [1-3 Eng.]; and 69:30-36 [31-37 Eng.].

34. The route of the divine warrior is conventionally portrayed as coming from the region of Edom—Teman, Mount Paran, Seir, etc.—to the defense of Israel (e.g., Deut. 33:2 and Judg. 5:4).

with an explosive flash of light that emanates from his hand (v. 4). He brings with him in his retinue *deber* who precedes him, and *rešep* who follows close behind (v. 5). *Rešep* is a proper name referring to the widely revered ancient Near Eastern god Resheph, as well as a common noun meaning both "flame" and "pestilence."[35] All of these meanings are perhaps connoted here. In ancient Near Eastern mythology, the divine warrior god is conventionally described as accompanied by a retinue of other auxiliary gods.[36] Elsewhere YHWH's advent is described as preceded by flames of fire (e.g., Ps. 97:3). Here, however, the poetic parallel with *deber*, which means "plague," emphasizes the reference of *rešep* to "pestilence." Pestilence and plague are here personified, as if they were YHWH's divine companions. Thus, YHWH brings with him, in a burst of cosmic energy, an outbreak of infectious diseases.

These two personifications of "plague" and "pestilence" do not explicitly reappear or play any part in the ensuing action, but neither do they completely disappear. Their role is to serve as a prelude to YHWH's subsequent actions, which follow from what their coming initiates. They are symptomatic of an imbalance in one aspect of the global ecosystem, which portends a larger disruption of the whole cosmos. The epidemics that accompany YHWH's advent are subsumed within the dynamics of the broader crisis as one among several simultaneously occurring ecological disturbances, such as drought and famine (v. 17) permeating earth, sky, and sea.

As YHWH takes his stand (v. 6) the earth begins to tremble, throwing the nations into turmoil. Earthquake is a conventional element in the description of YHWH's theophany (cf. Judg. 5:4-5; Pss 29:6-8; 97:5; 114:4-8). What is unusual here—as has already been mentioned above—is the prophet's own first-person report of having seen the localized effects of the tremor (v. 7), which are described in terms of what happens to "the tents of Cushan" and "the curtains of the land of Midian." The location of Cushan is uncertain. Midian lies south of Edom, just west of the Gulf of Aqaba. "Tents" (*'ohālîm*) and "curtains" (*yərî'ôt*) are a formulaic word pair that forms a *merismus*, two contrasting terms referring to an entirety. This word pair figuratively represents all dwelling places in general, although it obviously reflects a nomadic rather than an urban setting, as in Jer. 4:20 (RSV):

---

35. Maciej M. Münnich, *The God Resheph in the Ancient Near East*, ORA 11 (Tübingen: Mohr Siebeck, 2013).

36. Shaul Bar, "Resheph in the Hebrew Bible," *JQR* 45 (2017): 121.

> Disaster follows hard on disaster,
>   the whole land is laid waste.
> Suddenly my tents are destroyed,
>   my curtains in a moment.

The dwelling places of the region from whence YHWH comes are "in trouble" (*taḥat 'āwen*) and are "trembling" (*yirgəzūn*). This report that the prophet has seen signs of the earthquake serves to affirm that YHWH's initiative is actually underway.

How could the prophet, presumably based in Judah, have "seen" something happening so far to the south? Scholars have long debated whether parts of Habakkuk are visionary because the superscription uses the verb *ḥāzâ* to describe the prophet's activity (1:1), and YHWH's reply to the prophet's oracular inquiry in 2:2 instructs him to "write the *ḥāzôn*." These terms can refer to visions in the strict sense, but they can also refer to revelations in general, which do not necessarily entail any specifically visionary experience.[37] In the superscription the verb *ḥāzâ* probably refers to the revelation represented by the book as a whole: "the oracle (*maśśā'* revealed to Habakkuk the prophet" (1:1).[38] In 2:2 the *ḥāzôn* to be transcribed is probably YHWH's response to the oracular inquiry in 2:4ff. The *ḥzh* terminology in 1:1 and 2:2 seems not to denote prophetic visionary experience, but v. 7 could nevertheless be a prophetic vision report.

The prophet explicitly states that his description of YHWH's actions is based on reports that he has "heard" about YHWH's exploits in the distant past (v. 2a; cf. v. 16a). But he also prays for these exploits to be re-actualized in the present, and the report in v. 7 affirms that he has "seen" this begin to happen. In other words, he has perceived something happening which indicates that current events are unfolding in the way suggested by a comparison with the mythic pattern in vv. 3-15 (see above). Vision reports are often explicitly identified by a formulaic introduction, such as "YHWH showed me" (with *rā'â* in the Hiphil, e.g., Amos 7:1; Zech. 3:1), or "I lifted my eyes and saw" (e.g., Zech. 5:1; 6:1). However, vision reports can also be introduced simply with "I saw" (*rā'îtî*, e.g., Isa. 6:1; Amos 9:1). It is thus plausible to suppose that the report of the re-actualization of the ancient mythic pattern in v. 7, using this same verb form, has a visionary basis. Ezekiel's visions of what is

---

37. D. Vetter, חזה, *TLOT* 1:400–403.

38. On the meaning of *maśśā'* see Michael H. Floyd, "The משא (*Maśśā'*) as a Type of Prophetic Book," *JBL* 121 (2002): 401–22; idem, "The Meaning of *Maśśā'* as a Prophetic Term in Isaiah," *JHS* 18, Article 9, DOI:10.5508/jhs.2018.v18.a9.

happening in the temple in Jerusalem, which he sees while in Babylon, are similarly characterized by clairvoyant perception of events at a distance (Ezek. 8:1–11:25).

Having taken his stand, YHWH engages his enemies (vv. 8-15). Initially, this is described in a way that echoes the god Baal's fight with his foes in the Ugaritic myths, as a struggle against rivers and sea (vv. 8-11). Convoluted syntax makes it difficult to discern the details of this encounter.[39] It is clear, however, that the earthquakes that accompanied YHWH's advent continue (v. 16a) and that in the course of the struggle YHWH unleashes devastating floods (vv. 9b, 10aβ). In the second phase of the battle (vv. 12-15) YHWH again takes his stand (v. 12) and attacks the foe that is oppressing his own people (v. 13a). This time the opposition takes the form of an unnamed sea monster, echoing the god Marduk's struggle against the monster Tiamat in the Babylonian creation story, *Enuma Elish*, as well as YHWH's struggle against the monsters Rahab and Leviathan in parallel Israelite traditions (Pss 74:14-16; 89:9-10; Job 26:12; Isa. 27:1; 51:9-10). Again, obscure phraseology makes it difficult to discern precisely how YHWH disposes of the monster and its carcass (vv. 13b-14),[40] but in so doing victory is decisively achieved over the sea as well as its monstrous metamorphosis.

From the way YHWH is portrayed in Habakkuk 3, four conclusions can be drawn that are particularly significant for present purposes. First, the scope of YHWH's action is cosmic. The focus of the book is initially on the effect of Babylon's intervention primarily on Judah (1:1-4). Then the perspective is gradually broadened to include the nations as a whole (1:5–2:20). In ch. 3 the perspective is extended still more to all creation. This relativizes the unjust situation with which the prophet is concerned. His question is still on the table, but seen in a much larger context. YHWH is delivering his people by bringing about the downfall of Babylon, but he accomplishes this by destroying and re-creating the entire world order. Babylon is the most immediate manifestation of a global system that unjustly exploits the world's natural resources as well as its human populations (2:8, 17). The process of destruction and renewal encompasses and affects all the earth.

---

39. See the analysis of problems and an interesting proposed solution in Aron Pinker, "God's C³ in Habakkuk 3," *ZAW* 112 (2000): 261–5.

40. Hiebert, *God of My Victory*, 101–9; J. J. M. Roberts, *Nahum, Habakkuk, and Zephaniah*, OTL (Louisville: Westminster John Knox), 56–7; Walter Dietrich, *Nahum, Habakkuk, Zephaniah*, IECOT (Stuttgart: Kohlhammer, 2016), 163.

Second, YHWH not only battles against chaos, he also brings chaos. Because the actions that YHWH takes to deliver his people are a re-actualization of the actions he took to create heaven and earth, they show that creation is an ongoing and inherently chaotic process, in which destructive forms of chaos appear, and YHWH creatively uses other forms of chaos to contain, eliminate, or transform them. This is how YHWH is always breaking down whatever power structures thwart his desire for a just world, and always recreating new ones that have the potential for better fulfilling this desire.

Third, the prophet can realistically hope for an end to Babylonian domination, despite all indications to the contrary, precisely because he sees that YHWH wields as well as contends with chaos. He recognizes that, in the chaotic upheaval that he sees all around him, there are creative forces as well as destructive forces in play. Although YHWH's victory over the threatening forces is not yet fully realized, the prophet can be confident that it will finally be accomplished because this is how creation evolves in the hands of the Creator.

Fourth, the realistic expectation of deliverance from Babylonian domination does not altogether resolve the theodicy problem as it is posed in chs 1–2. By unleashing ecological catastrophes—epidemics, earthquakes, and floods, drought and famine—YHWH is able to counter the forces that are threatening his people, forces which arise from the interaction of a tyrannical international order with violent forces of the natural order. However, these catastrophes will affect the unjust and the just alike. YHWH will indeed visit on the oppressors their just deserts, but the means that YHWH employs to bring down the Babylonian tyranny and create the possibility of a new and more just world order will also bring undeserved suffering to the innocent, including his own people.

God in the Anthropocene

Of course, the world view of Habakkuk and the modern evolutionary world view are different, but when the crisis that Habakkuk confronted is considered in relation to his world view, and the crisis that we confront is considered in relation to our world view, the situations are analogous in four major respects.

First, both crises are the result of human greed. In Habakkuk's case, it is Babylon's addiction to imperialistic conquest, and in our case, it is our socio-economic system's addiction to fossil fuels that has brought the world order to a breaking point.

Second, both crises, when viewed in cosmic perspective, appear to be caught in an interplay of superhuman forces because greedy humans have violated the moral order of creation. For Habakkuk, YHWH is reordering the world because the Babylonians have transgressed the cosmic principle of justice ($ṣədāqâ$). In our case, rising temperatures are altering the planet's ecological life-support systems because we have resisted what Martin Luther King Jr. called "the moral arc of the universe," which "is long but tends toward justice."[41]

Third, both crises bring on chaos. Chaos results from the wrongdoing of greedy humans, and chaos is unleashed by the superhuman forces that are enforcing the moral order of creation. Chaos is thus both destructive and creative. It disintegrates the oppressive power structures and also makes it possible for new, more just alternatives to emerge.

And fourth, as both crises unfold, the onset of chaotic conflict produces a spectacle that evokes both terror and amazement. For Habakkuk, envisioning the eventual downfall of Babylon in mythic terms produces visceral fear and trembling (3:16a), and at the same time enables him to maintain his confidence in the outcome despite drought and famine (3:16b-17). Even as he trembles in fear, he also ecstatically exults in the still-incomplete manifestation of YHWH's power (3:18-19a). For us, the superhuman forces that are bringing us ineluctably to the point of ecological collapse are terrifying in their destructiveness, but also amazing in the intricacies of their interaction as they struggle to maintain the web of life.

In light of these similarities, we can sketch a view of God in relation to the global warming crisis and the ethical challenge that it poses for people of faith. This will be a view that is informed by Habakkuk's description of YHWH in action, but framed in terms of our present situation.

Following Habakkuk, we see a God who is intimately involved in the world, including the events of human history as well as natural phenomena. God is continually creating out of chaos. Some of the chaos is unleashed by the powers that threaten life and impose injustice, and some of the chaos is unleashed by God's own self. In this conflict of forces, the powers that promote life and foster justice are affirmed and reinforced. Salvation happens within the conflictive and creative evolution of the cosmos. In the process, random suffering occurs, but God does not remain unaffected. God struggles and, by implication, suffers, too.

---

41. King quoted this saying of the nineteenth-century preacher Theodore Parker in several of his articles and speeches, beginning with "Out of the Long Night," in *The Gospel Messenger* (Elgin, IL: General Brotherhood Board, Church of the Brethren, February 8, 1958), beginning on p. 3.

When the relationship between God and the world is imagined in this way, the ecological catastrophe that we face is ambiguous. On the one hand, it can be seen as the destructive reaction of the earth and its Creator against the unjust use of natural resources and exploitation of people, the inevitable result of human mismanagement of the earth. On the other hand, it can also be seen as the creative initiative of the earth and its Creator, clearing away the debris of the old way of life and making the necessary preparation for the emergence of a new way of life. The challenge is to maintain these two perspectives in creative tension, fully acknowledging the coming disaster and the suffering that it will bring, but not becoming so demoralized by this dismal prospect that we lose all hope in new possibilities.

The motivation for maintaining this delicate balance comes from viewing our situation in cosmic perspective. When we look back at our planet from outer space, which we can now do with photographs taken by astronauts, the view is both sobering and amazing. It is sobering because we can see that the divisions that seem so important and divisive here below—between nations, races, economic classes, and even species— are insignificant within the larger picture. This view of earth as a global community is conducive to an ethical attitude that values the solidarity of human beings with one another and with all living things. In the fallout from global warming, some are indeed more vulnerable and disadvantaged than others, but, in the final analysis, all are in the same danger of extinction. As Benjamin Franklin put it, in relation to a quite different crisis, "We must all hang together, or, most assuredly, we shall all hang separately."[42]

The view from outer space of "this fragile earth, our island home"[43] is amazing because we can see how contingent and beautiful life is. Our globe appears literally pulsing with the energy and color of life. It is highly unlikely that life is unique to our planet, but among the immense number of planets in the universe those that could support life are few and far between. As we face the consequences of global warming, planetary life-support systems cannot be taken for granted. This view is conducive to an ethical attitude rooted in gratitude and appreciation for life, which values life-affirming practices and policies. As the neurologist Oliver Sacks put it, reflecting on his terminal illness, "Above all, I have been a

---

42. Attributed to Benjamin Franklin at the signing of the US Declaration of Independence (August 2, 1776), cited in John Bartlett, *Familiar Quotations*, 10th ed. (Boston: Little, Brown & Co., 1919), quotation 3949.

43. "Eucharistic Prayer C," in *The Book of Common Prayer*, 370.

sentient being, a thinking animal, on this beautiful planet, and that in itself has been an enormous privilege and adventure."[44]

When we peer outward into the universe at large, we become aware of how life on earth is an integral part of an immense evolutionary process, in which creation is continually emerging out of chaos. In a recent NASA "Astronomy Picture of the Day" email there was a photograph of the Orion Nebula, an immense interstellar molecular cloud some 1,500 light years away. According to the caption, within this nebula "unspeakable beauty and unimaginable bedlam can be found together" as stars are being born. This spectacle beckons to us, inviting us to participate in the process of bringing beauty out of bedlam.

The ethical challenge of the Anthropocene Age is framed in terms of whether we will make a positive contribution to the creative evolution of the universe, as it plays out here on earth. In the face of the global warming disaster will we retreat into closed communities, monopolizing scarce resources in order to feed our consumeristic addictions, remaining indifferent to the fate of others less advantaged? Or will we stand in solidarity with fellow creatures, taking life-affirming action for the common good, deconstructing the socio-economic structures of fossil fuel civilization, and building from its debris the infrastructure for a new, more just way of life?

Habakkuk shows that the latter alternative is possible and more compelling. He models how we can imagine God reacting creatively to oppressive domination. On the one hand, the prophet fully experiences the chaos caused by the oppressors and the chaos with which God responds. On the other hand, he also remains confident and engaged in the possibility that this conflict will result in the overthrow of the oppressors and their replacement with a more just regime.

It is mere coincidence that the onset of the Babylonian crisis and the onset of the global warming crisis are both marked by an epidemic outbreak. However, in both the mythic pattern that informs Habakkuk's view of his situation and the climate change process that we are beginning to experience, epidemics are a veritable omen of what is to come. The coincidence can thus be a suggestive symbol of the real analogies between his situation and ours, which can inform our present outlook.

For Habakkuk, plague was a sign of YHWH's involvement in a convulsive world situation, which he knew would get substantially worse before it got any better. Because of YHWH's creative involvement he could nevertheless confidently hope that it would get better, and he could

44. Oliver Sacks, "My Own Life," in *Gratitude* (New York: Knopf, 2015), 20.

be inspired to keep contributing to that outcome. Could the COVID-19 pandemic be a similar sign for us, pointing to God's involvement in a convulsive world situation, which we know will get substantially worse before it gets any better? And because of God's creative involvement in defense of nature, could we nevertheless be confidently hopeful that it will get better, and also be inspired to keep contributing to that outcome?

Chapter 10

CREATING AND BRIDGING THE GAP:
ASSYRIA AND BABYLON IN THE PRESENTATION
OF THEODICY AND HOPE IN THE BOOK OF THE
TWELVE

Mark J. Boda

Julia O'Brien, in her study of the Twelve, argues that Hosea–Zephaniah provides the witness referred to as the "earlier prophets" within the book of Zechariah at 1:4-6 and 7:7, 12.[1] These prophetic books provide evidence for the recalcitrance of the "ancestors" who rejected the message of the "earlier prophets," as well as proof of how the nations used to discipline Israel and Judah were destined for judgment for exceeding their mandate (1:14-17; 2:4 [1:21 Eng.]). O'Brien sees in Nahum and Habakkuk references to the two key empires used by Yahweh to discipline Israel and Judah; Nahum addresses the demise of Assyria and Habakkuk addresses Babylon. Helpful in her work is identification of the role that Hosea–Zephaniah in general and Nahum–Zephaniah in particular play in the presentation of theodicy and hope in Zechariah.

One issue, however, that is not addressed by O'Brien relates to the presentation of Assyria and Babylon in Zechariah and in the books which precede it. Hosea–Zephaniah grants far greater space in its presentation to Assyria's rise and fall. In contrast, Babylon is largely ignored with little to no mention in general. For the Yehudite community recovering after the Babylonian period, one would expect greater emphasis on Babylon, the

---

1. Julia M. O'Brien, "Nahum, Habakkuk, Zephaniah: Reading the 'Former Prophets' in the Persian Period," *Int* 61 (2007): 168–83.

disciplinary agent of Yahweh against Judah and Jerusalem, and increased prominence on the demise of Judah and Jerusalem at its hands. This present contribution reflects on the greater emphasis on Assyria rather than Babylon in the Book of the Twelve and how this relates to the presentation of theodicy and hope in the collection as a whole.

Assyria and Babylon in Hosea–Zephaniah

The historical notation which begins the book of Zephaniah, דְּבַר־יהוה אֲשֶׁר הָיָה אֶל ("the word of Yahweh which came to"), is identical to two earlier prophets in the Twelve: Hosea (1:1) and Micah (1:1) and similar to Amos (1:1; דִּבְרֵי עָמוֹס אֲשֶׁר־הָיָה). This evidence of similarities between these four superscriptions laid the foundation for the theory that these four books were an original prophetic collection associated with the Deuteronomic renewal at the time of Josiah.[2] This collection contains three prophets (Hosea, Amos, Micah) who spoke during the period of the rise of Assyrian hegemony over the Levant and concludes with a prophet (Zephaniah) who spoke during the period of the demise of Assyria at Babylonian hands. The two earlier prophets whose superscriptions are closest to that of Zephaniah (Hosea and Micah) contain multiple references to Assyria (Hos. 5:13; 7:11; 8:9; 9:3; 10:6; 11:5, 11; 12:1; 14:4 [3 Eng.]; Mic. 5:4-5 [5-6 Eng.]) and Assyria is also featured in the book of Zephaniah, placed at the climactic end of the oracles against the nations in ch. 2 as Yahweh announces the destruction of Assyria and Nineveh (2:13-15).

This Assyrian theme dominates the book of Nahum, which also focuses on the destruction of Nineveh. However, between Nahum and Zephaniah lies the book of Habakkuk with its passing reference to the "Chaldeans" (כַּשְׂדִּים) in 1:6, a term associated with the Babylonians. Some have treated this reference as a late gloss or a cipher for the nations in general, and along with this date the book to the Hellenistic era.[3] Others use this reference to

2. James D. Nogalski, *Literary Precursors to the Book of the Twelve*, BZAW 217 (Berlin: de Gruyter, 1993), 176–8; Aaron Schart, *Die Entstehung des Zwölfprophetenbuchs*, BZAW 260 (Berlin: de Gruyter, 1998), 156–230; Jakob Wöhrle, "'No Future for the Proud Exultant Ones': The Exilic Book of the Four Prophets (Hos., Am., Mic., Zeph.) as a Concept Opposed to the Deuteronomistic History," *VT* 58 (2008): 608–27.

3. E.g., Anselm C. Hagedorn, "Diaspora or No Diaspora? Some Remarks on the Role of Egypt and Babylon in the Book of the Twelve," in *Perspectives on the Formation of the Book of the Twelve: Methodological Foundations, Redactional Processes, Historical Insights*, ed. Rainer Albertz, James Nogalski, and Jakob Wöhrle, BZAW 111 (Berlin: de Gruyter, 2012), 332. For an excellent recent review of issues related

locate the book at some point in the history of the Neo-Babylonian Empire
with many linking it to the late seventh century BCE, whether prior to
the fall of Nineveh or at the beginning of Neo-Babylonian hegemony.
In his review of these issues, Jones notes that "Habakkuk stands out as
a text that is more evocative than referential in its relation to historical
circumstances."[4] The evocative nature of this presentation in Habakkuk
along with its allusion to the Babylonians make its historical referentiality
malleable within its present position within the Twelve, making the books
surrounding it important to its historical placement.[5]

Several have noted how Nahum and Habakkuk betray signs that they
were preserved as a collection.[6] Both begin with similar oracular terms:
מַשָּׂא and חֲזוֹן (Nah. 1:1); מַשָּׂא and חָזָה (Hab. 1:1). Additionally, Nahum
begins and Habakkuk ends with theophanic hymns, which contain
verbal correspondences and which frame speeches against the nations
using a ring structure. This close literary connection along with the
reference to Babylon as an agent of discipline suggests that both Nahum
and Habakkuk are focused on the destruction of Assyria, with Nahum
declaring its destruction and Habakkuk identifying the Chaldeans as the
agent to enact this destruction. In the case of Habakkuk, the fall of Assyria
has implications for Judah and Jerusalem, which sets up the link between
the fall of Assyria and Jerusalem in this section of the Twelve. Placed just

---

to dating the books of Nahum, Habakkuk, and Zephaniah, see Barry A. Jones, "The
Seventh-Century Prophets in Twenty-First Century Research," *CBR* 14 (2016):
129–75.

4. Jones, "The Seventh-Century Prophets," 138.

5. Contra Dietrich who sees the sequence of books Nahum, Habakkuk, Zephaniah as conspicuous because of their respective relationship to the empires of the
day (Assyria–Babylon–Assyria); Walter Dietrich, "Three Minor Prophets and the
Major Empires: Synchronic and Diachronic Perspectives on Nahum, Habakkuk,
and Zephaniah," in Albertz, Nogalski, and Wöhrle (eds), *Perspectives on the
Formation of the Book of the Twelve*, 147–56. There is nothing odd with this
sequence if one understands that the rise of Babylon is key to the demise of Assyria
as well as Judah.

6. Schart posits a Nahum–Habakkuk collection, while Kessler speaks of "Zwei-
prophetenschrift" of Nahum–Habakkuk prior to inclusion in the Twelve. Baumann
identifies enough links between Nah. 1:2-8, Hab. 3, and Zephaniah to suggest a prior
collection comprising these texts. Schart, *Entstehung*, 246–51; Gerlinde Baumann,
*Gottes Gewalt im Wandel: Traditionsgeschichtliche und Intertextuelle Studien zu
Nahum 1,2-8*, WMANT 108 (Neukirchen–Vluyn: Neukirchener Verlag, 2005); Rainer
Kessler, "Nahum–Habakuk als Zweiprophetenschrift: Eine Skizze," in *Gotteserdung:
Beiträge zur Hermeneutik und Exegese der Hebräischen Bibel*, BWANT 170 (Stutt-
gart: Kohlhammer, 2006), 137–45; Dietrich, "Three Minor Prophets."

prior to Zephaniah within the Book of the Twelve, this Nahum–Habakkuk collection joins together with Zephaniah to announce the destruction of Assyria in the final quarter of the seventh century BCE—a destruction that has implications for the people of God.

It is noteworthy that while Hosea–Zephaniah refer to Assyria on many occasions, there is only passing mention of Babylon.[7] Babylon appears in one of the eighth-century BCE books—in Mic. 4:10 in reference to the exile of the population of Jerusalem, but this passage focuses on the rescue of this group from Babylon. The second reference, as noted above, is to the Chaldeans in Hab. 1:6, a people group that Habakkuk declares is being raised up to punish the Assyrians. There is very little focus on Babylon in Hosea–Zephaniah; instead the focus is squarely on Assyria: at its rise and its fall, concentrating then on the eighth and seventh centuries BCE.[8] What is not emphasized, however, are details on the Babylonian destruction of Judah and Jerusalem.

Allusions to this experience can be discerned in Habakkuk 2, which orients righteous readers to wait patiently for the appointed time, living by faithfulness through the coming ordeal of a force that "gathers to itself all the nations and collects to itself all the peoples" (Hab. 2:3-5). Habakkuk 3 again speaks of waiting quietly for the day of distress (Hab. 3:16). Such an approaching distressful day is announced in Zeph. 3:1-7. These verses proclaim a woe on a city in which Yahweh "is righteous in its midst" and whose destiny includes ruined corner towers, desolate streets, destroyed and uninhabited cities. No mention is made of the vessel that Yahweh will use for this judgment (Babylon), but the woe associates the demise of Jerusalem with the destruction of Assyrian Nineveh.

This association between Judean Jerusalem and Assyrian Nineveh is seen in connections between Zephaniah and Nahum. While Nahum is focused on Nineveh and Assyria entirely, and Zephaniah looks more broadly to various nations in the Levant and Africa, Zephaniah eventually turns its attention to Nineveh and Assyria, placing it in the final and climactic position at the end of ch. 2. Both books end with a woe oracle against an initially unmentioned city (Nah. 3:1; Zeph. 3:1). The identity of both becomes clear as the woe oracle proceeds; Nahum's city is Nineveh,

---

7. See further Mark J. Boda, "Babylon in the Book of the Twelve," *HBAI* 3 (2014): 225–48.

8. See my recent analysis of the geography in the Twelve and the connection between the eighth-century prophets (Hosea, Amos, Micah) and political dynamics of the Assyrian period; Mark J. Boda, "Geography in the Book of the Twelve," in *The Book of the Twelve: Composition, Reception, and Interpretation*, ed. Lena-Sofia Tiemeyer and Jakob Wöhrle, VTSup 184 (Leiden: Brill, 2020), 507–31.

while Zephaniah's is Jerusalem.[9] The association between these two endings to the respective books is further bolstered by the ambiguous structural distinction between the oracle against Nineveh in Zeph. 2:13-15 and the woe oracle against Jerusalem in Zeph. 3:1-7. This evidence highlights once again the importance of the fall of Assyria for the depiction of the demise of Jerusalem and Judah in the Twelve. The unnamed common denominator is the Babylonians and yet the details of the events of the first quarter of the sixth century BCE are largely passed over. There is reference to a coming destruction of Jerusalem at the beginning and end of Zephaniah, but the beginning is described in more cosmic terms (Zeph. 1) and the end utilizes a woe oracle with few details that focuses more on the close affinity between the demise of Nineveh and Jerusalem than on the Babylonians who were the means of divine judgment for both (Zeph. 3:1-7).

Before discussing Haggai–Malachi, one final piece of evidence must be mentioned. Assyria is also featured in the book of Jonah. Its placement among the eighth-century BCE prophets (Hosea, Amos, Micah) makes sense in light of the connection to Jeroboam II's reign in the tradition of 2 Kings (14:25). Its role in the Book of the Twelve has been explained in terms of its relation to the book of Nahum, especially in the key reversal of Yahweh's stance towards the city as one moves from Jonah to Nahum.[10] However, its presence with Joel among the eighth-century BCE prophets provides an additional way to understand its role in the Twelve. In both we find identical penitential traditions based on the character creed of Exodus 34, with one involving Jerusalem/Judah and the other the gentile city of Nineveh.[11] While the books of Nahum–Zephaniah

---

9. See Sweeney on the ambiguity of the transition and words in Zeph. 3:1-4 (contemptuous/fearsome, defiled/redeemed, oppressor/dove). OG reads 2:15 with ch. 3, so the city of ch. 3 is Nineveh (similarly Peshitta). Sweeney argues that it cannot be Nineveh because of the presence of God in it and trust in God from that city. Marvin A. Sweeney, *Zephaniah: A Commentary*, Hermeneia (Minneapolis: Fortress, 2003), 158–9.

10. See in particular the helpful review of the triangulation between Nahum, Jonah, and Joel in Klaas Spronk, "Jonah, Nahum, and the Book of the Twelve: A Response to Jakob Wöhrle," *JHS* 9 (2009): Article 8. Note also the words of O'Brien ("Reading the 'Former Prophets,'" 174): "when Jonah is read in retrospect, with the knowledge that Nineveh did indeed fall, the book assumes a particular meaning. If Nineveh fell, it could not be because YHWH did not care about non-Israelites."

11. See Mark J. Boda, "Penitential Innovations in the Book of the Twelve," in *On Stone and Scroll: A Festschrift for Graham Davies*, ed. Brian A. Mastin, Katharine J. Dell, and James K. Aitken, BZAW 420 (Berlin: de Gruyter, 2011), 291–308.

highlight similarities between the judgment that befell apostate Nineveh and Jerusalem, the earlier books of Joel and Jonah highlight similarities between the salvation of Jerusalem and Nineveh, a salvation rooted in repentance. This emphasizes further the importance of the Assyrian tradition in the Twelve, not only to explain the destruction of Jerusalem but also its restoration.

Assyria and Babylon in Haggai–Malachi

This absence of details surrounding the painful events of the first quarter of the sixth century BCE continues as one moves into the sixth- to fifth-century BCE prophetic collection in Haggai–Malachi.[12] There is initially little evidence of the exile of the people or of the people group(s) responsible (Haggai). The name "Zerubbabel" cryptically suggests both exile and Babylon (that he was seed born in Babylon). Nations are referred to in generic ways as a cosmic shaking leads to their contribution to the temple project (2:7-9) and their overthrow (2:20-23). More details are released as the collection progresses,[13] although Zech. 1:1-6 only suggests the annihilation of a former generation who did not heed the prophetic word. The first night vision (Zech. 1:7-17) finally clarifies that Jerusalem and Judah have undergone infrastructural devastation for a period of seventy years due to the actions of certain nations who are presently at ease and yet had overstepped their divine mandate. The second night vision (2:1-4 [1:18-21 Eng.]) refers to four horns that scattered Judah, Israel and Jerusalem, now shifting the focus from infrastructure to people. The reference to four horns suggests two large horned animals and along with the reference to Judah and Israel further suggests that these animals are Assyria and Babylon without providing specific details.[14] The oracle (2:10-17 [6-13 Eng.]) that follows the third night vision makes clear that an exile has taken place and the location is identified first as "the land of the north," but later particularized to the "daughter of Babylon." This oracle warns of coming judgment against

---

12. On this collection, its shape and development, see Mark J. Boda, *Exploring Zechariah: Volume 1—The Development of Zechariah and Its Role within the Twelve,* ANEM 16 (Atlanta: SBL, 2017).

13. See further Mark J. Boda, "Scat! Exilic Motifs in the Book of Zechariah," in *The Prophets Speak on Forced Migration,* ed. Mark J. Boda et al., AIL 21 (London: T&T Clark, 2015), 161–80.

14. See Mark J. Boda, "Terrifying the Horns: Persia and Babylon in Zechariah 1:7–6:15," *CBQ* 67 (2005): 22–41, and *The Book of Zechariah,* NICOT (Grand Rapids: Eerdmans, 2016), 155–66.

"the nations which plunder you," without naming Babylon itself. Another reference to Mesopotamia is used at the end of the seventh night vision (5:5-11) as the stork-winged beings remove the ephah with cultic figure to the "land of Shinar," a term identified with Babylon throughout the Hebrew Bible (Gen. 10:10; 11:2; 14:1; Isa. 11:11; Dan. 1:2). The final night vision (Zech. 6:1-8) contains echoes of the oracle in 2:10-17 [6-13 Eng.], referencing the "four winds/spirits of heaven" who emerge to target the "land of the north" for judgment. Babylon is then mentioned at the outset of the report of a prophetic sign act, which concludes the night vision section (6:9-15). Babylon here is the location from which the exiles have come.

Moving into the prose sermon collection in Zechariah 7–8, more details are given from the recent past. The reference to the seventy years of fasting and mourning in 7:3-5 brings back to the mind of the reader the association with the destruction of Jerusalem from the first night vision. This is affirmed immediately by the depiction of an earlier (and thus contrastive) era before the depopulation of Jerusalem, Judean cities, Negev and Shephelah in 7:7. Depopulation may refer to death and not to exile, but in light of the references to an exilic remnant in the name of Zerubbabel in Zechariah 2 and 6, this reference would activate this trope. By the end of Zechariah 7, however, the scattering of the community alongside the destruction of the land is clear (7:14). This focus on exile and return continues into the oracles of 8:1-8 and the sermon of 8:9-13. Zechariah 8:1-8 refers to saving God's people from "the land of the rising and the land of the setting" (east/west), and 8:9-13 refers to Judah and Israel "among the nations." Notable again is the reference to both Judah and Israel and to generic terminology for the exilic location.

This evidence from the beginning of the Haggai–Malachi collection reveals that the events of the first quarter of the sixth century BCE initially are only subtly referenced. Babylon is not explicitly identified with the destruction, only as the location of exile. More generic terminology is used when referring to the activity of destruction and plundering and subsequent punishment and this depiction comes to a climax in Zechariah 7, after which there is a shift to the return of exiles and restoration of the land. Idolatry is exported to Babylon, but the name used is that of Shinar. In two cases, both Israel and Judah are mentioned together; in one of these it is in a context that refers to two-horned animals that scattered the people of God, suggesting both Assyria and Babylon.

Reading beyond Haggai–Zechariah 1–8 in the Haggai–Malachi corpus, one finds no reference to Babylon and Assyria and little emphasis on the exile and destruction from the early sixth century BCE, except in

Zechariah 9–10. After the revelation to the Daughter of Zion/Jerusalem of her re-established Davidic king in 9:9-10, she is informed that her prisoners have been set free from the waterless pit (v. 11) and these prisoners are commanded to "return to the stronghold" (v. 12). This may refer to the release of exiles from afar, in light of the close association between the Daughter of Zion and the release of exiles from Babylon in the oracle of 2:10-17 [6-13 Eng.], but it is not made explicit. Little to no information is given here as to how these prisoners found their way into the pit. Another key allusion to the earlier period comes in Zech. 10:6-12. After the strengthening of the house of Judah, reference is made to the salvation of the house of Joseph/Ephraim who will be brought back from afar where God had sent them. Since those who have been sent among the nations are associated with the Northern Kingdom (Joseph/Ephraim) the location of their exile is identified as Egypt and Assyria and these are the nations that are targeted for judgment. When an exilic return is mentioned in Zechariah 9–14, instead of Babylon one finds references to Assyria and Egypt—that is, the geopolitical context of the eighth and seventh centuries BCE. This period saw the rise and demise of Assyria and Nineveh, recalling the emphasis of Hosea–Zephaniah in the Book of the Twelve.

Creating and Bridging the Gap

Zephaniah brings closure to the presentation of empire within the first nine books of the Twelve, a presentation that emphasized Assyria/Nineveh and their rise and fall and paralleled that with Judah's/Jerusalem's fate. Babylon's role in the destiny of both Nineveh and Jerusalem is rarely made explicit. The lack of details related to the events surrounding the fall of Jerusalem and especially the role of the Babylonians resonates with what is found in Haggai–Malachi, which at one point (Zech. 9–10) describes the political conditions that were in play in the final phase of the Assyrian Empire. This echoes the conclusion of Anselm Hagedorn, who argued: "within the internal chronology of the prophetic corpus, the Babylonian period is gapped and the books seem to jump from the end of the Assyrian period (Zephaniah) directly to Persian times (Haggai)."[15]

Evidence of a rhetorical strategy to bridge this gap between Hosea–Zephaniah and Haggai–Malachi can be discerned. In past work, I have identified two rhetorical features in the Twelve that suggest editorial

---

15. Hagedorn, "Diaspora or No Diaspora?" 331.

efforts to bridge the gap between the late Assyrian and early Persian periods of prophetic activity in the Twelve.[16] At three junctures in the latter half of the Twelve there appear "calls to silence," employing the Hebrew interjection הַס ("hush") followed by the preposition מִפְּנֵי ("before") and the divine name (or preposition pointing to an antecedent divine name) Yahweh:[17]

> But Yahweh is in his holy temple. Hush (הַס) before (מִפְּנֵי) him, all the earth. (Hab. 2:20)

> Hush (הַס) before (מִפְּ) the Lord Yahweh, for near is the day of Yahweh. (Zeph. 1:7)

> Hush (הַס), all flesh, before (מִפְּנֵי) Yahweh, for he has aroused himself from his holy habitation. (Zech. 2:17 [13 Eng.])

Additionally, at three junctures in this latter half of the Twelve there also appear "calls to joy" (*Aufruf zur Freude*), all addressed to בַּת־צִיּוֹן ("daughter of Zion"):

> Shout for joy, O daughter of Zion.
> Shout in triumph, O Israel.
> Rejoice and exult with all heart,
> O Daughter of Jerusalem! (Zeph. 3:14)

> Sing for joy and rejoice, O Daughter of Zion, for, take note, I am coming and I will dwell in your midst, declaration of Yahweh. (Zech. 2:14 [10 Eng.])

> Rejoice greatly, O Daughter of Zion!
> Shout in triumph, O Daughter of Jerusalem! (Zech. 9:9)

---

16. Mark J. Boda, "A Deafening Call to Silence: The Rhetorical 'End' of Human Address to the Deity in the Book of the Twelve," in *Exploring Zechariah: Volume 1*, 193–217.

17. See also Dietrich, "Three Minor Prophets," 155, for this trend. He considers Zeph. 1:7 the earliest instance, while Hab. 2:19, Zech. 2:17, and Amos 6:10 are inserted redactionally. He also sees Hab. 2:19 at the end of the Nahum–Habakkuk collection, Zech. 2:17 at the beginning of Haggai–Proto Zechariah collection, and then Amos 6:10 at the beginning of the entire corpus. In my opinion, Amos 6:10 stands out from the others which all use מִפְּנֵי and are liturgical in form. Amos 6:10 speaks very secularly: "keep quiet for the name of Yahweh is not to be mentioned/ invoked."

References to kingship, whether divine or human, follow all three of these calls to joy.[18]

Both of these sequences extend across the gap observed between Hosea–Zephaniah and Haggai–Malachi. The sequence of "calls to silence" begins in Habakkuk, crosses to Zephaniah, and ends in Zechariah, while the sequence of "calls to joy" begins in Zephaniah, crosses into Zechariah 2, and ends in Zechariah 9.

These sequences begin in the book of Habakkuk, a book focused on theodicy, after which human protest is quieted or challenged. Protest is left to the heavenly messenger of Yahweh who appears in the first night vision of Zechariah. A voice is allowed on the human plane, however, and it is that of Daughter of Zion, but only in the mode of joy, not protest.

These two triplets of calls intersect in two books within the Twelve, Zephaniah and Zechariah, and together they bridge the gap between the demise of Assyria and the rise of Jerusalem. As the readers are called to hush protest and shift to joy, the colourful details of the painful events surrounding the fall of Jerusalem are muted. The readers are being offered a particular strategy for dealing with the painful events of the demise of the nation: one that discourages rehearsal of the painful past and encourages the embrace of a joyous future.

This rhetorical strategy to bridge the gap provides some insight into how those responsible for the Twelve sought to shape the community's approach to theodicy and hope. However, the creation of the gap also plays a role. Why emphasize the Assyrian over the Babylonian tradition? On the one side, this is related to the explicit rhetorical strategy noted above, to reduce attention on the painful demise of the community during the Babylonian period. The protest voiced by the messenger of Yahweh in the first night vision focuses on the seventy-year tradition, which is inextricably linked with the Babylonian destruction of Jerusalem and Judah elsewhere in the Hebrew Bible. Thus, part of the silencing strategy is a reduction in the rehearsal of the Babylonian destruction tradition, subtly introducing it in depictions of the demise of Assyria/Nineveh and comparisons to Judah/Jerusalem. But in light of Zechariah 9–10 and its focus on an anticipated return of the northern tribes, facilitated by the initial return of Judeans, it may be that the Assyrian focus relates to a

---

18. On the role of kingship in the Twelve, see the helpful review of Paul Redditt, "The King in Haggai–Zechariah 1–8 and the Book of the Twelve," in *Tradition in Transition: Haggai and Zechariah 1–8 in the Trajectory of Hebrew Theology*, ed. Mark J. Boda and Michael H. Floyd, LHBOTS 475 (London: T&T Clark, 2009), 56–82.

community grappling with the enduring exile of the northern tribes for which Assyria was responsible.[19] With the southern tribes emerging from their Babylonian dystopia, attention turns to their northern compatriots who continue to languish in exile. Focusing on the Assyrian tradition turns the attention of those in Yehud to others who continue to languish in the exilic nightmare.

The Twelve among the Latter Prophets

These strategies for dealing with theodicy and hope evident in the Twelve can be compared and contrasted to those evident in other prophetic collections among the Latter Prophets. The book of Isaiah places great emphasis on the Assyrian period, focusing near the end of the first major section (chs 1–39) on a major defeat of Assyria. This depiction of Assyria's defeat is followed by gapping similar to what is found in the Twelve. Although there is explicit reference to Babylon plundering the treasury and exiling the royal house in Isaiah 39, any details of this experience are skipped in the transition from Isaiah 39 to 40. Babylon is the focus of the punishment in Isaiah 46–48 and the reason for the rise of Cyrus in Isaiah 44–45. However, the predicament of the people before the restoration is depicted in more detail in Isaiah than the Twelve. The overall shape of Isaiah highlights the importance of the Assyrian period for those living in the later Babylonian and Persian periods as the traditions of Isaiah of Jerusalem in chs 1–39 provide insight into how to live in faith in the midst of other great empires.[20]

19. One sees a similar strategy in the book of Chronicles, which, while focusing on the Southern Kingdom in its presentation of the history of Israel, also displays interest in the enduring role for the northern tribes in its vision for "all Israel." See the foundational works of Williamson and Japhet and the nuances provided in the more recent treatments of Sparks and Jonker: H. G. M. Williamson, *Israel in the Books of Chronicles* (Cambridge: Cambridge University Press, 1977); Sara Japhet, *The Ideology of the Book of Chronicles and Its Place in Biblical Thought*, BEATAJ 9 (Frankfurt am Main: Peter Lang, 1989); James T. Sparks, *The Chronicler's Genealogies: Towards an Understanding of 1 Chronicles 1–9*, Academia Biblica (Boston: Brill, 2008), 367; Louis C. Jonker, *Defining All-Israel in Chronicles: Multi-Levelled Identity Negotiation in Late Persian-Period Yehud*, FAT 106 (Tübingen: Mohr Siebeck, 2016).

20. See, e.g., the evidence of the impact of "the literary deposit of Isaiah of Jerusalem" on Deutero-Isaiah in H. G. M. Williamson, *The Book Called Isaiah: Deutero-Isaiah's Role in Composition and Redaction* (Oxford: Clarendon; New York: Oxford University Press, 1994), 30–94.

Jeremiah and Ezekiel, however, stand in stark contrast to Isaiah and especially the Twelve. Both provide direct reports of the fall of Jerusalem and the exile of the people and Babylon is clearly the main actor in the divine discipline of the people of God. Far from ignoring the painful experience of the period, the literary structures of these two prophetic books are marked by it.[21] In these books we find intimate portraits of prophets living in the midst of this painful period, seeking to intercede for the people but silenced by Yahweh's announcement that judgment is now certain for the people of God.[22]

Therefore, the strategies used within the Twelve to deal with the trauma of the sixth century BCE are not the only approach taken within the period that followed these painful events. One can discern variety within the Latter Prophets, with some justifying what happened and looking with hope to the future by muting painful memories and expressing hopeful joy. Others provided intricate details on the culpability of the people before shifting to promises of future hope. Still others could be found somewhere in between these two strategies. Those shaping the canonical section now called the Prophets and more particularly the Latter Prophets have provided their subsequent reading communities various ways to deal with pain and trauma. It may be that such strategies would be relevant to certain individuals or groups at varying points of removal from past communal pain, whether that is in terms of culpability or temporality.

---

21. Note the key literary hinge point in Jeremiah at Jer. 24–25 and in Ezekiel at Ezek. 33. See further Mark J. Boda, *A Severe Mercy: Sin and Its Remedy in the Old Testament*, Siphrut 1 (Winona Lake, IN: Eisenbrauns, 2009), 223–4, 256.

22. For Jeremiah, see further Mark J. Boda, "'Uttering Precious Rather than Worthless Words': Divine Patience and Impatience with Lament in Isaiah and Jeremiah," in *Why? How Long? Studies on Voice(s) of Lamentation Rooted in Biblical Hebrew Poetry*, ed. LeAnn Snow Flesher, Carol Dempsey, and Mark J. Boda, LHBOTS 552 (London: Continuum, 2014), 83–99. For Ezekiel, see further Boda, *A Severe Mercy*, 257–9.

Chapter 11

THE FAILURE OF DAVIDIC HOPE?
CONFIGURING THEODICY IN THE BOOK OF THE
TWELVE IN SUPPORT OF A DAVIDIC KINGDOM

George Athas

In 586 BCE, the Babylonians destroyed Jerusalem and its temple, bringing
to an end the state ruled by the Davidic royal dynasty in Judah. Despite
this, hopes for the restoration of both the temple and the Davidic state
were kept alive over the subsequent period of exile in Babylon. Seventy
years later, the temple in Jerusalem was rebuilt by a small community
of Judean pioneers who returned from Babylon for the task. However,
an independent state ruled by the Davidic dynasty was never achieved.
Considering the dynasty's centrality to the people of Yahweh in Judah,
and the magnitude of the promises of its restoration, this failure produced
significant theological dissonance. Was the Davidic dynasty still central
to the divinely announced program of restoration? If it was, how was the
failure to reinstate it explained? Did it cast aspersions upon the character
or ability of God, or was there another explanation? In this study, I wish to
investigate these questions, showing how the Book of the Twelve provides
us with key elements to understand the centrality of the Davidic dynasty
and the temple to God's restoration promises, as well as how it explains
the failure to restore a Davidic kingdom.

*Hope for the Davidic Kingdom in History
and the Book of the Twelve*

Early in the Persian Era, Judeans had begun migrating from Babylon back
to Jerusalem and its surrounding districts with the express purpose of

rebuilding the city and its institutions. As Lisbeth Fried has demonstrated, Jerusalem appears to have been resettled as a specific temple-community, rather than a generic urban settlement.[1] This is why specific connections are made to Cyrus' policy of repatriating conquered peoples and re-establishing the temples of previously captured deities (cf. Ezra 1:2-4; 2 Chron. 36:23).

However, a temple community in Jerusalem could be no *mere* temple community. Judean temple ideology meant that a temple in Jerusalem was necessarily steeped in Davidic significance. This was not just because Jerusalem had been the capital of the Davidic state before its destruction in 586 BCE. Even more than this, the Jerusalem temple was inextricably linked to Davidic kingship. We see this connection best expressed in 2 Samuel 7, which outlines the divinely ordained tenets of the role of the Davidic king, centering on the multivalent terminology of the "house" (בַּיִת). According to this prophetic oracle, there was a reciprocal relationship between Yahweh and the Davidic heir, based on each party building a "house" for the other: Yahweh would establish a permanent house (i.e., dynasty) for David, which necessarily extended to his progeny, and David's progeny would build a house (i.e., temple) for Yahweh. The immovability of the physical temple structure in Jerusalem (in contrast to the portability of the Tabernacle) was symbolic of the permanence of Yahweh's covenant with David. In other words, the permanence of the sanctuary was the earthly correlate of Yahweh's permanent commitment to David's dynasty, underscored in the oracle by the phrase עַד־עוֹלָם (2 Sam. 7:13, 16).

It is for this reason that the evaluations of the Davidic monarchs in 1 and 2 Kings center on their role as temple builders and maintainers, for this was the primary vital sign of the monarchy's health. To have a temple in Jerusalem was to have Davidic monarchy—one could not exist without the other.[2] The Jerusalem temple, therefore, was more than just

1. Lisbeth S. Fried, *The Priest and the Great King: Temple–Palace Relations in the Persian Empire*, Biblical and Judaic Studies 10 (Winona Lake: Eisenbrauns, 2004).

2. Of course, this raises the issue of David's reign ending without a temple being built. First, both Samuel and Chronicles present the temple as the brainchild of David. Second, and perhaps more importantly, the relationship between Yahweh and the Davidic king was filial—that is, the reigning Davidic descendant was considered the son of God by adoption at his enthronement (2 Sam. 7:14). This dynamic only describes David's descendants, and not David himself, for in the Davidic covenant, Yahweh himself became the father figure of the dynasty (though note the rhetoric in Ps. 89:21-28 [89:20-27 Eng.], which has David call God "my Father"). This could

a cultic installation. All the prerogatives of the cult associated with the Tabernacle certainly accrued to the Jerusalem temple, conveyed by the traditions that relate how the Ark of the Covenant was placed within it and the cloud of the presence entered the sanctuary (1 Kgs 8:6-11). But more than this, the temple was a sacrament of the Davidic covenant, meaning that the people of Israel assembled together at the one place (מָקוֹם) before Yahweh under the aegis of the Davidic king (cf. 1 Kgs 8:1-2), and Yahweh ruled and blessed his people through his adopted son—the Davidic king, who governed the people on his behalf (2 Sam. 7:14; cf. 1 Chron. 29:23). Priests and Levites were not superfluous to this situation, for they were required to minister at the altar and tend to daily functions. Yet, when David brought the Ark into his residence, he did so wearing the priestly garb of an ephod, after which he offered sacrifices and blessed the people in a priestly manner (2 Sam. 6:14, 17-18). He even appointed some of his own sons as priests (2 Sam. 8:18). There was a priestly aspect to Davidic kingship, though it was a royal priesthood, which Ps. 110:4 identifies as being in the order of Melchizedek, rather than the order of Levi. The priests and Levites were thus considered functionaries in a royal Davidic temple. In this regard, we note how the Chronicler presents David as the initiator, organizer, and patron of the entire priestly cult (1 Chron. 23–26), and that Solomon takes over this presidential role upon his enthronement. As Yahweh ruled Israel through the Davidic king, so the Davidic king enabled the cult by which Israel worshipped their God.[3] To borrow a New Testament turn of phrase, no one came to Yahweh except through the Davidic king at the Jerusalem temple.

This means that the reconstruction of the temple under Zerubbabel in the early Persian period was more than only the re-establishment of a cultic shrine. Being so steeped in royal Davidic significance, the temple necessarily implied the re-establishment of Davidic rule over Israel. The fact that Zerubbabel was the grandson of one of Judah's last reigning kings, Jehoiachin, is no historical accident, but a prophetic statement that the early pioneers in Persian-period Jerusalem were aiming to re-lay

---

only come into play once David had died, so that the son of David became the son of God (a dynamic picked up in the New Testament's claim about Jesus [Rom. 1:3-4]). The promise of the dynasty's permanence captures the temple within its purview also. It is for this reason that the fall of the Davidic kingdom coincides with the destruction of the temple in 586 BCE, and why, after the return from exile, the reconstruction of the temple but the failure to gain a Davidic king prompts the growth of messianic expectation.

3. Pivotal for understanding this is the statement that Solomon sat on the throne of Yahweh as king, and that Israel prospered as they obeyed him (1 Chron. 29:23).

the foundations of a Davidic state. Zerubbabel was reigniting Davidic ideology, which necessitated an independent kingdom of Judah (or Israel), centered on the Jerusalem temple. This was the larger, aspirational goal, but since the community around Zerubbabel was both small and subservient to the Persians, the reconstruction of the temple could only be the first stage of its realization. Thus, when Zerubbabel began building the temple to Yahweh in Jerusalem (Hag. 1:14-15), he was not only constructing a cultic site, but erecting the central monument of Davidic rule in the region—a politically momentous act.

In the Book of the Twelve, the concern to build the temple of Yahweh as a Davidic monument is seen most clearly in Haggai and Zechariah. However, it is flagged even earlier. Amos 9:11-12, for example, has Yahweh state:

בַּיּוֹם הַהוּא אָקִים אֶת־סֻכַּת דָּוִיד הַנֹּפֶלֶת וְגָדַרְתִּי אֶת־פִּרְצֵיהֶן וַהֲרִסֹתָיו אָקִים וּבְנִיתִיהָ
כִּימֵי עוֹלָם: לְמַעַן יִירְשׁוּ אֶת־שְׁאֵרִית אֱדוֹם וְכָל־הַגּוֹיִם אֲשֶׁר־נִקְרָא שְׁמִי עֲלֵיהֶם נְאֻם־
יְהוָה עֹשֶׂה זֹּאת:

> "On that day, I will raise the booth of David that has fallen, repair its breaches, and raise its ruins; I will rebuild it as in days gone by, so that they may possess the remnant of Edom and all the nations, over whom my name is called." Declaration of Yahweh, who will do this.[4]

These verses presume the fall of the Davidic dynasty and its temple, since the notions of a fallen booth, breaches, and ruins all recollect the destruction of the temple and the city of Jerusalem in 586 BCE, and the associated end of Judean statehood.[5] They also presume the migration of Edomites (Idumeans) into southern Judah, which occurred in the wake of Judah's collapse. The verses depict Yahweh as having the specific intention of reinstituting the Davidic dynasty in its native territory. This makes Haggai's prophecies of great significance, since they see Zerubbabel as the key player in the re-establishment of the Davidic dynasty. Not only does Zerubbabel re-lay the foundation of the temple (Hag. 1:14-15), but

---

4. All translations are my own.

5. Amos 9:11-15 has long been recognized as a redactional addition to Amos, since the situation it describes (the collapse of the Judean kingdom) did not prevail in Amos' day (mid-eighth century BCE), and was therefore irrelevant to his original audience. The verses come from a post-exilic hand, and function as a kind of mortar that enable the placement of Amos within the wall that is the Book of the Twelve—a post-exilic product. For a discussion of the redactional possibilities around Amos 9:11–15, see James Nogalski, *Literary Precursors to the Book of the Twelve*, BZAW 217 (Berlin: de Gruyter, 1993), 110–22.

Haggai identifies him as the signet ring on Yahweh's finger for "that day" when Yahweh shakes the heavens and the earth, and destroys the power of the nations (Hag. 2:20-23). The image of the signet ring, in particular, stands as an ostensible reversal of the rejection of Zerubbabel's grandfather, Jehoiachin, and the reinstatement of the Davidic dynasty in the purposes of Yahweh (Jer. 22:24-30).[6] The rebuilding of the temple thus represented an essential part of the recovery of Davidic ideology.

The Failure of Restoration

An independent Davidic state never materialized, though the opportunity to establish it certainly came rather quickly. The sudden death of Cambyses in 522 BCE and the murder of his brother, Bardiya, threw the entire Persian Empire into turmoil. The Persians were still something of a political novelty at this time, having ruled for barely a generation or so.[7] They had not had enough time to sink deep roots into the political soil of the ancient Near East, and so the power vacuum left by the deaths of Cambyses and Bardiya sparked the instant balkanization of the whole empire.[8] In his Behistun Inscription, Darius enumerates no fewer than nineteen "rebellions" that erupted in the eastern regions of the empire alone, including two within Persia itself, and three within Babylon—and this does not even take into account "rebellions" in the Levant or Egypt. Darius characterizes these as "rebellions" to show that his authority was never in doubt—a critical piece of his propaganda. He thus portrays himself as the one who quickly re-established order in the empire. But underlying his account is the reality that the world believed the Persian juggernaut had been sunk, and each sub-polity acted to secure its own viability in the wake of Persian collapse. As Briant recognizes, each so-called rebellion centered around a dynastic figure who declared himself

6. Matthew H. Patton, *Hope for a Tender Sprig: Jehoiachin in Biblical Theology*, BBRSup 16 (Winona Lake: Eisenbrauns, 2017), 58–69, 138–45.

7. In making this remark, I take Cyrus' conquest of Babylon in 539 BCE as the beginning of the "Persian period." The rise of Cyrus to imperial prominence had been occurring for over a decade before this, ever since he defeated Astyages, king of Media, in 550 BCE. But only with the conquest of Babylon can we state that Cyrus established Persia as a superpower.

8. A similar phenomenon is observed with the break-up of Alexander the Great's empire after his death. In both the Persian and Greek cases, the august achievements of the new imperial overlords were undermined by the novelty of their institutions and the unforeseen death of their primary agents.

"king."[9] That this occurred so widely across the empire, and repeatedly within certain centers (e.g., Babylon, Persia), demonstrates precisely how tenuous the Persians' grip on power was at this time. So many simultaneous and consecutive moves for independence would not have occurred if Persian power was seen as secure or inevitable.[10]

This balkanization of the Persian Empire in 522–518 BCE gave Zerubbabel an opportunity to attempt to secure Jerusalem's independence. When we understand Davidic ideology, particularly as it related to the Jerusalem temple, which Zerubbabel was himself rebuilding, we see that this was simply a logical next step in attaining the Jerusalem community's ultimate goal, namely the restoration of a Davidic kingdom. The presence of a Davidic temple without a Davidic king was, after all, an incongruity in Davidic ideology, and the turbulent years following the death of Cambyses provided a chance for Zerubbabel to correct it. In other words, as was to be expected on the grounds of both Davidic ideology and the political climate of the day, Zerubbabel acted as practically all other dynastic leaders of sub-polities acted, and declared the independence of a nascent Davidic state.

The difficulty we today have in seeing this comes from two factors. First, we are conditioned by the knowledge that Darius re-imposed Persian sovereignty over the lands of the Persian Empire. In this, we are led by his surviving propaganda, which stated that he established his rule after the removal of the "usurper," Gaumata, in September 522 BCE, and his persistent characterization of his opponents as "rebels," implying that they challenged an established sovereign entity whose power was never really in doubt. But this is the propaganda of the eventual victor, and must be evaluated in light of the wider facts, some of which even Darius had difficulty concealing. His version of events attempted to mask the pervasive political turmoil that gripped all the lands of the empire—turmoil that was actually captured in the earth-shattering imagery of Hag. 2:20-23, which provided the platform for Yahweh's promise to make Zerubbabel his signet-ring, reversing the judgment that had been inflicted on Zerubbabel's grandfather, Jehoiachin, and the loss of Judean statehood (Jer. 22:24-27).[11]

9. Pierre Briant, *From Cyrus to Alexander: A History of the Persian Empire*, trans. Peter T. Daniels (Winona Lake: Eisenbrauns, 2002), 120.

10. Ibid., 120–1.

11. We should furthermore note how the image of Jehoiachin as the signet ring that Yahweh removes from his finger comes within a larger section bemoaning the fate of the last kings of Judah and the loss of statehood and independence (Jer. 22). By

Second, there is no biblical passage that expressly stipulates that Zerubbabel either declared himself king, was anointed king, or was ever perceived to be king. It is, therefore, often doubted or simply overlooked. There were, however, good reasons for omitting such overt claims to kingship and diminishing the volume of collateral clues. Darius emerged from the political uncertainty of 522–518 BCE as the victor, and his reign was backdated to 522 BCE—the beginning of the crisis sparked by Cambyses' death. This certainty was then imposed on the dating formulae in the incipient book of Haggai–Zechariah (consisting of the kernel of Hag. 1 through to Zech. 8), despite the actual uncertainty that had prevailed immediately after Cambyses' death. Since Darius dealt harshly with any who challenged his authority, it is hardly surprising that a book, which was eventually timestamped with Darius' own regnal claims, would not broadcast any counterclaim to his kingship.

Furthermore, the timeline derived from Haggai shows that the Judean pioneers who returned from Babylonia to Jerusalem did so in the time of Cambyses.[12] A common assumption is that they returned during the reign of Cyrus, but this is, in fact, an unjustified assumption, rather than an assertion of any biblical text. Cyrus is credited with granting permission to return and build the temple (more on this below), but the return is never expressly dated to his reign. According to Ezra 3:1-6, the pioneers arrived in Jerusalem and the surrounding villages, and then built an altar in Jerusalem (with no sanctuary building yet) in the seventh month, without stipulating which year this was. Plans for constructing the sanctuary (but no actual construction) soon followed in the second month of the second year after their return, again without reference to any known ruler. In Hag. 1:13, we learn that the foundations of the temple were laid in Darius' second year (Hag. 1:12–2:5)—that is, 520 BCE—a decade after the death of Cyrus. Haggai also refers to drought and crop failures, especially olive trees failing to bear fruit (Hag. 1:6, 10-11), the cause of which was attributed to the community's failure to rebuild the temple of Yahweh (Hag. 1:4, 7-11). Since olive trees take three to five years after planting to bear fruit, we get a reasonably accurate timeline that shows the pioneers must have arrived in Jerusalem three to five years before Haggai's oracle, at which time they first undertook agricultural

---

focusing attention on Yahweh's purposes for Zerubbabel, Haggai's oracle compacts the wider hope for Judean statehood under a Davidic king into the person of Zerubbabel.

12. Cf. Bob Becking, *Ezra–Nehemiah*, HCOT (Leuven: Peeters, 2018), 22.

work. This places the return squarely in the reign of Cambyses, and implies his imprimatur upon it.

This posed a significant problem for the early returnees in Jerusalem. As we have seen, the reconstruction of the temple was not just the installation of a cultic shrine, but the building of a political monument to the Davidic dynasty, with all the ideological freight that came with it. When the Persians themselves eventually arrived in Jerusalem to re-impose their sovereignty (early 519 BCE), the temple reconstruction took them by surprise—they evidently did not know of any permission given by Cyrus—and the legitimacy of the endeavor was called into question (Ezra 5:3). The controversy was not merely over permission, as though a building license were at issue, but over the political significance of a Davidide (Zerubbabel) building a monument that expressed his aspirations (and that of the whole Jerusalem community) of establishing an independent state, at a time when most sub-polities were declaring their own independence on the assumption of Persia's collapse.

The arrival of the Persians in Jerusalem coincides with a delegation that Darius sent to Aryandes, the satrap of Egypt, to aid in recovering the country from the "rebel" Petubastis IV.[13] Ezra also tells us that the peoples around Jerusalem reported the building activities to the Persians as rebellious, and that the satrap of Abar-Nahara, Tattenai (Persian: Ushtanu), arrived in Jerusalem to investigate the issue (Ezra 4:1-2; 5:3-4).[14] These two operations occurred simultaneously as part of Darius' efforts to bring the western portions of the empire under his control. Whether Zerubbabel declared himself king or not, he was almost certainly perceived as having done so by the Persians by virtue of the significance of the temple he was building—an enterprise that Darius' regime had not authorized. In light of the political and ideological factors, it is likely that Zerubbabel did indeed create a nascent Davidic state, and for this, he was removed by the Persians (more on this below).

13. Olaf E. Kaper, "Petubastis IV in the Dakhla Oasis: New Evidence about an Early Rebellion against Persian Rule and Its Suppression in Political Memory," in *Political Memory in and after the Persian Empire*, ed. Jason M. Silverman and Caroline Waerzeggers, ANEM 13 (Atlanta: SBL, 2015), 125–49.

14. Tattanai/Ushtanu is first mentioned in March 520 BCE as the satrap of Abir Nahara. See Richard D. Parker, "Darius and His Egyptian Campaign," *AJSL* 58 (1941): 373–7. When the evidence of Ezra, Haggai, and Zechariah is taken into consideration, Tattenai must have arrived in Jerusalem approximately ten months later.

The political significance of the temple project was compounded by the fact that the community's return to Jerusalem was associated with Cambyses. As part of his legitimization strategy, Darius disparaged Cambyses in the Behistun Inscription by blaming the empire's near collapse on him (along with the evil mage, Gaumata), and portraying himself as the savior of the empire, who rescued it from the forces of evil that almost brought it down. Darius depicted himself as the rightful heir and restorer of Cyrus' legacy, which Cambyses (and Gaumata) had imperiled. When it became clear that Darius had won the day, the Jerusalem pioneers had to distance themselves from any association with Cambyses. They did this by adopting the very strategy that Darius himself did: they reached back to the legacy of Cyrus, claiming that he (rather than his son, Cambyses) was the one who had given them permission to rebuild the temple.

Darius' regime knew nothing of any permission granted by Cyrus for the temple in Jerusalem to be rebuilt. If they had, there would have been no investigation into who granted permission for its construction, or which locals were responsible for it (Ezra 5:3-4). But the lack of clarity necessitated such an investigation, sparking a major crisis in Jerusalem around the person of Zerubbabel. This is not to suggest that the Jerusalem community fabricated the claim that Cyrus had granted them permission to return and rebuild the temple. On the contrary, Ezra 6:1-2 states that a genuine decree was indeed discovered, albeit in Ecbatana rather than in the royal archives at Babylon, where one might have expected to find it. The Jerusalem community's claim regarding Cyrus was, therefore, upheld. Nonetheless, finding the proof of this claim in Ecbatana, rather than in Babylon, must have created an anxious delay for the Jerusalem community. And given the way Darius treated those he perceived as "rebels" (usually impalement), there is little chance that Zerubbabel remained as head of the community in the interim. Zerubbabel was most likely removed, though surprisingly he was not executed (see below).

This probability aligns with the rhetoric we read in Zechariah, and shows that the seeming lack of evidence about Zerubbabel's kingship is not absolute. There are indeed critical clues in biblical texts that point towards Zerubbabel having declared himself king in Jerusalem, and was subsequently remanded into Persian custody.

For example, Zechariah claims that Zerubbabel's hands began the work of the temple construction, and that his hands would complete it. Zechariah even pins his prophetic credentials on this eventuality (Zech. 4:8-9). If nothing had happened to Zerubbabel, this would hardly constitute a test of Zechariah's prophetic efficacy. The test only makes sense if Zerubbabel had been impeded in a major way. The political climate of the day strongly suggests that this was removal for the creation of a nascent but independent polity. In light of this, the divine oracle to Zerubbabel in Zech. 4:6 should be construed as a stern rebuke, rather than gentle guidance:

זֶה דְּבַר־יְהוָה אֶל־זְרֻבָּבֶל לֵאמֹר לֹא בְחַיִל וְלֹא בְכֹחַ כִּי אִם־בְּרוּחִי אָמַר יְהוָה צְבָאוֹת׃

This is the word of Yahweh to Zerubbabel: "Not by force, nor by prowess, but by my spirit," Yahweh of Ranks has said.

The economic syntax of two short negative clauses followed by a strong adversative (כִּי אִם) produces a stark contrast, further underlined by the persistent use of the preposition בְּ on both sides of the contrast. The pronominal suffix on רוּחִי ("my spirit") clearly identifies the spirit as belonging to Yahweh, which leads us to associate חַיִל ("force") and כֹחַ ("prowess") with Zerubbabel. In other words, Yahweh reprimands Zerubbabel here for the use of force and prowess in terms that speak of a political mistake that had tried to make something happen (and which ultimately backfired), when he should have allowed Yahweh to act instead. This is the rhetoric of rebuke. Yet, despite the mistake of Zerubbabel, Yahweh remains passionate for Zion (Zech. 1:5), and will therefore still enable Zerubbabel to complete the reconstruction of the temple.

Furthermore, part of the point of Zechariah's vision (Zech. 1:6–6:8) was to propose the promotion of Joshua, the High Priest, as Acting "Sprig" (צֶמַח). Before this time, no High Priest had ever headed the Judean community—that was a civic role reserved for the royal Davidic dynasty. Joshua's elevation to the role was a critical innovation. Zechariah insisted on promoting Joshua through a secret crowning ceremony, stipulating that Joshua would act as a priest on a royal throne (וְהָיָה כֹהֵן עַל־כִּסְאוֹ), while still maintaining the expectation that the actual "Sprig" would still come one day (Zech. 6:9-15). As Stead notes, the terminology used in this crowning of Joshua picks up on the very things that Jeremiah said had been removed from Jehoiachin: sitting, ruling, and a throne.[15] Joshua is, therefore, seen as occupying the place of the Davidic ruler.

Those who argue for identifying the "Sprig" as a single person understandably have trouble seeing either Zerubbabel or Joshua occupying the role, for Zerubbabel seems not to have amounted to much in the end,

---

15. Michael R. Stead, *The Intertextuality of Zechariah 1–8*, LHBOTS 506 (London: T&T Clark, 2009), 137.

while Joshua was a priest when the "Sprig" was clearly a royal designation (cf. Isa. 4:2; 11:1; Jer. 23:5; 33:15). Furthermore, the arrival of the "Sprig" is couched as a future event (Zech. 6:12-13).[16] But the "Sprig" was an office, not merely a person, and it was associated with Davidic kingship (Isa. 4:2; 11:1; Jer. 23:5; 33:15; cf. Isa. 53:2). It was, therefore, occupied by various individuals at various times, and was never thought of as referring to just a single individual in history, or designating a non-royal office. Zerubbabel was the "Sprig." In saying this, though, we should not take it to mean that he exhausted the significance of the role, or that the title only ever pertained to him. Rather, we mean that Zerubbabel held the royal office of "Sprig" as the primary Davidic descendant of his day. But this explains why he is likely to have declared himself king in the wake of the ostensible collapse of the Persian Empire (as many others in similar positions of local leadership did), and why he was removed for doing so by the authorities that established Darius' power. It is also why Joshua could act as a surrogate for Zerubbabel after his removal by the Persians, without undermining the fact that Zerubbabel was the actual "Sprig," or that other Davidides might occupy the office at later times (as they had at earlier times).

The imagery of Zechariah 4 reinforces these connections. In this vignette of Zechariah's vision, two olive trees flank a menorah of solid gold, and supernaturally provide it with olive oil to fuel its flames. The two trees are symbolically identified as "sons of olive oil" (Zech. 4:14), though their identities are never overtly disclosed. However, Zerubbabel

16. Anthony R. Petterson, "A New Form-Critical Approach to Zechariah's Crowning of the High Priest Joshua and the Identity of the 'Shoot' (Zechariah 6:9-15)," in *The Book of the Twelve and the New Form Criticism*, ed. Mark J. Boda, Michael H. Floyd, and Colin M. Toffelmire, ANEM 10 (Atlanta: SBL, 2015), 285–304. Petterson criticizes Stead for his assertion that Zerubbabel was the "Sprig" (or "Shoot"), arguing that (1) Stead reads Zech. 6:9-15 solely in relation to the events of 520–515 BCE, rather than the whole book of Zechariah; and (2) Stead "has a reduced view" of the role of the "Sprig" (293). Ironically, though, by ruling out Zerubbabel as the "Sprig," Petterson himself disconnects the concerns of the prophet Zechariah from the critical period of 520–515 BCE, which he addressed. He also reduces the nature of the "Sprig," assuming that it can be but a single historical person in the future (298–302), rather than an office occupied by various persons through history. This leads Petterson to the conclusion that Zechariah is concerned with the construction of an eschatological temple. While this is an idea that might be sustained in a later apocalyptic context, in which the "Sprig" has taken on more eschatological airs, it by no means precludes the understanding that the prophet himself was concerned with Zerubbabel (and Joshua) building the physical temple in 520–515 BCE.

is rightly identified as one of these "sons of olive oil." This unusual term is a periphrastic designation for anointed office, of which there were only two in Israel: king and High Priest. The other "son of olive oil" must be identified as Joshua the High Priest.[17] In the previous vignette (Zech. 3:1-10), Joshua was saved from disaster, given latitude before his attacker(s), and promoted to the defense of the temple courts—a role that no previous High Priest had ever had, for it was a civic role that belonged to the Davidic kings.[18] Indeed, the books of Kings evaluate the Davidic kings of Judah for the way they performed this very role. The imagery of this vignette, then, sees the High Priest Joshua mirroring the role of Zerubbabel. The reason for this duality and synergy is that Zerubbabel had most likely been removed from the Jerusalem community by the Persians, thus impeding the temple reconstruction and the restoration of a Davidic

17. Most commentators identify the two olive trees as Zerubbabel and Joshua, though there are some who opt for alternative interpretations. Boda, for example, opts for seeing them as the prophetic figures of Haggai and Zechariah. See Mark J. Boda, *Haggai, Zechariah*, NIVAC (Grand Rapids: Zondervan, 2004), 275. However, the arboreal imagery and the scene's association with anointing makes it implausible that the olive trees refer to anything other than the anointed royal office of the "Sprig" (an arboreal term) and, by association, the priestly office as its surrogate.

18. Zechariah 3 is usually read as removing the stain of exile from Joshua and thus commissioning him to function as High Priest. However, by February 519 BCE, when Zechariah's vision occurs, Joshua had already been functioning as High Priest for approximately five years. As Ezra 3:1-3 states, one of the first actions of the returnees in Jerusalem was the construction of an open-air altar, on which daily sacrifice was offered, implying that Joshua had been formally commissioned at that earlier point. It was completely redundant, therefore, to commission Joshua to act as High Priest again five years later. Zechariah 3 must, therefore, have another context and purpose in mind. Zechariah 3 sets the scene for why Joshua was the appropriate figure to act as surrogate for Zerubbabel during his absence. The crisis from which Joshua is saved in this visionary vignette is not exile, but the arrival of Darius' representatives in Jerusalem and their subsequent removal of Zerubbabel. Joshua had come close to a similar fate to that of Zerubbabel, since he was a leading figure in the Jerusalem community, but he had avoided it. Instead, the vision sees him dressed in civic garb—clothing that was worn by laity, rather than priestly garments. Isaiah 3:22 depicts the women of Zion as wearing the exact same garments (מַחֲלָצוֹת). Zechariah 3, therefore, presents the circumstances for seeing Joshua as an appropriate surrogate for Zerubbabel, which is then confirmed in Zech. 4 with the symbolism of the two sons of olive oil (Zech. 4:14). Cf. Jason M. Silverman, "Vetting the Priest in Zechariah 3: The Satan between Divine and Achaemenid Administrations," *JHS* 14, no. 6 (2014): 1–28; Shahpur Shahbazi, "CLOTHING ii. Median and Achaemenid Periods," *Encyclopaedia Iranica* V/7:723–37, http://www.iranicaonline.org/articles/clothing-ii.

kingdom, and Joshua was commissioned as the most appropriate person to function as acting "Sprig," since he too occupied an anointed office in Jerusalem. The arboreal imagery simply reinforces this fact. The synergy of the two olive trees in Zechariah 4 finds a more transparent analogy in the vision's epilogue (Zech. 6:9-15), which sees Joshua crowned like a king, seated on a throne from which he rules, and commanded to "branch out" (an allusion to the role of the "Branch" or "Sprig") and build the temple. The reference to peaceful counsel existing "between them both" (Zech. 6:13) would then refer to the synergy of (anointed) royal and priestly offices, which Joshua was to hold as both acting "Sprig" and High Priest.

Keeping Hope Alive

The appeal of the Jerusalem community to Cyrus' decree worked. Once Cyrus' permission for the construction of the Jerusalem temple was confirmed, Darius, in his eagerness to portray himself as the heir of Cyrus' legacy, allowed the construction to continue, and it was duly completed in 516 BCE (Ezra 6:2-15). Zerubbabel is not expressly named as being present at the completion in Ezra 6:15, but neither is Joshua the High Priest. We may surmise, however, that both men were indeed present, and Zechariah's prophetic credentials were proven right (Zech. 4:8-9), leading to the preservation of his oracles. Nonetheless, the hope for an independent Davidic kingdom had taken a significant blow, especially as Persian power persisted.

In light of these developments, the oracle of the king who returns to Zion (Zech. 9:9-12) should be understood, at least in its original redactional stage, as referring to Zerubbabel's release from Persian custody, and the survival of hope for a future Davidic kingdom.[19] Verses 9 and 12 are particularly pertinent to Zerubbabel's situation:

19. Of course, this raises the problem of the redaction and development of the book of Zechariah. Zech. 9 is seen by the majority as deriving from a later hand to that of the prophet Zechariah. It is my surmise that Zechariah 9 was originally composed as a description of Darius' menacing march to Egypt in 519 BCE, with the added twist of the release of Zerubbabel. This was then reworked in the light of Alexander the Great's campaign in 332 BCE, since Alexander's march through the Levant in order to reach Egypt recapitulated that of Darius two centuries earlier. The arrival of both kings had imperilled the local polities and created significant anxiety over the fate of Jerusalem and its temple. In both instances, the community of Jerusalem and its temple survived.

גִּילִי מְאֹד בַּת־צִיּוֹן הָרִיעִי בַּת יְרוּשָׁלַם
הִנֵּה מַלְכֵּךְ יָבוֹא לָךְ צַדִּיק וְנוֹשָׁע הוּא
עָנִי וְרֹכֵב עַל־חֲמוֹר וְעַל־עַיִר בֶּן־אֲתֹנוֹת:
וְהִכְרַתִּי־רֶכֶב מֵאֶפְרַיִם וְסוּס מִירוּשָׁלַם
וְנִכְרְתָה קֶשֶׁת מִלְחָמָה וְדִבֶּר שָׁלוֹם לַגּוֹיִם
וּמָשְׁלוֹ מִיָּם עַד־יָם וּמִנָּהָר עַד־אַפְסֵי־אָרֶץ:
גַּם־אַתְּ בְּדַם־בְּרִיתֵךְ
שִׁלַּחְתִּי אֲסִירַיִךְ מִבּוֹר אֵין מַיִם בּוֹ:
שׁוּבוּ לְבִצָּרוֹן אֲסִירֵי הַתִּקְוָה
גַּם־הַיּוֹם מַגִּיד מִשְׁנֶה אָשִׁיב לָךְ:

Celebrate heartily, Daughter Zion! Shout out, Daughter Jerusalem!
See, your king enters you. He is exonerated and liberated,
humbled, riding on a donkey—on a colt, the offspring of asses.
He wipes out chariotry from Ephraim, and cavalry from Jerusalem.
The war-bow is wiped out. He promises peace to the nations,
and his rule extends from sea to sea, from the River to the ends of the earth.
As for you, because of the blood of your covenant,
I have released your prisoners from a waterless dungeon.
Return to the stronghold, prisoners of hope!
This very day, I tell you, I am bringing you back a second time.

Of particular note here is the Niphal participle וְנוֹשָׁע (Zech. 9:9), which indicates that the king is the passive recipient of salvation, rather than one who actively bestows it on others. That is, the king is presented as one who has been saved, which in turn influences how we understand the description of him as צַדִּיק. The king has been declared righteous—that is, in right standing with the relevant authority (in this case, Darius' regime), and is thus exonerated and liberated. This designation is then backed up by four key images: (1) "Zion"—a term laden with Davidic significance, indicating that we are viewing a Davidic "king" who has been freed; (2) traditional terms of Davidic sovereignty and independence, indicating the restoration of hope for Davidic rule; (3) the release of prisoners, showing that the Davidic king has gone free from incarceration; and (4) a second return to the Davidic capital of Jerusalem. This last image is quite telling, as Zerubbabel's first return was his arrival from Babylon with the pioneering Jerusalem community. His second return was in the context of his release from incarceration after the confirmation of Cyrus' decree pertaining to the reconstruction of the Jerusalem temple.

Although Zerubbabel did indeed complete the reconstruction of the Jerusalem temple, he never ruled an independent Davidic state centered on Jerusalem. The reference to him as "king" (Zech. 9:9) is, therefore, more ideological than actual—a statement of the prophetic aspirations attached to his person and office, rather than the political functions he actually fulfilled. Davidic hope survived the crisis of Zerubbabel's removal. His ultimate passing from the stage of history did not, however, put an end to the prophetic hopes for a Davidic restoration. Indeed, the anonymity of the king in Zech. 9:9 provides flexibility, enabling the reader to apply the hopes associated with Davidic rule to others beyond Zerubbabel. The very compilation of the Book of the Twelve is testament to the survival of these hopes, not to mention the deliberate re-enactment of Zech. 9:9 performed by Jesus in the first century (Mt. 21:1-9). As such a restoration became more politically implausible, the hopes of those committed to it began to take on a more eschatological and apocalyptic quality.

In summary, all this evidence builds a profile of Zerubbabel, the Davidic descendant, occupying the royal office of "Sprig," and creating a nascent Davidic state in Jerusalem during the winter of 520/19 BCE as part of the prophetic restoration program. This was a logical step in light of the reconstruction of the temple—a monument to the Davidic covenant—and the apparent collapse of Persia's imperial structures after the death of Cambyses in 522 BCE, which had induced multiple sub-polities to declare their independence, also. However, no sooner had Zerubbabel made his political move than he fell afoul of the Persians, as Darius asserted his sovereignty over all the lands of the empire. Zerubbabel was removed from power, but unlike other dynasts who were executed for their actions, he was incarcerated, pending proof that Cyrus had permitted the construction of the Jerusalem temple, as the Jerusalem community claimed. Proof was indeed found in Ecbatana, and Darius permitted the construction to continue as part of his ambition to own the legacy of Cyrus. Zerubbabel thus earned a reprieve, and was released to complete the task, in fulfilment of Zechariah's prophecy. Zechariah does not contain overt mention that Zerubbabel declared himself king, because the book works with the assumption of Persian power and Darius' sovereignty. However, it is not devoid of clues about Zerubbabel's actions either. Analogously, we notice that Zechariah does not contain mention of the completion of the temple either, and yet there are distinct clues that the temple was indeed completed. The prophecy that Zerubbabel would be the one to complete it, the secret crowning of Joshua as Acting "Sprig," the notion of the return of the "Sprig," and the picture of Jerusalem's king returning "exonerated and liberated" (Zech. 9:9) all speak to its probability. Hope for a Davidic restoration was, therefore, kept alive and lived on for centuries beyond the time of Zerubbabel. All this means that the Book of the Twelve does not curb Davidic hope. On the contrary, it seeks ways to promote it, even in the face of very difficult historical circumstances that threatened to snuff it out. This is an important realization, since the Second Temple Era, in which the Book of the Twelve was finally compiled, did not see sustained Davidic leadership.

The Pivotal Failure of the Priesthood

If, then, the Book of the Twelve advocates continued hope for the restoration of a Davidic kingdom as God's express will, how does it deal with the fact that a Davidic kingdom did not materialize with either Zerubbabel or the generations after him? Had God failed, or should the finger of blame have been pointed elsewhere? Three points may be brought to bear on this issue.

First, the demise of the Davidic royal family was concomitant with the rise of the priestly caste in Jerusalem. This began with the High Priest Joshua, but continued throughout the remainder of the Second Temple Era. As time passed, the priests gained and sustained a hold on power in Jerusalem. Priests were no longer mere clerical adjutants to Judean royalty, but rather took a more central role in the life of the Jewish community. And as Jerusalem itself grew from a small temple community to a proper urban center and provincial capital, so the power of the priesthood grew. Ezra is perhaps the most obvious biblical example of this (Ezra 7:1-7), but multiple examples are known from extrabiblical sources also. When the enclave of Yahwists at Elephantine in Egypt saw their temple to Yahweh destroyed in 410 BCE, they wrote a letter to Jerusalem's High Priest, Yohanan, to seek support for its reconstruction (*TAD* A4.7, 1.18-19). The High Priest in Jerusalem was perceived to possess an authority that extended beyond the confines of his own temple's precincts. There was, as far as we know from the Elephantine documents, no concomitant appeal to any Davidic authority—a telling fact if, as I have argued, the temple in Jerusalem was initially reconstructed as a monument to the Davidic covenant.[20] In ca. 380 BCE, the same High Priest, Yohanan, wielded enough civic authority to mint his own coins.[21] Then, in ca. 350 BCE, Yohanan's sons, Jaddua and

20. Three years later, the Yahwists at Elephantine appealed also to the Judean governor, Bagohi, and to the two sons of the Samarian governor, Sanballat I, because of the lack of response from the High Priest Yohanan (cf. *TAD* A4.9). Although this shows that laity still held positions of civic power, Yohanan was perceived as having enough political clout to affect the sensitive political and religious situation of the Yahwists at Elephantine, though he declined to do so.

21. D. Barag, "A Silver Coin of Yohanan the High Priest and the Coinage of Judea in the Fourth Century B.C.," *INJ* 9 (1986): 4–21; Lisbeth S. Fried, "A Silver Coin of Yohanan Hakkôhēn," *Transeuphratène* 26 (2003): 65–85.

Manasseh, were involved in a controversy with the Samarian governor, Sanballat II. After Artaxerxes III's disastrous Egyptian campaign of 351 BCE, an imperial power vacuum prevailed, which saw the Tennes Revolt break out in Sidon and the neighboring Phoenician cities. Sanballat II took advantage of these conditions and attempted to form a regional coalition with Judah by marrying his daughter, Nicaso, to Manasseh (Josephus, *Ant.* 11.302-12).[22] The match was of great political consequence, despite Judah having a civic governor at the time (Hezekiah). Jaddua, however, as High Priest in Jerusalem, vehemently opposed the match. The coalition eventually came to naught when Artaxerxes III reasserted his sovereignty in the region. But, when Alexander the Great arrived in the Levant in 332 BCE, it was the High Priest Jaddua who was the recognized civic head of Judah (Josephus, *Ant.* 11.306-345).[23] Thereafter, the High Priests held both civic and religious authority (i.e., without a separate civic governor) right up until the Roman conquest of Judea (63 BCE).

Second, when Joshua was commissioned to lead the Jerusalem community in Zerubbabel's absence, he was admonished to obey Yahweh in order to enable Zerubbabel's return (Zech. 3:6-8):

וַיָּעַד מַלְאַךְ יְהוָה בִּיהוֹשֻׁעַ לֵאמֹר: כֹּה־אָמַר יְהוָה צְבָאוֹת אִם־בִּדְרָכַי תֵּלֵךְ וְאִם
אֶת־מִשְׁמַרְתִּי תִשְׁמֹר וְגַם־אַתָּה תָּדִין אֶת־בֵּיתִי וְגַם תִּשְׁמֹר אֶת־חֲצֵרָי וְנָתַתִּי לְךָ מַהְלְכִים
בֵּין הָעֹמְדִים הָאֵלֶּה: שְׁמַע־נָא יְהוֹשֻׁעַ הַכֹּהֵן הַגָּדוֹל אַתָּה וְרֵעֶיךָ הַיֹּשְׁבִים לְפָנֶיךָ כִּי־אַנְשֵׁי
מוֹפֵת הֵמָּה כִּי־הִנְנִי מֵבִיא אֶת־עַבְדִּי צֶמַח:

The messenger of Yahweh warned Joshua, "Thus has Yahweh of Ranks said: If you walk in my ways, and if you execute my commission, you will both govern my house and watch my courts, and I will give you leeway among those standing here. Listen, O Joshua, High Priest, you and your colleagues who sit before you. For they are symbolic men, for I am going to bring my servant, the Sprig!"

22. Josephus' account is riddled with chronological problems, exacerbated by the fact that he believed Samaria had possessed only one governor named Sanballat. In fact, there had been two. The first Sanballat was responsible for the construction of the Samarian temple on Mount Gerizim in the mid-fifth century BCE, but Josephus conflates this with the actions of Sanballat II in the mid-fourth century BCE. Once these chronological issues are untangled, a coherent picture of events emerges, allowing us to date the Manasseh Affair to ca. 350 BCE.

23. Although there are fanciful elements to Josephus' account of Jaddua's interaction with Alexander, the essential premise of Jaddua as the de facto ethnarch of the Judeans is sound.

The role of Joshua and his priestly colleagues was to follow the ways of Yahweh and guard the temple as the way to embody symbolically the return of the "Sprig." In other words, the moral rectitude of the priests was necessary for the fulfilment of Yahweh's purposes, which centered not on the priests themselves, but on the Davidic descendant. Since the priests were functionaries at the Davidic monument—the temple in Jerusalem— this expectation aligns with Davidic ideology. The Book of the Twelve, therefore, sees the priests as pivotal but not central to the restoration purposes of Yahweh. The Davidic descendant plays the central role in Yahweh's purposes, and the priests play a supporting role.

Third, it is precisely the failure of the priests in their supporting role that the Book of the Twelve identifies as the main issue in the seeming delay of restoration. Priests receive rebuke at various points throughout the Twelve and, on the whole, are characterized with great negativity. This characterization begins in Hos. 4:4, where Yahweh states:

אַ֥ךְ אִ֛ישׁ אַל־יָרֵ֖ב וְאַל־יוֹכַ֣ח אִ֑ישׁ וְעַמְּךָ֖ כִּמְרִיבֵ֥י כֹהֵֽן׃
וְכָשַׁלְתָּ֣ הַיּ֔וֹם וְכָשַׁ֧ל גַּם־נָבִ֛יא עִמְּךָ֖ לָ֑יְלָה וְדָמִ֖יתִי אִמֶּֽךָ׃
נִדְמ֥וּ עַמִּ֖י מִבְּלִ֣י הַדָּ֑עַת כִּֽי־אַתָּ֞ה הַדַּ֣עַת מָאַ֗סְתָּ וְאֶמְאָֽסְאךָ֙ מִכַּהֵ֣ן לִ֔י וַתִּשְׁכַּח֙ תּוֹרַ֣ת
אֱלֹהֶ֔יךָ אֶשְׁכַּ֥ח בָּנֶ֖יךָ גַּם־אָֽנִי׃
כְּרֻבָּ֖ם כֵּ֣ן חָֽטְאוּ־לִ֑י כְּבוֹדָ֖ם בְּקָל֥וֹן אָמִֽיר׃
חַטַּ֥את עַמִּ֖י יֹאכֵ֑לוּ וְאֶל־עֲוֺנָ֖ם יִשְׂא֥וּ נַפְשֽׁוֹ׃
וְהָיָ֥ה כָעָ֖ם כַּכֹּהֵ֑ן וּפָקַדְתִּ֤י עָלָיו֙ דְּרָכָ֔יו וּמַעֲלָלָ֖יו אָשִׁ֥יב לֽוֹ׃

Oh, let no one dispute, and let no one berate, that my dispute is with you, O priest!
As you stumbled in the day, so also the prophet stumbled with you in the night.
As I destroyed your mother, my people were destroyed without knowledge.
Since you have rejected knowledge, I will reject you as my priest.
You forgot the law of your God. I will in turn forget your sons.
As they increased, so they sinned against me. I will exchange their importance for insignificance.
They feed on the sin of my people, and put up with their guilt,
so that it has become, "Like people, like priest!"
I will deal their own ways back upon them, and repay them for their deeds.

This announces Yahweh's dispute with the priests as those responsible for leading the whole nation (northern and southern halves) astray, and it is a theme that will continue throughout the Book of the Twelve. Prophets are also mentioned here, and at other points in the Book of the Twelve (e.g. Zech. 13:2-6), as bearing some of the blame for the waywardness of the people. However, prophets were occasional figures, whereas the priests were part of a fixed, permanent, hereditary institution. They therefore have the lion's share of the blame. Hosea's setting is in the northern kingdom of Israel—that half of the nation that did not have Davidic leadership. This provides an analog for the readers of the Book of the Twelve, who were Judeans living in the Second Temple era, but without Davidic leadership. If the nation faced crisis and peril, and a Davidic state seemed a faraway dream, then the priests bore responsibility for the situation.

Joel presents a similar line of reasoning. In 1:13, the priests are called to initiate mourning and repentance:

חִגְרוּ וְסִפְדוּ הַכֹּהֲנִים הֵילִילוּ מְשָׁרְתֵי מִזְבֵּחַ
בֹּאוּ לִינוּ בַשַּׂקִּים מְשָׁרְתֵי אֱלֹהָי
כִּי נִמְנַע מִבֵּית אֱלֹהֵיכֶם מִנְחָה וָנָסֶךְ:

Gird yourselves and mourn, O priests! Wail, O ministers of the altar!
Come, spend the night in sackcloth, O ministers of my God!
For offering and libation are withheld from the house of your God.

Only after heartfelt repentance can there be a change of fortunes, which is captured in 2:1:

תִּקְעוּ שׁוֹפָר בְּצִיּוֹן וְהָרִיעוּ בְּהַר קָדְשִׁי
יִרְגְּזוּ כֹּל יֹשְׁבֵי הָאָרֶץ כִּי־בָא יוֹם־יְהוָה כִּי קָרוֹב:

Blow the trumpet in Zion, and shout on my holy mountain!
Let all the residents of the land quake, for the Day of Yahweh is coming—
for it is near.

The reference here to Zion is not merely an allusion to the temple as a cultic place. Since Zion was the name of the fortress originally captured by David, in which he took up residence (2 Sam. 5:7-9), the term connotes Davidic rule in Jerusalem over a united Israel. It is not devoid of cultic significance, but rather underscores that the temple—along with the priesthood that served within it—was an integral feature of Davidic ideology, and that Davidic kingship could not be legitimately separated from the Jerusalem temple and its cult. Thus, the repentance of the priests, and also the nation that they lead in the absence of a Davidic king, prompts the arrival of the Day of Yahweh.

Yet there is ambivalence as to what exactly the Day of Yahweh will entail. The imagery of Yahweh arriving at the head of his army is fearsome and threatening, and seems initially to spell disaster for the nation. But in the midst of his invasion, Yahweh issues a plea (Joel 2:12-14):

וְגַם־עַתָּה נְאֻם־יְהֹוָה
שֻׁבוּ עָדַי בְּכָל־לְבַבְכֶם וּבְצוֹם וּבְבְכִי וּבְמִסְפֵּד:
וְקִרְעוּ לְבַבְכֶם וְאַל־בִּגְדֵיכֶם
וְשׁוּבוּ אֶל־יְהֹוָה אֱלֹהֵיכֶם
כִּי־חַנּוּן וְרַחוּם הוּא אֶרֶךְ אַפַּיִם
וְרַב־חֶסֶד וְנִחָם עַל־הָרָעָה:
מִי יוֹדֵעַ יָשׁוּב וְנִחָם וְהִשְׁאִיר אַחֲרָיו בְּרָכָה
מִנְחָה וָנֶסֶךְ לַיהֹוָה אֱלֹהֵיכֶם: פ

"Even now," declares Yahweh,
"Return to me with all your heart—with fasting, weeping, and lamentation.
Rend your hearts, and not your garments,
and return to Yahweh your God."
For he is gracious and compassionate, slow to anger,
full of commitment and relenting from disaster.
Who knows—perhaps he will turn and relent, and leave behind him a blessing—
offering and libation to Yahweh your God?

Yahweh is described here in the classic terms of the national covenant (cf. Exod. 34:6; Deut. 4:31)—a characterization that will be repeated in Jon. 4:2. The implication is that Yahweh has not changed his character—a fact that will be stated even more overtly in Mal. 3:6, and given as the reason for why the nation of Israel has survived at all. Yahweh is thus presented as a deity desiring to restore his people and bless them, but repentance is lacking. Critically, it is the priests' role to bring the nation to repentance, and they have failed to do this. To underscore these connections, Joel repeats the call to repentance and its significance for Zion, noting the mediatory role of the priests (2:15-17):

תִּקְעוּ שׁוֹפָר בְּצִיּוֹן קַדְּשׁוּ־צוֹם קִרְאוּ עֲצָרָה:
אִסְפוּ־עָם קַדְּשׁוּ קָהָל קִבְצוּ זְקֵנִים
אִסְפוּ עוֹלָלִים וְיֹנְקֵי שָׁדָיִם
יֵצֵא חָתָן מֵחֶדְרוֹ וְכַלָּה מֵחֻפָּתָהּ:
בֵּין הָאוּלָם וְלַמִּזְבֵּחַ יִבְכּוּ הַכֹּהֲנִים מְשָׁרְתֵי יְהֹוָה
וְיֹאמְרוּ חוּסָה יְהֹוָה עַל־עַמֶּךָ
וְאַל־תִּתֵּן נַחֲלָתְךָ לְחֶרְפָּה לִמְשָׁל־בָּם גּוֹיִם
לָמָּה יֹאמְרוּ בָעַמִּים אַיֵּה אֱלֹהֵיהֶם:

Blow the trumpet in Zion! Declare a fast! Call a council!
Collect the people! Declare an assembly! Gather the elders!
Collect the children, and babes at breast!

Let the groom leave his chamber, and the bride her canopy.
Between the porch and the altar, let the priests weep—ministers of Yahweh—
and let them say, "Have mercy, O Yahweh, upon your people,
and do not put your estate to scorn—a byword among nations!
Why let them say among the peoples, 'Where is their God?'"

The priests are here identified as leaders with the responsibility of leading the nation in repentance. Once again, the importance of Zion and the temple in which the priests minister highlights the Davidic significance of their vocation. When seen through the lens of the Davidic covenant, we understand that the priests here stand on the property of the house that the Davidic heir builds for Yahweh, which itself symbolizes the permanent house that Yahweh builds for David. The whole people are gathered together in the one true place of worship under the putative aegis of the Davidic king, as per the Davidic covenant, but conspicuously absent is the king himself. The priests, therefore, are required to lead the nation in repentance to rectify this. A similar gathering is envisioned in Mic. 4:6-8, leading to the promise, "The former sovereignty will come, kingship to Daughter Jerusalem" (Mic. 4:8). In Hosea, the priests represent Yahweh to the people, while in Joel we see the priests representing the people to Yahweh. This critical position of the priests betwixt the deity and his covenant people is what makes them pivotal for both understanding God's intentions for the nation, and leading that nation to align itself with the divine will for a restoration of Davidic kingship.

Yet, the Book of the Twelve goes on to show that the priests fail in their role. Their obstinacy is embodied, for example, in the attitude of Amaziah, the priest of Bethel, in Amos 7:10-17. Amaziah was part of a rival Yahwistic cult, rather than a priest in Jerusalem. Nevertheless, like the priests in Hosea, Amaziah typifies the situation of having priests but no Davidic king. The incongruence of the situation is highlighted by the famous opening words of Amos (1:2):

יְהוָה מִצִּיּוֹן יִשְׁאָג וּמִירוּשָׁלַם יִתֵּן קוֹלוֹ
וְאָבְלוּ נְאוֹת הָרֹעִים וְיָבֵשׁ רֹאשׁ הַכַּרְמֶל:

Yahweh roars from Zion, and emits his voice from Jerusalem,
and the fields of the shepherds wither, and the summit of Carmel dries up.

Here we see Yahweh clearly situated in Zion and Jerusalem—the deity of the Davidic dynasty and its temple. The effect of his anger is the destruction of the domain of the shepherds—a common analogy for the leaders of the people, such as the priests. This helps frame the presentation of the obstinate Amaziah, who rejects Yahweh's prophet (Amos), and is thus confirmed in an oracle of destruction of both his own family and his nation (Amos 7:17). The destruction of the northern kingdom of Israel, which Amos then begins to describe in 8:1–9:10, thus serves as a threatening precedent for the judgment that can come upon the nation for its waywardness.[24] And this is, in turn, followed by the statement that God remains committed to restoring the fallen booth of David (Amos 9:11). Amos, therefore, is bookended by statements about God's connection to the Davidic dynasty, showing how the blame for the failure to restore the Davidic kingdom lies not with God, but with the priests who have led the nation astray.

As mentioned above, Zechariah is the key text for understanding the synergy that was meant to exist between the priesthood and the Davidic dynasty. The oracle in Zechariah 9–11 begins with buoyant hope for the restoration of a Davidic kingdom in the midst of international turmoil (Zech. 9:1-17), but ends with a note of dejection as the shepherds of the people are exposed as self-interested leaders who pursue wealth, leading them to abuse their flock and cause it great harm (Zech. 11:4-17). Despite God's stated desire to restore the Davidic kingdom, he instead raises up a stupid shepherd, who does not care for the flock, as a judgment (Zech. 11:15-17). This note of dejection then gives way to the apocalyptic-like oracle of Zechariah 12–14, which sees the only way for the nation to be rescued from oblivion being for Yahweh himself to step in and enact change.

This then leads on to the oracle of Malachi, which completes the bleak picture of the priesthood. Unlike Hosea and Amos, who lived centuries earlier when the kingdoms of Israel and Judah were still a reality, Malachi directly addresses priests within the post-exilic situation, when there was no local, native kingdom.[25] His condemnation of the priests is, therefore, perhaps the loudest voice in the Book of the Twelve. The chastising of the priests begins in Mal. 1:6:

---

24. A similar theme was taken up in the ministry of John the Baptist (Mt. 3:7-12).

25. It is entirely plausible that some of the words directed towards the priests in Hosea are the words of a later, post-exilic redactor. Nonetheless, this does not take away from the fact that both Hosea and Amos addressed a pre-exilic situation. Malachi's words, therefore, are more directly relevant to the context of a covenant community that lacks a Davidic king.

בֵּן יְכַבֵּד אָב וְעֶבֶד אֲדֹנָיו
וְאִם־אָב אָנִי אַיֵּה כְבוֹדִי
וְאִם־אֲדוֹנִים אָנִי אַיֵּה מוֹרָאִי
אָמַר יְהוָה צְבָאוֹת לָכֶם הַכֹּהֲנִים בּוֹזֵי שְׁמִי

> "Son honors father, and servant his master,
> So if I am father, where is my honor?
> And if I am master, where is my respect?"
> Yahweh of Ranks says to you, O priests, who despise my name.

Thus begins the tirade against the priests that is sustained practically throughout all of Malachi. In Mal. 1:11-12, the honor that the priests of Jerusalem's temple give to Yahweh is compared to the honor that is accorded to Yahweh's name by other nations. The verdict is that the nations do a better job honoring Yahweh's name than his own priests in Jerusalem do. In Mal. 2:1-2, the priestly attitude towards Yahweh draws rebuke and curse:

וְעַתָּה אֲלֵיכֶם הַמִּצְוָה הַזֹּאת הַכֹּהֲנִים: אִם־לֹא תִשְׁמְעוּ וְאִם־לֹא תָשִׂימוּ עַל־לֵב לָתֵת
כָּבוֹד לִשְׁמִי אָמַר יְהוָה צְבָאוֹת וְשִׁלַּחְתִּי בָכֶם אֶת־הַמְּאֵרָה וְאָרוֹתִי אֶת־בִּרְכוֹתֵיכֶם וְגַם
אָרוֹתִיהָ כִּי אֵינְכֶם שָׂמִים עַל־לֵב:

> Well now, this directive is to you, O priests: "If you do not listen, if you do
> not take it to heart to give honor to my name," says Yahweh of Ranks, "I will
> send against you the curse. I will curse your blessings, and curse it again,
> because you do not take it to heart."

The implication here is that the moral failures of the priesthood are the basis for the lack of blessing in God's covenant community. It is not that God has failed to make good on his promises to raise the fallen tent of David, or changed his mind. Indeed, God says in Malachi, "Because I am Yahweh, I have not changed, and you have not been destroyed" (Mal. 3:6). The survival of the nation is credited to Yahweh's consistent character, despite the waywardness of the priest—an important facet of the Book of the Twelve's theodicy. But the wickedness of the priests has forced God to bring judgment, rather than blessing, because the constancy of his character means he cannot be unjust. The priests were supposed to keep the covenant nation in a godly "holding pattern" until God finally acted to restore a Davidic kingdom. This dynamic was specifically flagged with the commissioning of Joshua as Acting "Sprig" in Zechariah 3, but the priests failed in this task. Thus, in Mal. 3:1-4, the hopes for restoration are put into the perspective of judgment:

הִנְנִי שֹׁלֵחַ מַלְאָכִי וּפִנָּה־דֶרֶךְ לְפָנָי וּפִתְאֹם יָבוֹא אֶל־הֵיכָלוֹ הָאָדוֹן אֲשֶׁר־אַתֶּם מְבַקְשִׁים
וּמַלְאַךְ הַבְּרִית אֲשֶׁר־אַתֶּם חֲפֵצִים הִנֵּה־בָא אָמַר יְהוָה צְבָאוֹת:
וּמִי מְכַלְכֵּל אֶת־יוֹם בּוֹאוֹ וּמִי הָעֹמֵד בְּהֵרָאוֹתוֹ כִּי־הוּא כְּאֵשׁ מְצָרֵף וּכְבֹרִית מְכַבְּסִים:
וְיָשַׁב מְצָרֵף וּמְטַהֵר כֶּסֶף וְטִהַר אֶת־בְּנֵי־לֵוִי וְזִקַּק אֹתָם כַּזָּהָב וְכַכָּסֶף וְהָיוּ לַיהוָה מַגִּישֵׁי
מִנְחָה בִּצְדָקָה: וְעָרְבָה לַיהוָה מִנְחַת יְהוּדָה וִירוּשָׁלָםִ כִּימֵי עוֹלָם וּכְשָׁנִים קַדְמֹנִיּוֹת:

See, I am sending my messenger, and he will trace the way before me.
Suddenly the master, whom you are seeking, will come into his palace—the
messenger of the covenant whom you are desiring. See him coming, says
Yahweh of Ranks. But who can contain the day of his coming? Who can
stand at his appearing? For he will be like refining fire, like launderers'
soap. He will take his seat while refining, purifying silver. He will purify
the sons of Levi, and refine them like gold and silver, that they may become
righteous bearers of offering to Yahweh. Then the offering of Judah and
Jerusalem will be pleasing to Yahweh, as in days of old, and yesteryear.

We see here that Yahweh fully intends to meet the community's expectations. A masterly figure will come with covenantal significance, enter a
palace and sit himself down. But this will be a moment of judgment, not
blessing. Indeed, only with the enactment of judgment can blessing ensue.

Conclusion

We see, then, that the Book of the Twelve continues to hold out hope for
the restoration of a Davidic Kingdom. Hope revolves primarily around
the figure of the "Sprig"—the office of the primary Davidic descendant.
In the first instance, this figure is identified with Zerubbabel in Haggai
and Zechariah during the early Persian period. But a Davidic kingdom
under Zerubbabel ultimately failed to materialize. This failure is not
blamed on God, but is initially placed at the feet of Zerubbabel himself.
He is reprimanded for the presumptuous use of force and prowess, rather
than waiting for Yahweh's Spirit to enact the necessary conditions for
full restoration. Zerubbabel's failure, however, did not scuttle Davidic
hope. Rather, it was temporarily focused on the priesthood as a surrogate.
The High Priest, Joshua, was commissioned to be Acting "Sprig" in
the wake of Zerubbabel's removal by the Persians. He was expressly
commanded to lead his priestly colleagues in following God's ways, in
order to facilitate the fulfilment of God's purposes regarding Davidic
hope. But the priesthood fails in this task. Throughout the Twelve, priests
are condemned for their moral and cultic failure, receiving sustained
criticism in Malachi. Thus, God has not failed or changed his mind. He is
still committed to fulfilling Davidic expectations. It is, rather, the human

leadership of his people that has caused the delay in fulfilment. The result is that God will still act to bring about a Davidic kingdom, but this will be concomitant with an act of judgment.

In the longer term, this situation contributed to the development of eschatological and apocalyptic messianic hope. As the centuries wore on, the likelihood of a Davidic kingdom becoming a reality grew smaller and smaller. The Persians, generally accorded respect in wider biblical depiction, gave way to the empire of Alexander, and the subsequent kingdoms of the Diadochi, and the goal of an independent Davidic state began to look politically impossible. Yet, the Book of the Twelve encouraged continued hope that God would still act, despite the imperial machinations of foreign powers. God was still to be trusted, because he himself had not changed. What he had said through the former prophets had come to pass, so he would make good on his promise to bring about a Davidic kingdom. But since normal political processes brought nothing but disappointment, and the nation's priestly leaders were not to be trusted, God himself would have to step into history to bring about the restoration. The emergence of apocalyptic thinking in the later Second Temple Period is testament to this development.

BIBLIOGRAPHY

Abel, Douglas Stephen. "The Marriage Metaphor in Hosea 4 and Jeremiah 2: How Prophetic Speech 'Kills Two Birds with One Stone.'" *Proceedings* 29 (2009): 15–27.

Abma, R. *Bonds of Love: Methodic Studies of Prophetic Texts with Marriage Imagery (Isaiah 50:1–3 and 54:1–10, Hosea 1–3, Jeremiah 2–3)*. SSN. Assen: Van Gorcum, 1999.

Achtemeier, Elizabeth. *Nahum–Malachi*. Atlanta: John Knox, 1986.

Adams, Karin. "Metaphor and Dissonance: A Reinterpretation of Hosea 4:13–14." *JBL* 127 (2008): 291–305.

Adler, Elaine June. "The Background for the Metaphor of Covenant as Marriage in the Hebrew Bible." PhD diss., University of California, Berkeley, 1990.

Ahn, John J., and Jill Middlemas (eds). *By the Irrigation Canals of Babylon: Approaches to the Study of the Exile*, LHBOTS 526. London: T&T Clark, 2012.

Albertz, Rainer. "Exile as Purification: Reconstructing the 'Book of the Four.'" In *Thematic Threads in the Book of the Twelve*, edited by Paul L. Redditt and Aaron Schart, 232–51. Berlin: de Gruyter, 2003.

Albertz, R., J. D. Nogalski, and J. Wöhrle (eds). *Perspectives on the Formation of the Book of the Twelve: Methodological Foundations, Redactional Processes, Historical Insights*. BZAW 433. Berlin: de Gruyter, 2012.

Allen, Leslie C. *The Books of Joel, Obadiah, Jonah, and Micah*. NICOT. Grand Rapids: Eerdmans, 1976.

Ames, Frank R. "Forced Migration and the Visions of Zechariah 1–8." In *The Prophets Speak on Forced Migration*, edited by Mark J. Boda et al., 147–59. Atlanta: SBL, 2015.

Andersen, Francis I. *Habakkuk*. AB 25. Garden City: Doubleday, 2001.

Andersen, Francis I., and David Noel Freedman. *Amos: A New Translation with Introduction and Commentary*. AB 24A. New York: Doubleday, 1989.

Andersen, Francis I., and David Noel Freedman. *Hosea: A New Translation with Introduction and Commentary*. AB 24. Garden City, NY: Doubleday, 1980.

Andersen, Francis I., and David Noel Freedman. *Micah: A New Translation with Introduction and Commentary*. AB 24E. New York: Doubleday, 2000.

Angus, Ian. *Facing the Anthropocene: Fossil Capitalism and the Crisis of the Earth System*. New York: Monthly Review Press, 2016.

Arnold, Bill T., and John H. Choi. *A Guide to Biblical Hebrew Syntax*. New York: Cambridge University Press, 2003.

Asad, Talal. *Genealogies of Religion: Discipline and Reasons of Power in Christianity and Islam*. Baltimore: Johns Hopkins University Press, 1993.

Assis, Elie. *The Book of Joel: A Prophet between Calamity and Hope*. LHBOTS 581. London: Bloomsbury, 2013.

Assis, Elie. "A Disputed Temple (Haggai 2,1-9)." *ZAW* 120 (2008): 582–96.

Auerbach, Erich. *Mimesis: The Representation of Reality in Western Literature*. Princeton: Princeton University Press, 1953.

Avishur, Yitzhak. *Studies in Hebrew and Ugaritic Psalms*. Jerusalem: Magnes, 1994.

Baker, David W. *Joel, Obadiah, Malachi*. NIVAC. Downers Grove: Zondervan, 2009.

Balentine, Samuel E. *Prayer in the Hebrew Bible: The Drama of Divine–Human Dialogue*. OBT. Minneapolis: Fortress, 1993.

Ball, Edward. "'When the Towers Fall': Interpreting Nahum as Christian Scripture." In *In Search of True Wisdom: Essays in Old Testament Interpretation in Honour of Ronald E. Clements*, edited by Edward Ball, 211–30. JSOTSup 300. Sheffield: Sheffield Academic, 1999.

Bar, Shaul. "Resheph in the Hebrew Bible." *JQR* 45 (2017): 119–26.

Barag, D. "A Silver Coin of Yoḥanan the High Priest and the Coinage of Judea in the Fourth Century B.C." *INJ* 9 (1986): 4–21.

Barker, Joel. *From the Depths of Despair to the Promise of Presence: A Rhetorical Reading of the Book of Joel*. Siphrut 11. Winona Lake: Eisenbrauns, 2014.

Barker, Kenneth L. "Zechariah." In *The Expositor's Bible Commentary 8: Daniel–Malachi*, edited by T. Longman III and D. Garland. Rev. ed. Grand Rapids: Zondervan, 2008.

Barth, Karl. *Church Dogmatics 2*. Translated and edited by Geoffrey W. Bromiley and Thomas F. Torrance. Edinburgh: T. & T. Clark, 1957.

Barton, John. *Ethics in Ancient Israel*. Oxford: Oxford University Press, 2014.

Barton, John. *Joel and Obadiah*. OTL. Louisville: Westminster John Knox, 2001.

Barton, John. "Prophecy and Theodicy." In *Thus Says the Lord: Essays on the Former and Latter Prophets in Honor of Robert R. Wilson*, edited by John J. Ahn and Stephen L. Cook, 73–86. New York: T&T Clark, 2009.

Barton, John. "Reading Texts Holistically: The Foundation of Biblical Criticism." In *Congress Volume Ljubljana 2007*, edited by André Lemaire, 367–80. VTSup 133. Leiden: Brill, 2010.

Bauckham, Richard J. *The Theology of the Book of Revelation*. NTT. Cambridge: Cambridge University Press, 1993.

Baumann, Gerlinde. *Gottes Gewalt im Wandel: Traditionsgeschichtliche und Intertextuelle Studien zu Nahum 1,2-8*. WMANT 108. Neukirchen-Vluyn: Neukirchener Verlag, 2005.

Baumann, Gerlinde. *Love and Violence: Marriage as Metaphor for the Relationship between YHWH and Israel in the Prophetic Books*. Translated by Linda M. Maloney. Collegeville: Liturgical Press, 2003.

Beaulieu, Paul-Alain (trans.). "Nabopolassar's Restoration of Imgur-Enlil: The Inner Defensive Wall of Babylon (2.121)." *COS* 2:307–8.

Beaulieu, Paul-Alain. "Mesopotamia." In *Religions of the Ancient World*, edited by S. I. Johnston, 165–72. Cambridge: Belknap Press of Harvard University Press, 2004.

Beck, M. *Der 'Tag YHWHs' im Dodekapropheton: Studien im Spannungsfeld von Traditions- und Redaktionsgeschichte*. BZAW 356. Berlin: de Gruyter, 2005.

Becker, Uwe. *Jesaja—von der Botschaft zum Buch*. FRLANT 178. Göttingen: Vandenhoeck & Ruprecht, 1997.

Becking, Bob. *Ezra-Nehemiah*. Historical Commentary on the Old Testament. Leuven: Peeters, 2018.

Ben Zvi, Ehud. "Reading Hosea and Imagining YHWH." *HBT* 30 (2008): 43–57.

Ben Zvi, Ehud. "Twelve Prophetic Books or 'the Twelve': A Few Preliminary Considerations." In *Forming Prophetic Literature Essays on Isaiah and the Twelve in Honor of John D.W. Watts*, edited by Paul R. House, James W. Watts, and John D. W. Watts, 125–56. JSOTSup 235. Sheffield: Sheffield Academic, 1996.

Bergler, Siefgried. *Joel als Schriftinterpret*. BEATAJ 16. Frankfurt am Main: Peter Lang, 1988.

Bergmann, Claudia D. *Childbirth as a Metaphor for Crisis: Evidence from the Ancient Near East, the Hebrew Bible, and 1QH XI, 1–18*. BZAW 382. Berlin: de Gruyter, 2008.

Bird, Phyllis. "'To Play the Harlot': An Inquiry into an Old Testament Metaphor." In *Gender and Difference in Ancient Israel*, edited by Peggy L. Day, 75–94. Minneapolis: Fortress, 1989.

Bird, Phyllis. "Prostitution in the Social World and Religious Rhetoric of Ancient Israel." In *Prostitutes and Courtesans in the Ancient World*, edited by Christopher A. Faraone and Laura K. McClure, 40–58. Madison: University of Wisconsin Press, 2006.

Bleibtreu, Erika. "Grisly Assyrian Record of Torture and Death." *BAR* 17 (1991): 52–61.

Boda, Mark J. "Babylon in the Book of the Twelve." *HebAI* 3 (2014): 225–48.

Boda, Mark J. *The Book of Zechariah*. NICOT. Grand Rapids: Eerdmans, 2016.

Boda, Mark J. "A Deafening Call to Silence: The Rhetorical 'End' of Human Address to the Deity in the Book of the Twelve." Pages 193–217 in *Exploring Zechariah: Volume 1—The Development of Zechariah and Its Role within the Twelve*. ANEM 16. Atlanta: SBL, 2017.

Boda, Mark J. *Exploring Zechariah: Volume 1—The Development of Zechariah and Its Role within the Twelve*. ANEM 16. Atlanta: SBL, 2017.

Boda, Mark J. "From Fasts to Feasts: The Literary Function of Zechariah 7–8." *CBQ* 65 (2003): 390–407.

Boda, Mark J. "Geography in the Book of the Twelve." In *The Book of the Twelve: Composition, Reception, and Interpretation*, edited by Lena-Sofia Tiemeyer and Jakob Wöhrle, 507–31. VTSup 184. Leiden: Brill, 2020.

Boda, Mark J. *Haggai, Zechariah*. NIVAC. Grand Rapids: Zondervan, 2004.

Boda, Mark J. "Penitential Innovations in the Book of the Twelve." In *On Stone and Scroll: A Festschrift for Graham Davies*, edited by Brian A. Mastin, Katharine J. Dell, and James K. Aitken, 291–308. BZAW 420. Berlin: de Gruyter, 2011.

Boda, Mark J. *A Severe Mercy: Sin and Its Remedy in the Old Testament*. Winona Lake: Eisenbrauns, 2009.

Boda, Mark J. "Scat! Exilic Motifs in the Book of Zechariah." In *The Prophets Speak on Forced Migration*, edited by Mark J. Boda et al., 161–80. Atlanta: SBL, 2015.

Boda, Mark J. "Terrifying the Horns: Persia and Babylon in Zechariah 1:7–6:15." *CBQ* 67 (2005): 22–41.

Boda, Mark J. "'Uttering Precious Rather than Worthless Words': Divine Patience and Impatience with Lament in Isaiah and Jeremiah." In *Why? How Long? Studies on Voice(s) of Lamentation Rooted in Biblical Hebrew Poetry*, edited by LeAnn Snow Flesher, Carol Dempsey, and Mark J. Boda, 83–99. LHBOTS 552. London: Continuum, 2014.

Boda, Mark J. et al. (eds). *The Prophets Speak on Forced Migration*. Atlanta: SBL, 2015.

Braaten, Laurie J. "Earth Community in Joel 1–2: A Call to Identify with the Rest of Creation." *HBT* 28 (2006): 113–29.

Braaten, Laurie J. "God Sows: Hosea's Land Theme in the Book of the Twelve." In *Thematic Threads in the Book of the Twelve*, edited by Paul L. Redditt and Aaron Schart, 104–32. New York: de Gruyter, 2003.

Bracke, John M. "šûb šebût: A Reappraisal." *ZAW* 97 (1985): 233–44.

Bratcher, Dennis Ray. "The Theological Message of Habakkuk: A Literary-Rhetorical Analysis." PhD diss., Union Theological Seminary in Virginia, 1984.

Briant, Pierre. *From Cyrus to Alexander: A History of the Persian Empire*. Translated by Peter T. Daniels. Winona Lake: Eisenbrauns, 2002.

Bright, John. *A History of Israel*. 4th ed. Louisville: Westminster John Knox, 2000.

Brueggemann, Walter. "Amos' Intercessory Formula." *VT* 19 (1969): 385–99.

Brueggemann, Walter. "The Recovering God of Hosea." *HBT* 30 (2008): 5–20.

Brueggemann, Walter. "Some Aspects of Theodicy in Old Testament Faith." *PRSt* 26 (Fall 1999): 253–68.

Brueggemann, Walter. *Tradition in Crisis: A Study in Hosea*. Richmond: John Knox, 1968.

Carroll R., M. Daniel. "'I Will Send Fire': Reflections on the Violence of God in Amos." In *Wrestling with the Violence of God: Soundings in the Old Testament*, edited by M. Daniel Carroll R. and J. B. Wilgus, 113–32. BBR Sup 10. Winona Lake: Eisenbrauns, 2015.

Carroll R., M. Daniel. "Hosea." In *The Expositor's Bible Commentary 8: Daniel–Malachi*, edited by T. Longman III and D. Garland. Rev. ed. Grand Rapids: Zondervan, 2008.

Carson, D. A. *How Long, O Lord? Reflections on Suffering and Evil*. 2nd ed. Grand Rapids: Baker Academic, 2006.

Castelo, Daniel. *Theological Theodicy*. Cascade Companions 14. Cascade: Wipf & Stock, 2012.

Chapman, Cynthia R. *The Gendered Language of Warfare in the Israelite–Assyrian Encounter*. HSM 62. Winona Lake: Eisenbrauns, 2004.

Chapman, Stephen B. "Martial Memory, Peaceable Vision: Divine War in the Old Testament." In *Holy War in the Bible: Christian Morality and an Old Testament Problem*, edited by H. A. Thomas, J. Evans, and P. Copan, 47–67. Downers Grove: InterVarsity Press Academic, 2013.

Childs, Brevard S. "Psalm Titles and Midrashic Exegesis." *JSS* 16 (1971): 137–50.

Chisholm, R. B., Jr., *Interpreting the Minor Prophets*. Grand Rapids: Zondervan, 1990.

Chisholm, R. B., Jr. "Retribution." In *Dictionary of the Old Testament Prophets*, edited by J. G. McConville and M. J. Boda, 671–6. Downers Grove: InterVarsity, 2012.

Christiansen, Duane. "Nahum." In *Harper's Bible Commentary*, edited by James L. Mays, 736–8. San Francisco: Harper & Row, 1988.

Cifarelli, Meghan. "Gesture and Alterity in the Art of Ashurnasirpal II of Assyria." *The Art Bulletin* 80 (1998): 210–28.

Clements, Roland E. "Patterns in the Prophetic Canon." In *Canon and Authority*, edited by G. W. Coats and B. O. Long, 42–55. Philadelphia: Fortress, 1977.

Clements, Roland E. *Prophecy and Covenant*. SBT 43. London: SCM, 1965.

Clendenen, E. Ray. "C. J. H. Wright's 'Ethical Triangle' and the Threefold Structure of Malachi." In *Annual Meeting of the Evangelical Theological Society 2003*, 1–16. Nashville: Broadman & Holman, 2003.

Clendenen, E. Ray. "The Structure of Malachi: A Textlinguistic Study." *CTR* (1987): 3–17.

Clendenen, E. Ray. "Textlinguistics and Prophecy in the Book of the Twelve." *JETS* 46 (2003): 385–99.

Clines, David J. A. (ed.). *The Dictionary of Classical Hebrew*. 9 vols. Sheffield: Sheffield Academic, 1993–2014.

Clines, David J. A. "Misapprehensions, Ancient and Modern, About Lions (Nahum 2:13)." In *Poets, Prophets, and Texts in Play: Studies in Biblical Poetry and Prophecy in Honour of Francis Landy*, edited by Ehud Ben Zvi, Claudia V. Camp, David M. Gunn, and Aaron W. Hughes, 58–76. LHBOTS 597. London: Bloomsbury T&T Clark, 2015.

Cogan, Mordechai. "'Ripping Open Pregnant Women' in Light of an Assyrian Analogue." *JAOS* 103 (1983): 755–7.

Collett, Donald C. "Prophetic Intentionality and the Book of the Twelve: A Study in the Hermeneutics of Prophecy." PhD diss. University of St. Andrews, 2007.

Cook, Stephen Derek. "'Who Knows?' Reading the Book of Jonah as a Satirical Challenge to Theodicy of the Exile." PhD diss., University of Sydney, 2019.

Corzilius, Björn. *Michas Rätsel: Eine Untersuchung zur Kompositionsgeschichte des Michabuches.* BZAW 483. Berlin: de Gruyter, 2016.

Creach, Jerome F. D. *Violence in Scripture.* Int. Louisville: Westminster John Knox, 2013.

Crenshaw, James L. "Introduction: The Shift from Theodicy to Anthropodicy." In *Theodicy in the Old Testament,* edited by James L. Crenshaw, 1–16. IRT 4. Philadelphia: Fortress; London: SPCK, 1983.

Crenshaw, James L. *Joel.* AB 24C. New York: Doubleday, 1995.

Crenshaw, James L. "Popular Questioning of the Justice of God in Ancient Israel." *ZAW* 82 (1970): 380–95.

Crenshaw, James L. *Prophetic Conflict: Its Effect Upon Israelite Religion.* BZAW 124. New York: de Gruyter, 1971.

Crenshaw, J. L. "Theodicy and Prophetic Literature." In *Theodicy in the World of the Bible,* edited by A. Laato and Johannes C. de Moor, 236–55. Leiden: Brill, 2003.

Crenshaw, J. L. "Theodicy in the Book of the Twelve." In *Thematic Threads in the Book of the Twelve,* edited by P. L. Redditt and A. Schart, 175–91. BZAW 325. New York: de Gruyter, 2003.

Crenshaw, James L. ed. *Theodicy in the Old Testament.* IRT 4. Philadelphia: Fortress, 1983.

Crouch, Carly. *War and Ethics in the Ancient Near East: Military Violence in Light of Cosmology and History.* BZAW 407. Berlin: de Gruyter, 2009.

Crutzen, Paul J., John R. McNeill, and Will Steffen. "The Anthropocene: Are Humans Now Overwhelming the Great Forces of Nature?" *AMBIO: A Journal of the Human Environment* 36 (2007): 614–21.

Da Riva, Rocio. *The Neo-Babylonian Royal Inscriptions: An Introduction.* Guides to the Mesopotamian Textual Record 4. Münster: Ugarit-Verlag, 2008.

Dangl, Oskar. "Habakkuk in Recent Research." *CBR* 9 (2001): 131–68.

Davies, Eryl W. "The Morally Dubious Passages of the Hebrew Bible: An Examination of Some Proposed Solutions." *CBR* 3 (2005): 197–228.

Davis, Mike. "Who Will Build the Ark?" *New Left Review* 61 (2010): 29–46.

Day, John. *God's Conflict with the Dragon and the Sea: Echoes of a Canaanite Myth in the Old Testament.* Cambridge: Cambridge University Press, 1985.

Day, Peggy L. "Adulterous Jerusalem's Imagined Demise: Death of a Metaphor in Ezekiel XVI." *VT* 50 (2000): 285–309.

De Roche, Michael. "Zephaniah 1:2-3: The 'Sweeping' of Creation." *VT* 30 (1980): 104–9.

Dearman, J. Andrew. *The Book of Hosea.* NICOT. Grand Rapids: Eerdmans, 2010.

Dearman, J. Andrew. "YHWH's House: Gender Roles and Metaphors for Israel in Hosea." *JNSL* 25 (1999): 97–108.

Dent, Nicholas "Good." In *The Oxford Companion to Philosophy,* edited by T. Honderich, 322. Oxford: Oxford University Press, 1995.

Derrida, Jacques. *The Animal That Therefore I Am.* Translated by David Wills. New York: Fordham University Press, 2008.

Derrida, Jacques. *The Beast and the Sovereign.* Volume 1. Chicago: University of Chicago Press, 2009.

Derrida, Jacques. *The Beast and the Sovereign.* Translated by Geoffrey Bennington. Volume 2. Chicago: University of Chicago Press, 2011.

Diaz, Robert J., and Rutger Rosenberg. "Spreading Dead Zones and Consequences for Marine Ecosystems." *Science* 321.5891 (2008): 926–9.

Dietrich, Walter. *Nahum Habakkuk Zephaniah.* Translated by Peter Altmann. IECOT. Stuttgart: Kohlhammer, 2016.

Dietrich, Walter. "Three Minor Prophets and the Major Empires: Synchronic and Diachronic Perspectives on Nahum, Habakkuk, and Zephaniah." In *Perspectives on the Formation of the Book of the Twelve: Methodological Foundations, Redactional Processes, Historical Insights,* edited by Rainer Albertz, James Nogalski, and Jakob Wöhrle, 147–56. BZAW 433. Berlin: de Gruyter, 2012.

Dooley, Robert A., and Stephen H. Levinsohn. *Analyzing Discourse: A Manual of Basic Concepts.* Dallas: SIL International, 2001.

Duff, R. Antony. "Punishment." In *Oxford Handbook of Practical Ethics,* edited by H. LaFollette, 331–57. Oxford: Oxford University Press, 2003.

Edenburg, Cynthia. "From Eden to Babylon: Reading Genesis 2–4 as a Paradigmatic Narrative." In *Pentateuch, Hexateuch, or Enneateuch? Identifying Literary Works in Genesis through Kings,* edited by Thomas B. Dozeman, Konrad Schmid, and Thomas Römer, 155–67. SBLAIL 8. Atlanta: SBL, 2011.

Eichrodt, Walther. "Faith in Providence and Theodicy in the Old Testament." Translated by Laurence L. Welborn. In *Theodicy in the Old Testament,* edited by James L. Crenshaw, 17–41. IRT 4. Philadelphia: Fortress, 1983.

Eichrodt, Walther. "Vorsehungsglaube und Theodizee im Alten Testament." In *Festschrift Otto Procksch zum sechzigsten Geburtstag am 9. August 1934,* edited by Albrecht Alt, 45–70. Leipzig: A. Deichert'sche Verlangsbuchhandlung / J. C. Hinrich'sche Buchhandlung, 1934.

Eidevall, Göran. *Amos: A New Translation with Introduction and Commentary.* AYB 24G. New Haven: Yale University Press, 2017.

Eidevall, Göran. *Grapes in the Desert: Metaphors, Models, and Themes in Hosea 4–14.* ConBOT 43. Stockholm: Almqvist & Wiksell, 1996.

Eidevall, Göran. "Lions and Birds as Literature: Some Notes on Isaiah 31 and Hosea 11." *SJOT* 7 (1993): 78–87.

Eli, Eduardo F. "The Presence of the Covenant Motif in Hosea: An Intertextual Approach for the Last Oracle in the Book." *JBQ* 45 (2017): 34–42.

Elliger, Karl. "Ein Zeugnis aus der jüdischen Gemeinde im Alexanderjahr 322 v. Chr." *ZAW* 62 (1950): 63–115.

Everson, Joseph A. "The Canonical Location of Habakkuk." In *Thematic Threads in the Book of the Twelve,* edited by Paul L. Redditt and Aaron Schart, 165–74. BZAW 325. Berlin: de Gruyter, 2003.

Exum, J. Cheryl. "Prophetic Pornography." In *Plotted, Shot, and Painted: Cultural Representations of Biblical Women,* 101–28. JSOTSup 215. Sheffield: Sheffield Academic, 1996.

Fabry, Heinz-Josef. *Nahum.* HThKAT. Freiburg im Breisgau: Herder, 2006.

Fales, Frederick M. *Guerre et paix en Assyrie: Religion et impérialisme.* Les conférences de l'École Pratique des Hautes Études. Paris: Cerf, 2010.

Fensham, F. C. "The Marriage Metaphor in Hosea for the Covenant Relationship between the Lord and His People (Hos. 1:2–9)." *JNSL* 12 (1984): 71–8.

Fischer, Georg. *Jeremia 1–25.* HThKAT. Freiburg: Herder, 2005.

Fitzmeyer, Joseph A. (trans.). "The Inscriptions of Bar-Gàyah and Matiʿel from Sefire." *COS* 2.82:214.

Floyd, Michael H. "The משא (*Maśśā'*) as a Type of Prophetic Book." *JBL* 121 (2002): 401–22.

Floyd, Michael H. "The Meaning of *Maśśā'* as a Prophetic Term in Isaiah." *JHS* 18, Article 9. DOI:10.5508/jhs.2018.v18.a9.

Floyd, Michael H. *Minor Prophets: Part 2*. FOTL 22. Grand Rapids: Eerdmans, 2000.

Franzmann, Majella. "The City as Woman: The Case of Babylon in Isaiah 47." *ABR* 43 (1995): 1–19.

Fretheim, Terrence E. "Jonah and Theodicy." *ZAW* 90 (1978): 227–37.

Fretheim, Terence E., *Reading Hosea–Micah: A Literary and Theological Commentary*. Macon: Smyth & Helwys, 2013.

Fried, Lisbeth S. "A Silver Coin of Yoḥanan Hakkôhēn." *Transeuphratène* 26 (2003): 65–85.

Fried, Lisbeth S. *The Priest and the Great King: Temple–Palace Relations in the Persian Empire*. Biblical and Judaic Studies 10. Winona Lake: Eisenbrauns, 2004.

Fuchs, Andreas. "Assyria at War: Strategy and Conduct." In *The Oxford Handbook of Cuneiform Culture*, edited by K. Radner and E. Robson, 380–401. Oxford: Oxford University Press, 2011.

Fuentes-Nieva, Ricardo, and Nick Galasso. "Working for the Few: Political Capture and Economic Inequality." Oxfam International Briefing Paper, January 2014.

Fuller, David J. *A Discourse Analysis of Habakkuk*. SSN 72. Leiden: Brill, 2019.

Galambush, Julie. *Jerusalem in the Book of Ezekiel: The City as Yahweh's Wife*. SBLDS 130. Atlanta: Scholars Press, 1992.

Garcia-Treto, Francisco O. "The Book of Nahum." In *The New Interpreter's Bible*, edited by L. E. Keck et al., 7:592–617. Nashville: Abingdon, 1996.

Garrett, Duane A. *Amos: A Handbook on the Hebrew Text*. Baylor Handbook on the Hebrew Bible. Waco: Baylor University Press, 2008.

Garrett, Duane A. *Hosea, Joel*. NAC 19A. Nashville: Broadman & Holman, 1997.

Gault, Brian. "Avenging Husband and Redeeming Lover? Opposing Portraits of God in Hosea." *JETS* 60 (2017): 489–509.

Geertz, Clifford. *The Interpretation of Cultures: Selected Essays*. London: Fontana, 1993.

Gelb, Ignace J. et al., eds. *The Assyrian Dictionary of the Oriental Institute of the University of Chicago*. 21 vols. Chicago: The Oriental Institute of the University of Chicago, 1956–2010.

Gerstenberger, Erhard S. *Psalms: Part I with an Introduction to Cultic Poetry*. FOTL 14. Grand Rapids: Eerdmans, 1988).

Gignilliat, Mark S. *Micah*. ITC. London: T&T Clark, 2019.

Goff, Stan. "Exterminism and the World in the Wake of Katrina." *From the Wilderness*, http://www.fromthewilderness.com/free/ww3/102305_exterminism_katrina.shtml.

Goswell, Gregory. "Davidic Rule in the Prophecy of Micah." *JSOT* 44 (2019): 153–65.

Grabbe, Lester L. (ed.). *Leading Captivity Captive: "The Exile" as History and Ideology*. JSOTSup 278. Sheffield: Sheffield Academic, 1998.

Grayson, A. Kirk. *Assyrian and Babylonian Chronicles*. Winona Lake: Eisenbrauns, 2000.

Green, Ronald M. "Theodicy." In *The Encyclopedia of Religion*, edited by M. Eliade, 430–41. New York: Macmillan, 1987.

Gruber, Mayer I. *Hosea: A Textual Commentary*. LHBOTS 653. London: Bloomsbury T&T Clark, 2017.

Hagedorn, Anselm. *Die Anderen im Spiegel: Israels Auseinandersetzung mit den Völkern in den Büchern Nahum, Zefanja, Obadja und Joel*. BZAW 414. Berlin: de Gruyter, 2011.

Hagedorn, Anselm C. "Diaspora or No Diaspora? Some Remarks on the Role of Egypt and Babylon in the Book of the Twelve." In *Perspectives on the Formation of the Book of the Twelve: Methodological Foundations, Redactional Processes, Historical Insights*, edited by Rainer Albertz, James Nogalski, and Jakob Wöhrle, 319–36. BZAW 111. Berlin: de Gruyter, 2012.

Hall, Gary. "Origin of the Marriage Metaphor." *Hebrew Studies* 23 (1982): 169–71.

Hall, Shannon. "Found: Thousands of Man-Made Minerals—Another Argument for the Anthropocene." *Scientific American*, March 1, 2017.

Halvorson-Taylor, Martien A. *Enduring Exile: The Metaphorization of Exile in the Hebrew Bible.* Leiden: Brill, 2011.

Hanley, Ryan C. "The Background and Purpose of Stripping the Adulteress in Hosea 2." *JETS* 60 (2017): 89–103.

Harper, Joshua L. *Responding to a Puzzled Scribe: The Barberini Version of Habakkuk 3 Analysed in the Light of the Other Greek Versions.* LHBOTS 608. London: Bloomsbury T&T Clark, 2015.

Hartenstein, Friedhelm. *Das Archiv des verborgenen Gottes: Studien zur Unheilsprophetie Jesajas und zur Zionstheologie der Psalmen in assyrischer Zeit.* BthSt 74. Neukirchen–Vluyn: Neukirchener Theologie, 2011.

Harvell, C. Drew et al. "Climate Warming and Disease Risks for Terrestrial and Marine Biota." *Science* 296, no. 5576 (2002): 2158–62.

Hasel, Gerhard F. "The Alleged 'No' of Amos and Amos' Eschatology." *Andrews University Seminary Studies* 29 (1991): 3–18.

Hatton, Peter. "A Cautionary Tale: The Acts—Consequence 'Construct.'" *JSOT* 35 (2011): 375–84.

Hayes, John H. *Amos The Eighth-Century Prophet: His Times and his Preaching.* Nashville: Abingdon, 1988.

Hayes, Katherine M. *"The Earth Mourns": Prophetic Metaphor and Oral Aesthetic.* SBLAB 8. Leiden: Brill, 2002.

Hiebert, Theodore. *God of My Victory: The Ancient Hymn in Habakkuk 3.* HSM 38. Atlanta: Scholars Press, 1986.

Hillers, Delbert R., *Micah.* Hermeneia. Philadelphia: Fortress, 1984.

Hoffman, Yair. "Theodicy and Protest in Micah 7." In *Theodicy and Protest: Jewish and Christian Perspectives*, edited by Beate Ego, Ute Gause, Ron Margolin, Dalit Rom-Shiloni, 45–53. Leipzig: Evangelische Verlagsanstalt, 2018.

Hope, Edward R. "Problems of Interpretation in Amos 3:4." *BT* 42 (1991): 201–5.

House, Paul R. "The Character of God in the Book of the Twelve." In *Reading and Hearing the Book of the Twelve*, edited by James D. Nogalski and Marvin A Sweeney, 125–45. SBLSymS 15. Atlanta: SBL, 2000.

House, Paul R. "Endings as New Beginnings: Returning to the Lord, the Day of the Lord, and Renewal in the Book of the Twelve." In *Thematic Threads in the Book of the Twelve*, edited by Paul L. Redditt and Aaron Schart, 313–38. BZAW 325. Berlin: de Gruyter, 2003.

House, Paul R. *The Unity of the Twelve.* JSOTSup 97. Sheffield: Sheffield Academic, 1990.

Hubbard, David Allan. *Joel and Amos.* TOTC. Downers Grove: InterVarsity, 1989.

Huffmon, Herbert B. "The Covenant Lawsuit in the Prophets." *JBL* 78 (1959): 285–95.

Im, Yohan, and Pieter M. Venter. "The Function of Zechariah 7–8 within the Book of Zechariah." *HTS* 69 (2013): 1–10.

Intergovernmental Panel on Climate Change. "Summary for Policy Makers." In *Climate Change 2014: Mitigation of Climate Change*, edited by Ottmar R. Edenhofer et al. Cambridge: Cambridge University Press, 2015.

Jacobs, Mignon R. *The Conceptual Coherence of the Book of Micah.* JSOTSup 233. Sheffield: Sheffield Academic, 2001.

Jamieson, Dale. *Reason in a Dark Time: Why the Struggle against Climate Change Failed—and What It Means for Our Future.* New York: Oxford University Press, 2014.

Janzen, J. Gerald. "Habakkuk 2:2-4 in the Light of Recent Philological Advances." *HTR* 73 (1980): 53–78.

Janzen, J. Gerald. "Metaphor and Reality in Hosea 11." *Semeia* 24 (1982): 7–44.

Japhet, Sara. *The Ideology of the Book of Chronicles and Its Place in Biblical Thought.* BEATAJ 9. Frankfurt am Main: Peter Lang, 1989.

Jeppesen, Knud. "'Because of You!': An Essay about the Centre of the Book of the Twelve." In *In Search of True Wisdom: Essays in Old Testament Interpretation in Honour of Ronald E. Clements*, edited by Edward Ball, 196–210. JSOTSup 300. Sheffield: Sheffield Academic, 1999.

Jeremias, Jörg. *The Book of Amos: A Commentary.* OTL. Louisville: Westminster John Knox, 1995.

Jones, Barry A. "The Seventh-Century Prophets in Twenty-First Century Research." *CBR* 14, no. 2 (2016): 129–75.

Jonker, Louis C. *Defining All-Israel in Chronicles: Multi-Levelled Identity Negotiation in Late Persian-Period Yehud.* FAT 106. Tübingen: Mohr Siebeck, 2016.

Kakkanattu, Joy Philip. *God's Enduring Love in the Book of Hosea.* FAT 2/14. Tübingen: Mohr Siebeck, 2006.

Kamionkowski, S. Tamar. "The Problem of Violence in Prophetic Literature: Definitions as the Real Problem." In *Religion and Violence: The Biblical Heritage*, edited by David A. Bernat and Jonathan Klawans, 38–46. Sheffield: Sheffield Phoenix, 2007.

Kaper, Olaf E. "Petubastis IV in the Dakhla Oasis: New Evidence about an Early Rebellion against Persian Rule and Its Suppression in Political Memory." In *Political Memory In and After the Persian Empire*, edited by Jason M. Silverman and Caroline Waerzeggers, 125–49. Ancient Near East Monographs 13. Atlanta: SBL, 2015.

Keefe, Alice A. "Hosea's (In)Fertility God." *HBT* 30 (2008): 21–41.

Keefe, Alice A. *Woman's Body and the Social Body in Hosea.* JSOTSup 338. London: Sheffield Academic, 2001.

Keesing, Felicia, et al. "Impacts of Biodiversity on the Emergence and Transmission of Infectious Diseases." *Nature* 648 (2010): 647–62.

Kelle, Brad E. *Hosea 2: Metaphor and Rhetoric in Historical Perspective.* SBLAB 20. Leiden: Brill, 2005.

Kelle, Brad E. et al. (eds). *Interpreting Exile: Displacement and Deportation in Biblical and Modern Contexts.* Atlanta: SBL, 2011.

Kelsey, Marian. "The Book of Jonah and the Theme of Exile." *JSOT* 45 (2020): 128–40.

Kessler, Rainer. *Micha.* HThKAT. 2nd ed. Freiburg: Herder, 2000.

Kessler, Rainer. "Nahum-Habakuk als Zweiprophetenschrift: Eine Skizze." In *Gottes-erdung: Beiträge zur Hermeneutik und Exegese der Hebräischen Bibel*, 137–45. BWANT 170. Stuttgart: Kohlhammer, 2006.

Kim, Brittany. "Yhwh as Jealous Husband: Abusive Authoritarian or Passionate Protector? A Reexamination of a Prophetic Image." In *Daughter Zion: Her Portrait, Her Response*, edited by Mark J. Boda, Carol J. Dempsey, and LeAnn Snow Flesher, 127–47. SBLAIL 13. Atlanta: SBL, 2012.

Knoppers, Gary N., et al. (eds). *Exile and Restoration Revisited: Essays on the Babylonian and Persian Periods in Memory of Peter R. Ackroyd.* LSTS 73. London: T&T Clark, 2009.

Ko, Grace. *Theodicy in Habakkuk.* Paternoster Theological Monographs. Milton Keynes: Paternoster, 2014.

Koch, Klaus. "Gibt es ein Vergeltungsdogma im Alten Testament?" *ZTK* 52 (1955): 1–42.

Kolbert, Elizabeth. *The Sixth Extinction: An Unnatural History.* New York: Henry Holt, 2014.

Kratz, Reinhard Gregor. "Die Worte des Amos von Tekoa". In *Prophetenstudien: Kleine Schriften II*, edited by Reinhard Gregor Kratz, 310–43. FAT 74. Tübingen: Mohr Siebeck, 2011.

Krell, David Farrell. *Derrida and Our Animal Others: Derrida's Final Seminar, "the Beast and Sovereign."* Bloomington: Indiana University Press, 2013.

Kuhrt, Amélie. *The Ancient Near East c. 3000–330 BC.* Routledge History of the Ancient World. 2 vols. London: Routledge, 1995.

Kwakkel, Gert. "Exile in Hosea 9:3-6: Where and for What Purpose?" In *Exile and Suffering: A Selection of Papers Read at the 50th Anniversary Meeting of the Old Testament Society of South Africa OTWSA/OTSSA Pretoria August 2007*, edited by Bob Becking and Dirk Human, 123–45. OtSt 50. Leiden: Brill, 2009.

Laato, Antti. *Josiah and David Redivivus: The Historical Josiah and the Messianic Expectations of Exilic and Postexilic Times.* ConBOT 33. Stockholm: Almqvist & Wiksell, 1992.

Laato Antti, and Johannes C. de Moor. "Introduction." In *Theodicy in the World of the Bible*, edited by Antti Laato and Johannes C. de Moor, vii–liv. Leiden: Brill, 2003.

Laato, Antti, and Johannes C. de Moor (ed.). *Theodicy in the World of the Bible.* Leiden: Brill, 2003.

Lallemon-de Winkel, Hetty. *Jeremiah in Prophetic Tradition: An Examination of the Book of Jeremiah in the Light of Israel's Prophetic Traditions.* CBET 26. Leuven: Peeters, 2000.

Landy, Francis. "Three Sides of a Coin: In Conversation with Ben Zvi and Nogalksi, *Two Sides of a Coin.*" *JHS* 10 (2010): article 11. Doi:10.5508/jhs.2010.v10.a11.

Laurel Lanner. *"Who Will Lament Her?" The Feminine and the Fantastic in the Book of Nahum.* LHBOTS 434. New York: T&T Clark, 2006.

LeCureux, Jason T. "Joel, the Cult, and the Book of the Twelve." In *Priests & Cults in the Book of the Twelve*, edited by Lena-Sofia Tiemeyer, 65–79. Atlanta: SBL, 2016.

LeCureux, Jason T. *The Thematic Unity of the Book of the Twelve.* HBM 41. Sheffield: Sheffield Phoenix, 2012.

Leigh, Ben Y. "A Rhetorical and Structural Study of the Book of Habakkuk." PhD diss., Golden Gate Baptist Seminary, 1992.

Leonhardt-Balzer, Jutta. "The Minor Prophets in the Judaism of the Second Temple Period." In *The Minor Prophets in the New Testament*, edited by Maarten J. J. Menken and Steve Moyise, 7–25. LNTS 377. New York: T&T Clark, 2009.

Leuchter, Mark, and George Athas. "Is Cambyses Also Among the Persians?" (forthcoming)

Lévêque, Jean. "L'interprétation des discours de YHWH (Job 38,1–42,6)." In *The Book of Job*, edited by W. M. Beuken, 203–22. BETL 114. Leuven: Leuven University Press, 1994.

Limburg, James. "The Root ריב and the Prophetic Lawsuit Speeches." *JBL* 88 (1969): 291–304.

Linville, James R. "Amos among the 'Dead Prophets Society;' Re-Reading the Lion's Roar." *JSOT* 25 (2000): 55–77.

Lo, Alison. "Remnant Motif in Amos, Micah and Zephaniah." In *A God of Faithfulness: Essays in Honour of J. Gordon McConville on His 60th Birthday*, edited by Jamie A. Grant, Alison Lo, and Gordon J. Wenham, 130–48. New York: T&T Clark, 2011.

Luckenbill, D. D. *Ancient Records of Assyria and Babylonia: Vol. 2, Historical Records from Assyria from Sargon to the End*. Chicago: University of Chicago Press, 1927.

Lundbom, Jack R. "The Lion Has Roared: Rhetorical Structure in Amos 1:2–3:8." In *Milk and Honey: Essays on Ancient Israel and the Bible in Appreciation of the Judaic Studies Program at the University of California, San Diego*, 65–75. Winona Lake: Eisenbrauns, 2007.

Macintosh, A. A. *A Critical and Exegetical Commentary on Hosea*. ICC. Edinburgh: T. & T. Clark, 1997.

Mackie, Penelope J. "Causality." In *The Oxford Companion to Philosophy*, edited by T. Honderich, 126–8. Oxford: Oxford University Press, 1995.

Marshall, Chris "Divine Justice as Restorative Justice." In *Prison: Christian Reflection*, edited by Robert B. Kruschwitz, 11–19. Waco: Baylor University Press, 2012.

Mathews, Jeanette. *Performing Habakkuk: Faithful Re-enactment in the Midst of Crisis*. Eugene: Pickwick, 2012.

Mays, James L. *Amos: A Commentary*. OTL. Philadelphia: Westminster, 1969.

Mays, James L. "Psalm 29." *Int* 39 (1985): 60–4.

McCann, Dennis. P. "Good, The." In *Dictionary of Scripture and Ethics*, edited by J. B. Green, 332–4. Grand Rapids: Baker Academic, 2011.

McConville, J. Gordon. *Deuteronomy*. AOTC 5. Leicester: Apollos, 2002.

McConville, J. Gordon. *Grace in the End: A Study in Deuteronomic Theology*. Grand Rapids: Zondervan, 1993.

McGary, Howard. "Groups, Moral Status of." In *Encyclopedia of Ethics*, edited by L. C. Becker and C. B. Becker, 635–9. London: Routledge, 2001.

McKane, William. *The Book of Micah: Introduction and Commentary*. Edinburgh: T. & T. Clark, 1998.

Mendenhall, George E. "Ancient Oriental and Biblical Law." *BA* 17 (1954): 26–46.

Merwe, Christo H. J. van der, Jacobus A. Naudé, and Jan H. Kroeze. *A Biblical Hebrew Reference Grammar*. 2nd ed. London: Bloomsbury T&T Clark, 2017.

Meyer, Birgit. "An Author Meets Her Critics: Around Birgit Meyer's 'Mediation and the Genesis of Presence: Toward a Material Approach to Religion'." *RelSoc* 5 (2014): 205–54.

Meyers, Carol L., and Eric M. Meyers. *Haggai, Zechariah 1–8*. AB 25B. New York: Doubleday, 1987.

Meyers, Carol L., and Eric M. Meyers, *Zechariah 9–14: A New Translation with Introduction and Commentary*. AB 25C. New York: Doubleday, 1993.

Miller, Patrick D., Jr. *Sin and Judgment in the Prophets: A Stylistic and Theological Analysis*. SBLMS 27. Chico: Scholars Press, 1982.

Miller, Patrick D. "'Slow to Anger': The God of the Prophets." In *The Way of the Lord: Essays in Old Testament Theology*, 269–85. Grand Rapids: Eerdmans, 2004.

Mills, Mary. "Divine Violence in the Book of Amos." In *The Aesthetics of Violence in the Prophets*, edited by Julia M. O'Brien and Chris Franke, 153–79. LHBOTS 517. New York: T&T Clark, 2010.

Milstein, Sara J. "'Who Would Not Write?': The Prophet as Yhwh's Prey in Amos 3:3–8." *CBQ* 75 (2013): 429–45.

Moon, Joshua N. *Hosea.* AOTC 21. London: Apollos, 2018.

Moore, Stephen D. "Introduction: From Animal Theory to Creaturely Theology." In *Divinanimality: Animal Theory, Creaturely Theology*, edited by Stephen D. Moore, 1–16. Transdiciplinary Theological Colloquia. New York: Fordham University Press, 2014.

Moughtin-Mumby, Sharon. *Sexual and Marital Metaphors in Hosea, Jeremiah, Isaiah, and Ezekiel.* Oxford: Oxford University Press, 2008.

Mowinckel, Sigmund. *The Psalms in Israel's Worship.* 2 vols. Translated by D. R. Ap-Thomas. New York: Abingdon, 1967.

Münnich, Maciej M. *The God Resheph in the Ancient Near East.* ORA 11. Tübingen: Mohr Siebeck, 2013.

Nahkola, Aulikki. "Amos Animalizing: Lion, Bear and Snake in Amos 5:19." In *Aspects of Amos: Exegesis and Interpretation*, edited by Anselm C. Hagedorn and Andrew Mein, 83–104. LHBOTS 536. London: Bloomsbury T&T Clark, 2011.

National Research Council. *Abrupt Impacts of Climate Change: Anticipating Surprises.* Washington, DC: National Academies Press, 2013.

Nogalski, James D. *The Book of the Twelve: Micah–Malachi* SHBC. Georgia: Smyth & Helwys, 2011.

Nogalski, James D. "God in the Book of the Twelve." In *The Oxford Handbook of the Minor Prophets*, edited by Julia M. O'Brien, 103–16. Oxford: Oxford University Press, 2021.

Nogalski, James D. *Literary Precursors to the Book of the Twelve.* BZAW 217. Berlin: de Gruyter, 1993.

Nogalski, James D. "Recurring Themes in the Book of the Twelve: Creating Points of Contact for a Theological Reading." *Int* 61 (2007): 125–36.

Nogalski, James D. *Redactional Processes in the Book of the Twelve.* BZAW 218. Berlin: de Gruyter, 1993.

Notarius, Tania. "Aspectual Markers." In *Encyclopedia of Hebrew Language and Linguistics*, edited by G. Khan, 1:218–20. 4 vols. Leiden: Brill, 2013.

O'Brien, Julia M. *Micah.* Wisdom Commentary 37. Collegeville: Liturgical, 2015.

O'Brien, Julia M. *Nahum Habakkuk Zephaniah Haggai Zechariah Malachi.* AOTC. Nashville: Abingdon, 2004.

O'Brien, Julia M. *Nahum.* 2nd ed. Readings. Sheffield: Sheffield Phoenix, 2009.

O'Brien, Julia M. "Nahum–Habakkuk—Zephaniah: Reading the 'Former Prophets' in the Persian Period." *Int* 61 (2007): 168–83.

Oded, Bustaney. *War, Peace and Empire: Justifications for War in Assyrian Royal Inscriptions.* Wiesbaden: Dr Ludwig Reichert Verlag, 1992.

Oldfield, Frank. "Introduction: The Holocene, a Special Time." In *Global Change in the Holocene*, edited by Anson McKay, Rick Batarbee, John Birks, and Frank Oldfield, 1–9. London: Arnold, 2005.

Olmo Lete, Gregorio del, and Joaquín Sanmartín. *A Dictionary of the Ugaritic Language in the Alphabetic Tradition.* Translated and edited by W. G. E. Watson. 3rd ed. 2 vols. Leiden: Brill, 2015.

Olson, Dennis T. "The Lion, the Itch and the Wardrobe: Hosea 5:8–6:6 as a Case Study in the Contemporary Interpretation and Authority of Scripture." *CurTM* 23 (1996): 173–84.

O'Neal, G. Michael. *Interpreting Habakkuk as Scripture: An Application of the Canonical Approach of Brevard S. Childs.* StBibLit 9. New York: Peter Lang, 2007.

O'Rourke Boyle, Marjorie. "The Covenant Lawsuit of the Prophet Amos: III 1–IV 13." *VT* 21 (1971): 338–62.

Orsi, Robert A. *Between Heaven and Earth: The Religious Worlds People Make and the Scholars Who Study Them.* Princeton: Princeton University Press, 2005.

Parker, Richard D. "Darius and His Egyptian Campaign." *AJSL* 58 (1941): 373–7.

Patterson, Richard D. "Joel." In *The Expositor's Bible Commentary 8*: *Daniel–Malachi*, ed. T. Longman III and D. Garland, 307–46. Rev. ed. Grand Rapids: Zondervan, 2008.

Patton, Corrine L. "'Should Our Sister Be Treated Like a Whore?': A Response to Feminist Critiques of Ezekiel 23." In *The Book of Ezekiel: Theological and Anthropological Perspectives*, edited by Margaret S. Odell and John T. Strong, 221–38. SBLSymS 9. Atlanta: SBL, 2000.

Patton, Matthew H. *Hope for a Tender Sprig: Jehoiachin in Biblical Theology.* BBR Sup 16. Winona Lake: Eisenbrauns, 2017.

Paul, Shalom M. *Amos.* Hermeneia. Minneapolis: Fortress, 1991.

Paul, Shalom M. "Amos 3:3-8: The Irresistible Sequence of Cause and Effect." *HAR* 7 (1983): 203–20.

Peterson, David L. "A Book of the Twelve?" In *Reading and Hearing the Book of the Twelve*, edited by James D. Nogalski and Marvin A. Sweeney, 3–10. SBLSymS 15. Atlanta: SBL, 2000.

Petersen, David L. "Prophetic Rhetoric and Exile." In *The Prophets Speak on Forced Migration*, edited by Mark J. Boda et al., 9–18. Atlanta: SBL, 2015.

Peterson, David L. *The Prophetic Literature: An Introduction.* Louisville: Westminster John Knox, 2002.

Petterson, Anthony R. *Behold Your King: The Hope for the House of David in the Book of Zechariah.* LHBOTS 513. New York: T&T Clark, 2009.

Petterson, Anthony R. "The Shape of the Davidic Hope Across the Book of the Twelve." *JSOT* 35 (2010): 225–46.

Petterson, Anthony R. "The Eschatology of Zechariah's Night Visions." In *'I Lifted My Eyes and Saw': Reading Dream and Vision Reports in the Hebrew Bible*, edited by Lena-Sofia Tiemeyer and Elizabeth R. Hayes, 119–34. LHBOTS 584. London: T&T Clark, 2014.

Petterson, Anthony R. "The Flying Scroll That Will Not Acquit the Guilty: Exodus 34.7 in Zechariah 5.3." *JSOT* 38 (2014): 347–61.

Petterson, Anthony R. *Haggai, Zechariah & Malachi.* AOTC 25. Nottingham: Apollos, 2015.

Petterson, Anthony R. "The Messiah in the Book of the Twelve: Glory Through Suffering." In *The Seed of Promise: The Sufferings and Glory of the Messiah. Essays in Honor of T. Desmond Alexander*, edited by Paul R. Williamson and Rita F. Cefalu, 219–41. Wilmore: GlossaHouse, 2020.

Petterson, Anthony R. "A New Form-Critical Approach to Zechariah's Crowning of the High Priest Joshua and the Identity of the 'Shoot' (Zechariah 6:9-15)." In *The Book of the Twelve and the New Form Criticism*, edited by Mark J. Boda, Michael H. Floyd, and Colin M. Toffelmire, 285–304. ANEM 10. Atlanta: SBL, 2015.

Bibliography

Pietersma, Albert. "Septuagintal Exegesis and the Superscriptions of the Greek Psalter." In *The Book of Psalms*, edited by Peter W. Flint and Patrick D. Miller, 443–75. VTSup 99. Leiden: Brill, 2005.

Pinker, Aron. "God's C3 in Habakkuk 3." *ZAW* 112 (2000): 261–5.

Pinker, Aron. "Nahum's Theological Perspectives." *JBQ* 32 (2004): 148–57.

Pitard, Wayne T. "The Combat Myth as a Succession Story at Ugarit." In *Creation and Chaos: A Reconsideration of Hermann Gunkel's Chaoskampf Hypothesis*, edited by JoAnn Scurlock and Richard H. Beal, 199–205. Winona Lake: Eisenbrauns, 2013.

Porter, Barbara N. "Ishtar of Nineveh and Her Collaborator, Ishtar of Arbela, in the Reign of Assurbanipal." *Iraq* 66 (2004): 41–4.

Potsdam Institute for Climate Impact Research and Climate Analytics. *Turn Down the Heat: Confronting the New Climate Normal.* Washington, DC: World Bank, 2014.

Prinsloo, Willem S. *The Theology of the Book of Joel.* BZAW 163. Berlin: de Gruyter, 1985.

Purdy, Jedediah. *After Nature: A Politics for the Anthropocene.* Cambridge: Belknap/Harvard, 2015.

Pyper, Hugh S. "The Lion King: Yahweh as Sovereign Beast in Israel's Imaginary." In *The Bible and Posthumanism*, edited by Jennifer L. Koosed, 59–74. Atlanta: SBL, 2014.

Radine, Jason. *The Book of Amos in Emergent Judah.* FAT 2. Tübingen: Mohr Siebeck, 2010.

Redditt, Paul L. "The King in Haggai–Zechariah 1–8 and the Book of the Twelve." In *Tradition in Transition: Haggai and Zechariah 1–8 in the Trajectory of Hebrew Theology*, edited by Mark J. Boda and Michael H. Floyd, 56–82. LHBOTS 475. London: T&T Clark, 2009.

Redditt, Paul L. "The Production and Reading of the Book of the Twelve." In *Reading and Hearing the Book of the Twelve*, edited by James D. Nogalski and Marvin A. Sweeney, 11–33. SBLSymS 15. Atlanta: Scholars Press, 2000.

Redditt, Paul L. "Theodicy." In *Oxford Encyclopedia of the Bible and Ethics*, edited by Robert L. Brawley, 348–53. Oxford: Oxford University Press, 2014.

Redditt, Paul L., and Aaron Schart (eds). *Thematic Threads in the Book of the Twelve.* BZAW 325. Berlin: de Gruyter, 2003.

Rendtorff, Rolf. "Alas for the Day! The 'Day of the LORD' in the Book of the Twelve." In *God in the Fray: A Tribute to Walter Brueggemann*, edited by Tod Linafelt and Timothy K. Beal, 186–97. Minneapolis: Fortress, 1998.

Rendtorff, Rolf. *The Canonical Hebrew Bible: A Theology of the Old Testament.* Translated by D. E. Orton. Tools for Biblical Studies 7. Leiderdorp: Deo, 2005.

Rendtorff, Rolf. "How to Read the Book of the Twelve as a Theological Unity." In *Society of Biblical Literature 1997 Seminar Papers*, 420–32. SBLSPS 36. Atlanta: SBL, 1997.

Ristau, Kenneth A. "Rebuilding Jerusalem: Zechariah's Vision within Visions." In *Exile and Restoration Revisited: Essays on the Babylonian and Persian Periods in Memory of Peter R. Ackroyd*, edited by Gary N. Knoppers, Lester L. Grabbe, and Deirdre N. Fulton, 195–213. LSTS 73. London: T&T Clark, 2009.

Roberts, J. J. M. *Nahum, Habakkuk, and Zephaniah.* OTL. Louisville: Westminster John Knox, 1991.

Roberts, Neil. *The Holocene: An Environmental History.* 3rd ed. Malden: Wiley-Blackwell, 2014.

Rockström, Johan et al. "The Unfolding Water Drama in the Anthropocene: Toward a Resilience-Based Perspective on Water for Global Sustainability." *Hydrology* 7 (2014): 1249–61.

Rom-Shiloni, Dalit. "Theodical Discourse: Theodicy and Protest in Sixth Century BCE Hebrew Bible Theology." In *Theodicy and Protest: Jewish and Christian Perspectives*, edited by Beate Ego, 55–74. Leipzig: Evangelische Veragsanstalt, 2018.

Roth, Martha T. *Law Collections from Mesopotamia and Asia Minor.* SBLWAW 6. 2nd ed. Atlanta: Scholars Press, 1997.

Sacks, Oliver. "My Own Life." In *Gratitude*, 13–20. New York: Knopf, 2015.

Sarot, Marcel. "Theodicy and Modernity: An Inquiry into the Historicity of Theodicy." In *Theodicy in the World of the Bible*, edited by Antti Laato and Johannes C. de Moor, 1–26. Leiden: Brill, 2003.

Sasson, Jack M. *Jonah.* AB 24B. New York: Doubleday, 1990.

Scalise, Pamela J. "Zechariah, Malachi." In *Minor Prophets II*, 177–366. Peabody: Hendrickson, 2009.

Schaab, Gloria L. "'I Will Love Them Freely': A Metaphorical Theology of Hosea 14." *JBT* 1 (2018): 227–52.

Schaefer, Konrad R. "Zechariah 14: A Study in Allusion." *CBQ* 57 (1995): 66–91.

Schart, Aaron. *Die Entstehung des Zwölfprophetenbuchs: Neubearbeitungen von Amos im Rahmen schriftenübergreifender Redaktionsprozesse.* BZAW 260. Berlin: de Gruyter, 1998.

Schart, Aaron. "The First Section of the Book of the Twelve Prophets: Hosea–Joel–Amos." *Int* 61 (2007): 138–52.

Schart, Aaron. "The Jonah-Narrative within the Book of the Twelve." In *Perspectives on the Formation of the Book of the Twelve. Methodological Foundations – Redactional Processes – Historical Insights*, edited by R. Albertz, J. Nogalski, and J. Wöhrle, 109–28. BZAW 433. Berlin: de Gruyter, 2012.

Schifferdecker, Kathryn. *Out of the Whirlwind: Creation Theology in the Book of Job.* HTS 61. Cambridge: Harvard University Press, 2004.

Schmid, H. H. *Gerechtigkeit als Weltordnung: Hintergrund und Geschichte der alttestamentliche Gerechtigkeitsbegriffes.* Tübingen: Mohr Siebeck, 1968.

Schmitt, John J. "The Wife of God in Hosea 2." *BibRes* 34 (1989): 5–18.

Schüngel-Straumann, Helen. "God as Mother in Hosea 11." In *A Feminist Companion to the Latter Prophets*, edited by Athalya Brenner, 194–218. FCB 8. Sheffield: Sheffield Academic, 1995.

Scott, James M. (ed.). *Exile: A Conversation with N.T. Wright.* Downers Grove: IVP Academic, 2017.

Seeman, Don. "Otherwise Than Meaning: On the Generosity of Ritual." *Social Analysis: The International Journal of Social and Cultural Practice* 48 (2004): 55–71.

Seitz, Christopher R. *Joel.* ITC. London: Bloomsbury T&T Clark, 2016.

Seitz, Christopher R. *Prophecy and Hermeneutics: Toward a New Introduction to the Prophets.* STI. Grand Rapids: Baker Academic, 2007.

Shahbazi, Shahpur. "CLOTHING II. Median and Achaemenid Periods." *Encyclopaedia Iranica* V/7:723–37.

Shepherd, Michael B. "Compositional Analysis of the Twelve." *ZAW* 120 (2008): 184–93.

Silverman, Jason M. "Vetting the Priest in Zechariah 3: The Satan between Divine and Achaemenid Administrations." *JHS* 14, no. 6 (2014): 1–28.

Slomovic, Eliezer. "Toward an Understanding of the Formation of the Historical Titles in the Book of Psalms." *ZAW* 91 (1979): 350–80.

Smith, Mark S., and Wayne T. Pitard. *The Ugaritic Baal Cycle: Introduction with Text, Translation and Commentary of KTU/CAT 1.3–1.4*. VTSup 114. Leiden: Brill, 2009.

Smith, Gary V. *Hosea, Amos, Micah*. NIVAC. Grand Rapids: Zondervan, 2001.

Smith, Ralph L. *Micah–Malachi*. WBC 32. Waco: Word, 1984.

Sparks, James T. *The Chronicler's Genealogies: Towards an Understanding of 1 Chronicles, 1–9*. Academia Biblica. Boston; Leiden: Brill, 2008.

Spronk, Klaas. "Jonah, Nahum, and the Book of the Twelve: A Response to Jakob Wöhrle." *JHS* 9 (2009): Article 8.

Stead, Michael R. *The Intertextuality of Zechariah 1–8*. LHBOTS 506. New York: T&T Clark, 2009.

Stern, Ephraim. *Archaeology of the Land of the Bible: Vol. 2, The Assyrian, Babylonian, and Persian Periods (732–332 B.C.E.)*. ABRL. New York: Doubleday, 2001.

Stienstra, Nelly. *YHWH is the Husband of His People: Analysis of a Biblical Metaphor with Special Reference to Translation*. Kampen: Kok Pharos, 1993.

Stovell, Beth M. "'I Will Make Her Like a Desert': Intertextual Allusion and Feminine and Agricultural Metaphors in the Book of the Twelve." In *The Book of the Twelve and the New Form Criticism*, edited by Mark J. Boda, Michael H. Floyd, and Colin M. Toffelmire, 37–61. ANEM 10. Atlanta: SBL, 2015.

Strawn, Brent A. *What Is Stronger than a Lion? Leonine Image and Metaphor in the Hebrew Bible and the Ancient Near East*. OBO 212. Göttingen: Vandenhoeck & Ruprecht, 2005.

Strømmen, Hannah M. *Biblical Animality after Jacques Derrida*. SemeiaSt 91. Atlanta: SBL, 2018.

Stuart, Douglas K. *Hosea–Jonah*. WBC 31. Waco: Word, 1987.

Stump, Eleonore. "The Problem of Evil and the History of Peoples: Think of Amalek." In *Divine Evil? The Moral Character of the God of Abraham*, edited by M. Bergmann, M. J. Murray, and M. C. Rea, 179–97. Oxford: Oxford University Press, 2010.

Sturch, R. L. "Theodicy." In *New Dictionary of Christian Ethics and Pastoral Theology*, edited by D. J. Atkinson, D. F. Field, A. Holmes, and O. O'Donovan, 954–5. Downers Grove: InterVarsity, 1995.

Sweeney, Marvin A. *The Twelve Prophets, Volume 1: Hosea, Jeol, Amos, Obadiah, Jonah.* Berit Olam: Studies in Hebrew Narrative & Poetry. Collegeville: Liturgical, 2000.

Sweeney, Marvin A. *The Twelve Prophets: Volume 2*. Berit Olam. Collegeville: Liturgical, 2000.

Sweeney, Marvin A., and Paul D. Hanson. *Zephaniah: A Commentary*. Hermeneia. Minneapolis: Fortress, 2003.

Talbott, Thomas. "Punishment, Forgiveness, and Divine Justice." *RelS* 29 (1993): 151–68.

Theodoret of Cyrus. *Commentaries on the Prophets, Volume 3: Commentary on the Twelve Prophets*. Translated by R. C. Hill. Brookline: Holy Cross Orthodox Press, 2006.

Thomas, Heath A. *Habakkuk*. THOTC. Grand Rapids: Eerdmans, 2018.

Thomas, Heath A. "Hearing the Minor Prophets: The Book of the Twelve and God's Address." In *Hearing the Old Testament: Listening for God's Address*, edited by Craig G. Bartholomew and David J. H. Beldman, 356–79. Grand Rapids: Eerdmans, 2012.

Thomas, Heath A. *Poetry and Theology in the Book of Lamentations: The Aesthetics of an Open Text.* HBM 47. Sheffield: Sheffield Phoenix, 2013.

Timmer, Daniel C. *A Gracious and Compassionate God: Mission, Salvation and Spirituality in the Book of Jonah*. NSBT 26. Downers Grove: InterVarsity, 2011.

Timmer, Daniel C. "Nahum's Representation of and Response to Neo-Assyria: Imperialism as a Multifaceted Point of Contact in Nahum." *BBR* 24, no. 3 (2014): 349–62.

Timmer, Daniel C. *The Non-Israelite Nations in the Book of the Twelve: Thematic Coherence and the Diachronic–Synchronic Relationship in the Minor Prophets*. BibInt 135. Leiden: Brill, 2015.

Timmer, Daniel C. "The Use and Abuse of Power in Amos: Identity and Ideology." *JSOT* 39 (2014): 101–18.

Toolan, David. *At Home in the Cosmos*. Maryknoll: Orbis, 2001.

Trimm, Charlie. *Fighting for the King and the Gods: A Survey of Warfare in the Ancient Near East*. SBLRBS 88. Atlanta: SBL, 2017.

Tugendhaft, Aaron. "Politics and Time in the Baal Cycle." *JANER* 12 (2012): 147–57.

Turner, Kenneth J. *The Death of Deaths in the Death of Israel: Deuteronomy's Theology of Exile*. Eugene: Wipf & Stock, 2011.

United Nations Development Program. *Human Development Report, 2007/2008: Fighting Climate Change, Human Solidarity in a Divided World*. New York: Palgrave McMillan, 2007.

United Nations Environment Programme. *Emissions Gap Report 2019*. Nairobi, 2019.

United Nations Food and Agriculture Organization. "General Situation of World Fish Stocks." http://www.fao.org/newsroom/common/ecg/1000505/en/stocks.pdf.

Ussishkin, David. "The 'Lachish Reliefs' and the City of Lachish." *IEJ* 30 (1980): 174–95.

Vanderhooft, David S. *The Neo-Babylonian Empire and Babylon in the Latter Prophets*. HSM 59. Atlanta: Scholars, 1999.

VanGemeren, Willem A., ed. *New International Dictionary of Old Testament Theology and Exegesis*. 5 vols. Grand Rapids: Zondervan, 1997.

Van Hecke, Pierre. "'For I Will Be Like a Lion to Ephraim': Leonine Metaphors in the Twelve Prophets." In *The Books of the Twelve Prophets: Minor Prophets – Major Theologies*, edited by Heinz-Josef Fabry, 387–402. BETL 295. Leuven: Peeters, 2018.

Van Leeuwen, Raymond C. "Scribal Wisdom and Theodicy in the Book of the Twelve." In *In Search of Wisdom: Essays in Memory of John G. Gammie*, edited by L. G. Perdue, B. B. Scott, and W. J. Wiseman, 31–49. Louisville: Westminster John Knox, 1993.

Vásquez, Manuel A. *More Than Belief: A Materialist Theory of Religion*. New York: Oxford University Press, 2011.

Verhoef, Pieter A. *The Books of Haggai and Malachi*. NICOT. Grand Rapids: Eerdmans, 1987.

Vermeulen, Karolien. "The Body of Nineveh: The Conceptual Image of the City in Nahum 2–3." *JHS* 17 (2017): 1–17.

Via, Dan. *Divine Justice, Divine Judgment: Rethinking the Judgment of Nations*. Facets. Minneapolis: Fortress, 2007.

Wacker, Marie-Theres. "Father-God, Mother-God—and Beyond: Exegetical Constructions and Deconstructions of Hosea 11." *Lectio difficilior* 2 (2012): 1–21. http://www.lectio.unibe.ch/12_2/pdf/wacker_marie_theres_father_god_mother_god_and_beyond.pdf.

Wagenaar, Jan A. *Judgement and Salvation: The Composition and Redaction of Micah 2–5*. SVT 85. Leiden: Brill, 2001.

Walker, Larry L. "Zephaniah." In *The Expositor's Bible Commentary 8: Daniel-Malachi*, edited by T. Longman III and D. Garland. Rev. ed. Grand Rapids: Zondervan, 2008.

Wallace, Paul. *Stars Beneath Us: Finding God in the Evolving Cosmos.* Minneapolis: Fortress, 2015.

Wallace-Wells, David. *The Uninhabitable Earth: Life After Warming.* New York: Tim Duggan, 2019.

Walsh, Jerome T. "Jonah 2:3-10: A Rhetorical Critical Study." *Bib* 63 (1982): 219–29.

Waltke, Bruce K. *A Commentary on Micah.* Grand Rapids: Eerdmans, 2007.

Wazana, Nili. "'War Crimes' in Amos's Oracles against the Nations (Amos 1:3–2:3)." In *Literature as Politics, Politics as Literature: Essays on the Ancient near East in Honor of Peter Machinist*, 479–501. Winona Lake: Eisenbrauns, 2013.

Weingart, Kristin. "Wie Samaria so auch Jerusalem: Umfang und Pragmatik einer frühen Micha-Komposition." *VT* 69 (2019): 460–80.

Wellman, James K., and Kyoko Tokuno. "Is Religious Violence Inevitable?" *JSSR* 43 (2004): 291–6.

Wenzel, Heiko. *Reading Zechariah with Zechariah 1:1-6 as the Introduction to the Entire Book.* CBET 59. Leuven: Peeters, 2011.

Weyde, Karl William. *Prophecy and Teaching: Prophetic Authority, Form Problems, and the Use of Traditions in the Book of Malachi.* BZAW 288. Berlin: de Gruyter, 2000.

Williamson, H. G. M. *The Book Called Isaiah: Deutero-Isaiah's Role in Composition and Redaction.* Oxford: Clarendon Press; New York: Oxford University Press, 1994.

Williamson, H. G. M. *Israel in the Books of Chronicles.* Cambridge: Cambridge University Press, 1977.

Willis, John T. "Hosea's Unique Figures of Yahweh." *ResQ* 61 (2019): 167–80.

Willis, John T. "'I Am Your God' and 'You Are My People' in Hosea and Jeremiah." *ResQ* 36 (1994): 291–303.

Wilson, Gerald H. *Job.* NIBC. Peabody: Hendrickson, 2007.

Wöhrle, Jakob. *Der Abschluss des Zwölfprophetenbuches: Buchübergreifende Redaktions-prozesse in den späten Sammlungen.* BZAW 389. Berlin: de Gruyter, 2008.

Wöhrle, Jakob. "'No Future for the Proud Exultant Ones': The Exilic Book of the Four Prophets (Hos., Am., Mic., Zeph.) as a Concept Opposed to the Deuteronomistic History." *VT* 58 (2008): 608–27.

Wolff, Hans W. "Guilt and Salvation: A Study of the Prophecy of Hosea." *Int* 15 (1961): 17–30.

Wolff, Hans W. *Hosea: A Commentary on the Book of the Prophet Hosea.* Hermeneia. Translated by Gary Stansell. Philadelphia/Augsburg: Fortress 1974.

Wolff, Hans W. *Joel and Amos.* Hermeneia. Philadelphia: Fortress, 1977.

Wolters, A. "Structure of Micah 3–5 and the Function of Micah 5:9-14 in the Book." *ZAW* 81 (1969): 191–214.

Wolters, A. *Zechariah.* HCOT. Leuven: Peeters, 2014.

Woodward, Alistair et al. "Climate Change and Health: On the Latest IPCC Report." *The Lancet* 383 (2014): 1185–9.

World Health Organization. *Global Urban Ambient Air Pollution Database (Update 2016).* http://www.who.int/phe/health_topics/outdoorair/databases/en/.

Yee, Gale A. "Hosea." In *Women's Bible Commentary*, edited by Carol A. Newsom and Sharon H. Ringe, 299–308. 3rd ed. Louisville: Westminster John Knox, 2012.

Youngblood, Kevin J. *Jonah: God's Scandalous Mercy.* Grand Rapids: Zondervan, 2013.

Zehnder, Markus. *Umgang mit Fremden in Israel und Assyrien: Ein Beitrag zur Anthropo-logie des 'Fremden' im Licht antiker Quellen.* BWANT 168. Stuttgart: Kohlhammer, 2005.

Zevit, Ziony. "The Search for Violence in Israelite Culture and in the Bible." In *Religion and Violence: The Biblical Heritage*, edited by D. A. Bernat and J. Klawans, 16–37. Sheffield: Sheffield Phoenix, 2007.

Zimran, Yisca. "The Notion of God Reflected in the Lion Imagery of the Book of Hosea." *VT* 68 (2018): 149–67.

INDEX OF REFERENCES

Index of Authors

Keefe, A. A. 69, 74, 82, 86
Keesing, F. 199
Kelle, B. E. 40, 67, 68
Kelsey, M. 51
Kessler, R. 143, 144, 151, 152, 166, 216
Kim, B. 82
Klawans, J. 161
Knoppers, G. N. 40
Ko, G. 175, 178, 183
Koch, K. 96
Kolbert, E. 199
Koopmans, W. T. 55
Kratz, R. G. 142
Krell, D. F. 118
Krispenz, J. 6
Kroeze, J. H. 160, 190
Kuhrt, A. 166
Kuppevelt, J. van 6
Kwakkel, G. 45

Laato, A. 8, 59, 96–8, 115, 158, 159
Lallemon-de Winkel, H. 25
Landy, F. 4, 159
Lanner, L. 163
LeCureux, J. T. 6, 44, 45, 47, 52, 68, 76,
  80–3, 85, 180–2, 192
Leigh, B. Y. 178, 185
Leonhardt-Balzer, J. 173, 174
Leuchter, M. 37
Lévêque, J. 172
Levinsohn, S. H. 159
Limburg, J. 25
Linville, J. R. 127
Lo, A. 49
Luckenbill, D. D. 162
Lundbom, J. R. 127, 129, 138
Lynch, M. 16

Maat, H. W. L. P. 3
Macintosh, A. A. 71, 84
Mackie, P. J. 166
Maier, C. 15
Marshall, C. 162
Mathews, J. 175
Mays, J. L. 116, 196
McCann, D. P. 158
McConville, J. G. 46, 47
McGary, H. 170
McKane, W. 143, 145, 150, 152, 153
McNeill, J. R. 196

Mendenhall, G. E. 27
Merwe, C. H. J. van der 160, 190
Meyer, B. 114
Meyers, C. L. 62, 188
Meyers, E. M. 62, 188
Middlemas, J. 40
Miller, P. D. 88, 93, 98, 100, 161
Mills, M. 118
Milstein, S. J. 126, 127
Moon, J. N. 43, 69, 71, 73, 78, 79, 83, 84
Moor, J. C. de 4, 8, 96–8, 115, 158, 159
Moore, S. D. 119
Moughtin-Mumby, S. 71, 75, 77, 78,
  85–7
Mowinckel, S. 202
Muldoon, C. L. 2
Münnich, M. M. 206

Nahkola, A. 133
Naudé, J. A. 160, 190
Nielsen, K. 91
Nogalski, J. D. 4–7, 27, 33, 52, 63, 93,
  99, 105, 107–9, 111, 116, 122, 176,
  181–3, 191, 215, 229
Notarius, T. 160

O'Brien, J. M. 2, 13, 14, 148, 150–2,
  163, 174, 176, 214
O'Neal, G. M. 178
O'Rourke Boyle, M. 25
Oded, B. 168
Oldfield, F. 195
Olson, D. T. 73, 84, 85
Orsi, R. A. 114

Parker, R. D. 233
Patterson, R. D. 32, 33
Patton, C. L. 69
Patton, M. H. 230
Paul, S. M. 126, 132, 134
Perdue, L. G. 13
Person, R. F. 4
Petersen, D. L. 43, 48, 98, 117
Petterson, A. R. 50, 54, 56, 57, 60–2,
  174, 236
Pietersma, A. 202
Pinker, A. 172, 208
Pitard, W. T. 125
Porter, B. N. 162
Prinsloo, W. S. 90, 91, 180

:an be obtained
com
24
/22B/53